T0321897

Powering the Internet of Things With 5G Networks

Vasuky Mohanan
Universiti Sains Malaysia, Malaysia

Rahmat Budiarto
Albaha University, Saudi Arabia

Ismat Aldmour
Albaha University, Saudi Arabia

A volume in the Advances in
Wireless Technologies and
Telecommunication (AWTT) Book
Series

Published in the United States of America by
    IGI Global
    Information Science Reference (an imprint of IGI Global)
    701 E. Chocolate Avenue
    Hershey PA, USA 17033
    Tel: 717-533-8845
    Fax: 717-533-8661
    E-mail: cust@igi-global.com
    Web site: http://www.igi-global.com

Copyright © 2018 by IGI Global. All rights reserved. No part of this publication may be reproduced, stored or distributed in any form or by any means, electronic or mechanical, including photocopying, without written permission from the publisher.
Product or company names used in this set are for identification purposes only. Inclusion of the names of the products or companies does not indicate a claim of ownership by IGI Global of the trademark or registered trademark.

Library of Congress Cataloging-in-Publication Data

Names: Mohanan, Vasuky, 1970- editor. | Budiarto, Rahmat, 1961- editor. |
   Aldmour, Ismat, 1962- editor.
Title: Powering the internet of things with 5G networks / Vasuky Mohanan,
   Rahmat Budiarto, and Ismat Aldmour, editors.
Description: Hershey, PA : Information Science Reference, [2018] | Includes
   bibliographical references.
Identifiers: LCCN 2017010780| ISBN 9781522527992 (hardcover) | ISBN
   9781522528005 (ebook)
Subjects: LCSH: Internet of things. | Mobile communication systems.
Classification: LCC TK5105.8857 .P69 2018 | DDC 004.67/8--dc23 LC record available at https://
lccn.loc.gov/2017010780

This book is published in the IGI Global book series Advances in Wireless Technologies and Telecommunication (AWTT) (ISSN: 2327-3305; eISSN: 2327-3313)

British Cataloguing in Publication Data
A Cataloguing in Publication record for this book is available from the British Library.

All work contributed to this book is new, previously-unpublished material.
The views expressed in this book are those of the authors, but not necessarily of the publisher.

For electronic access to this publication, please contact: eresources@igi-global.com.

Advances in Wireless Technologies and Telecommunication (AWTT) Book Series

ISSN:2327-3305
EISSN:2327-3313

Editor-in-Chief: Xiaoge Xu, The University of Nottingham Ningbo China, China

MISSION

The wireless computing industry is constantly evolving, redesigning the ways in which individuals share information. Wireless technology and telecommunication remain one of the most important technologies in business organizations. The utilization of these technologies has enhanced business efficiency by enabling dynamic resources in all aspects of society.

The **Advances in Wireless Technologies and Telecommunication Book Series** aims to provide researchers and academic communities with quality research on the concepts and developments in the wireless technology fields. Developers, engineers, students, research strategists, and IT managers will find this series useful to gain insight into next generation wireless technologies and telecommunication.

COVERAGE

- Mobile Technology
- Broadcasting
- Mobile Communications
- Telecommunications
- Mobile Web Services
- Cellular Networks
- Digital Communication
- Virtual Network Operations
- Wireless Technologies
- Wireless Broadband

IGI Global is currently accepting manuscripts for publication within this series. To submit a proposal for a volume in this series, please contact our Acquisition Editors at Acquisitions@igi-global.com or visit: http://www.igi-global.com/publish/.

The Advances in Wireless Technologies and Telecommunication (AWTT) Book Series (ISSN 2327-3305) is published by IGI Global, 701 E. Chocolate Avenue, Hershey, PA 17033-1240, USA, www.igi-global.com. This series is composed of titles available for purchase individually; each title is edited to be contextually exclusive from any other title within the series. For pricing and ordering information please visit http://www.igi-global.com/book-series/advances-wireless-technologies-telecommunication-awtt/73684. Postmaster: Send all address changes to above address. Copyright © 2018 IGI Global. All rights, including translation in other languages reserved by the publisher. No part of this series may be reproduced or used in any form or by any means – graphics, electronic, or mechanical, including photocopying, recording, taping, or information and retrieval systems – without written permission from the publisher, except for non commercial, educational use, including classroom teaching purposes. The views expressed in this series are those of the authors, but not necessarily of IGI Global.

Titles in this Series

For a list of additional titles in this series, please visit:
http://www.igi-global.com/book-series/advances-wireless-technologies-telecommunication-awtt/73684

For an enitre list of titles in this series, please visit:
http://www.igi-global.com/book-series/advances-wireless-technologies-telecommunication-awtt/73684

701 East Chocolate Avenue, Hershey, PA 17033, USA
Tel: 717-533-8845 x100 • Fax: 717-533-8661
E-Mail: cust@igi-global.com • www.igi-global.com

Editorial Advisory Board

Khalid AlBegain, *Kuwait College of Science and Technology, Kuwait*
Abdullah Gani, *University of Malaya, Malaysia*
Ali Selamat, *Universiti Teknologi Malaysia (UTM), Malaysia*
Deris Stiawan, *Sriwijaya University, Indonesia*
Tole Sutikno, *Universitas Ahmad Dahlan (UAD), Indonesia*
Suleiman Y. Yerima, *Queen's University Belfast, UK*
Aymen I. Zerikat, *American University of the Middle East (AUM), Kuwait*

Table of Contents

Detailed Table of Contents

Cellular communications has evolved from 1G to 4G to cater for the various service offerings of voice communication, data exchange and web browsing. The coming generation, 5G, is aiming at the wider concept of the Internet of things (IoT). A broad consensus by industry and standards organizations is to introduce 5G around 2020 time frame. This chapter will overview 5G as a necessary platform for the success of the IoT. It provides an overview of 1G to 4G evolution and the demand issues behind 5G while discussing deficiencies of 4G LTE which prohibits it from rising up to the challenges presented in IoT. On the path to 5G, the chapter outlines the 5G Vision, its requirements, use cases, business models and value creation. Discussions of some of the 5G challenges are included in the chapter; its coexistence with current technologies, its strict latency and high spectrum requirements, and the performance and variability of the QoS requirements of 5G applications. Finally, an outline of 5G research activities and initiatives across the globe is provided.

In evolution towards a successful mobile communications, the radio technology plays major role and the chosen radio technology should be spectrally efficient, robust and reliable. OFDM provided the much needed spectral efficiency, reliability, robustness and scalability for LTE, compared to the previous access methods such as TDMA, FDMA, and CDMA. For 5G, we should look for more spectrally efficient and massively scalable radio technology to cater to IoT and high bandwidth applications.

The objective of this chapter is to introduce the 5G radio system, its challenges from both user and network perspective, and the key disruptive technologies for 5G – such as carrier aggregation, waveform engineering, full duplex, Multi-RAT, flexible networks, and Massive MIMO. Finally, the chapter discusses the current developments in 5G radio research.

Chapter 3

Vojislav Milosevic, University of Belgrade, Serbia
Branka Jokanovic, University of Belgrade, Serbia
Olga Boric-Lubecke, University of Hawaii – Manoa, USA
Victor M. Lubecke, University of Hawaii – Manoa, USA

This chapter presents an overview on the drivers behind the 5G evolution and explains technological breakthroughs in the microwave and millimeter wave domain that will create the 5G backbone. Extensions to millimeter wave frequency bands, advanced multi-antenna systems and antenna beamforming and simultaneous transmission and reception are some of the prospects that could lead to both architectural and component disruptive design changes in the future 5G. 5G is expected to include an innovative set of technologies that will radically change our private and professional lives, though applications of novel services, such as remote healthcare, driverless cars, wireless robots and connected homes, which will alter boundaries between the real and the cyber world.

Chapter 4

Ahmed Mahmoud Mostafa, Helwan University, Egypt

The Internet of Things (IoT) is defined by the International Telecommunication Union (ITU) and IoT European Research Cluster (IERC) as a dynamic global network infrastructure with self-configuring capabilities based on standard and interoperable communication protocols where physical and virtual "things" have identities, physical attributes and virtual personalities, use intelligent interfaces and are seamlessly integrated into the information network. Many of the applications and use cases that drive the requirements and capabilities of 5G are about end-to-end communication between devices. This chapter describes the enabling technologies for the Internet of Things, the IoT architecture, the network and communication infrastructure for IoT, and the importance of scalability for 5G based IoT systems. Also, naming and addressing issues in IoT is presented along with an overview of the existing data exchange protocols that can be applied to IoT based systems.

Chapter 5

Ahmed Mahmoud Mostafa, Al Baha University, Saudi Arabia

Connecting a large number of physical objects equipped with sensors to the Internet generates what is called "big data." Big data needs smart and efficient storage. The emerging and developing technology of cloud computing is defined by the US National Institute of Standards and Technology (NIST) as an access model to an on-demand network of shared configurable computing sources such as networks, servers, warehouses, applications, and services. The manual installation and management of IoT devices becomes impractical due to the large numbers involved. Specifically, there exists an inefficiency that can be resolved by minimizing user intervention. The manual maintenance of a large number of devices becomes inefficient, and demands the presence of intelligent and dynamic management schemes. In addition, Internet of Things systems cannot successfully realize the notion of ubiquitous connectivity of everything if they are not capable to truly include 'multimedia things'.

Chapter 6

Massimo Condoluci, King's College London, UK
Maria A. Lema, King's College London, UK
Toktam Mahmoodi, King's College London, UK
Mischa Dohler, King's College London, UK

The effective provisioning of industry verticals over the next-to-come 5G systems opens novel business opportunities for telco operators especially when considering the integration of Internet of Things (IoT) devices as enablers of business cases based on remote sensing and control. This chapter highlights the main features of IoT verticals with particular attention on healthcare, smart cities, industry automation and entertainment business cases. The aim of this Chapter is to derive the requirements such IoT verticals pose in terms of design features to be considered in the standardization of 5G systems. This chapter presents the state of the art on the contribution from the research community and standardization bodies to address the 5G design characteristics with particular attention to the features enabling a proper management of IoT-oriented business cases.

Chapter 7

Ahmed Alahmadi, Al Baha University, Saudi Arabia
Tami Alwajeeh, Al Baha University, Saudi Arabia
Vasuky Mohanan, INTI International College Penang, Malaysia
Rahmat Budiarto, Al Baha University, Saudi Arabia

The Internet of Things (IoT) is transforming the agriculture industry and enables farmers to deal with the vast challenges in the industry. Internet of Farming (IoF) applications increases the quantity, quality, sustainability as well as cost effectiveness of agricultural production. Farmers leverage IoF to monitor remotely, sensors that can detect soil moisture, crop growth and livestock feed levels, manage and control remotely the smart connected harvesters and irrigation equipment, and utilize artificial intelligence based tools to analyze operational data combined with 3rd party information, such as weather services, to provide new insights and improve decision making. The Internet of Farming relies on data gathered from sensor of Wireless Sensor Network (WSN). The WSN requires a reliable connectivity to provide accurate prediction of the farming system. This chapter proposes a strategy that provides always best connectivity (ABC). The strategy considers a routing protocol to support Low-power and lossy networks (LLN), with a minimum energy usage. Two scenarios are presented.

Chapter 8

    Adil Fahad Alharthi, Albaha University, Saudi Arabia
    Mohammed Yahya Alzahrani, Albaha University, Saudi Arabia
    Ismat Aldmour, Albaha University, Saudi Arabia
    Deris Stiawan, Universitas Sriwijaya, Indonesia
    Muhammad Fermi Pasha, Monash University Malaysia, Malaysia
    Rahmat Budiarto, Albaha University, Saudi Arabia

The network traffic of the Internet became huge and more complex due to the expansion of the Internet technology in supporting the convergence of IP networks, Internet of Things, and social networks. As a consequence, a more sophisticated network monitoring tool is desired in order to prevent an enterprise network from malware attacks, to maintain its availability as high as possible at any time, and to maintain the network's healthiness. This chapter offers a development of real-time network monitoring tool platform. The research component of this chapter attempts to answer the challenges of making the monitoring tool become smarter and more accurate by applying artificial intelligence techniques. In addition, a research on buffering techniques to speed up the traffic data acquisition process and micro-controller unit design for sensor-based applications are also carried out. In the development component, some ground works has already been done such as network traffic packets capturing modules, and packets decoding modules. The system development uses Java Eclipse platform.

With the advancement of wireless sensor networks (WSN) and the increasing use of sensors in various industrial, environmental and commercial fields, it is difficult to store and process the volume of generated data on local platforms. Cloud computing provides scalable resources to perform analysis of online as well as offline data streams generated by sensor networks. This can help to overcome the weakness of WSN in combining and analyzing heterogeneous and large numbers of sensory data. This chapter presents a comprehensive survey on state-of-the-art results in the context of cloud –enabled large-scale sensor networks. The chapter also discusses the objectives, architecture and design issues of the generic sensor-cloud platform.

Chapter 10

In recent years the Internet of Things (IoT) has rapidly become a revolutionary technological invention causing significant changes to the way both corporate computing systems, and even household gadgets and appliances, are designed and manufactured. The aim of this chapter is to highlight the security and privacy issues that may affect the evolution of IoT technology. The privacy issues are discussed from customer perspectives: first, the IoT privacy concern where the privacy debates on IoT and the IoT privacy that reflected from users' perspective based on the examination of previous researches results. In addition, the different architectures for IoT are discussed. Finally, the chapter discusses the IoT security concern by collecting, analyzing and presenting the major IoT security concerns in the literature as well as providing some potential solutions to these concerns.

Preface

Drivers of the different G's of mobile cellular networks are varied; for the move from the 1G to the digital 2G, voice quality was a main driver to overcome the low quality analog 1G voice, 3G came to provide data, which was not the main focus of 2G, while 4G targeted serving the thirst for higher data rates not originally targeted by 3G. Though 4G is not yet mainstream, a stringent need for a new generation is prominent with multidimensional requirements and challenges that the latest 4G was not designed for, henceforth, the need for a new G, 5G. By now, it is realized that the new era of 5G is the time to change the role of communication networks from the traditional paradigm of text, voice or video connecting ourselves, or enhancing social life and boosting our work by making knowledge, entertainment and socialization at our figure tips, to a paradigm with which communication networks will transform the way we live or do work. This means that communication networks will have to interconnect, other than ourselves, entities and things we live or work with; e.g. our cars, homes, appliances and road signs, as well as, our office equipment, factory machines and cargo tracking equipment. In short, it is requested to connect all things around to all other things or to ourselves anytime and anywhere. This is the Internet of Things (IoT) or the Internet of Everything as some like to call. This ambitious target imposes many requirements and challenges that 5G networks are expected to provide support for. For example, IoT will embed various things of various requirements for throughput, reliability, .etc, which have to be interconnected at unprecedented high densities and varied traffic requirements. Additionally, it is also widely acceptable that energy efficiency issue cannot be any more in the background of the interest of communications networks designers; especially with the expected explosion of interconnected battery powered things. The added complexity is another dimension of this communication revolution which has to be cost effective as well, as the communication part is not any more luxurious or superficial; it is rather a integral part of our cost of living or doing work.

5G: CHALLENGES AND TECHNOLOGIES

The road to IoT has to be paved by a strong 5G. However, 5G is not a mature technology and not yet standardized. 5G is challenged by its objectives of being the solution to all conflicting needs!; fiber like data rates while satisfying small bursty devices, ubiquitous coverage while having to satisfy high densities nodes, which can be intermittent, delay tolerant smart metering and very delay intolerant autonomous driving gadgets, .etc. As of these varied challenges, one would expect that 5G cannot be a simple upgrade to one technology or other, and no single solution can be a solution. For that, solutions at different layers has to be devised: Optimization of the use of the traditional sub 6GHz spectrum while higher lightly loaded centimetric and millimetric waves will be invaded (mm-Waves will form a radical new solution to 5G challenges, especially for super high rates), more complex antennas and more sophisticated multiple connection techniques, service at the spot or indoors using base stations within the facilities, the cooperation of all the radio access technologies present, more reliance on the smart node, etc.

INTERNET OF THINGS

Connecting things together had been accomplished here and there in the past to serve specific needs in generally isolated situations. A large-scale interconnection of things and people is what forms the IoT. IoT is THE technology will characterize the 5G era; an explosive number of connected things which collect and exchange data. Things will have to embed proper electronics and software interfaced to their sensing or actuating terminals on one side and to the network on the other side. As billions of things of different natures will be connected, IoT should be architected to be scalable, things easily accessible but secure, with proper protocols for establishing the communication. Also, things can be limited on resources of memory and processing power. Generally, IoT architecture will build on traditional wireless sensor networks, which are domain limited interconnection of physical devices, but will have to involve the cloud and autonomous computing to overcome inefficiencies and limitations and to reduce the need for user intervention to installation, management and maintenance. Meaningful information can be extracted to create smartness and useful applications by having the data collected from the various sensors at different locations, processed and analyzed in the cloud, rather than in the resource limited devices.

In the IoT/5G era, the IoT will be used in a wide range of cases, for example, homes will get automated, cities and its transport can be made smart, multimedia things and virtual reality will change education, remote surgeries and multimedia aids to health workers will transform healthcare industry and manufacturing may enjoy safer work environments, higher cost efficiencies, automation and remote control, and the agriculture industry will be transformed like never before by empowering farmers and growers to deal with the enormous challenges they face. The different use cases of IoT will inflect different requirements and this in turn will propel 5G networks differently. In 5G, it is suggested to have network sliced to serve the different varied use cases with each slice serving a use case or so. To support this, 5G networks are moving toward more softwarization and virtualization of its networks. Virtual networks and software defined networks lies in the core of 5G solution, so in a successful 5G, the application defines what the network should be in contrary to what we are used to in current pre-5G era where the network is disjoint from the application.

In the coming era of IoT, billions of devices will be interconnected, hence, increased number of entry points for intruders, while at the same time the things will most probably have firmwares developed at low cost by small companies with more probable vulnerabilities resulting in threats of different kinds. In comparison to today's issues, e.g. loosing data or shutting a web site service, issues of security breaches to IoT can be catastrophic, e.g. a loss of life due to smart vehicles being manipulated, or a power plant blackout. Henceforth, 5G networks are expected to have strong fundamentals in providing security and privacy as this will be a ultimate test in the success of IoT. Due to this, the architecture of IoT has an impact on the security and privacy of the involved stakeholders; networks need to be smarter and more effective in monitoring, reporting and controlling the bursts of data exchanged between the IoT devices. After all, trust and consumer confidence is essential for the fulfilment of the full 5G/IoT potential.

BOOK OBJECTIVE

This book, *Powering the Internet of Things With 5G Networks,* as its name implies, aims to introduce to the interested reader how 5G networks can be leveraged to support IoT. Researchers and standards organizations are having the internet of things in their minds while crafting the 5G. It is an objective of this book to help the reader realize how 5G, with its varied enabling technologies, provides the platform for IoT to flourish, while at the same time, IoT will be the driving force for more 5G solutions. The reader of this book will be journeyed from 5G requirements and challenges, especially those that are IoT related, to history and standards, different technologies and radio solutions contributing to the 5G including the millimetic waves. Also, the reader will be introduced to solutions on the network level, e.g. network slicing, softerization and virtualization solutions. Also IoT architecture to overcome the difficulties in including resource constrained devices into the IoT infrastructure and complexity issues such as scalability, addressing and naming.

Another objective of the book is to show how the expected use cases and markets requirements in health, entertainment, automation, etc, pushes 5G to come up with more solutions. Additionally, the current volume presents reports and discussions on some special cases in some areas of IoT, i.e. Internet of Multimedia Things as a means to provide multimedia based features and enhancements, Internet of Farming, transforming the agriculture industry like never before, smart real-time IoT network monitoring tool platform and a survey on state-of-the-art results in the context of cloud –enabled large-scale sensor networks. A final target is to present the security and privacy concerns of the IoT and how they may affect its evolution.

THE TARGET AUDIENCE

5G and IoT are hot topic nowadays. This is not only because they represent a revolution to technology, networks and communications, but also because of the impact they will inflect on personnel, societies, services and industries of different kinds. Hence, the book serves as a reference for interested researchers in 5G, IoT and 5G/IoT interrelationship. Hence, audience of this book will range from students, researchers and other scholars to industry, society and service leaders. Scholars and similar audience will find in the book basic information, challenges, and samples of research ideas and pending research issues which may help them to enhance their scholarly works. On the other hand, society, business and industry leaders will find in the book answers to some of the questions of how this technology revolution can and will impact their societies, works and the services they provide. This is essential to grow their business and improve societies and services.

BOOK OUTLINE

Powering the Internet of Things With 5G Networks is composed of a total of 10 chapters, authored by academics and practitioners from around the world, Here, brief descriptions of the content and the importance of each of the chapters are presented:

Chapter 1: 5G – The Platform

This chapter is about how 5G performs as a platform for IoT. The chapter reviews 1G TO 4G cellular communications evolution, a brief introduction about 4G-LTE developments, demand issues for 5G, LTE deficiencies and how to overcome these deficiencies if LTE is to be adopted by 5G. On the path to converting to 5G, the chapter presents the 5G vision and requirements. Key elements in 5G characterizations in terms of use cases, business models and value creation are outlined. The chapter moves to discuss the variability in 5G solution and details the potential key technologies that will flourish in 5G environment. The chapter reviews some of the issues of adopting 5G; how 5G can coexist with legacy technologies, latency targets in 5G and mission critical communication. Performance and variability of QoS for various applications under 5G and solutions on how to meet 5G spectrum requirements are also discussed. At the end, a comprehensive outline of worldwide 5G research activities and initiatives is presented together with information on 5G timelines for standardization and commercialization.

Chapter 2: 5G – Radio

This chapter starts by reviewing the challenges for 5G radio systems imposed by the demand for massive capacity, services and spectrum. The chapter provides an overview of the novel possibilities offered by denser and more heterogeneous Radio Access Technologies (RATs), how to support widely varying traffic needs efficiently and the need for new radio technologies. The chapter reviews the key technologies for 5G radio of massive MIMO, Carrier Aggregation, Centimetre and Millimeter Waves, Waveform Engineering, Shared Spectrum Access, Advanced Inter-node Coordination, Full Duplex Communication, Multi-RAT Support, Device-to-Device Communications, Efficient Transmission of Small Data, Integration of Wireless Backhaul/Access, Flexible Networks, Flexible Mobility, Information Centric Networking (ICN), Context Aware Networking and Moving Networks.

Chapter 3: Key Microwave and Millimeter Wave Technologies for 5G Radio

This chapter commences and builds on the previous chapter, 5G Radio, to focus on one aspect of 5G radio; the millimetric waves. The chapter outlines the drivers for mm-Waves in 5G as a radical new solution to 5G challenges, especially the IoT, together with other new radical solutions of advanced multi-antenna (MIMO) techniques; in-band full duplex and innovative network architecture. The chapter reviews history, current state and standardization of mm-Waves and notable applications, the automotive radar in particular, are discussed. Usage in communications is also covered, including links, upcoming wireless LAN and current and future standardization. Next, the RF wave propagation is discussed, with a special focus on mm-waves and recent measurements. Then the basics of antenna arrays are given, for the reasons set forth in the section where the mm-wave MIMO architectures are reviewed. The rest of the chapter deals with advanced antenna designs for 5G.

Chapter 4: IoT Architecture and Protocols in 5G Environment

This chapter details the architecture and protocols that are needed in the 5G environment to support IoT. The chapter begins by discussing the enabling technologies that are essential for IoT development; namely, identification, sensing and communication technologies, hardware and software platforms, knowledge extraction (semantics), and services related to identity, information aggregation, collaboration and ubiquity. How IoT will increase the complexity of networks and impact communications is then detailed. The role of device to device communication and networking is emphasized. Following is an outline of the IoT requirements to be supported by forthcoming 5G systems of energy efficiency, resiliency, interoperability, group communications, and cloud-based IoT service environment and the support to multimedia IoT. Discussion on IoT architecture that can overcome scalability, addressing and naming issues is presented in this chapter as well. Finally, IoT protocols that support data exchange between different domains are presented.

Chapter 5: The Role of Autonomous Computing, Cloud Computing, and Multimedia in IoT

This chapter looks at how research in IoT can help overcome the difficulties, e.g. the need for user intervention for installation, management and maintenance, incurred by including large number of constrained physical objects equipped with sensors and actuators into the IoT infrastructure. The chapter highlights how autonomous computing and cloud computing with shared configurable computing sources such as networks, servers, warehouses, applications, and services, can be leveraged to achieve this. Additionally, Internet of Multimedia Things as a means to provide multimedia based features and enhancements are also tackled in this chapter. Properties of each of the technique are highlighted and how they minimize user intervention in managing resource challenged devices are detailed.

Chapter 6: 5G IoT Industry Verticals and Networks

This chapter covers the main trends in the industry that uses IoT to tackle several problems or to improve outcomes in business and industry. The chapter presents some important 5G use cases highlighting the novel business opportunities for IoT in the next-to-come mobile systems with the aim to recognize the role of MTC in generating an added value to 5G business activity or consumer end. The main use cases highlighted are: healthcare, smart cities, industry automation and entertainment. For each use case, features and requirements they pose in the design of 5G networks are discussed. These requirements range from QoS (e.g., data rates, latency, jitter, and energy consumption) to more generic constraints from a network point of view related to network flexibility and customization. In addition to the analysis of requirements of 5G use cases, the chapter discuses the limitations of present 4G systems to support these use cases and surveys the contribution from the research community and standardization bodies to satisfy these requirements. The chapter summarizes the available literature focusing on the recent advances in terms of network slicing, virtualization and softwarisation, solution for supporting MTC traffic, device multi-connectivity and centralized/cloud radio access network (RAN).

Chapter 7: Wireless Sensor Network With Always Best Connection for Internet of Farming

Some of the most innovative and practical applications of the IoT are happening in the Industrial Internet of Things (IIoT) of different industry sectors. Ultimately, the implementation of IoT in agriculture can have the greatest impact. The IoT for agriculture is also called as Internet of Farming (IoF). IoF relies on data gathered from sensors interconnected through a Wireless Sensor Network (WSN). The WSN requires a reliable connectivity to provide accurate prediction data of the farming system. Modern farming utilized tractors equipped by sensors to gather data from soil and the crops itself. Those sensors are considered as mobile nodes in a WSN. This chapter proposes a strategy that provides always best connectivity (ABC). The strategy considers users as one of the stakeholders combined with a routing protocol to support Low-power and lossy networks (LLN), with a minimum energy usage. In addition, the strategy also takes into account the context of the sensor nodes. In the experiment two scenarios are presented. At the end of the chapter, authors discuss how 5G technologies can improve the network connectivity in WSN. The authors proposes to incorporate ABC mechanism in the architecture of communication layer of 5G.

Chapter 8: Smart Real-Time Internet-of-Things Network Monitoring System

This chapter presents the development of smart real-time IoT network monitoring tool platform. The chapter is divided into 3 components: Research, Development, and Commercialization. The research component attempts to answer the challenges of making the monitoring tool become smarter and more accurate by applying artificial intelligence techniques. The IoT carries a tsunami of data. IoT rollouts bring a proliferation of cheap, distributed sensors – resulting in a huge volume of data in a short amount of time. Thus, a research on buffering techniques to speed up the traffic data acquisition process and micro-controller unit design for sensor-based applications are introduced. The proposed system utilizes available existing elementary components such as network traffic packets capturing, packet filtering and packets decoding modules. Malwares are becoming smart and sophisticated. Now, the same malwares may attack smart TV connected to Internet. This matter triggers the need for a system that is capable of monitoring in real time fashion to detect any anomalies in the network and to pinpoint the sources of the malwares. The proposed monitoring system uses intelligent techniques for clustering the network traffic to distinguish anomalies from normal traffics and machine learning for adaptively learning the network traffic changes and adapt accordingly. An insider attack is one of the biggest threats faced by modern enterprise networks. Thus, the proposed monitoring system also acts as CCTV. The monitoring system uses Java Eclipse platform. Experiments using an IoT testbed are conducted to reveal attacks/anomalies patterns.

Chapter 9: Sensor Cloud – A Cloud-Based Sensor Network Data Gathering and Processing Platform

This chapter presents a comprehensive survey on state-of-the-art results in the context of cloud–enabled large-scale sensor networks. The chapter starts with giving an overview of Cyber Physical Cloud, Internet of Things and Sensor Cloud as a background. Then followed by sensor cloud description, and how the sensor cloud is designed through an adoption of the concept of cloud computing. To allow users to utilize many sources of data simultaneously, a framework is needed to define the geometric, dynamic, and observational characteristics of sensors such as location, accuracy and type of sensor nodes. Virtualization in sensor networks can provide flexibility and cost effective solutions for the availability and performance of physical sensors. The solutions are materialized by allowing heterogeneous sensor nodes to coexist over the common physical sensor substrate. Furthermore, a discussion on sensor virtualization as well as an architecture for sensor cloud are provided. Some examples of existing and future sensor cloud applications are presented together with discussions of some of the issues of integrating sensor network and cloud computing. Finally, the chapter ends with a suggestions on future works including designing and implementing event matching algorithms as well as a study on benefit of distributed optimization techniques to enable flexibility and agility in service provisioning while reduces the overall system costs

Chapter 10: Internet of Things Security and Privacy

This chapter focuses on the security and privacy concern that may affect the evolution of IoT technology. The different security architectures for IoT are discussed. Then, privacy issues are presented from two perspectives; the IoT privacy concern where the privacy debates on IoT and the IoT privacy that reflected from users' perspective based on the examination of previous researches results. The chapter starts with presenting the maturity of Internet of Things, followed by research direction in IoT with the aims to emphasis the importance of security and privacy in IoT. Then the security architecture for IoT is described over its three layers of *Perception layer, Network layer and Application layer*. Finally, IoT security concern is defined, by collecting, analysing and presenting the security concerns related to IoT, and exploring some potential solutions.

CONCLUSION

This book is about 5G, IOT, and their interrelationship. It clarify what is 5G, what is IoT and how 5G paves the way to a flourishing IoT while 5G pushes on 5G to come with solutions. The book discusses concepts of 5G networks as a platform for the IOT and its 5G radio concepts with a focus on millimetric waves; which will boost broadband for future high data rates applications. The book discusses IoT architecture and protocols in 5G environment, the role of autonomous computing, cloud computing, and multimedia in IoT and some of the main industries, such as health, entertainment, automation, intelligent transportation and smart cities and even implementation of IoT in agriculture. The book focuses on and discuss solutions to challenges that will result by the proliferation of interconnected things with 5G networks support brings new challenges to data gathering, networks monitoring, security, and privacy issues.

Acknowledgment

The editors would like to acknowledge the help of all the people involved in this project and, more specifically, to the chapters authors who contributed their time and expertise to this book. The editors like, as well, to acknowledge the valuable contributions of the reviewers regarding the improvement of quality, coherence, and content presentation of chapters. Most of the authors also served as referees; we highly appreciate their double task.

Vasuky Mohnnan
Universiti Sains Malaysia, Malaysia

Rahmat Budiarto
Albaha University, Saudi Arabia

Ismat Aldmour
Albaha University, Saudi Arabia

Chapter 1
5G:
The Platform

Ravi Sekhar Yarrabothu
Vignan's University, India

ABSTRACT

Cellular communications has evolved from 1G to 4G to cater for the various service offerings of voice communication, data exchange and web browsing. The coming generation, 5G, is aiming at the wider concept of the Internet of things (IoT). A broad consensus by industry and standards organizations is to introduce 5G around 2020 time frame. This chapter will overview 5G as a necessary platform for the success of the IoT. It provides an overview of 1G to 4G evolution and the demand issues behind 5G while discussing deficiencies of 4G LTE which prohibits it from rising up to the challenges presented in IoT. On the path to 5G, the chapter outlines the 5G Vision, its requirements, use cases, business models and value creation. Discussions of some of the 5G challenges are included in the chapter; its coexistence with current technologies, its strict latency and high spectrum requirements, and the performance and variability of the QoS requirements of 5G applications. Finally, an outline of 5G research activities and initiatives across the globe is provided.

INTRODUCTION

The cellular industry has already started working on the development of 5G, as the 4G deployments are getting completed across the world. However, there are few issues that are being discussed among research institutions, standards bodies, cellular operators, the supplier community, trade organizations and governments – What will be the 5G deployment time frame?, What will be the characteristics of

DOI: 10.4018/978-1-5225-2799-2.ch001

Copyright © 2018, IGI Global. Copying or distributing in print or electronic forms without written permission of IGI Global is prohibited.

the cellular networks beyond 2020?, and What will be the likely technologies that come in to picture for 5G?. This chapter is written in an attempt to address these questions in a systematic way.

5th Generation cellular communication networks are going to revolutionize current life styles by providing ubiquitous and reliable communication. Internet of Things (IoT) concept and Tactile Internet are the major drivers for 5G communications (Fettweis, & Alamouti, 2014) and its use cases. Thus, 5G Platform can be defined as "a cellular platform which provides a ubiquitous, reliable, low power and high data rate mobile communication network between smarter devices".

Keeping in view of the 5G Research the following high level Key Performance Indicators (KPI's) are proposed to frame the research activities (IWPC 2014, METIS, 2015):

- Providing 1000 times higher wireless area capacity and more varied service capabilities compared to current day.
- Saving up to 90% of energy per service provided.
- Reducing the average service creation time cycle from 90 hours to 90 minutes.
- Creating a secure, reliable and dependable Internet with a "zero perceived" downtime for services provision.
- Facilitating very dense deployments of wireless communication links to connect over 7 trillion wireless devices serving over 7 billion people.
- Enabling advanced user controlled privacy

Before we go in to the necessity of 5G, we will start with a very brief overview of existing cellular technologies, and their limitations.

1G TO 4G CELLULAR COMMUNICATIONS EVOLUTION

Ever since its birth in the 1980s, mobile communications have been undergoing more than three decades of explosive growth and the mobile network has become a basic information network connecting human society. It already has a major impact on people's daily lives, and also become an important engine for economy development and social informatization.

Cellular communications has evolved from 1G to 4G to cater to various service offerings. Analog voice services with mobility are provided by 1G and digital voice services with increased voice capacity in 2G; while 3G mobile broadband services enabled faster data rates and better connectivity. Now, 4G systems provide high speed data along with voice and multimedia services. Mobile communications evolving from 1G to 4G are shown in the Table 1.

Table 1. 1G to 4G evolution

Generation	Standard	Data Speed	Signal Type	Modulation Techniques	Application
1G	AMPS/TACS	2.4 Kbps	Analog	FM	Voice only
2G	GSM/CDMA	64 Kbps	Digital	PSK, GMSK	Voice and messaging
2.5G	GPRS/CDMA 2000	64-144 Kbps	Digital	QPSK, PSK	Data only
3G	UMTS	144 Kbps – 40Mbps	Digital	QPSK, QAM	Voice, Data, Messaging, Multimedia, Web browsing
4G	LTE	40 - 300 Mbps	Digital	QAM	High Data rates, HD Video streaming

Brief About 4G-LTE Developments

The most important feature of cellular is to provide coverage, i.e. connectivity no matter where the customer is positioned. Once connectivity is available and a connection has been established, the speed of data communications becomes the next prominent feature to be provided. LTE will be used over the coming years with its new orthogonal frequency-division multiple access (OFDMA) transmission scheme acting as a stepping stone for providing higher data rates in future improvements. Initially it had the data rates of the same order that HSPA+ within the same carrier bandwidth (BW). This repeats the case seen at the time of 3G UMTS (universal mobile telecommunications system) introduction, which was also done at data rates compatible with previous second-generation enhancements of 384kb/s EDGE (enhanced data rates for GSM evolution).

LTE Release 8 (R8) and Release 9 (R9) ideally offer data rates of up to 300Mb/s in the downlink and 75Mb/s in the uplink at the physical (PHY) layer without high level signaling. The push for higher data rates in the subsequent standard update R10 is mostly addressed by going from 4 to 8 transmit antennas in the downlink, and from 1 to 4 transmit antennas in the uplink, which is known as MIMO. R10 is thus compliant to the IMT-Advanced requirements and is known as LTE-Advanced (LTE-A). Even higher data rates (over 1 GB/s in downlink, and over 500Mb/s in uplink) will be possibly achieved through carrier aggregation. Inter-cell coordination like ICIC (inter-cell interference coordination, R10) as well as joint processing enabled by CoMP (Coordinated Multipoint) transmission/reception (R11) will further increase spectral efficiency. All such schemes seek for an evolutionary approach within a synchronous/orthogonal physical layer framework. In 10 years, following the progression of wireless throughputs, speeds in the order of 10 GB/s must be addressed.

Specific traffic needs of access devices such as smart phones, multimedia tablets or MTC devices have not been addressed in LTE R10 yet. Moreover, particularly MTC devices are currently viewed as a threat to network stability due to signaling overhead, and thus, restrictions are considered upon bringing in such devices into the network (network overload protection). MTC devices may have other special requirements such as low power operation, low data transmission, bursty and sporadic traffic profiles. A dedicated study group was formed within the 3rd Generation Partnership Project (3GPP) to work out signaling and protocol schemes to include MTC traffic into the LTE-A standard update (release R12), which enabled the creation of multimedia sensor networks at the service level. This contribution could be realized in terms of proposing specific definition of services, requirements, features, options, signaling, and many more. MTC, as a specific type of communication, has its special requirements, such as for example a strong need to minimize the power consumption at the end device. Other example features of MTC to be proposed and evaluated include mobile-only originated calls, low data transmission, low power transmission, low mobility scenarios (e.g. surveillance cameras), periodic data transmission, and delay tolerant services. Also here, a fundamental issue for working on MTC is to have an adequate and detailed model of the physical (PHY) and medium access (MAC) layers of the system. So far only the basic features and concept of MTC are included (3GPP, 2011) at the level of stage 1 specification. Physical layer techniques, however, as one of the main focus of the 5GNOW project proposal, which are not within the scope of 3GPP.

Finally, LTE-A is, in one way or another, dealing with some spectrum agility as a requisite to allow worldwide interoperability of devices in a fragmented spectrum, fuelled by ongoing spectrum auctions, license renewals and re-farming initiatives across a wide range of frequency band (3GPP, 2009). LTE is already implemented in many frequency bands: 700 MHz and AWS (Advanced Wireless Spectrum) bands in the USA, 800, 1800 and 2600 MHz in Europe, 2.1 GHz and 2.6 GHz in Asia. It is expected that the 2.6 GHz, 1800 MHz and 800 MHz bands to be the most widely used in Western Europe for 4G deployments. As a conclusion, the lack of spectrum harmonization is forcing vendors to find contour solutions to deliver, as far as possible, globally compatible LTE chipsets and devices (and OFDM spectrum property is not helping much to alleviate the analog signal processing challenges in the front-end).

WHY 5G

In this section the necessity of 5G is discussed. As the modern society is getting well connected, there is a huge demand issues in terms of data capacity and lower latencies. Due to the inherent design limitations, existing 4G networks are not suitable for IoT and Device to Device Communications.

Demand Issues

The Networked Society is taking shape and new applications brought together through connectivity are being put into operation every day. Remote monitoring techniques are being used to combat illegal logging and deforestation, trash cans are telling us when they need to be emptied, and machines operating in hazardous environments are being remote-controlled from a safe distance. These are just some of the applications that connectivity and evolved ICT technologies have already enabled. But it is not just business that is being transformed; people are becoming increasingly dependent on the millions of applications that cellular networks deliver to their smart phones and other mobile devices. Today, for example, more than 5 million videos are viewed on YouTube, and 67,000 images are uploaded to Instagram every minute as it is shown in infograph in Figure 1, (Qmee, n.d).

The way people do things is changing: People are moving away from consuming content in groups to a more individual experience (TV has shifted from the living room to the second screen, for example); connectivity is providing the means and smart devices are providing the interface. Users are doing more with less: by enabling

Figure 1. What we do over the network today in one minute
Qmee, n.d.

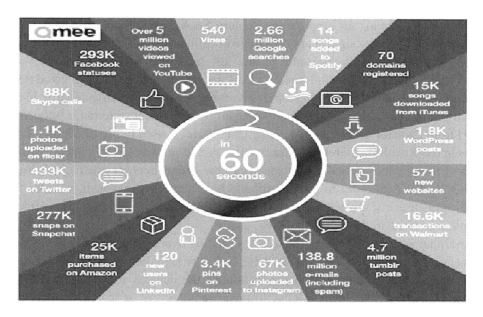

systems to track, monitor and interact with things, connectivity allows us to use the Earth's resources wisely – to share them, reuse them, and even dispose of them in a sustainable manner.

LTE Deficiencies

More than 50% of the data volume measured in cellular networks is generated by users consuming streaming applications. As high definition 3D streaming with user enabled vision angle control requires bandwidth on the order of 100Mb/s, and users expect even higher data rates for the simple transference of such files, it is possible *to see 10-100 Gb/s wireless connectivity* coming up as a target in future. Obviously, this does not lead to a need for a continuously sustainable very high bandwidth for one user over long periods of time. Instead, data rates of 100 GB/s will be shared via the wireless medium.

Sporadic access poses another second significant challenge to mobile access networks due to an operation known as *fast dormancy* [Nokia Networks 2011,and Huawei Technologies, 2010). Fast dormancy is used by handheld manufacturers to save battery power by using the feature that a mobile can break ties to the network individually and as soon as a data piece is delivered the smartphone changes from active into idle state. Consequently, when the mobile has to deliver more pieces of data it will always go through the complete synchronization procedure again. Actually, this can happen several hundred times a day resulting in significant control signalling growth and network congestion threat. Furthermore, with M2M on the horizon, a multitude of (potentially billions) MTC devices accessing asynchronously the network will dramatically amplify the problem. Such huge number of MTC devices will eventually pose a significant challenge in cellular networks for the envisioned higher density cells with thousands of low cost and energy efficient devices.

A third challenge for cellular networks is the variable usage of aggregated non-contiguous frequency bands, so-called *carrier aggregation* implemented to achieve much higher rates. Carrier aggregation means the use of separate radio frequency (RF) front ends for accessing different channels and is used to provide higher data rates in the downlink, thereby reinforcing the attraction of isolated frequency bands such as the L-Band. Actually, the search for new spectrum is very active in Europe and in the USA in order to provide mobile broadband expansion. It includes the opportunistic use of spectrum, which has been an interesting research area in wireless communications in the past decade.

Another issue that is closely related to signaling overhead is the complexity and power consumption of the M2M devices. The more signaling the cellular standard requires, the more complex and power-hungry the devices will be. Considering state-of-the-art device technologies, a power reduction of at least two orders of magnitude is still required (Fettweis et al, 2011). The design of new physical layer techniques can facilitate the required reduction in device complexity and power consumption and support heterogeneous connectivity, with various degrees of M2M device mobility and different data rate / bandwidth requirements in an optimal way.

How to Overcome the Deficiencies of LTE

It is identified that orthogonality and synchronism as common design principles of the underlying system architecture itself, pose as hindrance for realizing the 5G use cases. For example, MTC traffic generated by devices (including smartphones) should not be forced to be integrated into the bulky synchronization procedure which has been deliberately designed to meet orthogonal constraints. Instead, they optimally should be able to awake only occasionally and transmit their message right away and be only coarsely synchronized. By doing so, MTC traffic would be removed from standard uplink data pipes with drastically reduced signalling overhead. Therefore, alleviating the synchronism requirements can significantly improve operational capabilities and network performance as well as user experience and life time of smartphones and autonomous MTC nodes.

MTC traffic and the corresponding network congestion problems are primarily concerned with synchronism and orthogonality constraints on the LTE-A PHY layer uplink channels. However, LTE-A downlink is also involved when Coordinated Multipoint transmission (3GPP TR 36.819, 2011) is considered. CoMP is driven by the appealing idea to exploit the superior single-cell performance of the underlying synchronous orthogonal air interfaces enabling both uniform coverage and high capacity. However, such an approach entails huge additional overhead in terms of message sharing, base station synchronization, feedback of channel state information, and forwarding of control information etc. Additionally, the approach is known to lack robustness against the actual extent to what the delivered information reflects the current network state - in fact, it turns out that the achieved gains by CoMP transmission are still far away from the theoretical limits while even constraining the potential services in the network due to extensive uplink capacity used for control signalling (Wild, 2011). In addition, in a heterogeneous networking scenario HetNet with uncoordinated pico or femto cells and highly overlapping coverage, as in today's networks, it seems illusive to provide the required information to all network entities. Evidently, if the degree of coordination to maintain synchronism and orthogonality across layers (PHY, MAC/networking) is not attainable, the LTE-A PHY layer should not be forced into such strict requirements, calling for 5GNOW non-orthogonal waveforms for asynchronous signalling and also improved robustness in the downlink.

Finally, interference within the network is overlaid by inherently uncoordinated interference from other legacy networks due to carrier aggregation. Current systems impose generous guard bands to satisfy spectral mask requirements which either severely deteriorate spectral efficiency or even prevent band usage at all, which is again an artefact of strict orthogonality and synchronism constraints within the PHY layer. 5G standards need to address carrier aggregation by implementing sharp frequency notches in order not to interfere with other legacy systems and tight spectral masks.

Investigations are ongoing about the inherent tradeoffs between possible relaxation in orthogonality and synchronism and their corresponding impact on performance and network operation/user experience versus the required signal processing capabilities. 5GNow, a research project is thoroughly investigating the non-orthogonal waveforms to address the basic issues of LTE and the following waveform approaches have been developed:

- Generalized Frequency-Division Multiplexing (GFDM),
- Filter-Bank Multi-Carrier (FBMC) transmission,
- Universal Filtered Multi-Carrier (UFMC) transmission,
- Bi-orthogonal Frequency Division Multiplexing (BFDM).

These waveforms have been thoroughly investigated within 5GNOW, each particularly related to certain scenarios as described in detail in the next chapter.

PATH TO 5G

The fifth-generation (5G) mobile communications system will emerge to meet new and unprecedented demands beyond the capability of previous generation systems (Fettweis, 2012). 5G will penetrate into every element of future society and create an all-dimensional, user-centered information ecosystem as shown in Figure 2. 5G will break through the limitation of time and space to enable an immersive and interactive user experience. 5G will also shorten the distance between human and things and implement seamless integration to achieve an easy and smart interconnection between people and all things. 5G will provide users with fiber-like access data rate and "zero" latency user experience. 5G will be able to deliver a consistent experience across a variety of scenarios including the cases of ultra-high traffic volume density, ultra-high connection density, and ultra-high mobility. 5G will also be able to provide intelligent optimization based on services and users awareness, and will improve energy and cost efficiency by over a hundred times, enabling us all to realize the vision of 5G - "Information a finger away, everything in touch".

Figure 2. 5G vision
IMT 2020, 2015.

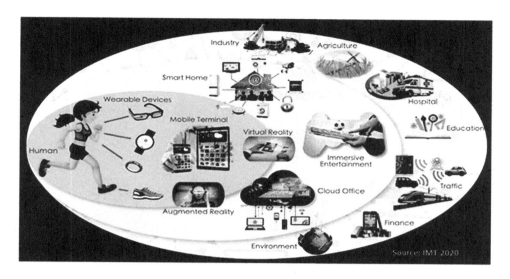

5G Vision

Next Generation Mobile Network(NGMN) is an alliance with a vision to expand the communications experience by providing a truly integrated and cohesively managed delivery platform that brings affordable mobile broadband services to the end user with a particular focus on 5G while accelerating the development of LTE-Advanced and its ecosystem.

NGMN forum defines the 5G Vision as *an end-to-end ecosystem to enable a fully mobile and connected society. It empowers value creation towards customers and partners, through existing and emerging use cases, delivered with consistent experience, and enabled by sustainable business models* (NGMN Alliance, 2016).

Mobile communications have profoundly changed everyday life, and people's desire for higher-performance mobile communications is never-ending. Going forward, several trends are on a path to exhaust the capabilities of existing wireless networks. These include: explosive growth of data traffic, massive increase in the number of interconnected devices and the continuous emergence of new services and application scenarios.

9

Requirements of 5G

As a result of research and initiatives undertaken by many industry and standardization organization on 5G, the requirements as depicted in Figure 3 are broadly accepted (IWPC 2014; METIS, 2015; GSMA Intelligence, 2014).

Characteristics of 5G Networks

The key elements of 5G characterization are:

- Use cases,
- Business Models,
- Value Creation.

Use Cases

In addition to supporting the evolution of the established mobile broadband use cases, 5G need to support innumerable emerging use cases with a high variety of applications and variability of their performance attributes: from delay-sensitive video applications to ultra-low latency, from high speed entertainment applications in a vehicle to mobility on demand for connected objects, and from best effort applications to reliable and ultra-reliable ones such as health and safety. Furthermore, use cases

Figure 3. 5G requirements

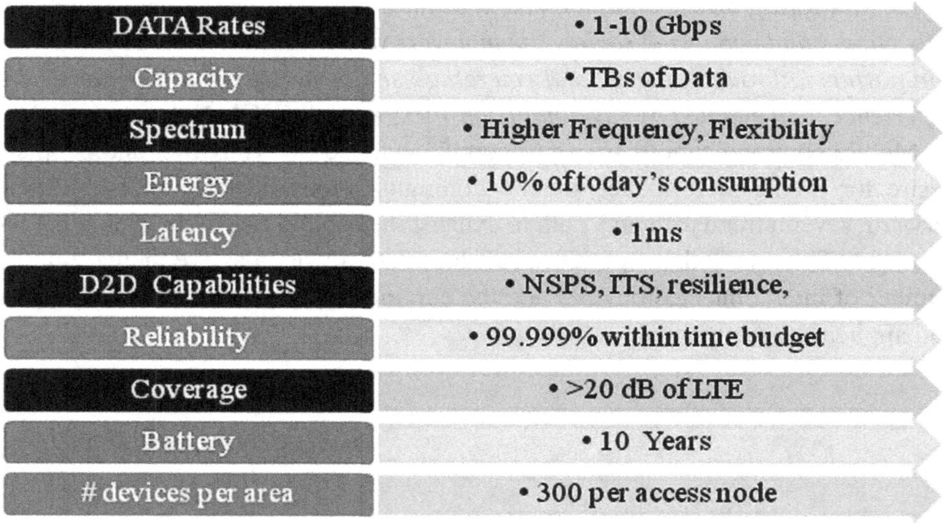

DATA Rates	• 1-10 Gbps
Capacity	• TBs of Data
Spectrum	• Higher Frequency, Flexibility
Energy	• 10% of today's consumption
Latency	• 1ms
D2D Capabilities	• NSPS, ITS, resilience,
Reliability	• 99.999% within time budget
Coverage	• >20 dB of LTE
Battery	• 10 Years
# devices per area	• 300 per access node

will be delivered across a wide range of devices (e.g., smartphone, wearable, MTC) and across a fully heterogeneous environment. NGMN has developed twenty five use cases for 5G (NGMN Alliance, 2016), as representative examples that are grouped into eight use case families. The use cases and use case families serve as an input for stipulating requirements and defining the building blocks of the 5G architecture. The diagram in Figure 4 shows the eight use case families with one example use case given for each family with a description of these families and use case examples.

Broadband Access in Dense Areas

This family highlights the broad range of growing and new use cases of the fully connected society. The focus is service availability in densely-populated areas (e.g., multi-storey buildings, dense urban city centres or events), where thousands of people per square kilometre (km^2) live and/or work. Communications are expected to be pervasive and part of everyday life. Augmented reality, multi-user interaction and three-dimensional (3D) services will be among the services which play an increasingly significant role in the 2020+ timeframe. Context recognition will be an essential aspect, at the network edge (i.e. close to the user), ensuring delivery of consistent and personalised services to the customers.

Figure 4. 5G use case families and related examples
NGMN Alliance, 2016.

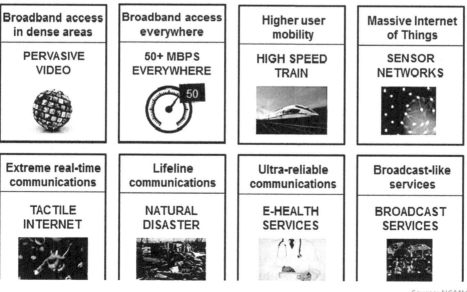

Source: NGMN

This family includes the following use cases:

1. **Pervasive Video:** Beyond 2020, person-to-person or person-to-group video communication with extremely high resolution will have a much wider usage with much more advanced and extreme capabilities. Customers will use video broadly in their everyday workflow. Examples include data delivery for optical head-mounted displays, collaboration in 3D cyber-real offices or operating rooms (with both physical and virtual presence) and customers' support by hologram services. An environment will emerge in which video is available to everyone, regardless of the physical location, the device being used, and the network connection. The number of concurrently active connections, combined with the performance required (data rate and the end-to-end latency) will present a challenging situation.

2. **Smart Office:** In a future office, it is envisioned that most of the devices will be wirelessly connected and the users will be interacting with them. This suggests a scenario in which hundreds of users require ultra-high bandwidth for services that need high-speed execution of bandwidth-intensive applications, processing of a vast amount of data in a cloud, and instant communication by video. Ultra-high traffic volume, and for some applications latency, is the main challenge applicable for this use case.

3. **Operator Cloud Services:** Cloud services provided by operators will become increasingly diversified, and further customized to each user, allowing operators to provide the user a full mobile "Smart life" experience. To support the future value added cloud services, there will be a need for higher QoE with user throughput consistency, fast and reliable networks, and seamless interworking across clouds, networks and devices.

4. **HD Video/Photo Sharing in Stadium/Open-Air Gathering:** This use case is characterised by a high connection density and potentially temporary use (e.g., in a stadium, concert, or other events). Several hundred thousand users per km2 may be served, possibly integrating physical and virtual information such as score, information on athletes or musicians, etc., during the event. People can watch high definition (HD) playback video, share live video or post HD photos to social networks. These applications will require a combination of ultra-high connection density, high date rate and low latency.

Broadband Access Everywhere

This family highlights the need to provide access to broadband service everywhere, including the more challenging situations in terms of coverage (from urban to suburban and rural areas). A consistent user experience with respect to throughput needs a minimum data rate guaranteed everywhere.

This family includes the following use cases:

1. **50+ Mbps Everywhere:** The mobile and connected society will need broadband access to be available everywhere. Therefore, 50 Mbps should be understood as the minimum user data rate and not a single user's theoretical peak rate. Furthermore, it is emphasized that this user rate has to be delivered consistently across the coverage area (i.e. even at cell edges). The target value of 50 (or possibly 100) Mbps everywhere is meant to be indicative, depending upon the 5G technology evolution to support these figures economically.

2. **Ultra-Low Cost Networks:** Deployment and operation of mobile networks infrastructure as well as cost of terminals are not economically sustainable to cover scarcely populated and some very-low ARPU areas of the world. 5G is expected to be flexible enough to be deployed under ultra-low cost requirements to offer Internet access in these areas and enable new business and new opportunities in underserved areas of the world.

Higher User Mobility

Beyond 2020, there will be a growing demand for mobile services in vehicles, trains and even aircrafts. While some services are the natural evolution of the existing ones (navigation, entertainment, etc.), some others represent completely new scenarios such as broadband communication services on commercial aircrafts (e.g., by a hub on board). Vehicles will demand enhanced connectivity for in-vehicle entertainment, accessing the internet, enhanced navigation through instant and real-time information, autonomous driving and safety and vehicle diagnostics. The degree of mobility required (i.e. speed) will depend upon the specific use case.

This family includes the following use cases:

1. **High Speed Train:** High speed train is used in various regions for inter-city transport and will further evolve beyond 2020; these high speed trains can reach speeds greater than 500 km/h. While travelling, passengers will use high quality mobile Internet for information, interaction, entertainment or work. Examples are watching a HD movie, gaming online, accessing company systems, interacting with social clouds, or having a video conference. Providing a satisfactory service to the passengers (e.g. up to 1000) at a speed of 500 km/h may be a great challenge. In addition, providing an acceptable end-to-end latency will become a challenge for office-like applications.

2. **Remote Computing:** Beyond 2020, remote computing is used on the go and at high speeds (such as vehicles or public transport), in addition to those indicated for stationary or low-mobility scenarios (such as smart office). Moreover,

automotive & transportation industry will rely on remote processing to ease vehicle maintenance and to offer novel services to customers with very short time-to-market. All this requires very low latencies with robust communication links together with availability close to 100%.

3. **Moving Hot Spots:** While moving vehicles or crowds (e.g., moving mass events such as walking/cycling demos or a long red-cycle of a traffic light) will generate capacity variation (from almost stationary to bursty), current radio planning determines hot spot areas, for optimization, assuming stationary hot spot. Therefore, non-stationary capacity demand will become a challenge in 2020+. 5G shall complement the stationary mode of planning of capacity, and incorporate non-stationary, dynamic and real-time provision of capacity.

4. **3D (Three Dimensional) Connectivity-Aircrafts:** Civil aviation will implement commercial connectivity services in 2020+, and the passenger services offered will comprise of similar applications to those available on the ground. Typical aircraft routes are up to 12 km in altitude, while other objects like helicopters will usually fly at much lower altitudes. Another example for 3D connectivity is support of sporting event live services where the user is moving physically in all 3 dimensions, e.g., balloonists, gliders, or skydivers.

Massive Internet of Things (IoT)

The vision of 2020 and beyond also includes a great deal of growing use cases with massive number of devices (e.g., sensors, actuators and cameras) with a wide range of characteristics and demands. This family will include both low-cost/long-range/low-power MTC as well as broadband MTC with some characteristics closer to human-type communication (HTC).

This family includes the following use cases:

1. **Smart Wearables (Clothes):** It is expected that the use of wearables consisting of multiple types of devices and sensors will become mainstream. For example, a number of ultra-light, low power, waterproof sensors will be integrated into people's clothing. These sensors can measure various environmental and health attributes like pressure, temperature, heart rate, blood pressure, body temperature, breathing rate and volume, skin moisture, etc. A key challenge for this use case is the overall management of the number of devices as well as the data and applications associated with these devices.

2. **Sensor Networks:** Smart services will become pervasive in urban areas, and usage will also grow in suburban and rural areas. Among others, metering (e.g., gas, energy, and water), city or building lights management, environment (e.g., pollution, temperature, humidity, noise) monitoring, and vehicle traffic control

represent prominent examples of services in a smart city. The aggregation of all these services leads to very high density of devices with very different characteristics expected to be combined in a common communication and interworking framework. Depending on the specific use cases, very low cost devices with very high battery life may be required.

3. **Mobile Video Surveillance:** In the coming years, mobile video surveillance may evolve to being available on aircrafts, drones, cars, and safety and security personnel for monitoring houses/buildings, targeted areas, special events, etc. These applications will leverage automated analysis of the video footage, not requiring human support. While they will not present constraints on the battery life and often use medium/high-end devices, these applications require a highly reliable and secure network with the right performance and instant interaction with back-end and remote systems

Extreme Real-Time Communications: Tactile Internet

This family covers use cases which have a strong demand in terms of real-time interaction. These demands are use-case specific and, for instance, may require one or more attributes such as extremely high throughput, mobility, critical reliability, etc.. For example, the autonomous driving use case that requires ultra-reliable communication may also require immediate reaction (based on real-time interaction), to prevent road accidents. Others such as remote computing, with stringent latency requirement, may need robust communication links with high availability.

Tactile Internet

Tactile interaction is referred to as a system where humans will wirelessly control real and virtual objects. Tactile interaction typically requires a tactile control signal and audio and/or visual feedback. One application falling into this category is the use of software running in the cloud in a way that the user, interacting with environment, does not perceive any difference between local and remote content. Robotic control and interaction include countless scenarios such as those in manufacturing, remote medical care, and autonomous cars. The main challenge in tactile interaction is the real-time reaction that is expected to be within sub-millisecond.

Lifeline Communication: Natural Disasters

Public safety and emergency services that are provided today are continuously improving. In addition to new capabilities for authority-to-citizen and citizen-to-authority communication for alerting and support, these use cases will evolve to include emerging and new applications for authority-to-authority communication, emergency prediction and disaster relief. Furthermore, there will be an expectation that the mobile network acts as a lifeline, in all situations including times of a more general emergency. Therefore, the use cases require a very high level of availability in addition to the ability to support traffic surges.

Natural Disasters

5G should be able to provide robust communications in case of natural disasters such as earthquakes, tsunamis, floods, hurricanes, etc. Several types of basic communications (e.g., voice, text messages) are needed by those in the disaster area. Survivors should also be able to signal their location/presence so that they can be found quickly. Efficient network and user terminal energy consumptions are critical in emergency cases. Several days of operation should be supported.

Ultra-Reliable Communications

The vision of 2020 and beyond suggests not only significant growth in such areas as automotive, health and assisted living applications, but a new world in which the industries from manufacturing to agriculture rely on reliable MTC. Other applications may involve significant growth in remote operation and control that will require extreme low latency as well (e.g., enterprise services or critical infrastructure services such as Smart Grid). Many of these will have zero to low mobility.

This family includes the following use cases:

1. **Automated Traffic Control and Driving:** In the coming years advanced safety applications will appear to mitigate the road accidents, to improve traffic efficiency, and to support the mobility of emergency vehicles (e.g., ambulances, fire trucks). These applications foresee not only a vehicle to vehicle or vehicle to infrastructure communication, but also communication with vulnerable road users such as pedestrians and cyclists. An application such as controlled fleet driving will require an ultra-low end-to-end latency for some warning signals, and higher data rates to share video information between cars and infrastructure. 5G should provide the high reliability, low latency, and high scalability required in this space.
2. **Collaborative Robots: A Control Network for Robots:** Automation will complement human workers, not only in jobs with repetitive tasks (e.g., production, transportation, logistics, office/administrative support) but also within the services industry. In order to enable these applications with completely diverse tasks in different environments, it will be essential to provide

an underlying control network with very low latency and high reliability. For many robotics scenarios in manufacturing a round-trip reaction time of less than 1ms is anticipated.

3. **eHealth: Extreme Life Critical:** While mobile applications of remote health monitoring will continue growing beyond 2020, other applications such as remote treatment will emerge. Such applications will include several devices, like sensors, e.g., for electrocardiography (ECG), pulse, blood glucose, blood pressure, temperature. The monitoring applications, including the surveillance of patients remotely, will further grow in terms of availability and new applications. Depending on the patient's device, treatment reactions may be required that are based on monitored data, and these should be immediate and (semi-)automatic. eHealth applications can be life critical and the system must be able to reserve/ prioritise capacity for the related communications including out of coverage warnings. Identity, privacy, security and authentication management must be ensured for each device.

4. **Remote Object Manipulation: Remote Surgery:** Remote surgery, available today using fixed networks, will be mobile in some scenarios such as in ambulances, for disaster-response, in remote areas, for the exploration of dangerous and hazardous areas, or during a leakage of radioactive material, etc. The technology necessary for providing the correct control and feedback for the surgeon entails very strict requirements in terms of latency, reliability and security.

5. **3D Connectivity - Drones:** Future 5G services will require ubiquitous coverage, including both terrestrial and up-in-the-air locations. For example drones may be used for logistics such as autonomous delivery of packages on routes with no/low civil population. An example is delivery of medicine to the addressee, with drones automatically finding the way using a remote control system that exploits a 5G communication.

6. **Public Safety:** The public safety organisations will need enhanced and secure communications. This, for instance, will include real time video and ability to send high quality pictures. The main challenge is to ensure (ultra) reliable communication over the entire footprint of the emergency services including land, sea, air, in-building and some underground areas such as basements and subway systems. It will also require priority over other traffic (in networks shared with other users), ability for direct communication between devices, and high security.

Broadcast-Like Services

While personalization of communication will lead to a reducing demand for legacy broadcast as deployed today, e.g. linear TV, the fully mobile and connected society will nonetheless need efficient distribution of information from one source to many destinations. These services may distribute content as done today (typically only downlink), but also provide a feedback channel (uplink) for interactive services or acknowledgement information. Both, real-time or non-real time services should be possible. Furthermore, such services are well suited to accommodate vertical industries' needs. These services are characterized by having a wide distribution which can be either geo-location focused or address-space focused (many end-users).

1. **News and Information:** Beyond 2020, receiving text/pictures, audio and video, everywhere and as soon as things happen (e.g., action or score in a football match) will be common. Customers in specific areas should simultaneously receive appropriate news and information regardless of the device they are using and their network connection.
2. **Local Broadcast-Like Services:** Local services will be active at a cell (compound) level with a reach of for example 1 to 20 km. Typical scenarios include stadium services, advertisements, voucher delivery, festivals, fairs, and congress/convention. Local emergency services can exploit such capabilities to search for missing people or in the prevention or response to crime (e.g. theft).
3. **Regional Broadcast-Like Services:** Broadcast-like services with a regional reach will be required, for example within 1 to 100 km. A typical scenario includes communication of traffic jam information. Regional emergency warnings can include disaster warnings. Unlike the legacy broadcast service, the feedback channel can be used to track delivery of the warning message to all or selected parties.
4. **National Broadcast-Like Services:** National or even continental/world-reach services are interesting as a substitute or complementary to broadcast services for radio or television. Also vertical industries will benefit from national broadcast like services to upgrade/distribution of firmware. The automotive industry may leverage the acknowledgement broadcast capability to mitigate the need for recall campaigns. This requires software patches to be delivered in large scale, and successful updates to be confirmed and documented via the feedback channel.

The post-2020 outlook, shown throughout the use cases above, is extremely broad in terms of variety of applications and variability of their performance attributes.

The use case families shown earlier represent both enriched service categories and also prospects for numerous new services.

Business Models

On top of supporting the evolution of the current business models, 5G will expand to new ones to support different types of customers and partnerships. Operators will support vertical industries, and contribute to the mobilization of industries and industry processes. Partnerships will be established on multiple layers ranging from sharing the infrastructure, to exposing specific network capabilities as an end to end service, and integrating partners' services into the 5G system through a rich and software oriented capability set. There is a need for flexibility and embedded functionality to enable these. Figure 5 shows examples of models that have to be supported by 5G.

Figure 5. 5G business model examples

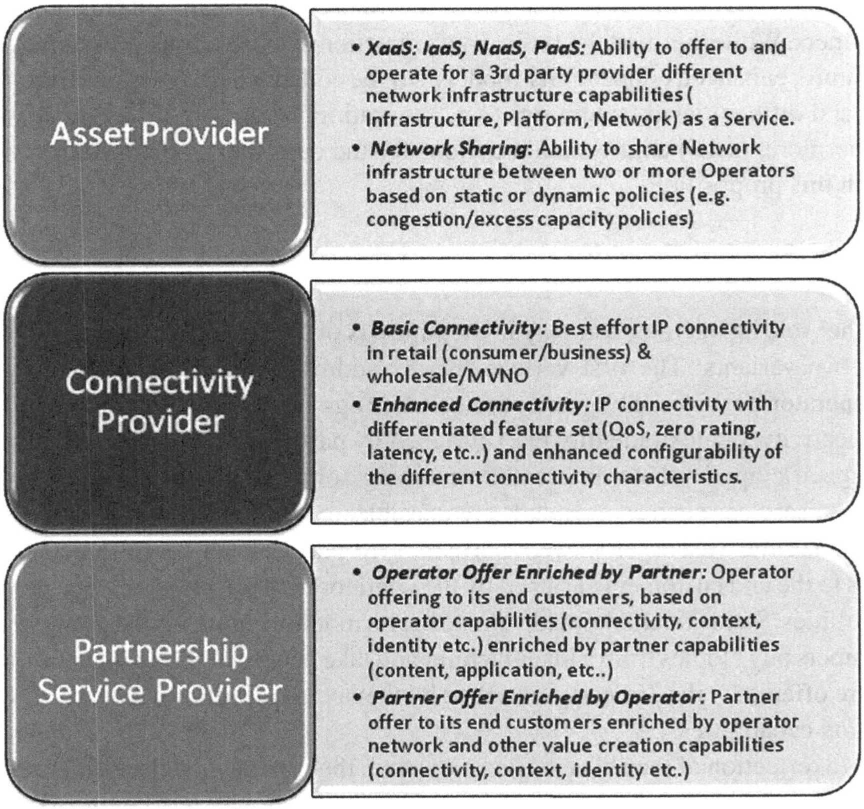

Asset Provider

- *XaaS: IaaS, NaaS, PaaS:* Ability to offer to and operate for a 3rd party provider different network infrastructure capabilities (Infrastructure, Platform, Network) as a Service.
- *Network Sharing:* Ability to share Network infrastructure between two or more Operators based on static or dynamic policies (e.g. congestion/excess capacity policies)

Connectivity Provider

- *Basic Connectivity:* Best effort IP connectivity in retail (consumer/business) & wholesale/MVNO
- *Enhanced Connectivity:* IP connectivity with differentiated feature set (QoS, zero rating, latency, etc..) and enhanced configurability of the different connectivity characteristics.

Partnership Service Provider

- *Operator Offer Enriched by Partner:* Operator offering to its end customers, based on operator capabilities (connectivity, context, identity etc.) enriched by partner capabilities (content, application, etc..)
- *Partner Offer Enriched by Operator:* Partner offer to its end customers enriched by operator network and other value creation capabilities (connectivity, context, identity etc.)

Asset Provider

One of the operator's key assets is infrastructure. Infrastructure usually is used by an operator to deliver own services to the end-customer. However, especially in the wholesale business it is common that parts of the infrastructure – so-called assets - can be used by a third party provider. Assets can be different parts of a network infrastructure that are operated for or on behalf of third parties resulting in a service proposition. Accordingly, one can distinguish between Infrastructure as a Service (IaaS), Network as a Service (NaaS) or Platform as a Service (PaaS). These may be summarized as Anything as a Service (XaaS). Another dimension of asset provisioning is real-time network sharing that refers to an operator's ability to integrate 3rd party networks in the MNO network and vice versa, based on a dynamic and context dependent policies (e.g., congestion/excess capacity policies).

Connectivity Provider

Another role an operator can play in the future is one of a Connectivity provider. Basic connectivity involves best effort IP connectivity for retail and wholesale customers. While this model is basically a projection of existing business models into the future, enhanced connectivity models will be added where IP connectivity with QoS and differentiated feature sets (e.g. zero rating, latency, mobility) is possible. Furthermore, (self-) configuration options for the customer or the third party will enrich this proposition.

Partner Service Provider

Another role an operator can play in the future is one of a partner service provider, with two variants: The first variant directly addresses the end customers where the operator provides integrated service offerings based on operator capabilities (connectivity, context, identity etc.) enriched by partner (3rd party / OTT) content and specific applications. Integrated streaming solutions can be an example here but even services such as payments are possible.

The second variant empowers partners (3rd parties / OTTs) to directly make offers to the end customers enriched by the operator network or other value creation capabilities. Smart wearables with remote health monitoring are a good example. The customers buy clothes from a manufacturer and take benefit of the health monitoring feature offered by the 3rd party, enriched by the operator's set of network and value creation capabilities.

As a reflection of the above business context, the pricing models will also evolve and adapt to represent different types of services and customer profiles, for example,

- Evolved usage-based pricing, which reflects the throughput, latency, data consumption and device movement.
- Event based / real-time charging which may cover e.g. bandwidth consuming services.
- Tiered offers based on differentiated customer profiles and services.

Linked to the business context, the operators' capability to meet customers' demands, will depend on spectrum availability, roaming and assets sharing policies, and differentiated capabilities exposure. These parameters impact operators' ability to develop new value propositions, and to provide quality service with consistent user experience throughout a wide range of scenarios. Therefore, it is evident that regulatory aspects will play a key role in 2020 and beyond.

Value Creation

5G will bring multiple propositions to all customers and at the same time provides an enhanced and unique proposition tailored to each one of them. The definition of the customer is not limited to the consumers and the enterprises as in today's environment but also expand to include verticals and other partnerships. Common to all types of use cases and spanning all customer types, 5G will provide the following value proposition:

- **Available Anywhere-Anytime:** Delivering faster connectivity, communication and content anywhere, anytime without user perceived delay.
- **Delivered With Consistent Experience:** Services are delivered with a consistent experience across time, space, technology and devices used.
- **Accessible on Multiple Devices/Interfaces:** User sessions are assumed to be portable from one device to another, in a transparent way to the user. Freedom to choose interfaces and forms of interaction (e.g., touch, speech, face and eye recognition).
- **Support Multiple Interaction Types:** Multi-device interactions within smart user spaces and personal clouds with the user's ability to create, communicate, control, manage and share.
- **Supported Transparently Across Technologies:** Full transparency and seamless connectivity for all customers regardless of the wireless or fixed accesses utilized.
- **Delivered in a Personalized and Contextual Fashion:** Services are enhanced by contextual and personalized attributes to provide a personalized experience

- **Enabled by Trusted and Reliable Communications:** Full trust, security and privacy supported.
- **Highly Reliable and Resilient Network:** Mobile communication will be assumed to be always available as a lifeline, and serve as means for smart socio-economic well-being, smart services and processes, smart automated industries, and smart remote operations.
- **Responsive and Real-Time:** Extreme communication with stringent requirements, from fast downloads to real-time multimedia and pervasive video, with ultra-high resolution, for personal interaction and peer-to-peer or multi-party.

For consumers, 5G will provide higher data rates and lower latencies required to support new and demanding applications. 5G as an engine of innovation will allow for faster development of new services delivered with consistent experience across time and space. Services and experience will be enhanced by contextual information leading to a very unique and personalized experience. On top of that, 5G should extend the battery life beyond today's norm.

For enterprises, 5G will provide differentiated capabilities to fulfil specific enterprise or enterprise application needs (security, privacy, reliability, latency, etc.). At the same time, through exposure of capabilities (e.g., location, analytics), enterprises can enrich and enhance processes and applications. Enterprise applications will enjoy the level of consistency of experience delivered by 5G.

For verticals, 5G will provide the required flexibility of functions and capabilities as it does for the enterprises. More specifically, 5G will provide the flexibility for verticals to operate their own applications in a profitable manner coming with a high degree of self service and at a cost level that allows sustainable business.

For 3rd party partners, 5G will foster innovation by flexible exposure of the network's value creation capabilities. This will enable partner-based propositions and allows for faster development and launch of these partner services at the benefit of all.

Operators' value creation propositions as outlined above will be enabled by capabilities that are flexibly integrated into the 5G system and easily exposed through APIs. This will be of significant benefit to all customers as it will allow for tailored and differentiated capability offering, enablement of new services, faster time to market and cost-efficient design.

As depicted in Figure 6, on top of network connectivity, the value creation capabilities cover trust, experience and service related attributes. Trust includes capabilities such as security, identity management and privacy. Experience of services will be seamless and personalized across technologies, devices, time and location. From a service perspective, capabilities such as quality of service, context,

Figure 6. 5G value creation

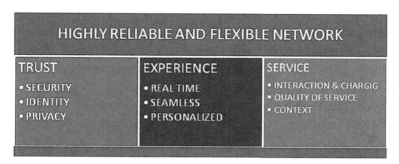

and a responsive interaction and charging design will enable a differentiated service offering to customers and other service partnerships.

The following definitions describe the respective value creation capabilities in more detail. The value creation capabilities are expected to be embedded in the 5G design right from the start, and designed for exposure to enable a fast pace of innovation.

- **Security:** The operator is the partner for state-of-the art data security, running systems that are hardened according to recognized security practices, to provide security levels for all communication, connectivity and (cloud) storage purposes.
- **Identity:** The operator is the trusted partner for one (master) identity, providing for secured, hassle-free single-sign-on and user profile management to fit all communication and interaction demands.
- **Privacy:** The operator is the partner to safeguard sensitive data, while ensuring their full handling transparency.
- **Real-Time Experience:** The operator enables perceived real-time connectivity to allow for instantaneous remote interaction among Things & People as if they are in close physical proximity.
- **Seamless Experience:** The operator provides a seamless experience by managing and hiding the complexity involved in delivering services in a highly heterogeneous environment (multiple access technologies, multiple devices, roaming, etc.)
- **Personalized Experience:** The operator is able to dynamically tailor delivered service experience based on customer context and a differentiated, customer configurable product portfolio.
- **Responsive Interaction and Charging:** The operator is able to maintain a close relation with its customers throughout the lifecycle, by pro-actively

triggering service or sales related transactions where and whenever relevant, and in real-time. This is enabled by a capability to identify events in real-time and apply the required business process in real-time (e.g. real-time charging).

- **Quality of Service:** The operator is able to guarantee an agreed QoS, reliability and connectivity levels towards end customers and partners, over time and across the service coverage.
- **Context:** The operator utilizes its contextual information asset to improve network operation and to enrich its service offering to end customers and partners.

5G CONCEPT: IT IS NOT A SINGLE CONCEPT OR A NEW AIR-INTERFACE

As the requirements for 5G cover both ultra broadband and low data rates of Device to Device communications such as sensor networks, a single concept may not serve the purpose. 5G networks should coexist with technologies like LTE and Wi-Fi, which necessitate that they support multiple air interfaces. Henceforth, a target for 5G integrated air interfaces is to efficiently combine various types of service and performance classes within a radio frame (from small packet service to high rate 'bit-pipe').The vision of 5G can be summarized as depicted in Figure 7:

Figure 7. Summary of 5G vision with requirements

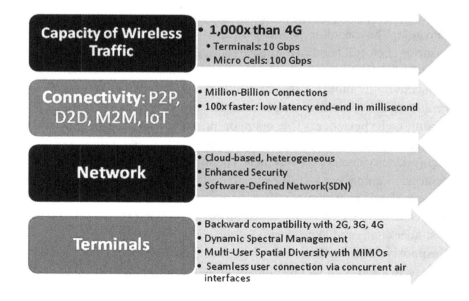

From a technical perspective it seems to be utmost challenging to provide *uniform service experience* to users under the premises of heterogeneous networks. So, to realize 5G, one concept or one new air interface is not sufficient to provide ubiquitous communications with wide ranging requirements of low and high data speeds, low and high latencies for applications. It involves new air interface concepts, networking models, battery technologies, back haul networks, antenna concepts and spectrum sharing techniques.

Potential key technologies for 5G to address the requirements and to realise the 5G vision are identified as follows (Ravi & Mohan, 2015; 4G America's, 2014):

- Massive MIMO,
- RAN Transmission at Centimetre and Millimetre Waves,
- New Waveforms,
- Shared Spectrum Access,
- Advanced Inter-node Coordination,
- Simultaneous Transmission Reception,
- Multi-RAT Integration and Management,
- Device-to-Device Communications,
- Efficient Small Data Transmission,
- Wireless Backhaul/Access Integration,
- Flexible Networks,
- Flexible Mobility,
- Context Aware Networking,
- Information Centric Networking (ICN),
- Moving Networks.

5G Coexisting With Legacy Technologies

Today, the evaluation of 3G/4G network performance is based on the metrics like peak data throughput, coverage, and spectral efficiency. In the 5G scenario, performance metrics will be centered around the user's quality of experience (QoE), including factors such as ease of connectivity with close-by devices and improved energy efficiency (Bangerter et al, 2014).

In the 5G era, many devices will use various Radio Access Technologies and modes ranging from device-to-device (D2D) communications based on WiFi or LTE, to short-range millimeter-wave (mm-wave) technologies such as WiGig, and even current day body area networks oriented toward wearable devices. Mobile operators would create a blend of pre-existing technologies covering 2G, 3G, 4G, Wi-Fi and others to allow broader coverage, and higher network density, with a key differentiator being greater connectivity to enable Machine-to-Machine (M2M) and the Internet of Things (IoT) services. Maintaining an optimum user experience in such a complex network environment will require closely coordinated RAT selection and management at both the network and device levels. In short, the 5G Era will achieve these needed improvements in network and service performance and efficiency by providing a technology framework where networks, devices, and applications are co-optimized.

Spectrum Requirements for 5G and Proposed Solutions

Much more spectrum will be needed to meet increased traffic demand. To date, spectrum for mobile communications has focused only on frequency ranges below 6 GHz. To meet demand in the 2020-2030 time frame, spectrum above 10 GHz and potentially up to 100 GHz will be needed. Depending on the carrier frequency, spectrum needs will include: large chunks of spectrum in high(er) bands, TDD mode in unpaired bands and flexible use of spectrum through advanced spectrum sharing techniques.

The 6 to 100 GHz range can be broadly split in two parts, centimeter wave and millimeter wave, based on different radio propagation characteristics and the carrier bandwidth possible in the different frequency ranges. The centimeter wave frequencies may be the next logical step for cellular access as they are closer to currently used frequency ranges, however, more research is needed to fully characterize radio propagation in these bands. In some ways, centimeter waves behave similarly to traditional cellular bands (e.g., reflections and path loss exponents), but some effects will be different, such as the overall path loss and diffraction, particularly at the higher end of the centimeter wave band. The contiguous bandwidth that is potentially available at centimeter wave, roughly 100-500 MHz, is wider than LTE-Advanced is designed for and the LTE air interface design, optimized at around 2 GHz, is not well suited for centimeter wave frequencies.

At the other end of the spectrum range are the millimeter wave frequencies which start at 30 GHz. At millimeter wave, the radio propagation and RF engineering is different from the sub-6 GHz spectrum range in some respects (Rappaport et al.2013), such as higher diffraction and higher foliage and structure penetration losses. However, recent measurements have shown that millimeter wave frequencies are also similar to those below 6 GHz in some other respects such as reflections and path loss exponents. There is still more experimentation required in these bands to understand the practical performance of the millimeter wave bands but the reward will be achievable carrier bandwidths of for example 1-2 GHz. Even though there is a well defined border of 30 GHz between centimeter wave and millimeter wave bands (1 cm wavelength), the radio propagation changes more smoothly and there is no sharp transition point in the radio propagation characteristics.

Figure 8 illustrates this differentiation of frequencies up to 100 GHz (Nokia Networks, 2015). One can foresee various different radio access components used with 5G, ranging from the evolution of LTE to completely new access technologies. The Radio communication Sector of the International Telecommunication Union (ITU-R), working on the global management of the radio spectrum, has recognized the relationship between IMT (International Mobile Telecommunication system) and "5G" and is working towards realizing the future "IMT2020" vision of mobile broadband communications.

Currently, WP 5D, an ITU-R sub group, is working on various reports to provide guidance on what may be expected in the future development of IMT for 2020 and beyond, including systems operating above 6 GHz. The World Radio Conference (WRC), which was happened in November 2015, had set the stage for the next WRC in 2019. This would then be able to identify frequency bands from 6 to 100 GHz for IMT use and facilitate global harmonization of the spectrum.

The World Radio Conference (WRC) in 2015 discussions have resulted in an agreement to include an agenda item for IMT-2020, the designated ITU-R qualifier for 5G, in WRC 2019. The conference also reached an agreement on a set of bands that will be studied for 5G. Many of the proposed bands are in the millimeter wave region and include:

- 24.25GHz to 27.5GHz, 37GHz to 40.5GHz, 42.5GHz to 43.5GHz, 45.5GHz to 47GHz, 47.2GHz to 50.2GHz, 50.4GHz to 52.6GHz, 66 GHz to 76GHz and 81GHz to 86GHz, which have allocations to the mobile service on a primary basis; and

Figure 8. Candidates for LTE-A and new 5G access (please note the non-linear x-axis)
NOKIA Networks 2015.

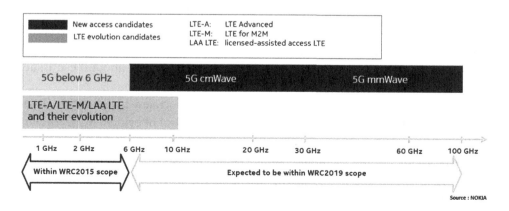

- 31.8GHz to 33.4GHz, 40.5GHz to 42.5GHz and 47GHz to 47.2GHz, which may require additional allocations to the mobile service on a primary basis.

WRC 2019 will be a unique opportunity to identify spectrum above 6GHz for mobile broadband (5G). Therefore it is important that WRC 2015 decides on the respective agenda item for the WRC 2019 to meet this opportunity. To help ensure the best spectrum is identified, several aspects related to new frequency bands need to be assessed and studied, including but not limited to:

- Frequency ranges that contain bands which already have worldwide primary allocation to Mobile Services should be considered as more likely options for possible spectrum designation and need to be further studied.
- Spectrum bands that are harmonized, at least regionally, should be given high priority.
- Current use of these frequency ranges should be further investigated.
- Minimum bandwidth requirements should also be considered as a criterion for the selection of frequency ranges.
- Coexistence with systems in the bands under consideration and in adjacent bands.
- Availability of contiguous spectrum (e.g. 500 MHz up to 1 GHz) should be taken into account.

It is essential that the industry and regulators work together to secure sufficient spectrum for mobile communications beyond 2020. It will facilitate the development of the technology and will improve society and economic development.

Latency Targets in 5G and Mission Critical Communication

Requirement of less than 1ms latency is a real challenge to achieve and industrial process automation and remote surgery are examples of use cases that will be possible in future 5G systems. They are called mission-critical machine type communication use cases and they require communication with very high reliability and availability, as well as very low end-to-end latency. This section discusses about these issues and the proposed solutions in detail.

Very low latency will be driven by the need to support new applications. Some envisioned 5G use cases, such as traffic safety and control of critical infrastructure and industry processes, may require much lower latency compared with what is possible with the mobile-communication systems of today.

To support such latency-critical applications, 5G should allow for an application end-to-end latency of 1ms or less, although application-level framing requirements and codec limitations for media may lead to higher latencies in practice. Many services will distribute computational capacity and storage close to the air interface. This will create new capabilities for real-time communication and will allow ultra-high service reliability in a variety of scenarios, ranging from entertainment to industrial process control.

Fundamentally, applications such as mobile telephony, mobile broadband and media delivery are about information for humans. In contrast, many of the new applications and use cases that drive the requirements and capabilities of 5G are about end-to-end communication between machines (Ericsson WP 2016). To distinguish them from the more human-centric wireless-communication use cases, these applications are often termed machine-type communication (MTC).

Although spanning a wide range of applications, MTC applications can be divided into two main categories – massive MTC and critical MTC – depending on their characteristics and requirements as shown in Figure 9.

Massive MTC refers to services that typically span a very large numbers of devices, usually sensors and actuators. Sensors are extremely low cost and consume very low amounts of energy in order to sustain long battery life. Clearly, the amount of data generated by each sensor is normally very small, and very low latency is not a critical requirement. While actuators are similarly limited in cost, they will likely have varying energy footprints ranging from very low to moderate energy consumption.

Figure 9. Massive MTC and critical MTC
Ericsson W P 2016.

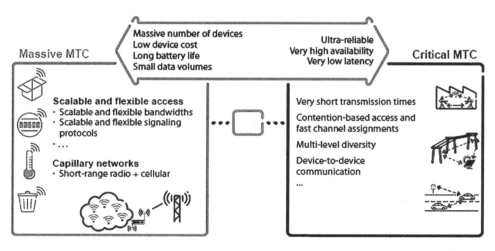

Source: Ericsson

Sometimes, the mobile network may be used to bridge connectivity to the device by means of capillary networks. Here, local connectivity is provided by means of a short-range radio access technology, for example Wi-Fi, Bluetooth or 802.15.4/6LoWPAN. Wireless connectivity beyond the local area is then provided by the mobile network via a gateway node.

Critical MTC refers to applications such as traffic safety/control, control of critical infrastructure and wireless connectivity for industrial processes. Such applications require very high reliability and availability in terms of wireless connectivity, as well as very low latency. On the other hand, low device cost and energy consumption is not as critical as for massive MTC applications. While the average volume of data transported to and from devices may not be large, wide instantaneous bandwidths are useful in being able to meet capacity and latency requirements.

There is much to gain from a network being able to handle as many different applications as possible, including mobile broadband, media delivery and a wide range of MTC applications by means of the same basic wireless-access technology and within the same spectrum. This avoids spectrum fragmentation and allows operators to offer support for new MTC services for which the business potential is inherently uncertain, without having to deploy a separate network and reassign spectrum specifically for these applications.

Performance and Variability of QoS for Various Applications

The main challenges for 5G system are the continued evolution of mobile broadband and the addition of new services e.g., massive sensor communication and vehicular to anything communication, requiring shorter setup times and delay, as well as reduced signaling overhead and energy consumption. Mobile broadband of the future will have significantly increased traffic volumes and data transmissions rates, but also many more use cases. They include not only traffic between humans and between human and the cloud, but also between humans, sensors, and actuators in their environment, as well as between sensors and actuators themselves.

5G Vision sets out an ambitious goal of enabling a world where services are provided wirelessly to the end device by a fixed and mobile (converged) infrastructure that functions across the whole geography, including indoors and outdoors, dense urban centers with capacity challenges, sparse rural locations where coverage is the main challenge, places with existing infrastructure, and also where there is none.

The foremost requirement is that the 5G infrastructure should be far more demand/ user/device centric with the ability to marshal network/spectrum resources to deliver "always sufficient" data rate and minimal user plane (UP) latency (subject to use-case) so as to give the end-user the perception of an infinite capacity environment. Thus a new architecture is expected to address enhancements in terms of:

- **Flexibility:** It should be easy to introduce new services, software upgrades and change traffic management policies and systems
- **Complexity:** Should be reduced in terms of implementation, deployment and costs structures
- **Performance:** Should be scalable, routing unlimited, UP and CP latency according to use case and traffic management made simple to set, monitor and adjust.

These enhancements are further mapped to the following five generic targets of the 5G vision, which are set to provide a route towards much higher performing networks and to a far more predictable Quality of Experience for users.

- Minimize End to End latency for services and use cases that need this to execute successfully and/or safely.

(e.g.: <=1ms IOT control activation turnaround such as Drone direction control adjustment)

(e.g.: <=1s for IoT meter report update)

- Maximize Quality of Experience.
- Enable new Applications.
- Make more efficient usage of all available communications resources at time of service request.
- Continue to minimize network OPEX and CAPEX.

Performance Targets for IMT-2020

The performance parameters for so-called 5G network which are identified by ITU-R with the following eight key capabilities as shown in Table 2 and the targets for IMT-2020(ITU-R, 2015), mostly from the radio access network points of view while they are still quite relevant to its network as well, which are subject to be changed according to future studies.

WORLDWIDE 5G RESEARCH ACTIVITIES AND INITIATIVES

Historically the ITU-R (International Telecommunications Union, Radio communication Sector) has led the industry in the definition of next generation wireless technologies through the IMT (International Mobile Telecommunications)

Table 2. IMT-2020 key capabilities in ITU-R

Parameters	Target
User experienced data rates	100 Mbps – 1Gbps
Peak data rates	20 Gbps
Mobility	up to 500 km/h with acceptable QoS
Latency (air interface)	1 ms
Connection density	10^6 /km^2
Network energy efficiency	100 times better than IMT-Advanced
Spectrum efficiency	3 times better IMT-Advanced
Area traffic capacity	10 Mbit/s/m^2

program (IMT-2000 and IMT-Advanced). Discussion of standardization beyond IMT-Advanced has been underway in the ITU since 2010. ITU does not officially use the nomenclature 4G or 5G, leaving this to industry marketing. Historically there has been an evolution of wireless technology every 10 years; ITU related vision in 2013-2015 and requirements in 2016-2018 for IMT 2020.

The industry is racing to 5G, but setting the standard for the technology won't be pretty, as the multitude of technologies involved in the standard for 5G, a whole host of standards organizations have stepped in - from traditional big players like the ITU to specialized groups focusing on standardizing a single piece of the 5G puzzle.

3GPP has been one of the first to make moves towards standardization, hosting a conference to discuss RAN options as research and development moves forward. Indeed, the 3GPP's founding members include forums like ETSI that draw in a massive number of global 5G players. Some of the main organizations that are working on 5G standards and regulations in order to better understand how their work overlaps, who they're partnering with and when we can expect changes to occur as 5G implementation draws nearer.

- **5GNOW:** 5GNOW is a European project pushing for a 5G specification to alter 4G and LTE's "strict" reliance on orthogonal frequency-division multiplexing (OFDM), trading it for waveforms that could handle not only the demand of large data packages (such as smartphones downloading video), but also bursts of data transmission related to the Internet of Things (5G Now, 2015). Its partners include the Fraunhofer Institute for Telecommunications, Alcatel-Lucent, France's Atomic Energy and Alternative Energies Commission, IS-Wireless, National Instruments and the Dresden University of Technology.

- **The FANTASTIC-5G:** Partnership is the EU's follow-up to 5GNOW, sharing some of the group's partners, including the Fraunhofer Institute, and adding players like Intel, Nokia, Samsung and Huawei. FANTASTIC-5G derives its name from its standards goal, which is a "flexible air interface for scalable service delivery within wireless communication networks of the 5th Generation."

- **3GPP:** The 3rd Generation Partnership Project, whose partners include a variety of telecom associations in Japan, India, China and more, is also planning for IMT-2020 deadlines.

- **ETSI:** As a founding member of 3GPP, ETSI has been at the forefront of 5G standardization, first mobile summit hosted on the topic in November 2013. The group has hosted several additional conferences since, with another happened in January 2016 with a focus on air interfaces and future radio technologies.

- **5G Infrastructure Public Private Partnership (5GPPP):** Considered one of the frontrunners of 5G standardization, 5GPPP has a broad scope of goals for network standards, as well as an umbrella of more focused sub-groups. 5GPPP's goals include 1000x increased capacity, 90 percent reduced energy (particularly in mobile), drastically reduced service creation time cycle, secure and ubiquitous coverage with negligible latency, dense wireless communication links and an increase in user security.

- **METIS-II EU:** A subset of 5GPPP, this project, like 3GPP, focuses on the design of radio systems, with the ambition of creating a "roadmap recommendation for 5G," as well as playing a key role in the development of 5G system architecture. Rather than developing its own technology, this project aims to unite other RAN-developing groups by the end of its duration in 2017. Partners include Ericsson, Telecom Italia, Orange, Deutsche Telecom and a variety of U.S. and European universities, among others.

- **5G Novel Radio Multiservice Adaptive Network Architecture (5G NORMA):** NORMA's focus is in end-to-end architecture and core networks with a goal, once again, to create a flexible architecture that not only successfully integrates previous standards, but uses software to ensure that it is "future-proof" as well. Group participants Nokia, Alcatel-Lucent, Azcom Technology, Real Wireless Limited and others are working to integrate SDN and NFV technology into the infrastructure of 5G by the project's end in 2017.

- **mmMAGIC:** The 5GPPP's millimeter-wave focused arm concentrates on the development of mobile radio access technology for millimeter wave bands. The consortium includes equipment and infrastructure vendors and universities including Rohde & Schwarz, Samsung, Ericsson, Alcatel-Lucent, Huawei and Nokia.

- **Next Generation Mobile Networks (NGMN) Alliance:** The Alliance has adopted a comprehensive approach to 5G, announcing plans to research infrastructure, frequency, business principles and more in addition to creating a 5G patent pool framework. NGMN, which includes wireless executives from companies like AT&T, U.S. Cellular and Verizon, aims to include operator voices in the 5G discussion, ensuring that standards and patents are compliant with the needs of all stakeholders.

- **International Telecommunication Union (ITU):** The ITU's IMT-2020 is largely being considered the definitive timeline of 5G development, citing early 2016 as the beginning point for discussions on technical performance requirements and evaluation criteria. According to the group's plan, standards proposals would begin in late 2017 through mid-2019, with consensus building beginning in 2018 and continuing into 2020. The group anticipates an outcome and definitive 5G standards to be in early stages by mid-2019. An ITU focus group met in Turin, Italy, in late September to cover network standardization requirements, with emphasis in lower latency, increased speed and diversity of use, as well as reliability comparable to that of fiber-optic networks.

- **IEEE:** In May 2015, the IEEE held a 5G Summit, which featured talks on everything from cloud-based networks to design fundamentals and even vocabulary associated with the IoT. The group has been active in research and standardization talks that promote the use of technology like WLAN and WPAN in order to allow mobile phones to use very high bandwidth.

- **National Institute of Standards and Technology:** As part of the U.S. Department of Commerce, NIST researchers are working to tackle three proposed elements of 5G: massive multi-user MIMO, millimeter-wave communications and ultra-dense networks. While the group has not announced any deadlines for completion, it has launched a 5G Millimeter Wave Channel Model Alliance to consolidate research participants.

- **4G Americas:** 4G Americas, a trade group focused on North and South America, has branded itself "the voice for 5G in the Americas," bringing in partners including AT&T, Sprint, T-Mobile US, Intel, Nokia, Qualcomm and more. The organization recommends a variety of 5G standards, including massive MIMO, network flexibility, millimeter-wave use and new waveforms. In its white papers, 4G Americas has featured both ITU's IMT-2020 and the 3GPP's timelines.

- **Federal Communications Commission (FCC):** The FCC is the U.S. agency for spectrum and telecommunications regulation. FCC would adopt a Notice of Proposed Rulemaking to further exploration into 5G, adding that 600 MHz spectrum, which has been auctioned in early 2016, could pave the U.S. leadership in 5G as the 700 MHz spectrum band did for 4G. The Commission proposed a variety of usable spectrum bands at the 2015 World Radio communication Conference.

- **5G Forum Korea:** 5G Forum was founded by the Korean Ministry of Science, ICT (information and communications technology) and Future Planning (MSIP) to lead the development of 5G mobile wireless communications and to commercialize 5G technology (5G Forum,2015). The forum cooperates internationally on standardization, research and development, and in creating an ecosystem for the next generation of wireless communications.

- **Small Cell Forum:** Following the 3GPP's recent workshop, the Small Cell Forum detailed three requirements for small cell involvement in 5G: multi-operator support, RAN virtualization and monetization through common APIs. In addition, the Forum announced six new small cell work programs focusing on license-exempt spectrum, virtualization, multi-operator applications, enterprise opportunities, HetNet and SON compatibility, and M2M and IoT. Each program will be researched alongside a Forum vendor; members include AT&T, Black & Veatch, Boingo, Cisco and Motorola, among others.

- **GSMA:** GSMA has taken on the task of defining 5G, publishing a white paper earlier in the year that defines what 5G both is and is not, as well as attempting to determine a generation-defining attribute. The GSMA has posited that NFV, SDN and HetNet developments are separate from 5G rather than integral to it. These findings are in contrast to many groups, some of which include GSMA members.

Figure 10. Timeline for the development of 5G

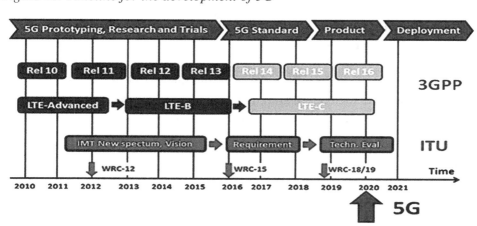

5G Timelines for Standardization and Commercialization

The development timeline for 5G, shown in Figure 10, provides a clear time-table for when 5G standards will be complete.

CONCLUSION

The IoT applications include vehicle infotainment, transportation and logistics, security and home automation, manufacturing, construction and heavy equipment, healthcare, and digital signage. The "smart city" concept is exploring ways to optimize pedestrian and vehicular traffic, smart utility meters, and smart trash containers that can inform when it becomes full.

Although IoT market is promising, it is also challenging, with varying communications requirements, long battery lifetimes, security concerns, cost sensitivity, unusable conventional networking protocols for few applications, and other factors that application developers must address. Streamlining processes and developing supporting infrastructure will take time. The IoT market is not monolithic, but ultimately will consist of thousands of markets.

The Internet of Things (IoT), Machine to Machine(M2M) and Tactile Internet requires a new kind of wireless communication platform because it cannot be served by the existing 4G cellular communication. The Requirements of the future networks as follows:

- Huge System Capacity(10's of Billions of IoT devices),
- Ubiquitous Ultra High Data Rates(up to 10GB/S),
- Extreme Low Latency(<1ms),
- Ultra-High Reliability And Availability,
- Very Cost Effective Devices Cost,
- Ultra Low Energy Consumption Devices,
- Energy-Efficient Networks.

The 5G platform is the necessity to power the Internet of Things, which is the future of our smarter societies. Currently researchers across the world are working towards consolidating the requirements, use-cases, and standardising the 5G platform.

REFERENCES

4G. America's. (2014b, October). *4G America's Recommendations on 5G Requirements and Solutions.* Available from http://www.5gamericas.org/files/2714/1471/2645/4G_Americas_Recommendations_on_5G_Requirements_and_Solutions_10_14_2014-FINALx.pdf

4G. America's. (2014a, June). *4G America's Summary of 5G Global initiatives.* Available from http://www.5gamericas.org/files/2114/0622/1680/2014_4GA_Summary_of_Global_5G_Initiatives__FINAL.pdf

Bangerter, B., Talwar, S., Arefi, R., & Stewart, K. (2014). Networks and Devices for the 5G Era. *IEEE Communications Magazine, 52*(2), 90–96. doi:10.1109/MCOM.2014.6736748

Ericsson White Paper. (2016, April). *5G Radio Access.* Available from https://www.ericsson.com/res/docs/whitepapers/wp-5g.pdf

Fettweis, G. (2012). A 5G Wireless Communications Vision. *Microwave Journal, 55*(12), 24–39.

Fettweis, G., & Alamouti, G. (2014, February). 5G: Personal Mobile Internet beyond What Cellular Did to Telephony. *IEEE Communications Magazine, 52*(2), 140–145. doi:10.1109/MCOM.2014.6736754

Fettweis, G., Denzin, F., Michailov, N., Schlöder, K., Seul, D., Wolff, I., & Zimmermann, E. (2011). *Wireless M2M – Wireless Machine-to-Machine Communications.* VDE Position Paper.

5G. Forum. (2014). *5G Vision and Requirements Of 5G Forum, Korea.* Available from https://www.itu.int/en/ITU-T/gsc/19/.../GSC-19_304_5_5_5GForum.pptx

3. GPP. (2009). *LTE-Advanced (3GPP Release 10 and beyond) - RF aspects.* Available from http://www.3gpp.org/ftp/workshop/2009-12-17_ITU-R_IMT-Adv_eval/docs/pdf/REV-090006.pdf

3. GPP. (2011). *Technical Specification 22.368 V11.2.0 (2011-06) Stage 1 (Release 11).* Available from http://www.3gpp.org/ftp/Specs/html-info/22368.htm

3. GPP TR 36.819 V11.1.0. (2011, December). *Coordinated Multi-point Operation for LTE Physical Layer Aspects.* Available from http://www.3gpp.org/dynareport/36819.htm

GSMA Intelligence Report. (2014). *ANALYSIS Understanding 5G: Perspectives on future technological advancements in mobile*. Available from http://www.gsma. com/network2020/volte/understanding-5g-perspectives-on-future-technological-advancements-in-mobile-gsmai-report-3/

Huawei Technologies. (2010). *Behaviour Analysis of Smartphone, White Paper*. Available from http://www.huawei.com/en/static/hw-001545.pdf

IMT2020. (2015, July). Available from https://www.itu.int/en/ITU-T/gsc/19/ Documents/201507/GSC-19_307_Research_Activities_of_IMT-2020_%20(5G)_ Promotion%20Group.pptx

ITU-R. (2015, September). *IMT Vision – Framework and overall objectives of the future development of IMT for 2020 and beyond*. Available from https://www.itu. int/dms_pubrec/itu-r/rec/m/R-REC-M.2083-0-201509-I!!PDF-E.pdf

IWPC. (2014, April 2). *IWPC Ultra High Capacity Networks White Paper Version 1.1*. Available from http://www.iwpc.org/WhitePaper.aspx?WhitePaperID=17

METIS. (2015). *Scenarios, requirements and KPIs for 5G mobile and wireless system*. Document number: ICT-317669-METIS/D1.1. Available from https://www. metis2020.com/wp-content/uploads/deliverables/METIS_D1.1_v1.pdf

NGMN Alliance. (2016). *NGMN 5G White Paper*. Available from https://www. ngmn.org/uploads/media/NGMN_5G_White_Paper_V1_0.pdf

Nokia Networks. (2015). *Nokia Networks white paper - 5G Radio Access System Design Aspects*. Available from http://resources.alcatel-lucent.com/asset/200009

Nokia Siemens Networks. (2011). *Understanding Smartphone Behavior in the Network, White Paper*. Available: http://www.nokiasiemensnetworks.com/sites/ default/files /document/Smart_Lab_WhitePaper_27012011_low-res.pdf

5G. Now. (2015). *Consistent 5G Radio Access Architecture Concepts*. Available from http://cordis.europa.eu/docs/projects/cnect/5/318555/080/deliverables/001-5GNOWD22v10.pdf

Qmee. (n.d.). Blog.Qmee.Com online. Retrieved from http://blog.qmee.com/online-in-60-seconds-infographic-a-year-later/

Rappaport, T., Shu Sun, , Mayzus, R., Hang Zhao, , Azar, Y., Wang, K., & Gutierrez, F. et al. (2013). Millimeter Wave Mobile Communications for 5G Cellular: It Will Work. *IEEE Access*, *1*, 335–349. doi:10.1109/ACCESS.2013.2260813

Ravi, S. Y., & Mohan, J. (2015). A Survey Paper On 5G Cellular Technologies - Technical & Social Challenges. *International Journal of Emerging Trends in Electrical and Electronics*, *11*(2), 98–100.

Wild, T. (2011, Sep). Comparing coordinated multi-point schemes with imperfect channel knowledge. *Proceedings of IEEE VTC Fall 2011*. doi:10.1109/VETECF.2011.6092923

KEY TERMS AND DEFINITIONS

CAPEX: Capital expenditure or capital expense ("CAPEX") is an expense where the benefit continues over a long period, rather than being exhausted in a short period. Such expenditure is of a non-recurring nature and results in acquisition of permanent assets. It is thus distinct from a recurring expense.

Long Term Evolution: LTE is commonly marketed as 4G LTE, and it is a standard for high-speed wireless communication for mobile phones and data terminals, based on the GSM/EDGE and UMTS/HSPA technologies.

Machine Type Communications: MTC is characterized by fully automatic data generation, exchange, processing and actuation among intelligent machines, without or with low intervention of humans. With the rapid penetration of embedded devices, MTC are becoming the dominant communication paradigm for a wide range of emerging smart services including healthcare, manufacturing, utilities, consumer goods and transportation.

Multiple Input Multiple Output: In radio, MIMO, is a method for multiplying the capacity of a radio link using multiple transmit and receive antennas to exploit multipath propagation.

OPEX: Operating expenditure or OPEX is an ongoing cost for running a product, business, or system. Its counterpart, a capital expenditure (CAPEX), is the cost of developing or providing non-consumable parts for the product or system.

Tactile Internet: Tactile interaction is referred to a system where humans will wirelessly control real and virtual objects. Tactile interaction typically requires a tactile control signal and audio and/or visual feedback.

Chapter 2
5G:
Radio

Ravi Sekhar Yarrabothu
Vignan's University, India

ABSTRACT

In evolution towards a successful mobile communications, the radio technology plays major role and the chosen radio technology should be spectrally efficient, robust and reliable. OFDM provided the much needed spectral efficiency, reliability, robustness and scalability for LTE, compared to the previous access methods such as TDMA, FDMA, and CDMA. For 5G, we should look for more spectrally efficient and massively scalable radio technology to cater to IoT and high bandwidth applications. The objective of this chapter is to introduce the 5G radio system, its challenges from both user and network perspective, and the key disruptive technologies for 5G – such as carrier aggregation, waveform engineering, full duplex, Multi-RAT, flexible networks, and Massive MIMO. Finally, the chapter discusses the current developments in 5G radio research.

INTRODUCTION

In the next few years, the demand for mobile broadband continues to increase, to cater the needs of delivering ultra-high definition video, tactile internet and IoT devices. 5G networks is going to be the platform enabling growth for many industries, ranging from the IT industry to the automotive, and manufacturing industries to entertainment.

As 5G is defined and requirements getting developed, it must include the entire 5G ecosystem (e.g., air interface, devices, transport, packet core). Future networks

DOI: 10.4018/978-1-5225-2799-2.ch002

Copyright © 2018, IGI Global. Copying or distributing in print or electronic forms without written permission of IGI Global is prohibited.

will need to be deployed much more densely than today's networks and, due to both economic constraints and the availability of sites. It needs to become significantly more heterogeneous and use multi Radio Access Technologies (RATs).

The operation of the network needs to be able to scale its operation even for short time periods depending on the widely varying traffic capacity needs and still remain energy efficient. Devices are no longer connected to just one single access node. The full picture consists of a combination of multiple physical interfaces based on the same or different radio technologies depending on the current situation and the actual used services. Fast selection and combining of all of the available interfaces supports an adaptive set of virtual interfaces and functions depending on applications.

5G networks enable newer applications such as autonomous driving, tactile applications and remote control of robots. At the same time, these applications bring a lot of challenges to the network. Few of these are related to ultra low latency in the order of few milliseconds and higher reliability comparable to fixed lines. But the biggest challenge for 5G networks will be that the services need to cater for a diverse set of services and their requirements. To achieve this, the goal for 5G networks will be to improve the flexibility in the architecture.

CHALLENGES FOR 5G RADIO SYSTEMS

5G networks need to present the opportunity for the operators to launch the new services, efficiently and cost-effectively, thus creating an ecosystem for technical and business innovation. In addition, the 5G infrastructures provides a customized network solutions to support vertical markets such as automotive, energy, food and agriculture, healthcare, etc. In addition, it is essential to accelerate the delivery of services to all the involved stakeholders. Compared to the evolution of earlier generations of mobile networks, 5G networks require not only improved networking solutions but involves sophisticated integration of massive computing and storage infrastructures

There are three fundamental requirements for building 5G wireless radio networks:

- Capabilities for supporting massive capacity and massive connectivity.
- Support for an increasingly diverse set of services, application and users all with extremely diverging requirements for work and life.
- Flexible and efficient use of all available non-contiguous spectrum for wildly different network deployment scenarios.

Challenges for 5G are broadly categorized into two:

- User-driven,
- Network-driven.

User Driven Challenges

To realize the 5G requirements discussed earlier, the challenges that are viewed from user perspective are as follows:

- Battery life,
- Data rate and latency,
- Robustness and flexibility,
- Seamless Mobility,
- Quality user experience,
- Context-aware networking.

Battery Life

Most of the IoT applications are based on battery operated sensor networks, deployed in the fields and transmit data occasionally. 5G-based IoT sensor networks would be possible only if much longer battery life and/or reduced energy consumption is guaranteed during their non-transmit period over a duration, which lasts for years.

User Data Rate and Latency

Typical data rate and round-trip delay of a network is defined by user data rate and latency attributes which ultimately decides the user experience and the types of applications that can be supported on a network. By 2020, there will be a new class of data-hungry services with low latency requirements. Applications such as 3D gaming, remote computing and "tactile Internet" require a 100x increase in data rates compared to the existing and a corresponding 5x to 10x reduction in latency (Fettweis & Alamouti, 2014). So, 5G networks need to be designed to meet these data-rate and latency requirements.

Robustness and Flexibility

By 2030, 5G networks may be used as the primary source of communication and will be the sunset for PSTN. So, 5G networks need to support emergency communications during and after disasters. In such cases, a key requirement is the network to be robust, reliable and flexible. And also the network need to be more secured against security attacks such as denial of service (DoS) for mission-critical applications such as public safety, natural gas and water distribution networks and smart grids.

Seamless Mobility

5G systems are going to support both low to no mobility and very high mobility scenarios (e.g., high-speed trains, planes). Therefore it will be a real challenge to cope efficiently with such extreme mobility with unique needs and capabilities.

5G networks will work across technologies, layers and frequency bands that seamlessly interwork when moving across networks, layers and/or frequencies. One more challenge is to design networks with interruption times less than 1 millisecond in both inter-RAT and intra-RAT handovers for the services such as UHD video or tactile Internet, whose latency requirement is in the order of 1 millisecond.

Quality User Experience

Current cellular systems provide very good data rates, but the quality varies substantially over the coverage area. For example, the data rates can be substantially lower for devices away from the base station site or in indoor locations. The daunting task for the 5G Networks is to deliver a much more consistent user experience, irrespective of the user's location.

Context-Aware Networking

With MTC and greater diversity in human communication devices, it becomes increasingly important for the network to provide the correct resources to meet the unique needs of each application and device. This is possible only if the network is context-aware and hence can dynamically adapt to meet those needs. This means, for example, that full mobility need not be provided to MTC devices that are stationary, that 3GPP mobility management and paging need not be provided for services that require only device-initiated communication and that resources are configured to support long battery life, high reliability, low latency, low cost, secure communications, global roaming and the like as is truly needed. Optimizing resource allocation in this manner makes possible simpler, lower cost, application-tailored devices and lower network costs because only the necessary resources are used. It also enables a better end-user/device experience.

Mobile operators gain additional abilities for creating service plans customized for individual customers, groups of customers or market segments. An example is creating one set of plans for MTC customers that use a limited amount of network resources, and a second set of plans for smart phones that use a large amount of network resources.

Context includes network awareness, such as the availability of alternative multi-RAT, small cell and macro networks of varying capabilities, application and device awareness with associated service requirements, subscription context such as operator preferences for providing service and subscriber analytics. Awareness of these attributes makes it possible for the network to dynamically adapt to the end user requirements.

Network Driven Requirements

To realize the 5G requirements discussed earlier, the challenges that are viewed from network perspective are as follows:

- Scalability,
- Network capacity,
- Cost efficiency,
- Self organization,
- Network flexibility,
- Energy efficiency,
- Coverage,
- Security,
- Diverse spectrum operation,
- Unified system framework.

Scalability

The success of 5G networks depends on the support for IoT use cases and high speed applications. It is expected that the number of devices will increase by 100-1000 fold, primarily due to M2M services. The networks should be able to scale up to cater to the demands of exponentially growing number of IoT devices and also handle small data transmissions from large number of devices.

It has another dimension, when it comes to support a mix of traffic from IoT applications and traditional services such as voice and video. M2M communication will have its own unique traffic pattern of both frequent and infrequent (bursty) data transmission that has to be supported in an efficient manner. For example, traffic pattern and transmission requirements (data rate, latency) of public safety (earthquake/tsunami warning sensors) networks will be quite different from traffic of a vending machine. So, 5G networks need to be scalable enough to cater to the dynamic requirements that can arise due to MTC and other disaster tracking networks.

Network Capacity

As the 5G gets deployed and use cases expand, we can expect a rise in traffic in the order of 1000x – 5000x (Fettweis & Alamouti, 2014, IWPC 2014, METIS, 2015) over the next decade. The key requirement for 5G networks will be handling such an explosive traffic, with massive increase in network capacity without compromising on QoS.

Cost Efficiency

The 5G mobile networks should be providing a significant cost benefit over the current generation to stay relevant and competitive. The cost benefit should be much better than 3G to 4G networks in terms of both the OPEX and CAPEX of delivering a byte of data to the subscriber with the help of technologies like Software Defined Radio(SDR) and Network Function Virtualization (NFV).

Self Organization

In 5G deployments, the network density is expected to significantly increase for a number of reasons including higher data volume density and the use of higher frequency spectrum. To better manage the CAPEX and OPEX of running a network with a much higher number of network nodes, a key requirement is that 5G networks will be able to self-configure as much as possible. As the MTC increase due to the larger number of IoT devices in the sectors like health care, smart city infrastructure, and smart home automation, the cost of signaling increase massively; and to avoid such situations, at local level self organizing networks is an essential part of 5G networking.

Flexibility

The 5G network architecture should allow the RAN and the core network to evolve and scale independently of each other. And additionally it should support multi-RAT connectivity efficiently and effectively. This includes the ability to:

- Provide an access-agnostic packet core across multi RAT (e.g., cellular, Wi-Fi) to support uniform authentication, session continuity and security.
- Provide plug-and-play capability to attach a new access technology with the packet core.

Energy Efficiency

One of the requirements for the 5G is energy consumption per bit (expressed in Joules/bit) that represents a measure of the energy efficiency should be 10X, along with maximizing spectral efficiency. Energy consumption of the 5G networks to the current traffic conditions should have significant energy savings in off-peak situations.

Coverage

5G has to take care in improving coverage for IoT-related applications and make it viable, although coverage is limited by the band in use. Generally, the coverage is largely depend on the frequency of operation and density of base stations, which has to ensure optimal coverage for services such as IoT, public safety and other critical systems.

Security

5G has to ensure security against mission-critical applications such as telemedicine, smart traffic control, smart grids, public safety and automotive. 5G should address the following security objectives:

- **Integrity:** Information should not be tampered either accidentally or deliberately during transmission. This includes the ability to authenticate the source of the received information and the ability to authenticate the recipient.
- **Confidentiality:** Information has to be shared with authenticated users only and the data protection should be ensured through encryption.

Diverse Spectrum Operation

5G is expected to operate in a diverse set of spectrum bands such as traditional sub-6 GHz cellular bands for better coverage and low-power operation and above-6 GHz bands for ultra-high speed data. 5G systems should accommodate the varying propagation characteristics and hardware implications in radio access, protocol and network architecture.

Unified System Framework

Use cases of 5G are very much diverse, and conflicting requirements. For example, sensor networks require low data rates and higher latencies are tolerable, where as applications such as telemedicine require high data rates and low latencies. 5G systems should be able to cater both types of use cases and also should support both the existing and future use case requirements.

KEY TECHNOLOGIES FOR 5G

This section describes the potential technologies for 5G to address the market drivers and use cases and the requirements for 5G identified. Specifically, this section will discuss the following potential technologies:

- Massive MIMO,
- Carrier Aggregation,
- Centimetre and Millimeter Waves,
- Waveform Engineering,
- Shared Spectrum Access,
- Advanced Inter-node Coordination,
- Full Duplex Communication,
- Multi-RAT Support,
- Device-to-Device Communications,
- Efficient Transmission of Small Data,
- Integration of Wireless Backhaul/Access,
- Flexible Networks,
- Flexible Mobility,
- Information Centric Networking (ICN),
- Context Aware Networking,
- Moving Networks.

Massive MIMO

MIMO means Multi In Multi Out antenna structure at the transmitter and receiver for increasing the spectral efficiency of a wireless link. The advantage of MIMO is serving multiple users simultaneously with the same time frequency. Both Single-user MIMO and multi-user MIMO are both part of the 4G standards.

Massive MIMO is an extension of classical multi-user MIMO by increasing the number of antennas employed at the base, as shown in the Figure 1. With hundreds of antennas serving tens of users simultaneously, spectral efficiency can increase 5x to 10x, while users on a cell's fringes can maintain high throughput (Marzetta, 2010).

Time-division duplexing is employed to overcome the major challenge of acquiring channel information at the transmitter. Orthogonal pilots are transmitted on the UL for estimating the UL channel and then use it for the conjugate beam-forming on

Figure 1. Massive MIMO

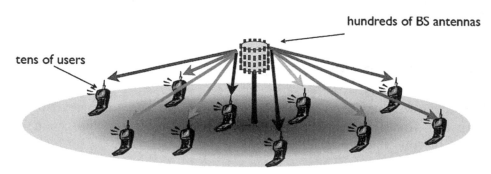

Figure 2. Pilot contamination

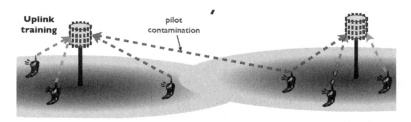

the DL (Marzetta, 2006). UL pilot transmissions need not be orthogonal across cells as few resources only devoted for pilot transmissions, which results in to "pilot contamination," producing channel estimation errors, as shown in Figure 2.

Pilot contamination can be mitigated by using pilot reuse. To deploy a large number of antennas at the base station, cost-effectively, advances in radio and antenna technology are required. One should note that Massive MIMO does not increase the peak rate for a single user significantly, as it inherently provides high spectral efficiency when multiple users are served simultaneously. The benefits of massive MIMO are:

- Simplified multiuser processing,
- Reduced transmit power,
- Thermal noise and fast fading vanish.

There are few critical issues in Massive MIMO, which need to be addressed:

- Gains are not that big with not-so-many antennas:
  - Require many antennas to remove interference,

◦   Need more coordination to remove effects of pilot contamination.
- Massive MIMO seems to be more "uplink driven":
  ◦   Certain important roles are reserved between base stations and users,
  ◦   A different layout of control and data channels may be required.
- Practical effects are not well investigated:
  ◦   Channel aging affects energy-focusing ability of narrow beams,
  ◦   Spatial correlation reduces effective DoFs as increasing number of antennas,
  ◦   Role of asynchronism in pilot contamination and resulting performance.

Carrier Aggregation

Carrier Aggregation (CA) is a key feature of LTE-Advanced which enables the operators to create "virtually" larger carrier bandwidths for LTE services by combining separate spectrum allocations in the sub 6 GHz frequencies that are currently getting used for 3G and 4G networks. CA is needed in LTE-Advanced since the requirement of larger bandwidths than those of currently used in LTE (up to 20 MHz), without compromising the backward compatibility towards LTE. The benefits of CA include higher peak data rates and increased average data rates for users (4G America's, 2014).

CA enables the combination of up to five LTE Release 8 compatible carriers (20MHz each) and this enables operators to provide high throughput without worrying about contiguous frequency band allocations. CA combinations are specified within 3GPP RAN Working Group 4. CA combinations are divided into intra-band (contiguous and non-contiguous) and inter-band. Intra-band contiguous and inter-band combinations, aggregating two Component Carriers (CCs) in downlink, are specified in 3GPP Rel-10. 3GPP Rel-11 offers many more CA configurations, including non-contiguous intra-band CA and Band 29 for inter-band CA, which is also referred as Supplemental Downlink. Release 12 will include CA of FDD and TDD frequency bands, as well as support of aggregation of two CCs in uplink and three CCs in downlink.

CA can currently provide bandwidths up to 100 MHz in LTE. Aggregated carriers can be adjacent or non-adjacent even at different frequency bands. In some heterogeneous deployment scenarios, CA performance can be even better because flexible frequency reuse can be arranged between local area nodes to provide better inter-cell interference coordination.

CA has also been designed to be a future-proof technology, with great potential into and beyond LTE Release 12. By extending aggregation to more carriers and enabling aggregation of additional licensed spectrum, CA will play a key role in enabling both IMT-Advanced and 5G peak data rate requirements of: 3 Gbps DL and 1.5 Gbps UL. For 5G, the same concepts will be extended and expected to be extended for few GHz bandwidths.

Centimetre and Millimeter Waves

Till date mobile-communication networks have been operating on frequencies below 3 GHz. Ever growing demand for more spectrum, causes 5G look into higher frequency bands above 10 GHz. Generally, frequencies of 3 GHz to 30 GHz are known as centimeter waves and frequencies of 30 GHz to 300 GHz are known as millimeter waves.

The main benefit of frequencies above 10 GHz is availability of large amount of continuous spectrum chunks, which is needed to enable multi-Gbps data rates (mmMagic, 2016, Rappaport et al. 2013). The major drawback of using higher frequencies is higher path loss for line-of-sight conditions and can be partially overcome by using more advanced antenna configurations, using reduced size of antenna elements.

In mobile communications the typical propagation is non-line-of-sight, and there are additional path-loss-degrading factors such as:

- Reduced diffraction, leading to higher path loss due to shadowed locations.
- Higher attenuation when propagating through walls.

The focus of World Radio Conference (WRC) 2015 was on new spectrum for mobile communication below roughly 6.5 GHz. For WRC 2019, identification and assignment of spectrum above 10 GHz is going to be on the agenda and will be available for 5G initial deployments in 2020.

One of the options that is most likely to be incorporated into the 5G technologies that are being developed for the 5G cellular telecommunications systems is a millimeter wave capability. With spectrum being in short supply below 4GHz, frequencies extending up to 60GHz are being considered.

One of the interfaces being considered for 5G mobile communications uses millimeter wave frequencies. It is estimated that bandwidths of several GHz may be required by operators to provide some of the extremely high data rates being forecast. Currently frequency below 4GHz are being used by cellular communications systems, and by the very nature, these frequencies could only offer a maximum bandwidth of 4 GHz, even if they were all clear for use which is obviously not possible.

There are two issues that need to be resolved for millimeter wave to be used for 5G, which are discussed as follows:

- **5G Millimeter Wave Propagation:** The propagation characteristics of millimeter wave bands are very different to those below 4GHz.Typically, distances that can be achieved are very much less and the signals do not pass through walls and other objects in buildings. Typically millimeter wave communication is likely to be used for outdoor coverage for dense networks - typically densely used streets and the like. Here, ranges of up to 200 or 300 meters are possible. One of the issues of using millimeter wave signals is that they can also be affected by natural changes such as rain. This can cause a considerable reduction in signal levels for the duration of the precipitation. This may result in reduced coverage for some periods. Often these 5G millimeter wave small cells may use beamforming techniques to target the required user equipment and also reduce the possibility of reflections, etc.
- **Millimeter Wave Coverage:** Simulations have shown that when millimeter wave small cells are set up they provide a good level of coverage. Naturally, typically being lower down than macro cells, the coverage will not be as good, but when considering the level of data they can carry, they provide an excellent way forwards for meeting the needs of 5G systems. A further issue to be considered when looking at 5G millimeter wave solutions is that they will incur a much greater number of handovers than a normal macro cell. The additional signaling and control needs to be accommodated within the system. Also backhaul issues need to be considered as well.

Waveform Engineering

5G systems will be realized through new waveforms both orthogonal advanced multi-carrier transmission and non-orthogonal transmission. The radio access for LTE is based on OFDM technique, which is a multi-carrier transmission scheme, is one of the candidates for 5G as well. As the 5G requirements and use cases are widely varying in terms of speed, latency, several other multi-carrier transmission schemes are also under consideration for 5G radio access.

Investigations are ongoing on the inherent tradeoffs between possible relaxation in orthogonality and synchronism and their corresponding impact on performance and network operation/user experience versus the required signal processing capabilities. Some of the key requirements that need to be supported by the modulation scheme and overall waveform include:

- Capable of handling high data rate wide bandwidth signals.
- Able to provide low latency transmissions for long and short data bursts, i.e. very short Transmission Time Intervals, TTIs, are needed.

- Capable of fast switching between uplink and downlink for TDD systems that are likely to be used.
- Enable the possibility of energy efficient communications by minimizing the on-times for low data rate devices.

5GNow, a research project is thoroughly investigating the non-orthogonal waveforms to address the basic issues of LTE. These include (5GNOW, 2015 for more details):

- GFDM (Fettweis, 2014 & Michailow et al, 2014) can be seen as a more generic block oriented filtered multicarrier system that follows the Gabor principles. Basically, the parameterization of the waveform directly influences i) transmitter window; ii) time-frequency grid structure; as well as iii) transform length and can hence provide means to emulate a multitude of conventional multi-carrier systems.
- FBMC-OQAM (Boroujeny, 2011 & Doré et al, 2014) belongs to the family of filter-bank based waveforms. The principles revolve around filtering the subcarriers in the system while retaining orthogonality. As the name suggests, the essence of this candidate waveform is offset modulation, which allows avoiding interference between real and imaginary signal components.
- BFDM (Kasparick et al, 2014 & Wunder et al 2014) directly relates to the theory of Gabor frames. Signal generation can be considered a Gabor expansion while the bi-orthogonal receive filter constitutes a Gabor transform.
- In UFMC (Vakilian et al, 2013) a pulse shaping filter is applied to a group of conventional OFDM subcarriers. This approach can be also represented in the context of the Gabor frame.

GFDM Advantages and Disadvantages

GFDM features the following advantages:

- Lower PAPR compared to OFDM.
- Low out-of-band radiation due to adjustable Tx-filtering.
- Frequency and time domain multi-user scheduling comparable to OFDM.
- White space aggregation even in heavily fragmented spectrum regions.
- Block-based transmission using cyclic prefix insertion and efficient FFT-based equalization.

GFDM disadvantages are:

- Complicated receiver design.
- Matched filter with successive interference cancellation to remove ICI/SIS from filtering needed or alternatively OQAM must be used which again makes MIMO more difficult.
- Symbol time offset (STO) estimation, Carrier frequency offset (CFO) estimation.
- To suppress inter-subcarrier interference, high-order filtering and tail biting are needed. Pre-cancellation or successive interference cancellation is also required to alleviate the inter-subcarrier interference that still exists after filtering.

FBMC Advantages and Disadvantages

The good localization of FBMC enables several scenarios targeted with 5G:

- Asynchronous transmission, no need for perfect synchronization like timing advance in LTE.
- Well suited for fragmented spectrum or cognitive radio.
- Robustness against high mobility.
- Efficient adaptation of basic parameters like SC spacing or symbol duration within one band possible.

Disadvantage of FBMC are:

- Scattered pilot become more complex.
- MIMO schemes like Alamouti (space-time coding) do not work easily.
- 1 carrier guard between users needed in uplink or for frequency selective beamforming.
- Inefficient for short bursts due to long filter tails.

UFMC Advantages and Disadvantages

UFMC provides promising advantages:

- Good spectral efficiency similar to FBMC.
- Less overhead required compared to FBMC.
- Well suited for short burst transmissions.
- Enabling low latency modes.

Disadvantages are:

- As the complex orthogonality is partly lost, UFMC may not be suited for very high data rates.
- With high delay spread, multi-tap equalizers are to be applied.
- Larger FFT size at receiver increases complexity.
- Interference from partly overlapping sub-bands.

BFDM Advantages and Disadvantages

BFDM provides promising advantages:

- Transmission is very robust to (even negative) time offsets.
- Side effects such as spectral regrowth due to periodic are negligible.

Disadvantage is:

- Suitable only for sporadic traffic.

Shared Spectrum Access

New spectrum is required to sustain capacity expansion required to meet anticipated growth in wireless data traffic, but available resources are limited. So, cellular community decided to pursue shared spectrum access as a way to free up spectrum. Secondary users would be allowed to use the spectrum when the primary or incumbent is not using the spectrum in a given geography at a given time. The FCC has published a three-tier spectrum access in the 3.5 GHz band: incumbent, protected and general authorized access. A spectrum access server (SAS) manages the spectrum allocation between these tiers.

5G needs new technologies for mobile networks to utilize the shared spectrum efficiently:

- The Radio Access Network must be capable of interfacing with the SAS for spectrum allocations, and provide with spectrum-sensing information of the base stations to the SAS.
- The 5G base stations must be spectrum agile and capable of spectrum sensing.

Advanced Inter-Node Coordination

Interference is the biggest hurdle for current wireless networks and extreme densification of 5G cells complicate this problem. It necessitates specific solutions, for both network and the device sides. Current inter-cell interference coordination schemes (LTE Rel. 8) as well as Coordinated Multi-Point (CoMP) (LTE Rel. 11 and 12) is based on exchange of information between network side schedulers to mitigate interference.

However these solutions are not that much effective because of a number of drawbacks:

- Needs an upgrade in backhaul transport networks.
- CoMP-based solutions suffer from inter-cluster interference.

Research in 5G is targeted to overcome the above issues and facilitate inter-node coordination with legacy backhaul networks. One approach is to allow the interference between nodes to a certain extent, so that the inter-node coordination burden is relaxed and is handled at the receiver. Another approach is to reduce the signaling burden by centralizing radio processing and hence an efficient inter-node coordination is achieved.

Full Duplex Communication

Current wireless communication systems are not full duplex in real sense as dedicated spectral or temporal resources are allocated to Uplink and Downlink channels. Simultaneous transmission reception would enable a more efficient use of the available spectrum and in theory the current link capacity could be doubled. The gain may be less when compared with the 5G capacity needs and when it is combined with techniques like massive MIMO impact will be huge. The simultaneous transmission reception in 5G not only helps in its capacity gains, but also helps in improving in signaling and control layers. By thinking out of box and without having a notion of separate uplink and downlink, 5G systems could be designed with a new approach and possibly may lead to the achievement of 5G goals which may not be obvious now (Choi, et al. 2012)

The advantages of full duplex systems are:

- **Doubles Spectrum Efficiency:** A full duplex system using a single channel to transmit data to and from the base station rather than two for an FDD scheme, which effectively doubles the spectrum efficiency.
- **Fading Characteristics:** As the same channel is used in both uplink and downlink, the fading or propagation characteristics will be exactly same and the difficulties that can arise using an FDD scheme and the other will be less.
- **Filtering:** FDD requires filters to be used to ensure that the transmitted signal did not enter the receiver and desensitize it. As more bands were added, more filters were required with a resulting increase in loss and drop in performance.

By using single channel full duplex system, this issue can be overcome as techniques used have been shown to be capable of use over a wide bandwidth.

- **Novel Relay Solutions:** The techniques used for full duplex on a single channel enable the simultaneous re-use of spectrum in backhaul as well as the main user access can allow for almost instantaneous retransmission and high throughput mesh operation for heterogeneous networks.
- **Enhanced Interference Coordination:** The simultaneous reception of feedback information while transmitting data, possible using full duplex system reduce the air interface delays and provide much tighter time / phase synchronisation for techniques like Coordinated Multipoint, CoMP (which is also part of the 4G LTE standard).

The concept of full duplex using a single channel has been thought impossible for many years. The level of interference cause to the receiver by the transmitter has been thought to be far too great to make the concept of single frequency full duplex possible. However many researchers have spent years investigating since 1998 (Chen et al, 1998, D. Bliss et al, 2007, Radunovic et al, 2009, Choi et al, 2010, Jain et al, 2011, Khojastepour et al, 2011, Sahai et al, 2011 & Sahai et al, 2012) in developing the technology and now it seems likely that full duplex can be used as part of the 5G communications system. So far, researchers are successful in getting this interference reduced up to 85 dB (Duarte, 2012), and it has been achieved through a combination of analog, hardware and digital cancellation techniques. This achieved interference reduction is sufficient for Wi-Fi-type systems over very short distances and not enough for current cellular systems, which operates at much higher transmit powers and in greater path-loss environments.

The current results in achieving full duplex using a single channel in Wi-Fi-like scenarios are encouraging, but they are nowhere close to practical implementation in a cellular environment. Refinements of the existing interference cancellation methods and may be completely new interference cancellation techniques are necessary to make full duplex transmission reception practically possible.

There are two main technologies involved in full duplex:

- **Electrical Balance Isolation:** The isolation technique employed effectively uses the same technology as used in landline telephones to provide isolation between the incoming and outgoing signals and this is obviously modified for RF. It can provide around 20dB or so of isolation. The scheme uses a hybrid that has four ports, between three of them the phase shift is 0°, but the fourth has 180°. Balance is achieved when balancing impedance matches that of the antenna.

- **RF Self-Interference Cancellation:** The main amount of reduction of the transmitted signal is provided by using RF cancellation techniques - often referred to as self-interference cancelation, SIC. Much investigation work has been ongoing to improve the performance and enable 5G full duplex in a single channel to be a realistic option.

Using a combination of both the electrical balance isolation and the SIC it is possible to operate a single channel full duplex system for 5G. Single channel full duplex is an exciting technology that will bring many benefits in terms of operation, cost and efficiency to 5G mobile communications systems. Once fully developed, the implementation may be able to provide cost reductions when compared to the filters currently needed for FDD systems that are the most widespread for of duplex used.

Multi-RAT Support

As the wireless communications are growing exponentially in each and every domain of the life with multiple radio access technologies supported, it is crucial to consider multi-RAT integration and management issues. Coexistence of both 3GPP and non-3GPP such as Wi-Fi, WiMAX, and BT is a necessity in the 5G eco system. 5G's user-driven requirements such as ultra-high-definition video or tactile Internet, makes multi-RAT integration more critical. 5G eco systems need to support multiple, heterogeneous networks in ultra-high dense scenarios (e.g., 5G, LTE, 3G and Wi-Fi). Hence, de-coupling of the user and control planes is needed in order to differentiate the user signalling and user payload.

To support the multiple RAT systems, introduction of virtualization techniques can be used for enabling the network instantiation functions on demand, without changing the network topology and/or architecture. Software defined network functions can cope with different RATs by instantiating the necessary network functions upon demand, without the need to physically deploy additional network nodes for multi-RAT management.

Device-to-Device Communications

Direct device-to-device (D2D) communications was introduced for LTE in 3GPP Release 12, mainly focusing on public safety communication and proximity detection for general applications. However, in 5G discussions, D2D communication is getting included as a possible technology component, for integrated backhaul/access and more general multi-hop communication. Direct D2D communication should be considered as a part of 5G system, this includes:

- Efficient mode of transmission between nearby devices.
- Extension of coverage using device-based relaying.
- Cooperation between devices for "combined" transmission and/or reception for more efficient network-device communication, which is like a "CoMP" on the device, rather than the network side.

In 5G frame work, D2D communication is a key component of the overall wireless access solution, rather than "add-on" at a later stage. D2D communication should support both licensed and unlicensed spectrum under network control.

Efficient Transmission of Small Data

Connectionless access handles small data bursts most efficiently. Connectionless access is a contention based access, where a device wakes up and sends a shorter user plane data burst on a common carrier which eliminates the dedicated RRC and higher layer signaling. This results in reduction of power consumption in the devices and network resources usage. 5G radio system must support connectionless access coupled with scheduled access on a common carrier, and flexible resource allocation so that both the short data burst and continuous data transmission are taken care of.

OpenFlow Software Defined Networking (SDN)(Openflow, n.d.) procedures can be used to model the packet processing for connectionless access. To support connectionless access, the following steps are taken after the device attaches to the network.

- The device selects a base station and sends a user plane data burst.
- The base station sends the packet or packet header to the controller for validation, much as an OpenFlow switch would send a packet for which it had no flow table entry to an OpenFlow controller.
- The controller authorizes access and sends security context information to the base station along with forwarding instructions, much as an OpenFlow controller would provide a flow table entry to a switch.
- The base station deciphers the packet contents and forwards the packet according to the received instructions.

After a data burst has been sent, the device may wait for a response from the network and transition to a connected state as warranted by further transmissions.

Integration of Wireless Backhaul/Access

Across the world, wireless backhaul play a key role in cellular communications, where other solutions are not economically and/or technically feasible. Wireless backhaul is generally built on a proprietary radio link technology operating under line of sight propagation conditions and often uses frequencies in the 2 GHz range and even lower in the earlier days. Currently, backhaul networks are using the spectrum above 6 GHz, which includes the millimeter band (above 30 GHz). As 5G systems grow, the density of small cells will grow exponentially and wireless backhaul solutions that can operate under non-line-of-sight conditions becomes a norm. There is a strong feeling that the same operating spectrum and access technology could be used both for backhaul networks and the access (BS-UE) link. The following factors are taken into account to justify that:

• Considering the use of millimeter wave band for the access link.
• The use of Lower frequency bands for wireless backhaul.
• Flexibility to use the same spectrum for both mobile and backhaul.

In the case of integrated backhaul/access, one can see the access and backhaul link as just two radio links of the unified wireless access solution:

• The same radio-access technologies can be used on the access (BS-UE) link and the backhaul link.
• Both the backhaul and access link relies on the same spectrum pool.
• Management of radio resources, QoS and other tasks are done commonly for the backhaul and access links.

The main objective of access/backhaul integration is to achieve seamless use of technology and spectrum and improve the overall performance/quality of the end-to-end link.

Flexible Networks

Distributed computing and storage in data centers has created a need for highly dynamic networking that is being addressed by SDN. The major benefit of SDN is creation of on demand virtual private networks with configurable optical link capacity between enterprise premises and the data center through software components.

In the software defined network (SDN), the emphasis is on network programmability through open interfaces, a configurable framework for resource discovery and optimization and a separate SDN control framework apart from the

Figure 3. Network functions virtualisation relationship with SDN

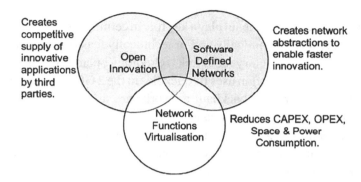

Creates competitive supply of innovative applications by third parties.

Open Innovation

Software Defined Networks

Creates network abstractions to enable faster innovation.

Network Functions Virtualisation

Reduces CAPEX, OPEX, Space & Power Consumption.

forwarding plane (Haleplidis et al, 2015, & Faq, n.d.). In the context of 5G, the application of SDN go beyond control of transport resources and it includes QoS management and application of forwarding plane functions, Mobility management, security, charging and optimization.

Another technology which 5G is looking for flexible networks is Network Functions Virtualization (NFV). NFV (4G Americas's Nov 2014) virtualizes network functions which are currently provided by dedicated core network components, media servers and management functions. NFV is already-part of 4G network implementations and so will be part of 5G as well. In the design of 5G networks, NFV concepts can be exploited, since the majority of the RAN and core functions are going to be virtualized, in order to meet varied demands of a large variety of applications. 5G will take advantage of SDN techniques for interconnection of the functions and programming of the forwarding plane to support mobility.

The orchestration framework is the key for realizing the cost saving virtualized implementations. Latency and networking requirements of 5G, makes it mandatory that virtualized functions are close proximity to each other and local data centers close to the subscriber. The MANO work group of ETSI NFV forum has defined an orchestration framework for 4G networks and it is going to be part of 5G network architecture as well.

As shown in Figure 3, Network Functions Virtualization is highly complementary to Software Defined Networking (SDN), but not dependent on it (or vice-versa). Network Functions Virtualization can be implemented without a SDN being required, although the two concepts and solutions can be combined and potentially greater value accrued

Network Functions Virtualization can be achieved using non-SDN mechanisms, relying on the techniques used in many datacenters. The approach defined by SDN, relying on the separation of the control and data forwarding planes can enhance

Table 1. Examples of flexible assignable mobility for 5G

Application	Idle Mode Mobility	Active Mode Mobility	Current Technology
Smart phones, Tables for mobile communication	Yes	Yes	3G/4G
Always-on, battery in-sensitive	None	None	Wi-fi
When the device need not be reachable from the network after idle transition and only the device initiates transactions (e.g., MTC long battery life)	None with sleep/ coma mode in device	None	-
For nomadic, long-battery life devices that must be reachable from the network	Yes	None	-
Always-on, battery insensitive with seamless continuity when active	None	Yes	-
When the device need not be reachable from the network after idle transition with seamless continuity when active	None with sleep/ coma mode in device	Yes	-

performance and compatible with existing deployments. Network Functions Virtualization aligns closely with the SDN objectives to use commodity servers and switches.

Flexible Mobility

Flexible mobility consists of two components: one for managing mobility of active devices and the other for tracking and reaching devices to support a power-saving idle mode. Assigned mobility can be either "active mode" mobility, with no support for idle mode similar to Wi-Fi or full support for active and idle mode mobility similar to mobile 3G/4G. Gradations of flexible mobility bridge the gap between these variations, allowing for independent assignment of idle-mode mobility on a per-device basis, and active mode mobility on a per-application basis as shown in the examples in Table 1.

Here idle mobility means the tracking of the device while in "sleep mode." Active mobility refers to establishment of IP anchors for seamless IP session continuity, when the UE moves between base stations.

Offering a range of mobility options that are not available in 4G enables a better match between the needs of the devices, applications and network resources. This has advantages for both the network and user/device. Specifically:

- **"No Idle Mode Mobility":** Means that no storage of context and state information for tracking the device and saving the resources. There are two cases for no idle mode mobility: The device will be always-on, no support for idle mode similar to Wi-Fi, and the second case is it supports a sleep mode whereby the device de-allocates Tx and Rx resources, hibernates until it initiates a transaction, suitable for a sensor-like device where battery life is very much important.

- **"No Active Mode Mobility":** Means that the network need not establish and maintain user plane tunnels and store related state information. IP addresses are allocated local to the base station, allowing for more efficient routing of locally available content. The user/device benefits from lower latency due to more direct routing when compared to active mobility with a centralized anchor. This mode is most appropriate for stationary and nomadic devices.

Flexible mobility is enabled by two critical technologies - one is context awareness and the other is SDN control of the transport path. The network required to know the context information of the device's capabilities and application's needs to assign the required level of active and idle mode mobility. Flexible active mode mobility is possible only if mobile anchors can be dynamically assigned at a central point, close to the device, in between or not at all, at the time an application is invoked. This requires a context-aware controller to establish tunnels wherever needed and forward the traffic by programming transport elements.

Information Centric Networking (ICN)

The fundamental design criteria for 5G networks should be based on new architectures and protocols to support mobility, security and content caching. Information Centric Networking (ICN) is realized in the Named-Data Networking (NDN) (Archoverview, n.d.) and Content-Centric Networking (CCN) (What-is-ccn, n.d.) programs – which can be potential architecture that can meet 5G network design criteria. ICN's focus is to support the future Internet evolution and new communication models of the distributed of information systems.

Rethinking of the key design principles of the Internet to incorporate the requirements of new application models such as scalable content distribution, mobility, security and trust as fundamental architectural design features. As such, key networking areas that are touched are summarized as follows:

- **Naming:** Focus on what content is of interest rather than where it is.
- **Routing:** Based on (hierarchical) names rather than addresses.
- **Mobility:** Now an intrinsic capability of networking layer.
- **Caching/Storage:** Information resides anywhere in the network at any time.
- **Security:** Secure content rather than communication channels.

ICN (NDN/CCN) redefines the role of the networking layer, to deliver named information to an endpoint that expresses an interest in it without explicitly getting directions of where that content is stored. At the network layer, ICN (NDN/CCN) facilitates the in-network caching, simplifies multicasting and enables a content security model. Expressions of interest are implemented using request-response mechanisms and a strategy mechanism to realize intelligent, control of context-aware content storage and delivery.

The basic concepts that are getting developed by the NDN/CCN community have a direct impact on the design of the 5G core network and may result in significant simplification.

Context Aware Networking

In near future, the networks cannot provide tailor made resources to serve a wide range of services and applications, without context information which is unavailable in 4G. Context awareness allows the network to adapt to the needs of applications within the framework of network constraints and operator policy. The user experience can be enhanced by using context awareness (e.g., historical usage pattern, subscriber preferences, and location) both at the network and device. Context awareness enables the concept of presenting the user automatically with most relevant and timely information, without wasting user's time by filtering out the irrelevant pieces of information.

Context awareness includes awareness of the following:

- **Network Analytics:** Including network layers (macro cell, Wi-Fi, small cell, mmWave), alternative RATs, and corresponding congestion levels, capabilities and performance characteristics.
- **Subscriber Analytics:** Including wireless activity level, subscription attributes, loyalty management status, historical subscriber activity, location history, current location, experience analytics, subscriber contacts, location context (e.g., work, home, mall) and application usage.
- **Device Attributes and Capabilities:** Including information of single function and multi-function devices, MTC subscriber devices, device support for specialized applications, and radio and network optimization capabilities.
- **Application Requirements:** Including QoS requirements (e.g., peak data rates, throughput, delay, latency), connection reliability, power consumption, access price and security level.
- **Operator Policies and Subscription Context:** Including allowed services, service attributes and QoS.

Context information can be gathered from the devices, network monitors, network elements, network databases and analytic platforms. It is processed by the network when a device attaches or an application is invoked and results in a determination of service attributes that govern how the device and application will be treated by the network. The service attributes for access may for example include cost, reliability, power consumption, security level, QoS and mobility. The service attributes for access may be mapped to configurable 5G features, which are then assigned by the network.

For example, context information may determine that low-cost access, with no support for active mobility and long battery life, is best for providing service to a nomadic sensor device that attaches to the network. The network as a result configures connectionless access with low priority, simple IP networking with no tunneling and an idle-mode wake-up period of one day.

Moving Networks

The requirements of mobility support in 5G will likely be at very high speeds, such as 350 km/h and beyond, which may include aircraft communications. In 5G, both the device and base station will be moving like in D2D, V2V or V2I scenarios. In the end, the concept of a cell diminishes in favour of a more general concept of ubiquitous connectivity. The management of nomadic and moving cells presents a number of issues – such as activation/deactivation of cells, trajectory prediction and handover optimization – because users will rapidly traverse multiple cells in a very short time. Additionally, the Doppler shift caused by very high relative movement between transmitter and receiver can challenge the use of millimeter waves.

LATEST DEVELOPMENTS IN 5G TECHNOLOGIES

As the mobile industry is working towards 5G, LTE capabilities will still continue to improve in LTE-Advanced through the rest of the current decade. Most of these enhancements will come through incremental network investments. 5G will sooner or later play an important role, but it should be timed appropriately so that the huge leap in capability justifies the new investment. Prior to full 5G availability, some of the features planned for 5G could be implemented as LTE-Advanced extensions.

The ITU, the standardization group of the United Nations, has set the following standardization timetable in its IMT-2020 project(ITU 2016):

- **2016-2017:** Definition of technical performance requirements, evaluation criteria and methods, and submission templates.
- **2018-2019:** Submission of proposals.
- **2019:** Evaluation of proposed technologies.
- **2020:** Publication of IMT-2020 specifications.

In 5G systems, massive MIMO and beamforming helps to mitigate the signal and path loss at higher frequency bands. Till now, millimetre-wave frequencies that were considered as unsuitable for many mobile applications and the availability of large amounts of freely available spectrum in the millimetre-wave frequency range also enables access to channels with larger bandwidths (in the order of 100s of MHz) and therefore higher data rates can be provided to end-user equipment. Exact bandwidth and data rate capability at certain frequencies have not been defined as yet in 5G. However, there have been a number of demonstrations, with some examples listed in Table 2.

CONCLUSION

The 5th generation communications systems will be the most critical building block of our "digital society" in the next decade. 5G will be the first instance of a truly converged network environment where wired and wireless communications will use the same infrastructure, driving the future networked society. It will provide virtually ubiquitous, ultra-high bandwidth, "connectivity" not only to individual users but also to connected objects. Wireless communication technology has progressed to the extent that considerable new advancements are inevitable, making 5G a possible alternative to wireline broadband for many subscribers (Rysavy, 2014). Therefore, it is expected that the future 5G infrastructure will serve a wide range of applications and sectors including professional uses (e.g. assisted driving, eHealth, energy management, possibly safety applications, etc).

Table 2. Examples of 5G demonstrations at millimetre wave frequencies

Demonstrator	Peak Data Rate	Frequency	Bandwidth
Nokia	10Gbps	73 GHz	1 GHz
Ericsson	5.8Gbps	15 GHz	400 MHz
Samsung	7.5Gbps, 1.2 Gbps(In Moving vehicle at 60mph)	28Ghz	800 MHz

REFERENCES

4G. America's. (2014, November). *4G America's Bringing Network Function Virtualization to LTE.* Available from http://www.5gamericas.org/files/1014/1653/1309/4G_Americas_-_NFV_to_LTE_-_November_2014_-_FINAL.pdf

4G. America's. (2014, October). *4G America's LTE Carrier Aggregation Technology Development and Deployment Worldwide.* Available from http://www.5gamericas.org/files/8414/1471/2230/4G_Americas_Carrier_Aggregation_FINALv1_0_3.pdf

Archoverview. (n.d.). *Named-data.net online.* Retrieved from http://named-data.net/project/archoverview/

Bliss, D. W., Parker, P., & Margetts, A. R. (2007). Simultaneous Transmission and Reception for Improved Wireless Network Performance. *IEEE/SP 14th Workshop on Statistical Signal Processing,* 478–482. doi:10.1109/SSP.2007.4301304

Boroujeny, B. F. (2011, April). OFDM versus filter bank multicarrier. *IEEE Signal Processing Magazine, 28*(3), 92–112. doi:10.1109/MSP.2011.940267

Chen, S., Beach, M., & McGeehan, J. (1998). Division-free duplex for wireless applications. In IEEE. *Electronics Letters, 34*(2), 147–148. doi:10.1049/el:19980022

Choi, J. I., Jain, M., Srinivasan, K., Levis, P., & Katti, S. (2010). Achieving single channel, full duplex wireless communication. *Proceedings of the sixteenth annual international conference on Mobile computing and networking,* 1–12. doi:10.1145/1859995.1859997

Choi. (2012, November). Beyond full duplex wireless. *Proceedings of Forty Sixth Signals, Systems and Computers (ASILOMAR) Conference,* 40 – 44. doi:10.1109/ACSSC.2012.6488954

Doré, J. B., Berg, V., Cassiau, N., & Kténas, D. (2014). FBMC receiver for multi-user asynchronous transmission on fragmented spectrum. *EURASIP Journal on Advances in Signal Processing, 41.* doi:10.1186/1687-6180-2014-41

Duarte, M. (2012, April). *Full-duplex Wireless: Design, Implementation and Characterization* (Ph.D. Thesis). Rice University.

FAQ. (n.d.). *Opendaylight online.* Retrieved from http://www.opendaylight.org/project/faq#1

Fettweis, G., & Alamouti, G. (2014, February). 5G: Personal Mobile Internet beyond What Cellular Did to Telephony. *IEEE Communications Magazine*, *52*(2), 140–145. doi:10.1109/MCOM.2014.6736754

Haleplidis, E., Pentikousis, K., Denazis, S., Salim, J. H., Meyer, D., & Koufopavlou, O. (2015, January). *Software-Defined Networking (SDN): Layers and Architecture Terminology*. RFC 7426, IETF, ISSN 2070-1721.

ITU. (2015 July). *ITU towards IMT for 2020 and beyond*. Available from http://www.itu.int/en/ITU-R/study-groups/rsg5/rwp5d/imt-2020/Pages/default.aspx

IWPC. (2014, April 2). *IWPC Ultra High Capacity Networks White Paper Version 1.1*. Available from http://www.iwpc.org/WhitePaper.aspx?WhitePaperID=17

Jain, M., Choi, J., Kim, T. M., Bharadia, D., Seth, S., Srinivasan, K., & Sinha, P. et al. (2011). Practical, real-time full duplex wireless. *Proceedings of the seventeenth annual international conference on Mobile computing and networking*, 301–312. Doi:10.1145/2030613.2030647

Kasparick, M., Wunder, G., Jung, P., & Maryopi, D. (2014 May). Bi-orthogonal Waveforms for 5G Random Access with Short Message Support. *European Wireless 2014- Conference Proceedings of 20th European Wireless, 1*(6), 14-16.

Khojastepour, M. A., Sundaresan, K., Rangarajan, S., Zhang, X., & Barghi, S. (2011). The case for antenna cancellation for scalable full-duplex wireless communications. *Proceedings of the 10th ACM Workshop on Hot Topics in Networks*, *17*, 1–17. doi:10.1145/2070562.2070579

Marzetta, T. (2006, October), How much training is required for multiuser MIMO. *Proceedings of Fortieth Signals, Systems and Computers (ASILOMAR) Conference*, 359 – 363. doi:10.1109/ACSSC.2006.354768

Marzetta, T. (2010, November). Noncooperative cellular wireless with unlimited numbers of base station antennas. *IEEE Transactions on Wireless Communications*, *9*(1), 3590–3600. doi:10.1109/TWC.2010.092810.091092

METIS. (2015). *Scenarios, requirements and KPIs for 5G mobile and wireless system*. Document number: ICT-317669-METIS/D1.1. Available from https://www.metis2020.com/wp-content/uploads/deliverables/METIS_D1.1_v1.pdf

Michailow, N., Matthe, M., Gaspar, I. S., Caldevilla, A. N., Mendes, L. L., Festag, A., & Fettweis, G. P. (2014, September). Generalized Frequency Division Multiplexing for 5th Generation Cellular Networks. *IEEE Transactions on Communications*, *62*(9), 3045–3061. doi:10.1109/TCOMM.2014.2345566 mmMagic. (2016, April). *Architectural aspects of mm-wave radio access integration with 5G ecosystem.* Available from https://bscw.5g-mmmagic.eu/pub/bscw.cgi/d100702/mm-wave_architecture_white_paper.pdf

5G. Now. (2015). *5G Waveform Candidate Selection, 5GNOW deliverable D3.1.* Available at http://www.5gnow.eu/node/52

Openflow, D. (n.d.). *Opennetworking online.* Retrieved https://www.opennetworking.org/sdn-resources/openflow

Radunovic, B., Gunawardena, D., Key, P., Singh, A. P. N., Balan, V., & Dejean, G. (2009). *Rethinking Indoor Wireless: Low power, Low Frequency, Full-duplex.* Technical report, Microsoft Research. Available from https://www.microsoft.com/en-us/research/wp-content/uploads/2016/02/TR-1.pdf

Rappaport, T., Shu Sun, , Mayzus, R., Hang Zhao, , Azar, Y., Wang, K., & Gutierrez, F. et al. (2013). Millimeter Wave Mobile Communications for 5G Cellular: It Will Work. *IEEE Access*, *1*, 335–349. doi:10.1109/ACCESS.2013.2260813

Rysavy Research. (2014, May). How will 5G compare to fiber, cable or DSL. *Fierce Wireless.* Available from http://www.rysavy.com/Articles/2014-05-5G-Comparison-Wireline.pdf

Sahai, A., Patel, G., & Sabharwal, A. (2011). *Pushing the limits of Full-duplex: Design and Real-time implementation.* Available from arXiv.org:1107.0607

Sahai, A., Patel, G., & Sabharwal, A. (2012). Asynchronous Full-duplex Wireless. *Proceedings of Fourth International Conference on Communication Systems and Networks (COMSNETS 2012)*, 1–9. doi:10.1109/COMSNETS.2012.6151328

Vakilian, V., Wild, T., Schaich, F., Brink, S. T., & Frigon, J. F. (2013, December). Universal-Filtered Multi-Carrier Technique for Wireless Systems Beyond LTE. *Proceedings of 9th International Workshop on Broadband Wireless Access(Globecom'13).* doi:10.1109/GLOCOMW.2013.6824990

What-is-ccn. (n.d.). *ccnx.org online.* Retrieved from http://ccnx.org/what-is-ccn/

Wunder, G., Jung, P., & Wang, C. (2014, June). Compressive Random Access for Post-LTE Systems. *IEEE ICC Workshop on Massive Uncoordinated Access Protocols*, 539-544. doi:10.1109/ICCW.2014.6881254

KEY TERMS AND DEFINITIONS

Content Centric Networking: In contrast to IP-based, host-oriented, Internet architecture, content centric networking (CCN) emphasizes content by making it directly addressable and routable. CCN is characterized by the basic exchange of content request messages (called "Interests") and content return messages (called "Content Objects"). It is considered an information-centric networking (ICN) architecture.

Filter Bank Multi-Carrier: FBMC has gained a high degree of interest as a potential 5G waveform candidate. FBMC has many similarities to CP-OFDM, (OFDM using a cyclic prefix, which is the specific variant used as the 4G waveform). Instead of filtering the whole band as in the case of CP-OFDM, FBMC filters each sub-carrier individually. FBMC does not have a cyclic prefix and as a result it is able to provide a very high level of spectral efficiency.

Generalized Frequency Division Multiplexing: GFDM is a non-orthogonal, digital multicarrier transmission method proposed to meet the emerging requirements of cellular communications system like efficient spectrum usage and machine-to-machine communication with special consideration to asynchronous low duty cycle transmission and exploration of non-continuous bandwidths.

Information-Centric Networking: ICN is an approach to evolve the Internet infrastructure away from a host-centric paradigm based on perpetual connectivity and the end-to-end principle, to a network architecture in which the focal point is "named information" (or content or data).

Network Functions Virtualization: NFV is a network architecture concept that uses the technologies of IT virtualization to virtualize entire classes of network node functions into building blocks that may connect, or chain together, to create communication services.

Software Defined Networking: SDN is an approach to computer networking that allows network administrators to programmatically initialize, control, change, and manage network behavior dynamically via open interfaces and abstraction of lower-level functionality.

Universal Filtered Multi-Carrier: UFMC is seen as a generalization of Filtered OFDM and FBMC (Filter Bank Multi-carrier) modulations. The entire band is filtered in filtered OFDM and individual subcarriers are filtered in FBMC, while groups of subcarriers (subbands) are filtered in UFMC. This subcarrier grouping allows one to reduce the filter length (when compared with FBMC). Also, UFMC can still use QAM as it retains the complex orthogonality (when compared with FBMC), which works with existing MIMO schemes.

Chapter 3
Key Microwave and Millimeter Wave Technologies for 5G Radio

Vojislav Milosevic
University of Belgrade, Serbia

Olga Boric-Lubecke
University of Hawaii – Manoa, USA

Branka Jokanovic
University of Belgrade, Serbia

Victor M. Lubecke
University of Hawaii – Manoa, USA

ABSTRACT

This chapter presents an overview on the drivers behind the 5G evolution and explains technological breakthroughs in the microwave and millimeter wave domain that will create the 5G backbone. Extensions to millimeter wave frequency bands, advanced multi-antenna systems and antenna beamforming and simultaneous transmission and reception are some of the prospects that could lead to both architectural and component disruptive design changes in the future 5G. 5G is expected to include an innovative set of technologies that will radically change our private and professional lives, though applications of novel services, such as remote healthcare, driverless cars, wireless robots and connected homes, which will alter boundaries between the real and the cyber world.

DOI: 10.4018/978-1-5225-2799-2.ch003

Copyright © 2018, IGI Global. Copying or distributing in print or electronic forms without written permission of IGI Global is prohibited.

INTRODUCTION

The fifth generation (5G) is the next major step in the development of mobile networks, which is expected to be implemented from 2020 and beyond. Apart from the empirically observed fact that every generation is succeeded after about 10 years, the motivation behind 5G is that current networks, despite their continued evolution, are approaching fundamental limits of their performance. Table 1 sums up key parameters of 4G networks (based on IMT-Advanced standard, not yet achieved) and what is expected for 5G (there is no official standard yet, but the given values are widely cited in the literature, e.g. (Boric-Lubecke, et al., 2015)). In addition to that, 5G is expected to improve reliability (up to 99.999%), coverage and capacity, support advanced machine-type communication (MTC), and to improve battery life of devices up to 10 times.

The demand for the stated goals of 5G has two main drivers; the first is evolution of existing services. Mobile data rates are going ever higher, driven by applications such as 4K video streaming. However 5G is about much more than just that speed, capacity and reliability are aimed to be significantly improved, compared to the current networks. The ultimate goal in this respect is to provide users with the perception of "infinite capacity", i.e. that any service can be run without delay wherever the user might be.

Second driver behind 5G are the emerging new applications. For example, virtual and augmented reality systems have received a lot of attention in recent years, as well as lots of investments from the industry and venture capitalists. It is envisioned that the users will be able to connect with others to participate in shared virtual environment, with the purpose of either gaming or business applications like smart office. In any case, along with high data rate, very low latencies are needed to provide realistic experience – less than 10 ms for visual and aural senses. If touch interaction is transmitted through network – the goal of the so-called Tactile internet – latency of less than 1 ms is required for users not to perceive delay (Simsek, et al., 2016).

Internet of Things (IoT) is another area which is seeing huge growth (more than 20 billion devices are predicted by 2020), and it could greatly benefit from 5G connectivity. Currently, there is significant fragmentation in IoT communication standards, with technologies like RFID, Bluetooth, WiFi and proprietary systems being used simultaneously. 5G networks, due to their scalability, have the potential to provide unified framework to integrate various IoT systems, paving the way for large-scale diverse applications like smart city. For some IoT applications, like autonomous vehicles, latency is critical parameter. The high data-rates of 5G could help improve battery life of sensors, as their duty cycles can be shorter.

Table 1. Comparison between the key requirements for 4G and 5G

	Fourth Generation (4G)	**Fifth Generation (5G)**
Data rate for stationary users	1 Gbps	50 Gbps
Data rate for moving users (pedestrians, vehicles)	100 Mbps	5 Gbps
Latency	10 ms	1 ms

The aforementioned goals present a huge challenge, and there is a wide consensus in the research community that they cannot be met by simple evolution of the current technology (Boccardi, Heath, Lozano, Marzetta, & Popovski, 2014). There is a necessity for radical new solutions, and in the authors' view the key enablers for 5G will be the following:

- Utilization of millimeter wave (mm-wave) spectrum;
- Advanced multi-antenna (MIMO) techniques;
- In-band full duplex;
- Innovative network architecture.

These technologies are not mutually exclusive; on the contrary, they go hand in hand and their synergetic effect will be able to provide huge performance gains required for 5G.

Millimeter Waves

The data-rate which can be transmitted over a radio link is ultimately limited by the available bandwidth, according to the Shannon-Hartley theorem:

$$C = B \log_2 \left(1 + \frac{S}{N} \right), \tag{1}$$

where C is the capacity (in b/s), B is the available bandwidth (in Hz), and S/N is the signal-to-noise ratio (SNR). All current cellular networks operate in the microwave range below 6 GHz, where the spectrum is heavily congested. The bandwidth of around 600 MHz is currently available for mobile networks, divided among operators. Although it is possible to increase the bandwidth through spectrum refarming and use of unlicensed bands, the improvement by factor of 2 can be expected in the best-case scenario. In contrast to that, there are huge amounts of unutilized or under-utilized spectral resources at millimeter wavelengths, at about

30 GHz and above. This is why mm-wave is a serious candidate for 5G, with a potential to achieve huge data rates, both for radio access and wireless backhaul. Numerous challenges still need to be solved; however, they are mostly related to higher propagation losses (Rappaport, et al., 2013).

It is not expected that 5G will rely on mm-waves exclusively; instead, they will be used, at least initially, to deliver high data rates in very dense areas (e.g. urban centers, office buildings, shopping malls, public gatherings etc.). In this case, propagation losses can actually be beneficial as they allow higher frequency reuse, permitting denser deployment of picocells. Overall, by combining the abundance of mm-wave spectrum with dense deployment, huge boost in network capacity can be achieved. In the frame of the proposed use cases for 5G by NGMN Alliance (2016), mm-waves best fit into "Broadband Access in Dense Areas" family, with example use cases including pervasive video, smart office and operator cloud services.

Multi-Antenna Techniques

Multiple-input, multiple-output (MIMO) systems use more than one antenna at transmitter and receiver sides, which enables them to exploit the spatial dimension. There are several ways to leverage this additional capability, most important of them being diversity, spatial multiplexing and beamforming. MIMO can be used to increase the wireless system reliability or capacity, and it is already deployed in current standards, but on a relatively small scale, with only several antennas. Future systems could achieve huge performance gains by using a much larger number of antennas, and this is facilitated in mm-waves, since many antennas can be integrated in small form factor, due to the small wavelength. Beamforming is regarded as essential for mm-waves, because it can be used to overcome high propagation losses (Wei, Hu, Qian, & Wu, 2014). It is based on combining multiple antennas to produce narrow directional beams, as it is shown in Figure 1. It results in improved SNR ratio, reduced interference, and better edge coverage. Adaptive beamforming can track the moving user, or create a null in the direction of the interferer to cancel it. It requires for the antennas to be sufficiently close together so that they experience the same (or closely correlated) radio channel. This principle underlays antenna arrays (or phased arrays), which will be discussed in section "Antenna arrays and beamforming".

In-Band Full Duplex

Mobile communication networks use the duplex mode to manage the isolation between the uplink and downlink, in order to prevent the transmitter saturating the receiver. In the frequency domain duplex (FDD), the uplink and downlink operate at the same time but at different frequencies, while in the time domain duplex (TDD), the transmitter and receiver transmit at the same frequency, but at different times. In the full duplex scheme both the transmitter and receiver operate at the same time achieving almost double capacity. Since the increase in overall capacity (spectrum efficiency) is very important for future mobile networks, it makes full duplex one of the key technologies for 5G. It is not clear if it is possible to achieve the required isolation of 136 dB between the transmitter and receiver within the timeframe of 5G deployment, keeping in mind that in current LTE networks the transmitter output power is about 23 dBm, the required receiver sensitivity is -113 dBm and that the best result reported until now is the isolation of 110 dB (Anritsu, 2015).

According to Figure 2., the sources of the transmitter-to-receiver leakage are: duplexer leakage due to practical limitations of the duplexer design and additional mismatch at the duplexer's output, antenna reflection due to mismatch between the transmission line impedance and the antenna input impedance and multipath reflection due to reflections in the surrounding environment. The transmitter leakage due to the antenna reflection can be suppressed by more than 35 dB using the antenna image impedance approach (Milosevic, Radovanovic, Jokanovic, Boric-Lubecke, & Lubecke, 2016), but multipath reflection, which requires both the analogue and digital stage cancellation, is still a big problem.

Network Architecture

Emerging technologies and applications pose a challenge to the traditional cellular paradigm. The IoT scenario envisages a huge number of devices which will transmit relatively low amounts of data in shorter time intervals, followed by longer intervals of "silence". Assigning and maintaining an orthogonal radio channel to a base station would be a huge overhead in such situations, with negative impact on battery life and base station capacity, so a non-orthogonal "smart" radio could be much better suited, possibly using a new waveform. Coverage problems of mm-waves can be offset with a heterogeneous network (HetNet) architecture, where smaller mm-wave cells would overlay larger microwave cells, to offload data-traffic in dense areas. Other approaches to improve the mm-wave coverage are relaying and cooperative diversity, and control and data plane splitting could prove to be beneficial (Choudhury, 2015).

This chapter focuses on mm-waves and enabling technologies. First, the history of mm-waves and notable applications, the automotive radar in particular, are discussed. Usage in communications is also covered, including links, upcoming wireless LAN and current and future standardization. Next, the RF wave propagation is discussed, with a special focus on mm-waves and recent measurements. Then the basics of antenna arrays are given, for the reasons set forth in the section where

Figure 1. Beamforming - all antennas are fed with the same signal, but with different time delays, so that their wavefronts add constructively in the arrow marked direction. The resulting gain is known as beamforming gain or array gain.

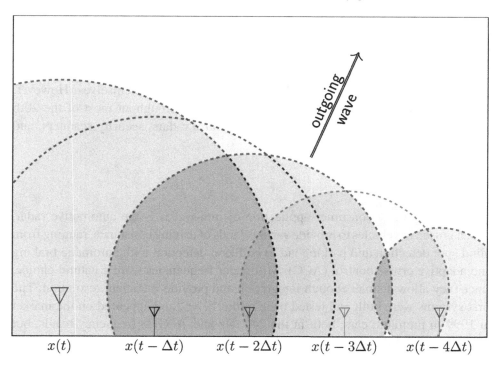

$x(t)$ $\quad$ $x(t-\Delta t)$ $\quad$ $x(t-2\Delta t)$ $\quad$ $x(t-3\Delta t)$ $\quad$ $x(t-4\Delta t)$

Figure 2. Sources of transmitter-to-receiver leakage

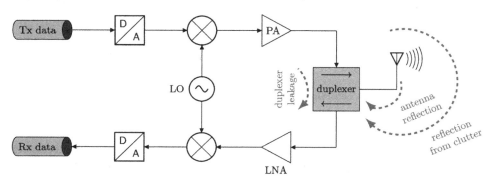

the mm-wave MIMO architectures are reviewed. The rest of the chapter deals with advanced antenna designs.

HISTORY, CURRENT STATE, AND STANDARDIZATION

First millimeter wave experiments were conducted by Bose in 1890s, so it can be said that they are as old as the wireless communications themselves. However, they were restricted to relatively niche applications throughout most of the 20th century, like radio-astronomy, military fire-control radars, security scanners, and police speed radars.

Automotive Radars

The first genuinely consumer application of mm-waves is the automotive radar, which is used in vehicles to provide various kinds of driving assistance, ranging from blind spot detection and parking aid to collision detection with automatic braking and adaptive cruise control (ACC). Millimeter frequencies were a natural choice, since they allow a small enough integration and provide sufficient resolution. The first systems were built and tested back in the 1970s, and appeared on the market in 1999 in premium cars, both in the 24 GHz and 76 GHz frequency bands, but only with recent development in the RF silicon technology they can be produced cheaply enough to become mainstream equipment (Menzel & Moebius, 2012; Slovic, Jokanovic, & Kolundzija, 2006).

Currently allocated frequency bands for automotive radars are: 76-77 GHz narrow band for far range applications (ITU-R M1452, ITU Footnote 5.150), 77-81 GHz UWB, 47 GHz narrow band (U.S.), 24 GHz narrow band (200 MHz bandwidth) and 24 GHz UWB (3 GHz bandwidth). In the near future almost all long or mid-range automotive radars will operate in the 76–81GHz band (Meinel, 2014; Brizzolara, 2013).

Since the European Decision in 2004 to open the 79 GHz band for automotive short range radars, various projects have been initiated with the aim to improve the silicon-based radar technology, in order to bring down the cost of 79 GHz automotive radar sensors significantly. One of them is the German government financed project "The Radar on Chips for Cars (RoCC)", which involves Daimler, BMW, Bosch, Infineon and Continental.

In France, the research and development of the 79 GHz ultra-wideband short range radar technology is taking place within the framework of three projects (RADAR ACC, ARPOD and RASSUR 79), financed by the French government.

Telecommunication Applications

First applications in telecommunications are high-speed point-to-point mm-wave links. In 2001 the Federal Communications Commission (FCC) allocated a continuous block of 7 GHz of unlicensed spectrum (57-64 GHz) for wireless communications. In 2008, WirelessHD was standardized as 60 GHz HDMI cable replacement. In 2012, IEEE 801.11ad was adopted for Wi-Fi networks at 60 GHz, and certified chips are now available for computers and phones, though they are still not mainstream.

In 2003, FCC opened up to 13 GHz of the E-band spectrum, at frequencies:

- 71 to 76 GHz,
- 81 to 86 GHz, and
- 92 to 95 GHz.

For shared government and nongovernment use, for short-range line-of sight radios. E-band contains sufficient space for digital transmission speeds comparable to optical systems (1.25-5 Gb/s) (Lehpamer, 2008).

In July 2016, FCC announced the allocation of approximately 11 GHz of spectrum above 24GHz for flexible, mobile and fixed wireless broadband, comprising 7 GHz of unlicensed spectrum from 64 to 71 GHz and 3.85 GHz of licensed spectrum, designated as a new "upper microwave flexible use" service, in three bands:

- 27.5 to 28.35 GHz,
- 37 to 38.6 GHz, and
- 38.6 to 40 GHz.

The FCC intention was to set a strong foundation for the rapid advancement of the next-generation 5G networks and technologies in the United States (FCC, 2016).

In 2005, the Commission for European Post and Telecommunications (CEPT) released a European-wide frequency channel plan for fixed service systems in the E bands. The 10 GHz of bandwidth between 70 and 80 GHz is of particular interest. Allocated 5 GHz bands at 71-76 GHz and 81-86 GHz allow full duplex transmission, which is enough to transmit a gigabit of data even with the simplest modulation schemes. With more spectrally efficient modulations, full duplex data rates of 10 Gb/s (OC-192, STM-64 or 10 GigE) can be achieved.

In FP7, the European Commission has already launched more than 10 EU projects to explore available technological options which can lead to the future generation of "wired" (optical) and "wireless" communications.

Some of the EU financed projects include:

- "Millimeter-wave Evolution for Backhaul and Access" (MiWEBA), with the aim to bring millimeter-wave technology into the mobile radio world,
- "Mobile and wireless communications Enablers for Twenty-twenty (2020) Information Society" (METIS), with the objective to develop the overall 5G radio access network design and to provide the technical enablers needed for an efficient integration and use of various 5G technologies,
- "5th Generation Non-Orthogonal Waveforms for Asynchronous Signaling" (5GNOW), with the aim to develop new PHY and MAC layer concepts, better suited to meet the upcoming needs with respect to service variety and heterogeneous transmission setups.

The overall EU investments dedicated to research on future networks amounted to more than €600 million from 2007 to 2013, half of which was allocated to wireless technologies contributing to development of 4G and beyond 4G. In 2013, the European Commission announced €50 million worth of grants for research aimed at delivering 5G mobile technology by 2020, with the ambition to place Europe back in the lead position of the global mobile industry.

Propagation

Microwaves and mm-waves used for cellular communications fall into a broader category of radio-frequency (RF) waves, which again represents one portion of the electromagnetic (EM) wave spectrum (the other being infrared, visible, X-rays etc.). We will start the discussion by considering the free-space propagation from a localized source – antenna. Under such conditions, all EM waves will have a spherical wave front (Figure 3), and their power will depend on the, distance according to the

Figure 3. Transmission between two antennas (left), some effects of the realistic environment causing multipath propagation (right)

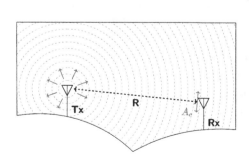
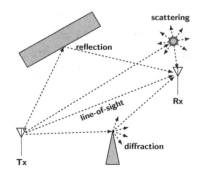

inverse square law (i.e. $P \sim 1 / R^2$, where R is the distance from the source). An idealized antenna which radiates power equally in all directions is called the isotropic radiator. Antenna performance is often quantified using gain, which is the ratio of its radiated power in a given direction to that of the isotropic radiator. Frequently, the gain is specified just as a number, when the direction of maximal power is assumed.

The receiving antenna performance is often defined by its effective area or aperture, which represents the area of the incoming wave front it can absorb. Due to reciprocity, the effective aperture, A_e, and gain, G, are related in the following way

$$A_e = \frac{G\lambda^2}{4\pi}. \tag{2}$$

where λ is the wavelength (which is related to frequency as $\lambda = c / f$, where c is the speed of light).

Considering the above, the received power sent from the transmitter through two antennas, in free space at a distance R, will be:

$$P_r = G_t G_r \left(\frac{\lambda}{4\pi R}\right)^2 P_t, \tag{3}$$

where $G_{t,r}$ are transmit and receive antenna gains, and $P_{t,r}$ are transmitted and received power, respectively. The expression (3) is known as the Friis formula. It should be noted that transmission is proportional to the wavelength (i.e. inverse proportionality to frequency). This results in frequent saying that "mm-wave free space path loss is higher than at microwaves", which is strictly speaking not true, because all EM waves decay according to inverse square law, as it was said earlier. The wavelength dependence in (3) actually comes from (2), since the aperture of the isotropic antenna will decrease when frequency increases.

However, if the receiving aperture is constant, the transmitted power will be frequency-independent. For many types of antennas, the aperture is roughly proportional to their physical size, so it is possible to have comparable aperture sizes at higher frequencies without increasing the form-factor. Consequently, the antenna gain at higher frequencies can be much higher with the same physical size. This is illustrated in Figure 4, where it is shown that a single patch antenna at 3 GHz ($G = 7.45\ dBi$) has roughly the same size as the 8x8 patch array at 30 GHz ($G = 23.1\ dBi$ when they are fed in-phase).

This additional gain can be used to counter the higher propagation loss, as it is shown in the right hand side of Figure 4. Here, propagation loss according to the Friis formula is calculated at 3 and 30 GHz, for isotropic radiators and for antennas shown in the figure. It can readily be seen that the losses for isotropic radiators at 30 GHz are 20 dB higher than at 3 GHz. However, when the array is used for reception, there is only about 4 dB additional loss compared to the patch at 3 GHz. If the array is used for transmission also, losses can be reduced by further 23 dB.

The trade-off when using high gain antennas is that they produce narrow beams, which have to be precisely steered to ensure their potential benefit. The simplest beam steering is realized mechanically; for fixed links, such as for wireless backhaul, this is a viable option. However, the radio access network has to accommodate moving users, and adaptive electronic beam steering is necessary. This requires additional complexity in many system aspects, like hardware and signal processing, which will be discussed subsequently.

Free space propagation is not a good model of a radio channel; however, since in practice RF waves are influenced by complex and dynamic environment, especially in dense urban areas. Their propagation is then governed by the following phenomena (see Figure 3):

- Reflection from large surfaces, such as buildings or ground,
- Refraction on interfaces between two media,
- Diffraction, i.e. bending of waves into shadow regions,
- Scattering on smaller objects, and
- Attenuation in various absorbing media, such as walls of the buildings.

Figure 4. From left to right: patch antenna at 3 GHz, 8x8 patch array at 30 GHz, distance dependent free space path calculated for several Tx/Rx antenna pairs

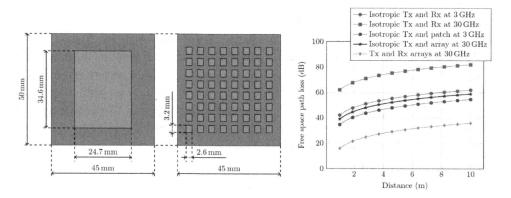

All these effects are generally frequency dependent, and different RF bands have very different propagation – for instance, longer wavelengths follow the Earth's curvature and extend way beyond optical visibility, and easily pass through obstacles. As the frequency increases (and wavelength decreases), propagation tends to be more "optics-like", i.e. possible only when there is direct line of sight (LoS) between the transmitter and the receiver. In microwave range, due to higher penetration and diffraction, significant non line of sight (NLoS) propagation is also possible, and this is expected to be diminished in mm-waves (actual measurements are discussed at the end of the current section).

Unlike at lower frequencies, atmospheric absorption is significant in mm-waves (Figure 5). It is caused by molecular resonance of some common gasses (oxygen, water vapor); scattering on the droplets of rain also causes attenuation. This is important for longer range links, but when typical cell size in the urban environment is taken into account (several hundred meters), these effects turn out to be minimal, of the order of just a few dB. In some cases, atmospheric absorption can actually be desirable, because it allows higher frequency reuse and more secure communication.

A useful concept for visualizing propagation, coming from geometric optics, is that of *rays*, i.e. imagining RF waves to travel along straight lines, and experience reflection and refraction on the interfaces between different media. This is an approximation,

Figure 5. Atmospheric absorption across mm-wave frequencies in dB/km
After McMillan (2006).

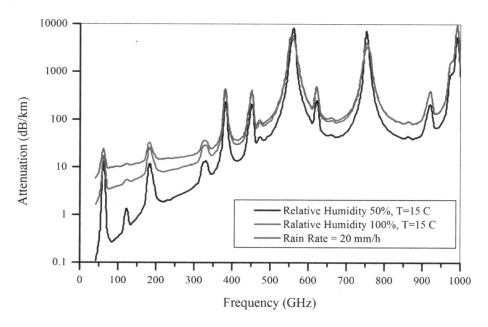

because these are actually vector fields, so it fails to take diffraction and scattering into account. However, it is easily visualized and intuitively understood; it also allows accurate calculations under certain conditions (namely, that the wavelength is small compared to the surrounding objects, which is generally true for mm-waves). The received signal is then a combination of multiple possible paths, which can interfere constructively or destructively; this is called a multi-path propagation.

In practice, analytical modeling of the above effects is too complex, of course, and empirical models for RF path loss are used. They break the losses into three components:

1. **Distance Based Path Loss:** Represented by a monotonic function of distance between BS and MS only. It gives the mean signal strength depending on the distance.
2. **Large-Scale Fading:** Deviations of the mean signal strength caused (mainly) by shadowing. It is modeled by log-normal random distribution, slowly varying, or constant in time.
3. **Small-Scale Fading:** Strong variations of signal strength over short periods of time, or when moving over short distances. Caused by multi-path propagation, it is frequently modeled by Rayleigh or Ricean distribution.

Availability of accurate channel models is essential in wireless communications. It allows network planning and deployment, for instance for calculating cell radii, number of users and throughput. It also enables simulation of new technologies, such as new waveforms, and optimization of various system aspects (for instance, certain types of fading can be mitigated with appropriately designed receivers).

Rappaport et al. (2013) presented the results of an extensive measurement campaign, which resulted in characterizing mm-wave channels. Frequency bands at 28 GHz were used in the dense urban environment in Manhattan, and at 38 GHz in the suburban environment in Austin, Texas. Penetration loss through common building materials, such as concrete, was measured and found to be very high (up to 40 dB), making communication with an outside base station difficult. However, losses from the indoor materials, such as drywall, are much lower, which makes placing picocells inside buildings practical (indoor and outdoor networks would seemingly have to be separated). Outdoor measurements found that the mean path loss exponent for LoS is 2.55, which is comparable to microwaves, and for NLoS 5.76, which is significantly higher. However, if the best directional antenna orientation is used, NLoS is reduced to 4.58, which is practically the same as for microwaves, giving further motivation for beamforming. An average of 7 significant multipath components could be resolved. Small scale fading was found to be not so significant. Overall, a typical urban microcell size of about 200 m is feasible.

ANTENNA ARRAYS AND BEAMFORMING

Based on the discussion in the last section on propagation of mm-waves, we conclude that antennas with large apertures are needed to create narrow directional beams, and obtain gain for countering propagation losses. There are several ways of accomplishing this; some antennas have intrinsically large apertures, in other cases reflector surfaces can be used. However, the most flexible solution is to use an array of lower gain elements; due to their mutual interference, they can produce a narrow beam in the desired direction. The key feature is that if the phase of each element can be controlled, the shape of the beam can be changed dynamically – to point at certain direction, or to put a null in the direction of interference, for example. The array theory basics will be reviewed in this section.

An array pattern is a combination of two factors – individual element pattern and array factor. An individual pattern depends on the used antennas, but even if they are all the same, it can be different due to the mutual coupling (Mailloux, Electronically Scanned Arrays, 2007). However, for initial considerations it is reasonable to assume that all the elements are isotropic. The array radiation pattern in the far field can be shown to be:

$$F_A\left(\vartheta, \varphi\right) = \sum_n a_n e^{jk\hat{r}\cdot\vec{r}_n},$$

(4)

where k is the wavenumber, $\hat{r}$ is the spherical unit vector (in ϑ, φ direction), and a_n and $\vec{r}_n$ are the weighting factor and position of the n-th element, respectively. It is often convenient to put weightings in vector form, $a = \left(a_1, \ldots, a_N\right)^T$, which is called the steering vector. The simplest array form is the uniform linear array (ULA), where all elements have the same displacement d along the z coordinate (for simplicity, because the pattern will then be independent from φ). Then the far field pattern will be:

$$F_A\left(\vartheta\right) = \sum_n a_n e^{jknd\cos\vartheta},$$

(5)

which is actually the discrete Fourier transform (DFT) of the beam steering vector a. To point a beam to angle ϑ_0, all individual patterns have to add in-phase in that direction, which can be achieved by using the equal phase shift between elements,

$$a = \left(1, e^{-j\theta}, e^{-j2\theta}, \ldots, e^{-j(N-1)\theta}\right)^T, \theta = kd\cos\vartheta_0.$$

Then, the (normalized) radiation pattern will be:

$$F_A(\vartheta) = \frac{\sin\left[\dfrac{N\pi d}{\lambda}\left(\cos\vartheta - \cos\vartheta_0\right)\right]}{N\sin\left[\dfrac{\pi d}{\lambda}\left(\cos\vartheta - \cos\vartheta_0\right)\right]}, \tag{6}$$

which will have a maximum for $\vartheta = \vartheta_0$. This function (Figure 6) is known as periodic sinc (p-sinc), and it is very similar to the sinc function ($\sin x \, / \, x$, which is the pattern of the continuously illuminated aperture). However, the difference is that for the large arguments it can have grating lobes (beams which have the same power as the main beam), which is one of the reasons why the element spacing is usually half of the wavelength. Gain is proportional to the number of elements. The side lobes are relatively high, -13.2 dB, which can be reduced by using non-uniform (tapered) amplitude distribution. An example of the theoretical radiation pattern for ULA with different number of elements, using eq. (6) for $\vartheta_0 = 90^o$, is shown in Figure 6.

Figure 6. Normalized radiation pattern for uniformly fed ULA with a varying number of elements

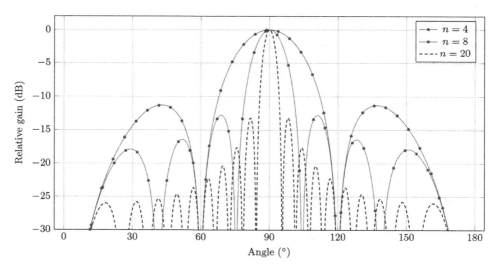

The array feeding network's task is to excite each antenna with the appropriate amplitude and phase. In its simplest form, it can be built using power dividers and transmission line sections of appropriate length; this will result in a fixed array, without the beam steering capability (Boskovic N., Jokanovic, Oliveri, & Tarchi, 2015).

Antenna Beamforming

Adaptive beam steering can be implemented with appropriately positioned phase shifters, or with switchable transmission line sections. If time delay is used for steering, the main beam direction will be independent from frequency, but its width will change. If phase shifting is used, the main beam direction is frequency dependent (beam squint), which is why it can be used in narrow band systems only.

To illustrate this, examples of radiation patterns of two dipole antennas with varying phase difference between them are given in Figure 7.

In Figure 8 an example of the 8x4 array of pentagonal dipoles is given, which can be scanned in one plane if the phase difference between elements changes.

Beamforming Networks

Another important class of array feeds has the ability to form multiple independent beams; they are called beamforming networks. This is clearly a desirable property in a communication system, and it will be discussed in more detail in the next section "MM-wave MIMO". First, we will review the design of beamforming networks themselves. They have a number of input ports, each of which corresponds to a beam of different direction. It is often desirable for adjacent beams to have a high

Figure 7. Examples of different null positions in 3D radiation patterns of two pentagonal dipoles (positions marked by crosses) fed by the following steering vectors: $a = \left(1e^{j\pi/4}\right)^T$ *(left),* $a = \left(1e^{-j\pi/4}\right)^T$ *(right)*

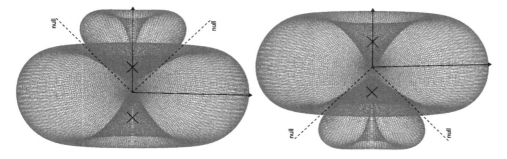

Figure 8. 2D array composed of 32 pentagonal dipoles (left), H-plane scanning due to phase change between the dipoles in four linear arrays (right)
Boskovic, Jokanovic, & Nesic, 2015.

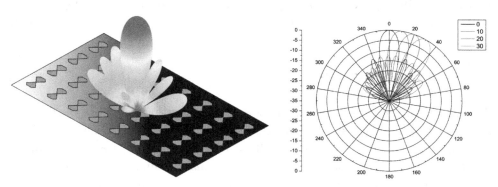

crossover level (i.e. overlap), to achieve sufficient gain at any spherical angle. Another important property is beam orthogonality. If the beams are orthogonal, they can be used to synthesize any possible beam for a given array. Also, it has been shown that the beamforming network which produces orthogonal beams has minimal losses (Mailloux, Electronically Scanned Arrays, 2007).

The Butler matrix is a classical microwave beamforming network, which consists of alternating rows of hybrid couplers and phase shifters (Figure 9). It has an equal number of input and output ports, which has to be a power of two – 4x4 and 8x8 matrices are most common, with up to 64 x 64 reported in the literature. When fed to a single input, it will give equal amplitude and constant phase shift at output ports, thereby producing a p-sinc radiation pattern. Its beams are orthogonal, and it can be made to have low losses. Due to the use of phase shifters it exhibits frequency dependent squint. One fabrication problem is that it requires crossovers, which are difficult to implement. It has been noted that Butler matrix actually represents an analog implementation of the Fast Fourier transform (FFT) algorithm, which is why

Figure 9. Beamforming networks: Butler matrix (left), Rotman lens (right)

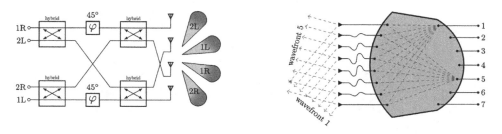

it requires less elements than other comparable networks. Multiple Butler matrices can be stacked to allow beam steering in two dimensions.

Another type of multi beam systems uses quasi-optical beamformers; a number of primary radiators (such as horn antennas) are used as input, and then a reflector or lens is used to collimate the beam. These are true time-delay devices, so they can be used in wide bands, and for feeding arbitrarily large arrays. Lenses offer more design freedom than reflectors (since there are two surfaces which can be optimized). They can be dielectric (including metamaterial lenses) and *constrained*, with antennas on both faces, so energy is guided between them via transmission lines, whose length can be optimized.

One of the most frequently used types is the Rotman lens (Figure 9), which is a 2D constrained lens with a flat front face, designed to have three perfect focus points (one on the axis, and two symmetrically displaced). Design equations are available in the literature (Hansen, 2009). The Rotman lens consists of the parallel-plate region (shaded area in the figure), where a freely propagating wave carries the excitation from the primary feed to the back face probes, and the constrained portion, where transmission lines guide the excitation to the front face array. The length of the lines is chosen such that a wave from the central input will arrive to all the antennas in phase. It can be simply fabricated in planar technologies, such as microstrip (Archer, 1984) and SIW (Lee, Kim, & Yoon, 2011; Tekkouk, Ettorre, Sauleau, & Casaletti, 2012).

There are numerous other lens types, such as miniaturized element frequency selective surface (MEFSS) lens (Li, Al-Joumayly, & Behdad, 2013), Luneburg lens, flat dielectric lens (Imbert, Romeu, Jofre, Papió, & Flaviis, 2014), and other metamaterial lenses. Transformation optics techniques can be used to reduce the lens size (Roberts, Kundtz, & Smith, 2009).

MM-WAVE MIMO

MIMO Techniques

Multiple-input multiple-output (MIMO) stands for communication systems which employ multiple transmitter and receiver antennas. They can be used to increase the radio link spectral efficiency or reliability. The key MIMO techniques are:

- **Diversity:** Which can be used at transmission or reception for redundancy; if the antennas are sufficiently far from each other, the fading which they experience will be uncorrelated, therefore there is an extremely small probability that they will be in deep fade simultaneously. Some diversity techniques are simple, and some are sophisticated, like Alamouti's code.

- **Beamforming:** Which uses multiple antennas to create a directional beam between communicating terminals, as it is shown in Figure 1. It allows RF power saving, receiver signal-to-noise ratio (SNR) increase, cell edge coverage improvement and interference reduction. Beamforming uses the same principle which underlies antenna arrays, and it requires antennas that are sufficiently close together, so their channels are correlated.

- **Spatial Multiplexing:** Which sends simultaneous parallel data streams through multiple antennas to increase the capacity. The receiver can distinguish these data streams through their different spatial signatures. Another option is to use precoding to maximize the SNR at each receiving antenna, which requires channel knowledge at the transmitter. To work optimally, it requires a rich scattering environment with many multipath components. It can be used in point-to-point links and point-to-multipoint, as when a base station serves multiple users. The latter is particularly relevant, because it allows the usage of the same frequency and time slot for different users, increasing the overall efficiency.

The key benefit of spatial multiplexing is that the number of streams, and correspondingly, the capacity, is linearly proportional to the number of antennas. If we use beamforming to increase the SNR, the capacity will depend logarithmically on the number of antennas, according to (1). Therefore, for low SNR channels, it will be most beneficial to use beamforming; however, above a certain threshold, spatial multiplexing will yield maximal capacity. In mm-waves, due to high propagation losses, we expect the most emphasis on beamforming, but spatial multiplexing can also be exploited to serve multiple users and to increase data link capacity. Even single-user-spatial multiplexing can be viable if uncorrelated channels can be established, e.g. by exploiting different polarizations. Before considering practical mm-wave MIMO implementations, the basic theory will be briefly discussed.

Channel Modeling

Consider a communication system which has n antennas at the transmitter and m at the receiver. The relationship between the input signals, $x_1, \ldots, x_n$, and the output signals, $y_1, \ldots, y_m$, can be conveniently written in matrix notation:

$$y = Hx + n \tag{7}$$

where x, y and n are input, output, and noise vectors, respectively, and H is the channel matrix, which represents couplings between all transmit and receive antennas (see Figure 10). The matrix H is also known as channel state information (CSI), and its estimation at the transmitter and/or receiver can be used to improve the system's performance. On the other hand, the knowledge of the statistical properties of H, for a given channel type, is necessary for capacity prediction and optimal system design. In particular, the spatial multiplexing gain which can be achieved is proportional to the (effective) channel rank, $rang(H)$.

If we represent a mm-wave channel as a sum of multipath components, then the channel matrix, H, in the frequency domain, will have following (time-dependent) form (Heath, González-Prelcic, Rangan, Roh, & Sayeed, 2016):

$$H(t, f) = \sum_{l=1}^{N_p} \alpha_l e^{j2\pi(\nu_l t - \tau_l f)} a_R\left(\vartheta_{R,l}, \varphi_{R,l}\right) a_T^*\left(\vartheta_{T,l}, \varphi_{T,l}\right), \tag{8}$$

where N_p is the total number of multipath components, and each component is described by its gain α_l, delay τ_l, Doppler shift ν_l, angle of arrival $\left(\vartheta_{R,l}, \varphi_{R,l}\right)$ and angle of departure $\left(\vartheta_{T,l}, \varphi_{T,l}\right)$. Here a_R and a_T^* are the receive and transmit array steering vectors, which are a function of the selected component angles of arrival and departure. If the channel is slowly-varying and narrowband, then its response can be assumed as approximately constant in time. The effective channel rank is expected to be proportional to the number of significant multipath components.

The expressions (7) and (8) represent the channel in the antenna space, i.e. inputs and outputs are individual antenna signals. This is well suited for current MIMO implementations with several antennas, each having its own RF chain, and where all the processing is done in the baseband. However, at mm-waves, we may

Figure 10. Channel representation in antenna space (left); beam space (right)

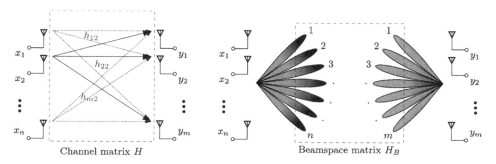

Channel matrix H　　　　　　Beamspace matrix H_B

use arrays with hundreds of antennas, due to smaller form-factor and the need to achieve high gains to overcome propagation losses. Hence, the **H** matrix will be quite large. However, its effective rank will be much lower, since the mean number of multipaths, even in a dense urban environment, is around 7 (Rappaport, et al., 2013). Also, in order to reduce complexity, beamforming can be done by analog or a combination of analog and digital processing, which will be discussed in more detail in the next subsection. Therefore, not all antenna signals may be directly available.

In this situation, it could be more natural to use the alternative channel representation in beam space and the corresponding concept of beam space MIMO (Brady, Behdad, & Sayeed, 2013). In this approach, spatial angles of transmit and receive arrays are sampled into a discrete number of characteristic beams, equal to the number of antennas (Figure 10). If they form a complete set, then every possible wave emanating from the transmit array (and, correspondingly, impinging wave at the receive array) can be expanded into these characteristic beams, multiplied by appropriate coefficients. In other words, the complete array state is given in terms of characteristic beams; correspondingly, the channel can be represented by the beam space matrix H_B which couples transmit and receive ends.

The beam space MIMO is also significant because it provides the connection between the MIMO and the array theory, and it can easily accommodate analog beamforming techniques (Sayeed, 2002). The beam space representation of uniform linear arrays (ULAs) will now be derived; an extension to 2D arrays is straightforward, but it is also possible to include arbitrary array geometries (Heath, González-Prelcic, Rangan, Roh, & Sayeed, 2016). For ULA with N elements, the beam space is defined with a set of N uniformly spaced spatial angles:

$$\vartheta_i = \frac{i\pi}{N}, i = 0 \dots (N-1), \tag{9}$$

which corresponds to the beam steering vectors with a constant phase shift:

$$a_i = \left(1, e^{j\theta_i}, e^{j2\theta_i}, \dots, e^{j(N-1)\theta_i}\right)^T, \theta_i = kd \cos \vartheta_i. \tag{10}$$

They define an orthonormal basis in the antenna space. Now, the channel response in the beam space can be found by applying the change of basis:

$$H_b(t,f) = U_R^* H(t,f) U_T, \tag{11}$$

where $U_{R,T}$ are the appropriate receiver and transmitter transformation matrices, respectively. The advantage is that the channel sparsity will be represented in H_b, which is expected to have just several significant elements. For narrowband channels, this can be easily understood as that only the matrix elements which correspond to angles of arrival and departure of significant multipath components will have nonzero values. A low-dimensional channel subspace can be formed by taking only significant factors of H_b, and uniform beam steering vectors represent approximate eigenvectors of such subspace. This low-dimensional channel nature has implications on MIMO implementation, which will be discussed next.

MIMO Architectures

With the characteristics of mm-wave MIMO channel in mind, possible architectures of MIMO processing (i.e. feeding each antenna element with appropriate signal) will be considered. They are (shown schematically in Figure 11):

- **Digital:** When each antenna has a complete transceiver chain, and all processing is done in the baseband DSP;
- **Analog:** When there is a single antenna input with a single transceiver, and analog RF circuits are used to feed each element with appropriate phase;

Figure 11. MIMO architectures: digital (top left), analog (top right) and hybrid, where p<n, (bottom)

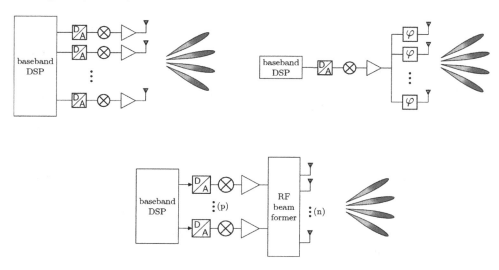

- **Hybrid:** It combines both of the above; there are multiple transceiver chains (but less than the number of antennas) which are then connected to some type of analog beamforming network.

Digital architecture offers the most flexibility, and that is how it is done in current standards like IEEE 802.11c and LTE-Advanced. However, they use a small number of antennas (<10), while at mm-waves we may use arrays of hundreds of elements, due to smaller form factor and the need to overcome the losses. Also, power is the major concern, because the DAC/ADC amplifier consumption can be very high at mm-wave, and having so many high data-rate channels will pose serious baseband DSP processing requirements. Overall, it would be impossible to simply scale the existing approach to mm-waves; however, the research is being done with low-resolution low-power ADCs (Heath, González-Prelcic, Rangan, Roh, & Sayeed, 2016).

Although it is not strictly relevant for mm-waves, it should be noted that a significant research direction is the so-called *Massive MIMO*, which aims to implement digital MIMO architecture in sub-6 GHz microwave frequencies, but on a much larger scale, with more than hundred antennas at base station. With so many degrees of freedom it is possible to use aggressive spatial multiplexing for unprecedented spectral efficiency, and recent massive MIMO prototype has set a world record of 145.6 bits/s/Hz (University of Bristol, 2016). Moreover, due to favorable asymptotics of large numbers, hardware conditions can be relaxed, so more efficient and lower cost components can be used (like power amplifiers and DAC/ADCs), and simple signal processing (like maximum ratio transmission) can achieve near-optimal performance. In Figure 12, antenna arrays for two practical massive MIMO testbeds are schematically shown, with form-factors that are fully practical for base stations. It should be noted that, theoretically, massive MIMO is applicable at any frequency, but due to current technological constraints discussed above, it would be very difficult to implement at mm-waves. Also, the abundance of mm-wave spectrum makes possible efficiency gains of massive MIMO much less compelling than at lower frequencies, where the spectrum is heavily congested.

Returning to the mm-wave MIMO, purely analog beamforming is the simplest for implementation; it relies on the classical antenna array beam steering techniques, typically by using phase shifters. These pose some design challenges, since active phase shifters consume power, have noise and nonlinearity, while passive phase shifters have higher loss which must be compensated using additional amplifiers. Since this architecture has a single transceiver, the use of other multi-antenna techniques, such as spatial multiplexing and diversity, is prohibited, as there is only one data-stream.

Considering the limitations of purely analog or digital solutions, there is clear motivation for choosing a hybrid approach, which tries to combine best from both worlds. In this architecture, there is small number of transceivers (usually less than

Figure 12. Massive MIMO array, left, and schematic of antenna array for massive MIMO testbed operating at 3.7 GHz, right
After Gao, Edfors, Rusek, & Tufvesson (2011); Vieira, et al. (2014).

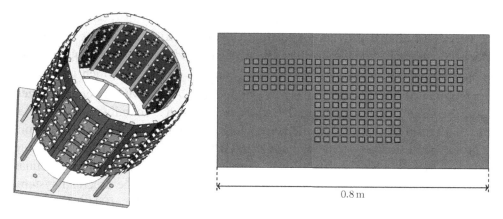

10), which are connected to the analog beamforming network. This way, processing is split between analog and digital domains, which relaxes requirements for DSP and the number of power consuming RF circuits, while still being able to use advanced MIMO techniques. Based on the previous discussion, due to the low channel rank, the number of MIMO streams which can be sent independently is small, so, in this terms, nothing is lost with a small number of transceivers. Also, hybrid precoding can be used in DSP to account for errors in analog beamforming (Heath, González-Prelcic, Rangan, Roh, & Sayeed, 2016). The trade-off is increased complexity compared to the purely analog solution.

Roh et al. (2014) present a hybrid beamforming scheme prototype which uses transmit and receive antennas with two RF channels, each representing a 32 microstrip patch array. The carrier frequency is 27.925 GHz, which allows a small footprint of 30x60 mm. Each array is split into 4 subarrays of 8 patch antennas, with a single RF unit per subarray. This architecture significantly reduces the hardware complexity, at the expense of reduced gain, scanning range and higher side lobe levels. However, it was found to be an acceptable trade-off. The resulting antenna parameters are the 18 dB gain, corresponding to the 10° horizontal/20° vertical 3 dB beamwidths, and the ±30° scanning range in the horizontal plane. To facilitate the processing, a set of beams with unique identifiers was selected. The appropriate phase shifts for each shifter are then loaded from the predefined matrix. An algorithm was implemented to select the best beam at both the transmitter and the receiver, with a refresh rate of 45 ms, which allows to sustain the beamforming gain even for high-mobility users. The measurements have shown that such a setup is capable of establishing a few hundred meters long links having data rates over 500 Mbps, both outdoors and indoors, under LoS and NLoS conditions.

Brady, Behdad, and Sayeed (2013) studied the Continuous Aperture Phased (CAP) MIMO concept theoretically. It considers an antenna with a constant aperture A; based on the linear array approximation, it is concluded that it supports $n \approx 2A/\lambda$ independent spatial modes (which are actually beams). However, only a small number of transmitter and receiver beams actually couple, $p_{max} \ll n$, which is why the conventional MIMO architecture is not optimal. The CAP-MIMO system is realized using the Discrete Lens Aperture (DLA) antenna, which is actually a metamaterial lens, built from sub-wavelength elements which approximate the phase distribution. A prototype of such a system was built at 10 GHz, using an 8 layer DLA consisting of a total of 4489 phase shifting pixels. Single dipole or waveguide horn antennas were moved in the focal plane to simulate multiple feeds in the practical system. Measurements have supported that spatial multiplexing can be effectively used in such a system, with 4 beams in the broadside direction showing significant coupling. When the beam is scanned away from the broadside, the DLA performance decreases, but 2 usable beams were found at 60° off-broadside scan. The usable bandwidth was determined to be 10% of the operating frequency. However, there is still a lot of work to be done towards realizing practical CAP-MIMO mm-wave systems. Other types of lenses, such as a perforated dielectric flat lens, were also investigated for communications (Imbert, Romeu, Jofre, Papió, & Flaviis, 2014).

ADVANCED ANTENNA SYSTEMS FOR 5G

Reconfigurable Metamaterial Antenna

Scanning antennas based on electromagnetic metamaterials that use the reconfigurable holographic approach is a very promising technology for the design of 5G base station antennas. This type of antenna is originally developed for high throughput (1 Gbp/s) satellite communications at 26.5 GHz. The antenna is composed of tens of thousands of individual meta-atoms (Figure 13) that are individually controlled in order to produce a high-gain beam capable of dynamically scanning in a broad angular range (Johnson, Brunton, Kundtz, & Kutz, 2015).

When tunable metamaterial elements are electrically activated, they scatter RF energy and generate a beam holographically. Changing the pattern of activated elements changes the beam direction and width as shown in Figure 13. Antenna reconfigurability is built into metamaterial elements using tunable dielectric-liquid crystal, which dynamically adjust the resonant frequency of meta-atoms. When the frequency of operation is close to the element's resonant frequency. it scatters strongly, and when the resonance frequency is tuned away from the operating frequency the meta-atom scatters very weakly. It can be seen (Figure 13) that activated antenna elements work together through constructive interference, to form a far-field pattern. The selected elements are activated by applying software controlled voltages.

Top-view of the KYMETA high-gain metamaterial antenna is shown in Figure 14. The antenna is composed of more than 10000 unit cells (seen in the inset) fed by parallel rectangular waveguides beneath the unit cells. Each column of cells is fed by one waveguide which runs from the top to bottom in Figure 14. Besides the hardware, a very important part of this antenna system is the software control algorithm which provides optimal beam performances.

Figure 13. Above: complementary electric inductive-capacitive resonators (CELCs) as radiative meta-atoms tunable with liquid crystal; below: different holographic images on the array surface produce beams in different directions
After Schurig, Mock, & Smith (2006); Johnson, Brunton, Kundtz, & Kutz (2015).

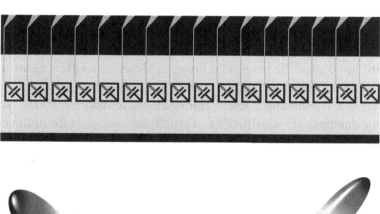

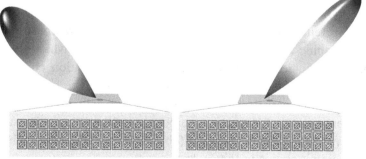

Figure 14. KYMETA holographic metamaterial antenna with overall dimensions of 50 λ x 20λ
After Johnson, Brunton, Kundtz, & Kutz (2015).

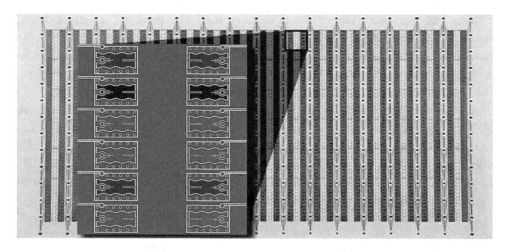

Scanning Holographic Antenna System

The first idea of a holographic antenna was published by Checcacci, Russo, & Scheggi (1970), but due to the low aperture efficiency and difficult feeding by an external horn antenna, further research in that field was almost stopped for many years. In the last decade the interest for holographic antennas grew again, due to the discovery of the efficient feeding by surface-wave launchers (Hammad, Antar, & Freundorfer, 2001; Mahmoud, Antar, Hammad, & Freundorfer, 2003). Nowadays, holographic antennas are considered as a promising candidate for millimeter-wave applications, due to their simplicity and very good integration capabilities.

The holographic technique is based on interference and it is used to record and reconstruct object images in 3D. The holographic principle extension to the microwave and mm wave range offers a new solution for various problems, like the antenna aperture reduction, feeding network simplification, directivity improvement, etc. The holographic antenna is a kind of aperture antenna which transforms the source antenna radiation performance into specific radiation characteristics of the target antenna by means of a holographic structure. The hologram forms the radiating aperture and consists of metal stripes periodically positioned at the roots of the interference pattern formed by superposition of the propagating surface-wave (reference wave) and the radiated wave (object wave). The holographic principle for antenna design is shown in Figure 15.

Figure 15. Holographic principle for the antenna design
After Rusch, Schäfer, Gulan, Pahl, & Zwick (2015).

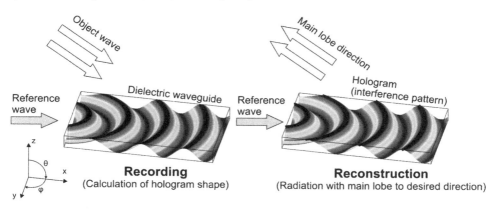

The holographic antenna exhibits the inherent frequency scanning property, since it is in fact a periodic leaky-wave antenna (Rusch, Schäfer, Gulan, Pahl, & Zwick, 2015). It is also suitable for 2D scanning in combination with the phase control feeding of the surface-wave launcher array using the Butler-matrix or Rotman lens.

A 2D-beam steering holographic antenna combined with the Rotman lens operating at 60 GHz is shown in Figure 16 (Rusch, Schäfer, Guian, & Zwick, 2014). Changing the phase difference between the antipodal Vivaldi antennas by using the Rotmans lens, the TE_0 surface-wave can be controlled, which results in the change of the main beam direction in free space. There are different ways to control the phase of the surface-wave launcher array, like integrated phase shifters which are able to control the phase of every single launcher independently and continuously, but they are complex for the system integration, since they need biasing. On the other side, passive phase control networks like Butler matrix (Tseng, Chen, & Chu, 2008) and Rotman lens are easy to implement, but provide a limited number of phase shifts which depend of the number of input ports. With respect to the Butler matrix, the Rotman lens provides better design flexibility in choosing the phase shift range and the phase step variation within that range, so it is a very good choice for the design of the phase control feeding network for 5G antenna systems.

Antenna Beam Steering Using Dielectric Flat Lens

For high data rate communications at mm-wave frequencies, high gain antennas are required in order to overcome high path loss attenuation. Also, in mobile communications, where we can count with high mobility users, antennas with 2D electronic beam steering are needed. One of the promising solutions with respect

Figure 16. 2D scanning holographic antenna system: top view of the antenna with the antipodal Vivaldi array and Rotman lens as the phase control feeding network (above) and side view of the antenna system (below)
After Rusch, Schäfer, Guian, & Zwick (2014).

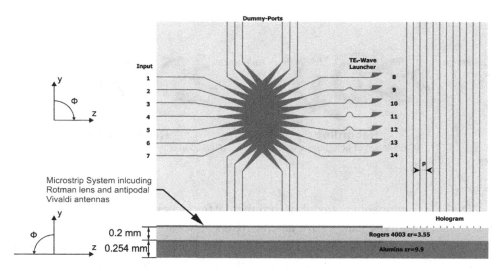

to the expensive and bulky phased-array antenna concepts, is the switched-beam array which has multiple fixed beams that can be selected individually (Imbert, Romeu, Jofre, Papió, & Flaviis, 2014). Switched-beam antenna systems consist of a 2D planar antenna array in which every single element can be switched ON/OFF individually, and a dielectric flat lens to seer and enhance radiation in a certain direction, placed in front of the planar array (Figure 17). The total number of possible beams is equal to the number of radiating array elements, but for each operating mode only one element of the array is selected and only one beam exists. The focusing beam direction depends on the position of the selected active element, so the scan in both ϑ and φ directions is possible.

The design and fabrication of the dielectric flat lens is a very demanding issue. The lens can be designed using multiple concentric rings with different permittivities in order to obtain the desired phase delays for the required beam directions. Due to difficulty of fabrication of the lens consisting of different materials, the alternative design, based on perforating a single dielectric layer, is proposed. Changing the diameter of the holes and the distance between them, which are kept small in respect to wavelength, the effective permittivity of the lens is changed. Dielectric permittivity is maximum at the center of the lens and decreasing toward its exterior edge, so the maximum beam inclination is obtained by activating the peripheral elements of the antenna array.

Figure 17. Principle of the switch-beam antenna array
After Imbert, Romeu, Jofre, Papió, & Flaviis (2014).

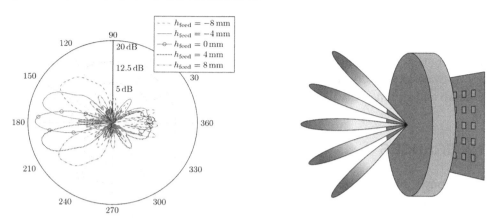

Recently, electromagnetic metamaterials have also been used to design planar microwave lenses using complementary split ring resonators or negative-refractive-index transmission lines. A very promising design of a low-profile planar lens which consists of miniature spatial phase shifters entirely composed of sub-wavelength, non-resonant periodic structures is also proposed (Al-Joumayly & Behdad, 2011). Due to subwavelength dimensions of the unit cells, the effective electromagnetic parameters of the structure can be determined using the generalized approach given by Milosevic, Jokanovic, & Bojanic (2013).

CONCLUSION

In this chapter we reviewed the major drivers that stand behind the 5G, such as ever-growing demand for data, virtual/augmented reality and Internet of Things. Key enabling technologies, namely the extension to mm-wave frequency bands, advanced multi-antenna systems, antenna beamforming and simultaneous transmission and reception, are discussed. New mm-wave frequency bands are already allocated between 71 GHz and 95 GHz, for short-range line-of-site radios in Europe and the United States in order to facilitate the rapid development of 5G networks. Allocated bands allow full-duplex data rate of 10 Gb/s that is comparable with optical transmission.

There is strong evidence which suggests that huge data rates expected in 5G will require radical new technologies. Mm-waves are extremely promising, because huge amounts of bandwidth are readily available; however, implementation is challenging, due to high propagation losses. They can be overcome by using a large number of antennas to obtain beamforming gain, which is facilitated by small antenna sizes at mm frequencies. Considering MIMO and massive MIMO architectures, a hybrid approach seems most promising, and working prototypes are already built and tested. Novel antenna systems, which are too bulky at lower frequencies, can find applications at mm frequencies, such as lens or holographic antennas. The future of mm-wave communications now seems secured, and there will be tremendous research and commercial opportunities in this field for both academia and industry.

REFERENCES

Al-Joumayly, M. A., & Behdad, N. (2011, December). Wideband Planar Microwave Lenses Using Sub-Wavelength Spatial Phase Shifters. *IEEE Transactions on Antennas and Propagation*, *59*(12), 4542–4552. doi:10.1109/TAP.2011.2165515

Anritsu. (2015). *Understanding 5G*. Retrieved from https://pages.anritsu-emearesponse.com/Understanding-5G-Guide.html

Archer, D. H. (1984, September). Lens-fed multiple beam arrays. *Microwave Journal*, *27*, 171.

Boccardi, F., Heath, R. W., Lozano, A., Marzetta, T. L., & Popovski, P. (2014, February). Five disruptive technology directions for 5G. *IEEE Communications Magazine*, *52*(2), 74–80. doi:10.1109/MCOM.2014.6736746

Boric-Lubecke, O., Lubecke, V. M., Jokanovic, B., Singh, A., Shahhaidar, E., & Padasdao, B. (2015, Oct). Microwave and wearable technologies for 5G. *Telecommunication in Modern Satellite, Cable and Broadcasting Services (TELSIKS), 2015 12th International Conference on*, 183-188. doi:10.1109/TELSKS.2015.7357765

Boskovic, N., Jokanovic, B., & Nesic, A. (2015). Frequency scanning antenna arrays with pentagonal dipoles of different impedances. *Serbian Journal of Electrical Engineering*, *12*(1), 99–108. doi:10.2298/SJEE1501099B

Boskovic, N., Jokanovic, B., Oliveri, F., & Tarchi, D. (2015). High gain printed antenna array for FMCW radar at 17 GHz. *Telecommunication in Modern Satellite, Cable and Broadcasting Services (TELSIKS), 2015 12th International Conference on*, 164-167. doi:10.1109/TELSKS.2015.7357760

Brady, J., Behdad, N., & Sayeed, A. M. (2013, July). Beamspace MIMO for Millimeter-Wave Communications: System Architecture, Modeling, Analysis, and Measurements. *IEEE Transactions on Antennas and Propagation*, *61*(7), 3814–3827. doi:10.1109/TAP.2013.2254442

Brizzolara, D. (2013). Future trends for automotive radars: Towards the 79 GHz band. *ITU News Magazine,* (4).

Checcacci, P., Russo, V., & Scheggi, A. (1970, November). Holographic antennas. *IEEE Transactions on Antennas and Propagation, 18*(6), 811–813. doi:10.1109/TAP.1970.1139788

Choudhury, D. (2015, May). 5G wireless and millimeter wave technology evolution: An overview. *2015 IEEE MTT-S International Microwave Symposium,* 1-4. doi:10.1109/MWSYM.2015.7167093

FCC. (2016). Use of Spectrum Bands Above 24 GHz for Mobile Radio Services, et al. Federal Communications Commission.

Gao, X., Edfors, O., Rusek, F., & Tufvesson, F. (2011, Sept). Linear Pre-Coding Performance in Measured Very-Large MIMO Channels. *Vehicular Technology Conference (VTC Fall), 2011 IEEE,* 1-5. doi:10.1109/VETECF.2011.6093291

Hammad, H. F., Antar, Y. M., & Freundorfer, A. P. (2001). Uni-planar slot antenna for TM slab mode excitation. *Electronics Letters, 37*(25), 1. doi:10.1049/el:20011009

Hansen, R. C. (2009). *Phased Array Antennas.* Hoboken, NJ: Wiley. doi:10.1002/9780470529188

Heath, R. W., González-Prelcic, N., Rangan, S., Roh, W., & Sayeed, A. M. (2016, April). An Overview of Signal Processing Techniques for Millimeter Wave MIMO Systems. *IEEE Journal of Selected Topics in Signal Processing, 10*(3), 436–453. doi:10.1109/JSTSP.2016.2523924

Imbert, M., Romeu, J., Jofre, L., Papió, A., & Flaviis, F. D. (2014, July). Switched-beam antenna array for 60 GHz WPAN applications. *2014 IEEE Antennas and Propagation Society International Symposium (APSURSI),* 1672-1673. doi:10.1109/APS.2014.6905162

Johnson, M. C., Brunton, S. L., Kundtz, N. B., & Kutz, J. N. (2015, April). Sidelobe Canceling for Reconfigurable Holographic Metamaterial Antenna. *IEEE Transactions on Antennas and Propagation, 63*(4), 1881–1886. doi:10.1109/TAP.2015.2399937

Lee, W., Kim, J., & Yoon, Y. J. (2011, February). Compact Two-Layer Rotman Lens-Fed Microstrip Antenna Array at 24 GHz. *IEEE Transactions on Antennas and Propagation, 59*(2), 460–466. doi:10.1109/TAP.2010.2096380

Lehpamer, H. (2008). *Millimeter-Wave Radios in Backhaul Networks. Tech. rep.* Communication Infrastructure Corporation.

Li, M., Al-Joumayly, M. A., & Behdad, N. (2013, March). Broadband True-Time-Delay Microwave Lenses Based on Miniaturized Element Frequency Selective Surfaces. *IEEE Transactions on Antennas and Propagation, 61*(3), 1166–1179. doi:10.1109/TAP.2012.2227444

Mahmoud, S. F., Antar, Y. M., Hammad, H. F., & Freundorfer, A. P. (2003). Optimum excitation of surface waves on planar structures. *Antennas and Propagation Society International Symposium, 2*, 88-91. doi:10.1109/APS.2003.1219186

Mailloux, R. J. (2007). *Electronically Scanned Arrays*. Williston, VT: Morgan & Claypool.

McMillan, R. W. (2006). Terahertz imaging, millimeter-wave radar. In *Advances in sensing with security applications* (pp. 243–268). Heidelberg, Germany: Springer. doi:10.1007/1-4020-4295-7_11

Meinel, H. H. (2014, April). Evolving automotive radar #x2014; From the very beginnings into the future. *The 8th European Conference on Antennas and Propagation (EuCAP 2014)*, 3107-3114. doi:10.1109/EuCAP.2014.6902486

Menzel, W., & Moebius, A. (2012, July). Antenna Concepts for Millimeter-Wave Automotive Radar Sensors. *Proceedings of the IEEE, 100*(7), 2372–2379. doi:10.1109/JPROC.2012.2184729

Milosevic, V., Jokanovic, B., & Bojanic, R. (2013, August). Effective Electromagnetic Parameters of Metamaterial Transmission Line Loaded With Asymmetric Unit Cells. *IEEE Transactions on Microwave Theory and Techniques, 61*(8), 2761–2772. doi:10.1109/TMTT.2013.2268056

Milosevic, V., Radovanovic, M., Jokanovic, B., Boric-Lubecke, O., & Lubecke, V. M. (2016, Oct., accepted paper). Tx Leakage Cancellation Using Antenna Image Impedance for CW Radar Applications. *2016 European Microwave Conference (EuMC)*. doi:10.1109/EuMC.2016.7824370

NGMN Alliance. (2016). *NGMN 5G White Paper*. Retrieved from https://www.ngmn.org/

Rappaport, T. S., Sun, S., Mayzus, R., Zhao, H., Azar, Y., Wang, K., & Gutierrez, F. et al. (2013). Millimeter Wave Mobile Communications for 5G Cellular: It Will Work! *IEEE Access, 1*, 335–349. doi:10.1109/ACCESS.2013.2260813

Roberts, D. A., Kundtz, N., & Smith, D. R. (2009, September). Optical lens compression via transformation optics. *Optics Express, 17*(19), 16535–16542. doi:10.1364/OE.17.016535 PMID:19770868

Roh, W., Seol, J. Y., Park, J., Lee, B., Lee, J., Kim, Y., & Aryanfar, F. et al. (2014, February). Millimeter-wave beamforming as an enabling technology for 5G cellular communications: Theoretical feasibility and prototype results. *IEEE Communications Magazine, 52*(2), 106–113. doi:10.1109/MCOM.2014.6736750

Rusch, C., Schäfer, J., Guian, H., & Zwick, T. (2014, April). 2D-scanning holographic antenna system with Rotman-lens at 60 GHz. *The 8th European Conference on Antennas and Propagation (EuCAP 2014)*, 196-199. doi:10.1109/EuCAP.2014.6901725

Rusch, C., Schäfer, J., Gulan, H., Pahl, P., & Zwick, T. (2015, April). Holographic mmW-Antennas With rm TE_0 and rm TM_0 Surface Wave Launchers for Frequency-Scanning FMCW-Radars. *IEEE Transactions on Antennas and Propagation, 63*(4), 1603–1613. doi:10.1109/TAP.2015.2400458

Sayeed, A. M. (2002, October). Deconstructing multiantenna fading channels. *IEEE Transactions on Signal Processing, 50*(10), 2563–2579. doi:10.1109/TSP.2002.803324

Schurig, D., Mock, J. J., & Smith, D. R. (2006). Electric-field-coupled resonators for negative permittivity metamaterials. *Applied Physics Letters, 88*(4), 041109. doi:10.1063/1.2166681

Simsek, M., Aijaz, A., Dohler, M., Sachs, J., & Fettweis, G. (2016). 5G-Enabled Tactile Internet. *IEEE Journal on Selected Areas in Communications, 34*(3), 460–473. doi:10.1109/JSAC.2016.2525398

Slovic, M., Jokanovic, B., & Kolundzija, B. (2006). High Efficiency Patch Antenna for 24 GHz Anticollision Radar. *Microwave Review, 12*(1), 50-53.

Sun, S., Rappaport, T. S., Heath, R. W., Nix, A., & Rangan, S. (2014). MIMO for millimeter-wave wireless communications: Beamforming, spatial multiplexing, or both? *IEEE Communications Magazine, 52*(12), 110–121. doi:10.1109/MCOM.2014.6979962

Tekkouk, K., Ettorre, M., Sauleau, R., & Casaletti, M. (2012, March). Folded Rotman lens multibeam antenna in SIW technology at 24 GHz. *2012 6th European Conference on Antennas and Propagation (EUCAP)*, 2308-2310. doi:10.1109/EuCAP.2012.6206347

Tseng, C. H., Chen, C. J., & Chu, T. H. (2008). A Low-Cost 60-GHz Switched-Beam Patch Antenna Array With Butler Matrix Network. *IEEE Antennas and Wireless Propagation Letters, 7*, 432–435. doi:10.1109/LAWP.2008.2001849

University of Bristol. (2016, May 17). *Bristol and Lund once again set new world record in 5G wireless spectrum efficiency*. Retrieved from http://www.bristol.ac.uk/ engineering/news/2016/bristol-and-lund-set-new-world-record-in-5g-wireless.html

Vieira, J., Malkowsky, S., Nieman, K., Miers, Z., Kundargi, N., Liu, L., & Tufvesson, F. (2014). *A flexible 100-antenna testbed for massive MIMO*. *In 2014 IEEE Globecom Workshops* (pp. 287–293). GC Wkshps.

Wei, L., Hu, R. Q., Qian, Y., & Wu, G. (2014, December). Key elements to enable millimeter wave communications for 5G wireless systems. *IEEE Wireless Communications*, *21*(6), 136–143. doi:10.1109/MWC.2014.7000981

KEY TERMS AND DEFINITIONS

Beamforming: A technique of using multiple antennas (antenna array) to create the desired radiation pattern.

Holographic Antenna: The antenna which uses interference pattern – hologram – excited by the surface wave, to create a desired wave front, and consequently radiation pattern.

Lens Antenna: Quasi-optical system which uses some type of lens (e.g. dielectric, constrained, metamaterial) to collimate the beam from primary radiator.

Metamaterials: Artificial electromagnetic composites, based on sub-wavelength inclusions, that have properties which are difficult or impossible to obtain in nature.

Millimeter Waves, Mm-Waves: Electromagnetic radiation with wavelengths in millimeter region, from about 30 GHz to 300 GHz.

MIMO: Multiple-input multiple-output, communication systems which utilize multiple antennas in order to exploit spatial dimension.

Multipath Propagation: The effect of transmitted signal coming to receiver through multiple paths (e.g. due to reflections), causing fading.

Spatial Multiplexing: A technique of sending multiple parallel data streams, which can be distinguished at the receiver by different spatial signatures, to increase the communication system capacity.

Chapter 4
IoT Architecture and Protocols in 5G Environment

Ahmed Mahmoud Mostafa
Helwan University, Egypt

ABSTRACT

The Internet of Things (IoT) is defined by the International Telecommunication Union (ITU) and IoT European Research Cluster (IERC) as a dynamic global network infrastructure with self-configuring capabilities based on standard and interoperable communication protocols where physical and virtual "things" have identities, physical attributes and virtual personalities, use intelligent interfaces and are seamlessly integrated into the information network. Many of the applications and use cases that drive the requirements and capabilities of 5G are about end-to-end communication between devices. This chapter describes the enabling technologies for the Internet of Things, the IoT architecture, the network and communication infrastructure for IoT, and the importance of scalability for 5G based IoT systems. Also, naming and addressing issues in IoT is presented along with an overview of the existing data exchange protocols that can be applied to IoT based systems.

INTRODUCTION

The Internet of Things (IoT) is a global infrastructure for the information society, enabling advanced services by interconnecting (physical and virtual) things based on existing and evolving interoperable information and communication technologies. Many of the IoT-based applications are about end-to-end communication between devices. In order to distinguish them from the more human-centric applications such as mobile telephony and mobile broadband, these applications are often labeled

DOI: 10.4018/978-1-5225-2799-2.ch004

Copyright © 2018, IGI Global. Copying or distributing in print or electronic forms without written permission of IGI Global is prohibited.

machine-type communication (MTC). Improved provisioning, device management, and service enablement will bring a wider range of potential IoT applications. Some predictions forecast that there will be 15 billion connected MTC devices by 2021, a nearly 40-fold increase over the number of currently deployed MTC devices. Although spanning a wide range of different applications, IoT can be divided into two main categories, massive MTC and critical MTC, depending on their characteristics and requirements. Each brings its own challenges and requirements for standardization. Enabling technologies for the Internet of Things considered in can be grouped into three categories (Friess & Vermesan, 2013): i) technologies that enable "things" to acquire contextual information, ii) technologies that enable "things" to process contextual information, and iii) technologies to improve security and privacy. The first two categories can be jointly understood as functional building blocks required for building "intelligence" into "things", which are indeed the features that differentiate the IoT from the usual Internet. The third category is not a functional but rather a de facto requirement, without which the security penetration of the IoT would be severely increased. Internet of Things developments implies that the environments, cities, buildings, vehicles, clothing, portable devices and other objects have more and more information associated with them and/or the ability to sense, communicate, network and produce new information. In addition, the network technologies have to cope with the new challenges such as very high data rates, dense crowds of users, low latency, low energy, low cost and a massive number of devices. The 5G scenarios that reflect the future challenges and will serve as guidance for further work are outlined by the EC funded METIS project.

The IoT should be capable of interconnecting billions or trillions of heterogeneous objects through the Internet, so there is a critical need for a flexible layered architecture. The ever increasing number of proposed architectures has not yet converged to a reference model. From the pool of proposed models, the basic model is a 3-layer architecture (R. Khan, S. U. Khan, Zaheer, & S. Khan, 2012; Yang et al., 2011; Wu, Lu, Ling, Sun, & Du, 2010) consisting of the Application, Network, and Perception Layers.

Mobile traffic today is driven by predictable activities such as making calls, receiving email, surfing the web, and watching videos (Friess & Vermesan, 2013). Over the next 5 to 10 years, billions of IoT devices with less predictable traffic patterns will join the network, including vehicles, machine-to-machine (M2M) modules, video surveillance that requires all the time bandwidth, or different types of sensors that send out tiny bits of data each day. The rise of cloud computing requires new network strategies for fifth evolution of mobile the 5G, which represents clearly a convergence of network access technologies. The architecture of such network has to integrate the needs for IoT applications and to offer seamless integration. To make the IoT and M2M communication possible there is a need for fast, high-capacity networks. 5G networks will deliver 1,000 to 5,000 times more capacity than 3G and 4G networks today and will be made up of cells that support peak rates of between 10 and 100Gbps. They need to be ultra-low latency, meaning it will take data 1–10 milliseconds to get from one designated point to another, compared to 40–60 milliseconds today. Another goal is to separate communications infrastructure and allow mobile users to move seamlessly between 5G, 4G, and WiFi, which will be fully integrated with the cellular network.

Existing wireless networks may have challenges in dynamic crowded IoT scenarios, one of these challenges is guaranteeing the requested quality of service. This problem will rise in cellular networks, where human-oriented and MTC shall be accommodated in the same infrastructure. Despite the recent efforts by The 3rd Generation Partnership Project (3GPP) to efficiently support MTC in LTE-A, several challenges remain to be faced in the view of full 5G based IoT systems. These include, avoiding congestion in connection access, providing a high system capacity, guaranteeing efficient radio resource allocations and efficiently handling small size data communications (Shariatmadari et al., 2015).

Identification is very important for the IoT to name and match services with their requesters. Object ID refers to its name such as "M5" for a particular motion sensor and object's address refers to its address within a communications network. Object IDs are not globally unique, while addressing assists to uniquely identify objects (Al-Fuqaha, Guizani, Mohammadi, Aledhari, & Ayyash, 2015).

To use the full features of IoT, the interconnected devices need to communicate using light weight protocols that don't require extensive use of resources. The IoT nodes use IoT gateways to supplement the low-intelligence node. This chapter provides an overview of the existing data exchange protocols that can be applied for data exchange among various IoT nodes. Two important architectures of data exchange protocols; bus-based and broker-based.

IoT ENABLING TECHNOLOGIES

IoT has a set of enabling technologies. This section discusses the most relevant ones and outline the role of each of them.

Identification, Sensing, and Communication Technologies

"Anytime, anywhere, anymedia" has been for a long time the vision pushing forward the advances in communication technologies (Atzori, Iera, & Morabito, 2010).

One of the key components of the IoT will be RFID systems (Finkelzeller, 2003), which are composed of one or more reader(s) and several RFID tags. Tags are described by a unique identifier and are applied to objects (even persons or animals). Readers request the tag transmission by generating an appropriate signal, which represents a query for the possible presence of tags in the surrounding area and for the reception of their IDs. Accordingly, RFID systems can be used to monitor objects in real-time, without the need of being in line-of-sight. Therefore, they can be used in an incredibly wide range of application scenarios, spanning from logistics to e-health and security. Physically, RFID tag is a small microchip attached to an antenna (that is used for both receiving the reader signal and transmitting the tag ID).

Usually, RFID tags are passive. This means that they do not have onboard power supplies and borrow the energy required for transmitting their ID from the query signal transmitted by RFID reader. Usually, the power gain characterizing such systems is very low. By using directive antennas utilized by the readers, tags ID can be correctly received within a radio range that can be as long as a few meters.

Also, there are RFID tags getting their power using batteries. So, we can distinguish between two types of RFID tags; namely: semi-passive and active RFID tags. In semi-passive RFIDs, batteries power the microchip while receiving the signal from the reader. In active RFIDs, the battery powers the transmission of the signal as well. Therefore, the radio coverage for active tags is higher than semi-passive RFID tags even if this is achieved at the cost of higher production costs.

Sensor networks can cooperate with RFID systems to enhance tracking the status of things, i.e., their location, temperature, movements, etc. Sensor networks have several applications, such as environmental monitoring, e-health, intelligent transportation systems, military, and industrial plant monitoring. Sensor networks consist of set of sensing nodes communicating wirelessly. Today, most of commercial wireless sensor network solutions are based on the IEEE 802.15.4 standard, which defines the physical and MAC layers for low-power, low bit rate communications in wireless personal area networks (WPAN). IEEE 802.15.4 does not include specifications on the higher layers of the protocol stack, which is necessary for the seamless integration of sensor nodes into the Internet. This is a difficult task for several reasons:

- Scarce availability of IP addresses.
- The largest physical layer packet in IEEE 802.15.4 has 127 bytes which is too small when compared to typical IP packet sizes.
- In many scenarios sensor nodes spend a large part of their time in a sleep mode to save energy and cannot communicate during these periods. This is absolutely anomalous for IP networks.

Computation

Many hardware platforms were developed to run IoT applications such as Arduino, ARM, Intel Galileo, Raspberry PI, and many more. Also, many software platforms are used to provide IoT functionalities. Among these platforms, Operating Systems are the most important since they run for the whole time of using a device. There are several Real-Time Operating Systems (RTOS) that are good candidates for the development of IoT applications. For instance, the Contiki RTOS has been used widely in IoT scenarios. Contiki has a simulator called Cooja which allows researcher and developers to simulate and emulate IoT and wireless sensor network (WSN) applications. Moreover, some industry leaders with Google established the Open Auto Alliance (OAA) and are planning to bring new features to the Android platform to accelerate the adoption of the Internet of Vehicles (IoV) paradigm. Cloud Platforms form another important computational part of the IoT. These platforms provide facilities for smart objects to send their data to the cloud, for big data to be processed in real-time, and eventually for end-users to benefit from the knowledge extracted from the collected big data.

Services

There are four main types of IoT services: Identity-related Services, Information Aggregation Services, Collaborative-Aware Services and Ubiquitous Services.

- Identity-related services are the most basic and important services that are used in other types of services. Every application that needs to bring real world objects to the virtual world has to identify those objects.
- Information Aggregation Services collect and summarize raw sensory measurements that need to be processed and reported to the IoT application.
- Collaborative-Aware Services act on top of Information Aggregation Services and use the obtained data to make decision and react accordingly.
- Ubiquitous Services, however, aim to provide Collaborative-Aware Services anytime they are needed to anyone who needs them anywhere.

Semantics

Semantic in the IoT refers to the ability to extract knowledge smartly by different machines to provide the required services. Knowledge extraction includes discovering and using resources and modeling information. Also, it includes recognizing and analyzing data to make sense of the right decision to provide the exact service. Thus, semantic represents the brain of the IoT by sending demands to the right resource.

IoT ARCHITECTURE

The Internet of Things domain encompasses a wide range of technologies. Therefore, single reference architecture cannot be used for all possible implementations. While a reference model can probably be identified, which is a 3-layer architecture consisting of the Application, Network, and Perception Layers, some other models have been proposed that add more abstraction to the IoT architecture. One common architecture the 5-layer middleware-based model. The middleware is a software layer or a set of sub-layers inserted between the technological and the application levels, used for hiding the details of different technologies and to free the programmer from issues that are not directly related to her/his focus, which is the development of the specific application enabled by the IoT infrastructures.

The middleware architectures proposed in the last years for the IoT often follow the Service Oriented Architecture (SOA) approach. The adoption of the SOA principles allows for decomposing complex systems into applications consisting of simpler and well-defined components. SOA approach also allows for software and hardware reusing, because it does not impose a specific technology for the service implementation (Pasley, 2005).

A middleware sketch that tries to encompass all the functionalities addressed in past works dealing with IoT middleware issues is shown in Figure 1. It is quite similar to the scheme proposed in (Spiess et al., 2009), which addresses the middleware issues with a complete and integrated architectural approach.

Figure 1. SOA-based architecture for the IoT middleware
Atzori et al., 2010.

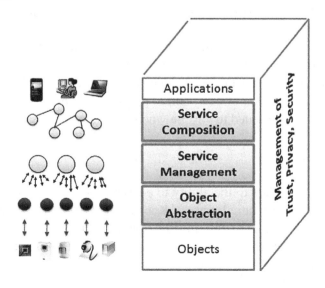

1. **Applications:** Applications are on the top of the architecture, exporting all the system's functionalities to the final user. Indeed, this layer is not considered to be part of the middleware but exploits all the functionalities of the middleware layer. Through the use of standard web service protocols and service composition technologies, applications can realize a perfect integration between distributed systems and applications.

2. **Service Composition:** Provides the functionalities for the composition of single services offered by networked objects to build specific applications. On this layer there is no notion of devices and the only visible assets are services. An important insight into the service landscape is to have a repository of all currently connected service instances, which are executed in run-time to build composed services.

3. **Service Management:** This layer provides the services for each object and their management in the IoT scenario. A basic set of services encompasses: object dynamic discovery, status monitoring, and service configuration. This layer might enable the remote deployment of new services during run-time, in order to satisfy application needs.

4. **Object Abstraction:** The IoT relies on heterogeneous set of objects. So, there is a need for an abstraction layer capable of organizing the access to the different devices with a common language and procedure.

    Accordingly, unless a device offers discoverable web services on an IP network, there is the need to introduce a wrapping layer, consisting of two main sub-layers: the interface and the communication sub-layers. The first one provides a web interface exposing the methods available through a standard web service interface and is responsible for the management of all the incoming/outgoing messaging operations involved in the communication with the external world. The second sub-layer implements the logic behind the web service methods and translates these methods into a set of device-specific commands to communicate with the real-world objects.

5. **Trust, Privacy, and Security Management:** Automatic communication of objects represents a danger in the future. Indeed, unseen by users, embedded RFID tags in our personal devices, clothes, and groceries can be unknowingly triggered to reply with their ID and other information. The middleware must then include functions for the management of the trust, privacy and security of all the exchanged data in a manner that does not affect system performance or introduce any overheads.

NETWORKS AND COMMUNICATION

Based on the research of the growing network complexity, caused by the Internet of Things, predictions of traffic and load models will have to guide further research to the increased complexity of real networks, their standards and on-going implementations. The number of body area networks and the networks integrated into clothes and further personal area networks – all based on Internet of Things devices - will be of the order of the current human population. In this way networks will grow on their current access side by extending these outermost nodes into even smaller, attached networks, spanning the Internet of Things in the future.

Device-to-Device (D2D) Communications

Due to the heterogeneity of devices, technologies, and interaction modalities (machine-to-machine, machine-to-human, and machine-to-cloud) involved in IoT, severe challenges concerning the communication process will be arising (Militano, Araniti, Condoluci, Farris, & Iera, 2015). So, a wide variety of low-power short-range wireless technologies, such as IEEE 802.15.4, Bluetooth Low Energy, IEEE 802.11ah, have been designed to provide efficient connectivity among IoT devices and to the Internet. Recently, also long-range cellular networks are being considered as promising candidates to guarantee the desired internetworking of IoT devices, thanks to the offered benefits in terms of enhanced coverage, high data rate, low latency, low cost per bit, high spectrum efficiency, etc. (S. Andreev et al., 2015).

The Third Generation Partnership Project (3GPP) has introduced novel features to support machine-type communications (MTC) (3GPP TS 22.368, 2014) by accounting for the battery-constrained capabilities of IoT devices and the related traffic patterns (e.g., small data packets). At the same time, the efforts of academic, industrial and standardization bodies are pushing towards the fulfillment of IoT requirements through the next-to-come fifth generation (5G) wireless systems (Gupta & Jha., 2015). 5G will not only be a sheer evolution of the current network generations but, more significantly, a revolution in the information and communication technology field (Soldani & Manzalini, 2015) with innovative network features (Boccardi, Heath, Lozano, Marzetta, & Popovski, 2014). Figure 2 shows the most important features of 5G [7].

D2D communications refers to the technology where devices communicate directly with each other without routing the data paths through a network infrastructure. In wireless scenarios this means bypassing the base station (BS) or access point (AP) and relaying on direct inter-device connections established over either cellular resources or over Wi-Fi/Bluetooth technologies. This approach has recently gained momentum as a means to extend the coverage and overcome the limitations of

Figure 2. 5G features
Friess & Vermesan, 2013.

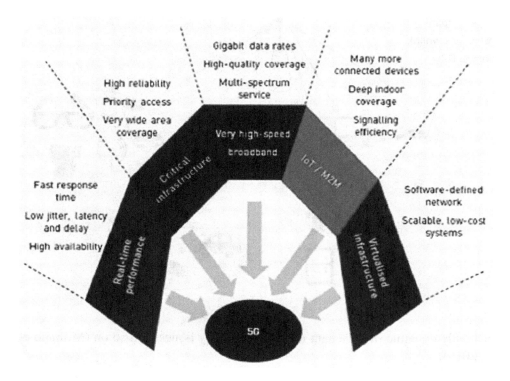

conventional cellular systems. The main benefits it can introduce are (Zhou, Hu, Huang, & Chen, 2013): (i) high data rate transmissions supported also by devices remotely located from the BS/AP; (ii) reliable communications also in case of network failure, as may be the case of disaster scenarios; (iii) energy saving since devices in close proximity can interact at a lower transmission power level; (iv) traffic offloading that reduces the overall number of cellular connections; (v) heterogeneous connectivity accounting that direct communications among devices does not only rely on cellular radio interface, but can be established through alternative radio technologies; (vi) instantaneous communications between a set of devices in the same way that walkie-talkies are used for emergency services.

Needless to say, these same features make D2D a very appealing solution to satisfy also the exacting requirements imposed by IoT in emerging 5G network scenarios (a possible IoT internetworking scenario is depicted in Figure 3) (Militano et al., 2015).

Nonetheless, when considering the possibility of D2D-based interconnection of IoT devices in cellular environment, severe challenges still need to be faced, such as efficient device discovery in heterogeneous environment, optimized link selection

Figure 3. D2D communications in 5G IoT networks
Militano et al., 2015.

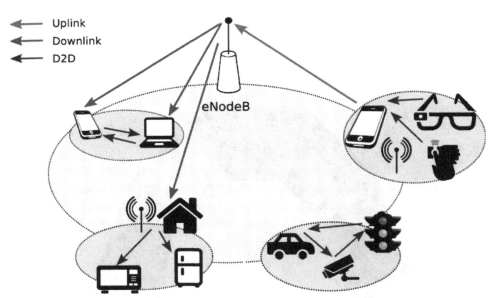

for highly dynamic multi-tenant networks, security issues, and so on (Militano et al., 2015).

Device-to-Device Communication: Approaches, Enabling Technologies, and Standards

A good taxonomy of D2D communications is given in (Asadi, Qing & Mancuso, 2014). There are two classes inband communication and outband communication. The inband solution, D2D and cellular communications can share the same licensed cellular spectrum or uses a dedicated spectrum resources for avoiding interference problems. The outband solution aims to eliminate the interference between D2D and cellular link, but needs extra interfaces such as Wi-Fi Direct or Bluetooth.

In the following, some details about Wi-Fi Direct, Bluetooth, Radio Frequency Identification (RFID) and IEEE 802.15.4 are given, before going into the details of the cellular D2D technology (named LTE-Direct) and the 3GPP standardization achievement concerning D2D services.

Wi-Fi Direct

Wi-Fi Direct (Alliance, 2009) allows mobile devices to directly connect over unlicensed bands and transfer content or share applications anytime and anywhere. Wi-Fi Alliance has recently certified Wi-Fi Direct to support peer-to-peer (P2P) communications between 802.11 devices by jointly exploiting the potentialities of ad-hoc and infrastructure modes. Wi-Fi Direct allows devices to implement the role of either a client or an access point (AP), and hence to take advantage of all the enhanced QoS, power saving, and security mechanisms typical of the infrastructure mode. Wi-Fi Direct devices can connect for a single exchange, or they can retain the memory of the connection and link together each time they are in proximity. Data communication is accomplished by creating a P2P group, where a device with a role of P2P group owner (P2P GO) can allow a cross-connection of devices belonging to its P2P group to an external network. Finally, to address the requirements of M2M communication, standardization activities have recently proposed IEEE 802.11ah, which aims to increase the number of possible devices in the network and to lower energy consumption.

Bluetooth

Bluetooth, together with WiFi, is the most widely known D2D technology working at the 2.4GHz unlicensed band. Bluetooth intends to provide wireless connectivity in personal area networks. In order to enable short-range communications, one device becomes the master of the connection(s) serving up to seven slaves (clients) to form a piconet. Bluetooth Low Energy (BLE) has recently been standardized for IoT devices.

NFC – RFID

RFID is a family of radio technologies which provides fast identification of objects through the interaction between transponders, also known as tags, and readers. The former answer with their identification codes when requested by the reader, which manages the overall data exchange process.

For short-range communications, NFC technology (Coskun, Ozdenizci, & Ok, 2013) plays a prominent role for its wide adoption, as it is natively included in modern smartphones. In addition to interacting with tags, it foresees a peer-to-peer mode by which devices can directly exchange any kind of data. On the other hand, UHF RFID systems are the most promising solution for long-range object identification and worldwide supply chain management.

Zigbee

Zigbee is a protocol stack tailored for resource constrained wireless sensor networks. It is built upon IEEE 802.15.4, which defines physical and MAC layers. Several enhancements have been proposed by introducing time synchronization and channel hopping.

3GPP Standardization for Cellular D2D Communications

Cellular D2D communications technology has been addressed in the Release 12 of 3GPP (Astely, Dahlman, Fodor, Parkvall, & Sachs, 2013), and it is expected to have a complete standardization of proximity services in next 3GPP releases 13 and 14 (Ericsson, 2016). 3GPP has been initially targeted to allow LTE becoming a competitive broadband communication technology for public safety networks used by first responders. 3GPP Radio Access Network (RAN) working group has proposed in TR 36.843 Rel. 12 (3GPP TR 36.843, 2014) two basic functions for supporting discovery and communications over the LTE radio interface. Discovery allows a User Equipment (UE) to identify other UEs in proximity. Two kinds of discovery exist, namely restricted and open; the difference consists in whether the permission is necessary or not for the discovery for a UE. The native support of D2D communications becomes crucial in 5G systems where the increasing data traffic exchanged over radio mobile systems requires novel communications paradigms. An example of research activities in this field is provided by Qualcomm Company, which developed a mobile communication system called FlashLinq (Wu et al., 2013). FlashLinq allows cellular devices to automatically and continuously discover thousands of other FlashLinq enabled devices within 1 kilometer and communicating peer-to-peer, at broadband speeds and without the need of intermediary infrastructures.

IoT Requirements to Be Supported by Forthcoming 5G Systems

In this Section, the main requirements and challenges to be met to exhaustively support IoT in the next-to-come 5G cellular systems are discussed (Militano et al., 2015).

Energy Efficiency

Energy efficiency in communications is important to IoT devices, typically relying on either small batteries or on harvesting technologies. This is even more important to application scenarios involving remote areas, which are difficult to reach and make it hard or almost impossible to recharge or replace the objects power supply.

A large set of short-range wireless technologies are already adopted to guarantee local connectivity among the IoT devices, while wireless gateways typically provide remote connectivity to the Internet. Recently, also wide area wireless technology with enhanced coverage capability, such as the modern LTE-A cellular networks, are being considered as enablers of the IoT.

Resiliency

Wireless IoT systems require guarantee of system continuity in exceptional conditions, including lack of the network infrastructure connectivity. This will appear in cases of congestion due to crowded events, failures of network node, bad wireless link conditions, and disastrous events. This should not prevent the correct functional behavior of IoT solutions. A connection failure could cause tremendous consequences for critical applications, such as safety road data dissemination, health alarm systems, and automated industrial processes. Also, real-time interactive application, e.g., multimedia IoT, could undergo a significant reduction of user quality of experience. Therefore, advanced and reliable IoT systems shall foresee a high-level network recovery capacity, quickly identify connectivity failures, and automatically establish alternative communication paths.

Interoperability

The IoT is populated by highly heterogeneous objects. One of the key requirements is to manage this heterogeneity to provide seamless integration of different types of devices, technologies, and services. IoT heterogeneity should manage the different radio technologies involved in the support of low-power devices. An emerging trend is promoting cellular communication for IoT devices in the view of an all-inclusive 5G framework. Also from the application point of view, common interfaces to access services offered by IoT mobile devices are required. This requires appropriate virtualization techniques to abstract from the underlying networking protocol and to provide syntactic and semantic interoperability (I. Khan, 2015).

Group Communications

In IoT, data provided by a single object may not be reliable to support specific applications and the desired Quality-of-Information. Group communications can be provided by multicast and unicast-oriented approaches. The former case is the most challenging, as the network needs to support simultaneous packet delivery to a group of receivers. This reduces network traffic and enhances Fefficient resource usage. However, multicast communication has a main drawback: it does not provide reliable service in IP network. 5G systems shall provide efficient support for group IoT communication, by optionally leveraging on proximity communications to reduce energy consumption and traffic congestion.

Cloud-Based IoT Service Environment

On-demand processing and storage resources, provided by Cloud data centers, represent an underground to develop and deploy scalable IoT platforms. For example, virtualization of IoT devices, offloading of computationally intensive applications, such as complex sensor event processing, and addressing the so-called Big Data challenge. However, cloud services could suffer from high delays in interacting with remote data centers, and cause an increase of data traffic. Thus, the network provider becomes highly interested to exploit novel form of communications, which accommodate IoT devices' requirements in terms of delay and energy saving.

Support to Multimedia IoT

Smart multimedia devices shall be properly included to sustain multimedia services. Sample use-cases include patient monitoring based on telemedicine, integrated monitoring systems of smart homes, and multimedia surveillance of smart cities. Also, the so-called "Internet of Multimedia Things" (Alvi, Afzal, Shah, Atzori, & Mahmood, 2015) introduces features and network requirements that are different from those of the typical resource-constrained IoT landscape. Multimedia things require higher computation capabilities and also communications are more focused on bandwidth, jitter, and loss rate to guarantee acceptable delivery of multimedia contents. Low-power radio technologies are not well suited to support these types of traffic, whereas cellular networks provide better performance for multimedia flows. 5G shall include novel efficient techniques to meet both machine and human requirements, e.g., by leveraging on edge content caching and proximity content distribution.

5G: The Internet for Everyone and Everything

5G networks must accommodate many more users and devices while delivering more data to each user at any instant in time. The cellular technology has evolved by increasing capacity and data rates to ultimately arrive where we are today. After the mobile Internet becomes a reality, researchers envision not only a 5G network with unprecedented data rates and mobile access but also to accommodate a wealth of new and diverse connected devices.

5G targets peak data rates per user in the range of 10 Gb/s (over 1,000X 4G). User can download an HD video in 40 minutes using the highest speed networks in good conditions. With 5G, the same video can be downloaded in a few seconds. But, there are many challenges to achieving this. Today's networks use spectrum anywhere from 700 MHz to almost 3 GHz, and a variety of public and private entities already claim this spectrum. This challenge can be met in two ways: (1) explore new spectrum or (2) develop new technologies to send more bits to users in the currently allocated spectrum.

Industry analysts predict that 50 billion devices will be connected to mobile networks by 2020. Embedded devices, servers, and the cloud will account for a large percentage of the devices. These devices may include sensors to measure pressure, temperature, or stress and may also include actuators to turn on and off devices. Buildings, bridges, and roads could be monitored continuously for structural health. Corporations and governments could use air-pollution monitoring data to regulate emissions. Patient vital sign data could be logged and monitored to better understand the cause and effect of certain health conditions.

The 5G systems needed to turn these applications into realities are composed of heterogeneous devices which present a significant design challenge. Also, 5G must address network response times (latency). It's estimated that latency on current networks is on average in the tens of milliseconds range with a very wide standard deviation. If researchers succeed in reducing latency, then connected devices can be controlled and operated remotely or autonomously in the cloud.

New 5G waveforms attempt to address spectrum efficiency using the existing network infrastructure to accommodate more users and devices. The Technical University in Dresden (TU-Dresden) has prototyped one of these new waveforms called generalized frequency-division multiplexing and prototyped a complete link. TU-Dresden realized 30 percent improvement in data rates compared to 4G.

New network topologies such as Cloud RAN or C-RAN enable service operators to locate their equipment in the cloud, which significantly reduces the heating and cooling costs of locally deployed equipment as well as the power consumption of a network.

New base station technologies such as massive multiple input, multiple output (MIMO) promise more bandwidth and energy efficiency. Massive MIMO base stations incorporate hundreds of antenna elements to focus the energy per user, which increases data rates and improves the quality of the communication links.

The scalability of the IoT refers to the ability to add new devices, services and functions for customers without affecting the quality of existing services. The IoT applications must be designed to enable extensible services and operations. A generic

IoT architecture has been presented in (Sarkar, Nambi, Prasad & Rahim, 2014) by introducing an IoT daemon consisting of three layers: Virtual Object, Composite Virtual Object, and Service layer. Presenting these layers featured with automation, intelligence, and zero configuration in each object guarantees scalability as well as interoperability in IoT environment.

NAMING AND ADDRESSING IN IoT

Internet of Things (IoT) has different naming schemes. Some are based on IP structure and others are new schemes part of future Internet architectures aiming to solve the tricky problems such as mobility and security.

Naming Scheme Based on IP

IP is the fundamental structure of today's Internet and IPv6 is expected to be the base of IoT in the future. An IP address is an identifier as it reveals the location and identity of a host or network interface. The Domain Name System (DNS) enables people to use Uniform Resource Identifier (URI), which is friendlier compared to IP address, to connect to certain web resource without knowing the IP address of it. As the information technology evolves, a lot of efforts has been done to adjust and extend IP addresses to keep them usable in the future Internet. IPv6 is the final solution for the very limited IPv4 address space. By providing 10^{38} possible addresses, IPv6 will meet the needs of not only the constant growing Internet nowadays, but also IoT which will contain 50 to 100 billion connected things by 2020.

Small and low power sensors and devices will also be an important part of IoT. This requires IPv6 to be extended to cope with these kind of devices. IPv6 over Low power Wireless Personal Area Networks (6LoWPAN) (Kushalnagar, Montenegro & Schumacher, 2007) is a solution provided by the Internet Engineering Task Force (IETF). The way 6LoWPAN extends IPv6 to these devices is to allow IP packets to be transmitted over IEEE 802.15.4 based networks through encapsulation and header compression mechanisms.

One of 6LoWPAN's disadvantage is that it has a relatively long overhead which highly limits the size of payload within an IEEE 802.15.4 frame. 6LoWPAN requires a 26-41 bytes overhead. Taking the 25 bytes with the extended MAC address into account, overhead will occupy up to 52% of the 127 byte-long Maximum Transfer Unit (MTU) provided by IEEE 802.15.4 standard. This will cause the system to be severely inefficient.

New Naming Schemes

New schemes are being developed via several major methods that will play an important role in future Internet architecture. Identification is one of several functions performed by a name. In IoT this function is the most important one because finding one object is very hard when there are billions of things available. Identifier can be globally unique, like fingerprint, or unique only within a certain scope, like zip code. Identifiers are usually the target of naming schemes related to IoT. In (Martin Bauer & et.al., 2013), authors listed four primary methods used to construct an identifier. They are random data, hierarchy identifier, encoding additional information (e.g. manufacturer, locator), by cryptographic operations (e.g. hash of public key). When defining a new name scheme, generally there are two approaches, reusing a scheme already there or define a new one. The latter approach requires a mapping mechanism to integrate itself into an existing scheme in order to provide service in a much broader scope.

Named Data Networking (NDN)

Named Data Networking (NDN) is a future Internet architecture project aims to replace the TCP/IP communication paradigm with a content/data-centric network structure. A new naming scheme which are similar to URI is at the center of this trial. The name of the data will perform several key functions such as routing, securing and content delivery.

NDN follows the idea of Content-Centric Network first proposed by Van Jacobson (Baid, Vu & Raychaudhuri, 2012). In a content-centric network architecture to retrieve the content, they need to send request with name. The web server listening to an incoming request with certain name prefix will create and send back the data packet directly based on the name of the content. In other words, the name of the content or the data will replace IP in the future Internet and act as the universal component in Internet protocol stack.

A name in NDN is a hierarchically structured name. Flat names are also allowed in the NDN when the data is local. The routing system knows the name without interpreting the meaning of it. Consequently, choice of the name is up to the corresponding application.

NDN has many challenges. The global service provided by NDN demands that the name should be unique globally. This uniqueness may eliminate certain names that can be very useful within a specific scope. A new name space management strategy is wanted. Also, since NDN directly routes data packets on the name and IoT will have billions of objects that needs to be named, the routing table will grow to a size no commercial router can support if the naming scheme fails to constrain the complexity of the name structure. Security is another issue associated with the naming scheme. On a data-centric network, the best way to secure the content is to tie a key to the name of the data and the key is signed into the data when the data is going to be transmitted.

NDN has been proved to be much more feasible in the context of IoT. Nonetheless, if NDN wants to be the basic architecture of the future Internet, more solutions including a comprehensive naming scheme are needed.

IoT PROTOCOLS

The most important thing for any protocol is the ability to convey the information contained in a particular domain to another one. This section provides an overview of the existing data exchange protocols that can be applied for data exchange among various domains.

Today there are two dominant architectures for data exchange protocols; bus-based, and broker-based. In the broker-based architecture (Friess & Vermesan, 2013), the broker controls the distribution of the information. For example, it stores, forwards, filters and prioritizes publish requests from the publisher (the source of the information) client to the subscriber (the consumer of the information) clients. Clients switch between publisher and subscriber roles depending on their objectives. Examples of broker –based protocols include Advanced Message Queuing Protocol (AMPQ), Constrained Applications Protocol (CoAP), Message Queue Telemetry Transport (MQTT) and Java Message Service API (JMS). Figure 4 shows Broker based architecture for data exchange protocols.

In the bus-based architecture, clients publish messages for a specific topic which are directly delivered to the subscribers of that topic. There is no centralized broker or broker-based services. Examples of bus-based protocols include Data Distribution Service (DDS), Representational State Transfer (REST) and Extensible Messaging and Presence Protocol (XMPP). Figure 5 shows Bus-based architecture for data exchange protocols.

Message Queue Telemetry Transport (MQTT)

MQTT is an open-sourced protocol for passing messages between multiple clients through a central broker. It was designed to be simple and easy to implement. The MQTT architecture is broker-based, and uses long-lived outgoing TCP connection to the broker. MQTT can be used for two-way communications over unreliable networks where cost per transmitted bit is high. It is also compatible with low power

Figure 4. Broker based architecture for data exchange protocols

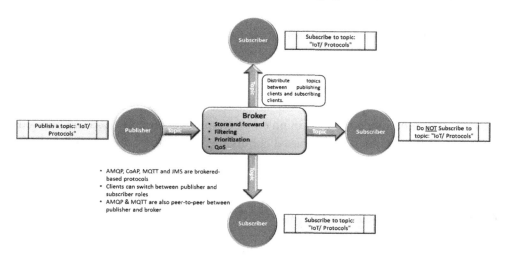

Figure 5. Bus-based architecture for data exchange protocols

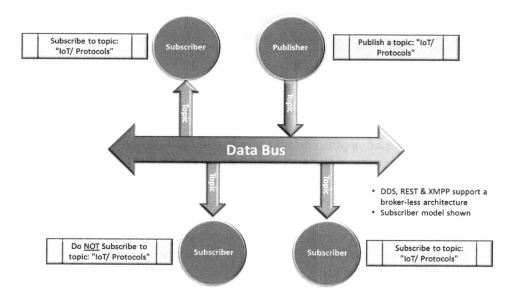

consumption devices. With MQTT, only partial interoperability between publishers and subscribers can be guaranteed because the meaning of data is not negotiated. Clients must know message format up-front. In addition, it does not support labeling messages with types or metadata.

Constrained Applications Protocol (CoAP)

CoAP is an internet-based client/server model document transfer protocol similar to HTTP but designed for constrained devices. A sensor is typically a "server" of information and the "client" the consumer. It supports a one-to-one protocol for transferring state information between client and server. CoAP utilizes User Datagram Protocol (UDP), and supports broadcast and multicast addressing. It does not support TCP. CoAP communication is through connectionless datagrams, and can be used on top of SMS and other packet-based communications protocols. CoAP supports content negotiation and discovery. CoAP supports monitoring resource state changes as they occur, so it is best suited to a state-transfer model.

Advanced Message Queuing Protocol (AMQP)

AMQP is an application layer message-centric brokered protocol that emerged with the objective of replacing proprietary and non-interoperable messaging systems. The key features of AMQP are message orientation, queuing, routing (including point-to-point and publish-and-subscribe), reliability and security. Discovery is done via the broker. It provides flow controlled, message-oriented communication with message-delivery guarantees such as at-most-once, at-least-once, and exactly-once.

Java Message Service API (JMS)

JMS is a message oriented middleware API for creating, reading, sending, receiving messages between two or more clients, based on the Java Enterprise Edition. It was meant to separate application and transport layer functions and allows the communications between different components of a distributed application to be loosely coupled, reliable and asynchronous over TCP/IP. JMS supports both the point to point and publish/subscribe models using message queuing, and durable subscriptions (i.e., store and forward topics to subscribers when they "log in"). Subscription control is through topics and queues with message filtering. Discovery is via the broker (server). The same Java classes can be used to communicate with different JMS providers by using the Java Naming and Directory interface for the desired provider.

When considering JMS API, keep in mind that it cannot guarantee interoperability between producers and consumers using different JMS implementations. Also, systems with more than a thousand nodes may result in poor performance and increased complexity.

Data Distribution Service (DDS)

DDS is a data-centric middleware language used to enable scalable, real-time, dependable high performance and interoperable data exchanges. The original target applications were financial trading, air traffic control, smart grid management and other big data, mission critical applications. It is a decentralized broker-less protocol with direct peer-to-peer communications between publishers and subscribers and was designed to be language and operating system independent. DDS sends and receives data, events, and command information on top of UDP but can also run over other transports such as IP Multicast, TCP/IP, shared memory etc. DDS supports real-time many-to-many managed connectivity and also supports automatic discovery. Applications using DDS for communications are decoupled and do not require intervention from the user applications, which can simplify complex network programming. QoS parameters that are used to configure its auto-discovery mechanisms are setup one time. DSS automatically handles hot-swapping redundant publishers if the primary publisher fails. Subscription control is via partitions and topics with message filtering. DDS Security specification is still pending. Implementers should be aware that DSS needs DSSI ("wire-protocol") to make sure all implementations can interoperate. DSS is available commercially and a version of it has been made "open" in as much as a "public" version is available.

Representational State Transfer (REST)

REST is a language and operating system independent architecture for designing network applications using simple HTTP to connect between machines. It was designed as a lightweight point-to-point, stateless client/server and cacheable protocol for simple client/server (request/reply) communications from devices to the cloud over TCP/IP. Use of stateless model supported by HTTP and can simplify server design and can easily be used in the presence of firewalls, but may result in the need for additional information exchange. It does not support Cookies or asynchronous, loosely coupled publish-and-subscribe message exchanges. Support for systems with more than a thousand nodes may result in poor performance and complexity.

Extensible Messaging and Presence Protocol (XMPP)

XMPP is a communications protocol for message oriented middleware based on XML (formally "Jabber"). It is a brokerless decentralized client-server (as previously defined) model and is used by text messaging applications. It is near real-time and massively scalable to hundreds of thousands of nodes. Binary data must be base64 encoded before it can be transmitted in-band. It is useful for devices with large and potentially complicated traffic, and where extra security is required. For example, it can be used to isolate security to between applications rather than to rely on TCP or the web. The users or devices (servers) can keep control through preference settings. New extensions being added to enhance its application to the IoT, including Service Discovery (XEP-0030), Concentrators for connecting legacy sensors and devices (XEP-0325), SensorData (XEP-0323), and Control (XEP-0322) and the Transport of XMPP over HTTM (XP-0124).

CONCLUSION

The emerging idea of the Internet of Things (IoT) is rapidly finding its path throughout our modern life, aiming to improve the quality of life by connecting many smart devices, technologies, and applications. Overall, the IoT would allow for the automation of everything around us. In fact, it is clear that the current Internet paradigm, which supports and has been built around host-to-host communications, is now a limiting factor for the current use of the Internet. It has become clear that Internet is mostly used for the publishing and retrieving of information (regardless of the host where such information is published or retrieved from) and therefore, information should be the focus of communication and networking solutions. This leads to the concept of data-centric networks. 5G technologies and the Internet of Things are among the main elements which will shape the future of the Internet in the coming years. Differently from previous cellular technologies which were designed essentially for broadband, the requirements which the future 5G networks will have to satisfy, and particularly those for MTC make 5G communications a particularly good fit for IoT applications. By offering lower cost, lower energy consumption and support for very large number of devices, 5G is ready to enable the vision of a truly global Internet of Things. This chapter presented an overview of IoT, its enabling technologies, protocols, architecture, communication technologies deployed, naming and addressing techniques, and the recent emerging 5G technology and its support for IoT.

REFERENCES

Al-Fuqaha, A., Guizani, M., Mohammadi, M., Aledhari, M., & Ayyash, M. (2015). Internet of things: A survey on enabling technologies, protocols, and applications. *IEEE Communications Surveys and Tutorials*, *17*(4), 2347–2376. doi:10.1109/COMST.2015.2444095

Alliance, W. F. (2009). *Wi-fi peer-to-peer (p2p) technical specification v1. 0*. Wi-Fi Alliance.

Alvi, S. A., Afzal, B., Shah, G. A., Atzori, L., & Mahmood, W. (2015). Internet of multimedia things: Vision and challenges. *Ad Hoc Networks*, *33*, 87–111. doi:10.1016/j.adhoc.2015.04.006

Andreev, S., Galinina, O., Pyattaev, A., Gerasimenko, M., Tirronen, T., Torsner, J., & Koucheryavy, Y. et al. (2015). Understanding the IoT connectivity landscape: A contemporary M2M radio technology roadmap. *IEEE Communications Magazine*, *53*(9), 32–40. doi:10.1109/MCOM.2015.7263370

Asadi, A., Wang, Q., & Mancuso, V. (2014). A survey on device-to-device communication in cellular networks. *IEEE Communications Surveys and Tutorials*, *16*(4), 1801–1819. doi:10.1109/COMST.2014.2319555

Astely, D., Dahlman, E., Fodor, G., Parkvall, S., & Sachs, J. (2013). LTE release 12 and beyond. *IEEE Communications Magazine*, *51*(7), 154–160. doi:10.1109/MCOM.2013.6553692

Atzori, L., Iera, A., & Morabito, G. (2010). The internet of things: A survey. *Computer Networks*, *54*(15), 2787–2805. doi:10.1016/j.comnet.2010.05.010

Baid, A., Vu, T., & Raychaudhuri, D. (2012, March). Comparing alternative approaches for networking of named objects in the future Internet. In *Computer Communications Workshops (INFOCOM WKSHPS), 2012 IEEE Conference on* (pp. 298-303). IEEE. doi:10.1109/INFCOMW.2012.6193509

Bauer, M. (2013). *Catalogue of IoT Naming, Addressing and Discovery Schemes*. IERC Projects V1.7. IERC-AC2-D1.

Boccardi, F., Heath, R. W., Lozano, A., Marzetta, T. L., & Popovski, P. (2014). Five disruptive technology directions for 5G. *IEEE Communications Magazine*, *52*(2), 74–80. doi:10.1109/MCOM.2014.6736746

Buckl, C., Sommer, S., Scholz, A., Knoll, A., Kemper, A., Heuer, J., & Schmitt, A. (2009, May). Services to the field: An approach for resource constrained sensor/ actor networks. In *Advanced Information Networking and Applications Workshops, 2009. WAINA'09. International Conference on* (pp. 476-481). IEEE.

Coskun, V., Ozdenizci, B., & Ok, K. (2013). A survey on near field communication (NFC) technology. *Wireless Personal Communications*, *71*(3), 2259–2294. doi:10.1007/s11277-012-0935-5

EU FP7 Internet of Things Architecture Project. (2014, Sep. 18). Retrieved from http://www.iot-a.eu/public

Finkelzeller, K. (2003). *The RFID handbook*. Academic Press.

Friess, P. (2013). *Internet of things: converging technologies for smart environments and integrated ecosystems*. River Publishers.

3. GPP TR 36.843. (2014). *Study on LTE device to device proximity services; Radio aspects*. 3GPP.

3. GPP TS 22.368. (2014). *Service Requirements for Machine-Type Communications (MTC)*. 3GPP.

Gupta, A., & Jha, R. K. (2015). A survey of 5G network: Architecture and emerging technologies. *IEEE Access, 3*, 1206-1232.

IEEE 802.15 Working Group for WPAN. (n.d.). Retrieved June 1, 2016, from http://ieee802.org/15

Khan, I., Belqasmi, F., Glitho, R., Crespi, N., Morrow, M., & Polakos, P. (2016). Wireless sensor network virtualization: A survey. *IEEE Communications Surveys and Tutorials, 18*(1), 553–576. doi:10.1109/COMST.2015.2412971

Khan, R., Khan, S. U., Zaheer, R., & Khan, S. (2012, December). Future internet: the internet of things architecture, possible applications and key challenges. In *Frontiers of Information Technology (FIT), 2012 10th International Conference on* (pp. 257-260). IEEE. doi:10.1109/FIT.2012.53

Kushalnagar, N., Montenegro, G., & Schumacher, C. (2007). *IPv6 over low-power wireless personal area networks (6LoWPANs): Overview, assumptions, problem statement, and goals* (No. RFC 4919). RFC.

Medagliani, P., Leguay, J., Duda, A., Rousseau, F., Duquennoy, S., Raza, S., ... Monton, M. (2014). *Internet of Things Applications-From Research and Innovation to Market Deployment*. Academic Press.

Militano, L., Araniti, G., Condoluci, M., Farris, I., & Iera, A. (2015). *Device-to-device communications for 5G internet of things*. EAI.

Pasley, J. (2005). How BPEL and SOA are changing Web services development. *IEEE Internet Computing, 9*(3), 60–67. doi:10.1109/MIC.2005.56

Ericsson. (n.d.). *Whitepaper: Release, L. T. E. 13*. Retrieved June 1, 2016, from http://www.ericsson.com/res/docs/whitepapers/150417-wp-lte-release-13.pdf

Sarkar, C., Nambi, S. A. U., Prasad, R. V., & Rahim, A. (2014, March). A scalable distributed architecture towards unifying IoT applications. In *Internet of Things (WF-IoT), 2014 IEEE World Forum on* (pp. 508-513). IEEE. doi:10.1109/WF-IoT.2014.6803220

Shariatmadari, H., Ratasuk, R., Iraji, S., Laya, A., Taleb, T., Jäntti, R., & Ghosh, A. (2015). Machine-type communications: Current status and future perspectives toward 5G systems. *IEEE Communications Magazine, 53*(9), 10–17. doi:10.1109/MCOM.2015.7263367

Soldani, D., & Manzalini, A. (2015). Horizon 2020 and beyond: On the 5G operating system for a true digital society. *IEEE Vehicular Technology Magazine, 10*(1), 32–42. doi:10.1109/MVT.2014.2380581

Spiess, P., Karnouskos, S., Guinard, D., Savio, D., Baecker, O., De Souza, L. M. S., & Trifa, V. (2009, July). SOA-based integration of the internet of things in enterprise services. In *Web Services, 2009. ICWS 2009. IEEE International Conference on* (pp. 968-975). IEEE.

Wu, M., Lu, T. J., Ling, F. Y., Sun, J., & Du, H. Y. (2010, August). Research on the architecture of Internet of things. In *Advanced Computer Theory and Engineering (ICACTE), 2010 3rd International Conference on* (Vol. 5, pp. V5-484). IEEE.

Wu, X., Tavildar, S., Shakkottai, S., Richardson, T., Li, J., Laroia, R., & Jovicic, A. (2013). FlashLinQ: A synchronous distributed scheduler for peer-to-peer ad hoc networks. *IEEE/ACM Transactions on Networking (TON), 21*(4), 1215-1228.

Yang, Z., Yue, Y., Yang, Y., Peng, Y., Wang, X., & Liu, W. (2011, July). Study and application on the architecture and key technologies for IOT. In *Multimedia Technology (ICMT), 2011 International Conference on* (pp. 747-751). IEEE.

Zhou, B., Hu, H., Huang, S. Q., & Chen, H. H. (2013). Intracluster device-to-device relay algorithm with optimal resource utilization. *IEEE Transactions on Vehicular Technology, 62*(5), 2315–2326. doi:10.1109/TVT.2012.2237557

KEY TERMS AND DEFINITIONS

Communications Protocol: A defined set of rules and regulations that determine how data is transmitted in telecommunications and computer networking.

Device-to-Device (D2D) Communications: Direct communication between devices using any communications channel, including wired and wireless.

Interoperability: A characteristic of a product or system, whose interfaces are completely understood, to work with other products or systems, present or future, in either implementation or access, without any restrictions.

IoT: The internet of things (IoT) is the network of physical devices, vehicles, buildings and other items—embedded with electronics, software, sensors, and network connectivity that enables these objects to collect and exchange data.

Resilience: The ability of a system to cope with change.

Scalability: The capability of a system, network, or process to handle a growing amount of work, or its potential to be enlarged in order to accommodate that growth.

Chapter 5
The Role of Autonomous Computing, Cloud Computing, and Multimedia in IoT

Ahmed Mahmoud Mostafa
Al Baha University, Saudi Arabia

ABSTRACT

Connecting a large number of physical objects equipped with sensors to the Internet generates what is called "big data." Big data needs smart and efficient storage. The emerging and developing technology of cloud computing is defined by the US National Institute of Standards and Technology (NIST) as an access model to an on-demand network of shared configurable computing sources such as networks, servers, warehouses, applications, and services. The manual installation and management of IoT devices becomes impractical due to the large numbers involved. Specifically, there exists an inefficiency that can be resolved by minimizing user intervention. The manual maintenance of a large number of devices becomes inefficient, and demands the presence of intelligent and dynamic management schemes. In addition, Internet of Things systems cannot successfully realize the notion of ubiquitous connectivity of everything if they are not capable to truly include 'multimedia things'.

INTRODUCTION

Internet of Things (IoT) is playing a major role in extending the reach of the existing communication systems to include resource constrained devices. Many exciting research works for IoT have been proposed for management of such devices such that human intervention is minimized. This is a challenge due to the high heterogeneity,

DOI: 10.4018/978-1-5225-2799-2.ch005

Copyright © 2018, IGI Global. Copying or distributing in print or electronic forms without written permission of IGI Global is prohibited.

high complexity of the devices and the lack of dynamic management schemes (Ashraf & Habaebi, 2015). This chapter introduces the paradigm of autonomic computing to be used for such dynamic yet secure management in IoT. The adoption of the autonomy in IoT architecture can prove to be a valuable addition to IoT systems.

The IoT employs a large number of embedded devices, like sensors and actuators that generate big data which in turn requires complex computations to extract knowledge. Big data is so huge such that it exceeds the capability of commonly used hardware environments and software tools to capture, manage, and process them within an acceptable slot of time. Cloud computing enables researchers and businesses to use and maintain many resources remotely, reliably and at a low cost. Therefore, the storage and computing resources of the cloud present the best choice for the IoT to store and process big data.

Cloud computing has been established as one of the major building blocks of the Future Internet. New technology enablers have progressively fostered virtualization at different levels and have allowed the various paradigms known as "Applications as a Service", "Platforms as a Service" and "Infrastructure and Networks as a Service" (Friess, 2013). Such trends have greatly helped to reduce cost of ownership and management of associated virtualized resources, lowering the market entry threshold to new players and enabling provisioning of new services. With the virtualization of objects being the next natural step in this trend, the convergence of cloud computing and Internet of Things will enable unprecedented opportunities in the IoT services arena (Hassan, Song & Huh., 2009). As part of this convergence, IoT applications (such as sensor-based services) will be delivered on-demand through a cloud environment. This extends beyond the need to virtualize sensor data stores in a scalable fashion. It asks for virtualization of Internet-connected objects and their ability to become orchestrated into on-demand services (such as Sensing-as-a-Service).

IoT systems cannot successfully realize the notion of ubiquitous connectivity of everything if they are not truly capable to include 'multimedia things'. Sample use-cases include ambient assisted living and patient monitoring based on telemedicine, integrated monitoring systems of smart homes, advanced multimedia surveillance of smart cities involving real-time sensor data acquisition. However, the current research and development activities in the field do not mandate the features of multimedia objects, thus leaving a gap to benefit from multimedia content based services and applications. Besides, the so-called "Internet of Multimedia Things" (IoMT) (Alvi, Afzal, Shah, Atzori & Mahmood, 2015) introduces features and network requirements that are different from those of the typical resource-constrained IoT landscape. IoMT is a novel paradigm in which smart heterogeneous multimedia things can interact and cooperate with one another and with other things connected to the Internet to facilitate multimedia based services and applications that are globally available to the users.

AUTONOMOUS COMPUTING IN INTERNET OF THINGS

In the next few years, the Internet of Things (IoT) will interconnect a huge number of "things". While IoT has many benefits to change our way of life to the best, it will also exponentially increase the scale and the complexity of existing computing and communication systems. It is impossible for humans to manage manually this huge amount of things. So, such "things" need to adapt automatically to the ever-changing environment and requirements. The future research trend is the development of intelligent and autonomic things, such as autonomic vehicles/robots/networks and smart electronics.

Autonomic computing (Computing, 2006), inspired by biological systems, has been proposed as a grand challenge that will allow the systems to self-manage this complexity, using high-level objectives and policies defined by humans. The objective is to provide some self-x properties to the system, where x can be adaptation, organization, optimization, configuration, protection, healing, discovery, description, etc (Friess, 2013).

Properties of Autonomic IoT Systems

The following properties are particularly important for IoT systems and need further research (Friess, 2013):

- **Self-Adaptation:** Self-adaptation is an essential property that allows the communicating nodes, as well as services using them, to react in a timely manner to the continuously changing context in accordance with business policies or performance objectives that are defined by humans. IoT systems should be able to reason autonomously and give self-adapting decisions.
- **Self-Organization:** In IoT systems, the network topology is continuously changing. The network should therefore be able to re-organize itself against this evolving topology. Self-organizing has an important role to provide seamless data exchange throughout the highly heterogeneous networks. When working on self-organization, it is also very important to consider the energy consumption of nodes and to come up with solutions that maximize the communication efficiency within that system.
- **Self-Optimization:** Optimal usage of the constrained resources (such as memory, bandwidth, processor, and most importantly, power) of IoT devices is necessary for sustainable and long-living IoT deployments.
- **Self-Configuration:** Configuration of the IoT system is very complicated and difficult to be handled by hand. Self-management applications should be able to automatically configure necessary parameters based on the

needs of the applications and users. It consists of configuring device and network parameters, installing/uninstalling/upgrading software, or tuning performance parameters.

- **Self-Protection:** Due to its wireless and ubiquitous nature, IoT system will be vulnerable to numerous malicious attacks. The IoT system should autonomously tune itself to different levels of security and privacy, while not affecting the quality of service.
- **Self-Healing:** The autonomous IoT system should be able is to detect and diagnose problems as they occur and to fix them immediately.
- **Self-Description:** Sensors and actuators should be able to describe themselves in an expressive manner in order to allow other communicating things to interact with them. Self-description is a fundamental property for implementing plug and play resources and devices.
- **Self-Discovery:** The self-discovery characteristic plays an essential role for dynamically discovering IoT resources in a seamless and transparent manner.
- **Self-Matchmaking:** The IoT system should be able to exploit the huge availability of underlying objects. They also need to find suitable objects alternatives in case of failure, unreachability etc. Such environments will require self-matchmaking features (between services and objects and vice versa).
- **Self-Energy-Supplying:** Energy harvesting techniques (solar, thermal, vibration, etc.) should be used as a power supply, rather than batteries that need to be replaced regularly, and that have a negative effect on the environment.

Autonomic Framework

A framework was proposed (Ashraf & Habaebi, 2015) to make the management of systems easier. The framework consists of two important functions, namely, 1) Managed Resource and 2) Autonomic Manager.

The managed resource is the less complex entity whereas the autonomic manager is more complex and provides the central control functionality. In addition to these two entities, an effector interface in the managed resource allows for the manipulation of the environment by the system. Effectors are essentially actuators which act upon command to change the current state in the system and environment.

Autonomy in the managed resource and the managed elements is implemented through the control loop of monitor, analyze, plan and execute. These modules are presented in Figure 1. The monitor component is responsible to collect details from a managed resource element. On the other hand, the analyze components allows to analyze the monitored data, and extract useful patterns and information. This enables the system to learn about the environment and predict future events. The

Figure 1. The autonomic control loop
Ashraf & Habaebi, 2015.

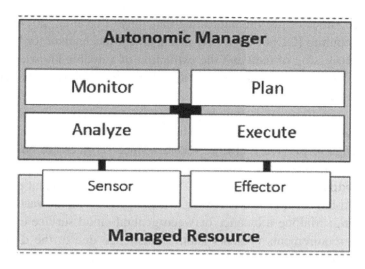

plan component provides higher level policies to guide the different actions, in order to achieve goals and objectives. Finally, the execute component controls execution of predefined plans and interfaces with the managed resource.

THE ROLE OF CLOUD COMPUTING IN INTERNET OF THINGS

Big data is used by businesses to extract knowledge by which a business can achieve competitive advantage (Al-Fuqaha, Guizani, Mohammadi, Aledhari, & Ayyash, 2015). There are some platforms for big data analytics like Apache Hadoop and SciDB. However, these tools are hardly strong enough for big data needs of IoT (Tsai, Lai, Chiang, & Yang, 2014). The amount of IoT data generally is too huge to be processed by the available tools. For an IoT system, these platforms should work in real-time to serve the users efficiently. For example, Facebook has used an improved version of Hadoop to analyze billions of messages per day (Borthakur et al., 2011). A lot of smart devices offer computing capabilities that can be used to perform parallel IoT data analytic tasks (Mukherjee, Paul, Dey & Banerjee, 2014).

A recent research has proposed an IoT big data analytics service known as TSaaaS using time series data analytics to perform pattern mining on a large amount of collected sensor data (X. Xu et al., 2014). Their analytic service relies on the Time Series Database service and is accessible by a set of RESTful interfaces.

Existing approaches like principle component analysis (PCA), pattern reduction, dimensionality reduction, feature selection, and distributed computing methods can be used to keep track of just the interesting data only (Tsai et al., 2014).

Cloud computing (CC) offers a new management mechanism for big data that enables the processing of data and the extraction of valuable knowledge from it. Employing CC for the IoT is not an easy task due to the following challenges (Al-Fuqaha et al., 2015):

- **Synchronization:** Synchronization between different cloud vendors presents a challenge to provide real-time services since services are built on top of various cloud platforms.
- **Standardization:** Standardizing CC also presents a significant challenge for IoT cloud-based services due having to interoperate with the various vendors.
- **Balancing:** Making a balance between general cloud service environments and IoT requirements presents another challenge due to the differences in infrastructure.
- **Reliability:** Security of IoT cloud-based services presents another challenge due to the differences in the security mechanisms between the IoT devices and the cloud platforms.
- **Management:** Managing CC and IoT systems is also a challenging factor due to the fact that both have different resources and components.
- **Enhancement:** Validating IoT cloud-based services is necessary to ensure providing good services that meet the customers' expectations.

Nimbits is an example, which is an open source Platform as a Service (PaaS) that connects smart embedded devices to the cloud and also performs data analytics (Nimbits, 2014). Moreover, it connects to websites and can store, share and retrieve sensors' data in various formats including numeric, text based, GPS, JSON or XML.

Cloud Services Management

Cloud must support appropriate levels of service performance to many diverse users and so cloud management is a very complex task (Rochwerger et al., 2009)). Several providers have products designed for cloud computing management (VMware, OpenQRM, CloudKick, and Managed Methods), along with the big players like BMC, HP, IBM Tivoli and CA.

Cloud Data Management

As the use of cloud computing services and applications increases, cloud data management technologies are emerging as alternatives to traditional on-premises software. An emerging method for cloud data management, is the use of formal languages as a tool for information exchange between the diverse data and information systems participating in cloud service provisioning. These formal languages rely on an inference plane (J. Strassner, Foghlú, Donnelly & Agoulmine, 2007; Serrano, Strassner & Foghlú, 2009) for example. By using semantic decision support and enriched monitoring information management, decision support is enabled and facilitated. As a result of using semantics, a more complete control of service management operations can be offered. This semantically-enabled decision support gives better control in the management of resources, devices, systems and services, thereby promoting the management of cloud with formal models.

Cloud Data Monitoring

Cloud data monitoring is an important requirement for automatic adaptation to the current data load, as well as to provide feedback on service logic. Cloud monitoring requires monitoring application-level information in addition to monitoring the system usage data that current tools already provide (Friess, 2013).

There are several related works in this area. Lattice is a distributed monitoring framework, which was exercised and validated in computing clouds (Clayman et al., 2010) and in network clouds (Shao, Wei, Wang & Mei, 2010). DSMon (Clayman, Galis & Mamatas, 2010) introduces system monitoring for distributed environments and mainly focuses on fault tolerant aspects; NWS (Wolski, Spring & Hayes, 1999) also provides a distributed framework for monitoring and has the ability of forecasting performance changes.

GoogleApp engine (Google, 2010) and Hyperic (Hyperic, 2010) both provide monitoring tools for system status such as CPU, memory, and processes resource allocations. Such system usage data can be useful for general purpose cloud monitoring, but they may not be sufficient enough for an application level manager to make appropriate decisions.

Cloud Data Exchange

Federation in the cloud would imply a requirement where user's applications or services shall still be able to execute across a federation of resources stemming from different cloud providers (Chapman, Emmerich, Marquez, Clayman, & Galis, 2012). It also refers to the ability for different cloud providers to scale their service offerings and to share capabilities to combine efforts and provide a better quality of service for their customers. This approach requires users and multiple providers to both delegate, share and consume each other resources in a peer-to-peer manner in a secure, managed, monitored and auditable fashion, with a particular focus on interoperability between management and resource description approaches (Friess, 2013).

Self-Organizing Cloud Architecture

Cloud infrastructures are deployed in a distributed manner to support service applications. In consequence, the development of self-configuration systems over these infrastructures are necessary. Cloud computing typically is characterized by large enterprise systems containing multiple virtual distributed software components that communicate across different networks and satisfy particular but secure personalized services requests (Shao et al., 2010).

In Figure 2 (Friess, 2013), a cloud management architecture following the design principles for cloud services control loop is depicted. Exact component's performance modeling is difficult to achieve since it depends on the used technology. To simplify this complexity, the cloud service lifecycle model rather focuses on standard performance analysis such as available memory, CPU usage, system bus speed, and memory cache thresholds. Instead of exact performance it is also

Figure 2. Self-organizing management architecture
Friess, 2013.

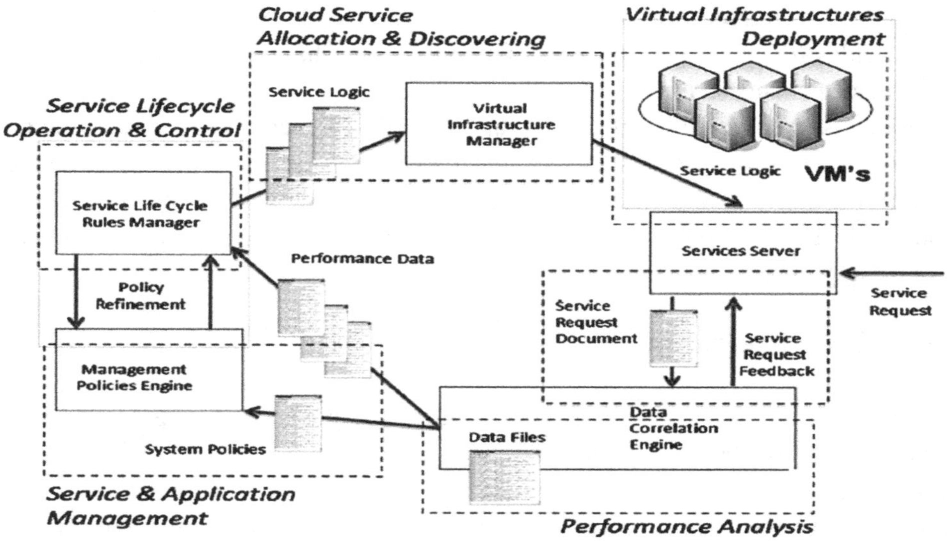

most practical to use an estimated model calculated based on monitored data from the Data Correlation Engine represented in Figure 2 (Holub, Parsons, Sullivan & Murphy, 2009).

Management of operations leads to modifying the cloud service lifecycle control loop according to user demands. Quality of service and reliability, play a critical role in the design of the management systems due to the inherent complexity associated with the management processes of the infrastructure itself.

Cloud Advanced Radio Access Network (C-RAN)

(Bangerter, Talwar, Arefi & Stewart, 2014) show that baseband signals from many cells can be received and processed at a centralized server platform with low-latency and high-rate backhaul. Figure 3 shows the C-RAN architecture. This architecture, known as Cloud RAN (C-RAN), creates a super base station with distributed antennas supporting multiple RAN protocols and dynamically adapting its signal processing resources based on the varying traffic load within its geographical coverage.

The technique of C-RAN depends on real-time low latency virtualization, which provides a pool of resources that can be dynamically allocated for baseband processing. C-RAN architecture saves on operational cost by locating all the processing of multiple base stations in one unit and enhanced intercell interference coordination (eICIC) by centralizing baseband.

The evolution of C-RAN will include even more advanced techniques such as joint processing and demodulation of multiple users' signals, and joint resource allocation across multiple Radio Access Technologies (RATs) to further increase 5G capacity.

Figure 3. C-RAN architecture
Bangerter et al., 2014.

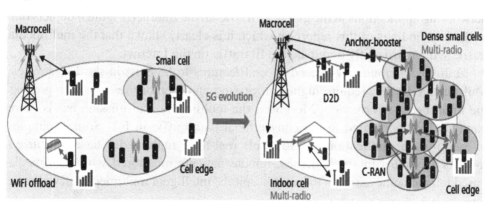

Figure 4. Global Internet traffic usage and forecast
Alvi et al., 2015.

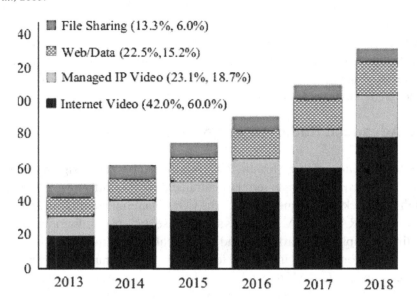

SUPPORT TO MULTIMEDIA IoT

Multimedia traffic have been increased on the global inter-network, due to the huge interest in development and usage of multimedia based applications and services. Real-time multimedia applications such as video conferencing, remote video-on demand, telepresence, real-time content delivery, and online-gaming have contributed to the exponential growth of the Internet multimedia traffic. The existing balance between non-multimedia data traffic and multimedia-traffic is now shifting away towards an increase in multimedia content specifically in terms of video content (Alvi et al., 2015). Cisco carried out an initiative to forecast the trends of the visual networking applications in the global IP traffic on the Internet. Figure 4 depicts one of the key findings of this report, in which it is clearly shown that the multimedia traffic will significantly dominate the IP traffic on the Internet.

Multimedia content will need special features to be exist in the IoT devices. Multimedia devices require higher processing and memory resources to process the multimedia information. Moreover, the multimedia transmission needs more bandwidth as compared to the conventional data traffic in IoT. Some examples of multimedia applications in IoT are: real-time multimedia based security/ monitory systems in smart homes, remote patients monitored with multimedia based telemedicine services in smart hospitals, intelligent multimedia surveillance

Figure 5. Typical wireless multimedia system architecture
Alvi et al., 2015.

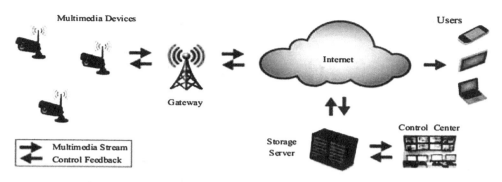

systems deployed in smart cities, transportation management optimized using smart video cameras, remote multimedia based monitoring of an ecological system, etc. Integrating IoT systems with multimedia devices and content is not a simple task and requires the introduction of additional functionalities which will bring us to a specialized subset of IoT, which we refer to with 'Internet of Multimedia Things' (IoMT) (Alvi et al., 2015).

Wireless Multimedia Systems (WMS) have been implemented to provide services and applications in several fields, such as surveillance, transportation, telemedicine. The design of WMS is depicted in Figure 5. If we consider a wireless multimedia based surveillance and monitoring system, the multimedia devices can be camera nodes, harvesting the multimedia information from the environment and reporting back to the control center using the underlying wireless technology. The control center gives feedback to alter the camera state or change the camera position to change the view of interest.

There are significant limiting factors which restrict the ubiquitous adaption of traditional wireless multimedia systems. Firstly, the scope of these systems is strictly limited to the deployment scenario. Secondly, the multimedia devices are generally powered by main energy source. Thus, there is no restriction on energy usage so that the deployed solutions are not energy-efficient. Thirdly, the multimedia devices possessing similar communication stacks are not meant to communicate with other network devices performing different tasks. Fourthly, in cloud based multimedia systems the multimedia content is globally available to users for streaming or processing. As a last point, the cost of multimedia devices is still very high, restricting their large scale deployment and widespread usage in everyday life.

Figure 6 shows the reference architecture for Wireless Multimedia Sensor Networks (WMSNs), where the multimedia sources have usually limited functionalities and send the content through a WSN.

Figure 6. Typical wireless multimedia sensor network architecture
Alvi et al., 2015.

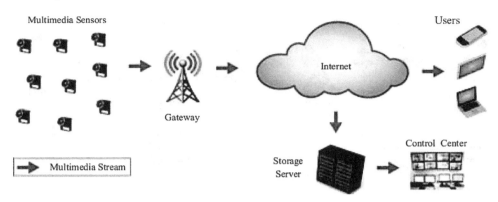

Due to the fixed architecture of WMSNs (Akyildiz, Melodia & Chowdhury, 2007), the individual multimedia devices are not addressable nor they are equipped with any context-awareness or application specific intelligence, that is why a WMSN behave like a single entity to the system.

From the above discussion, the IoMT can be defined as the global network of interconnected multimedia things which are uniquely identifiable and addressable to acquire sensed multimedia as well as possessing capability to interact and communicate with other multimedia and not multimedia devices and services, with or without direct human intervention (Alvi et al., 2015).

The operation of an IoMT based service can be described with the help of a four-stage IoMT architecture as shown in Figure 7.

In the first stage, the multimedia data are acquired. In the second stage, the multimedia content is sent to the cloud by incorporating efficient communication and addressing techniques. In the third stage, the multimedia content is stored, processed and disseminated as per end-user demand at the cloud. Lastly, the computational tasks may be carried out at the cloud according to the application/ service requirements (Alvi et al., 2015).

THE ROLE OF 5G IN IoT APPLICATIONS

Autonomic computing enables operational efficiency for networks and services. It needs to be operated based on principles for dynamically adaptive "automated" and "autonomic" management & control of operations. Three main objectives for the 5G standard have been established:

Figure 7. IOMT architecture
Alvi et al., 2015.

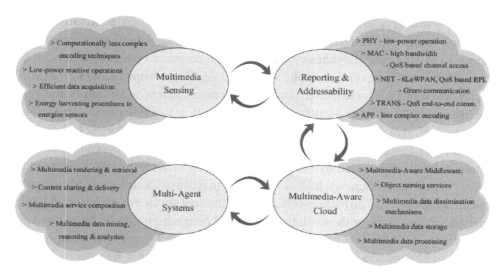

1. It should be capable of delivering a 1Gbps downlink to start with and multi-gigabits in future.
2. Latency must be brought under one millisecond.
3. It should be more energy efficient than its predecessors (though there's no agreement yet on just how much more).

5G will have many innovative network features:

•   Native support of Machine Type Communication to efficiently handle the cellular transmission of small packets by reducing latency and energy consumption.
•   Small-cell deployments to extend coverage and capacity and to reduce energy consumption.

IoT applications that generate small data with large volume and fast velocity will need 5G with characteristics of high data rate and low latency to transmit such data faster and cheaper. On the other hand, those data also need Cloud to process and to store and furthermore, Software Defined Networks (SDN) to provide scalable network infrastructure to transport this large volume of data in an optimal way.

CONCLUSION

Autonomy in IoT is still in infant stages, however researchers have started to recognize the importance of minimizing user intervention. The introduction of autonomic theory in IoT to achieve dynamic management of resource constrained devices by minimizing user intervention is one such solution. Also, some of the key state of the art developments on federated cloud service management and its applicability to the Internet of Things are discussed along with a self-organizing cloud architecture. With the arrival of the mobile Internet era, today's RAN architecture is facing more and more challenges that the mobile operators need to solve: mobile data flow increase drastically caused by the popularization of smart terminals, very hard to improve spectrum efficiency, lack of flexibility to multi-standard, dynamic network load and expensive to provide ever increasing internet service to end users. Mobile operators must consider the evolution of the RAN to a high efficient and lost cost architecture. C-RAN is a promising solution to the challenges mentioned above. Internet of Multimedia Things represents a specialized subset of Internet of Things, enabling the integration and cooperation among heterogeneous multimedia devices with distinct sensing, computational, and communication capabilities and resources. As compared to IoT, the realization of IoMT rather has some additional challenges and stringent requirements. The current task group activities for IoT do not mandate the features of multimedia things, thus leaving a gap to benefit from IoMT paradigm.

REFERENCES

Akyildiz, I. F., Melodia, T., & Chowdhury, K. R. (2007). A survey on wireless multimedia sensor networks. *Computer Networks*, *51*(4), 921–960. doi:10.1016/j.comnet.2006.10.002

Al-Fuqaha, A., Guizani, M., Mohammadi, M., Aledhari, M., & Ayyash, M. (2015). Internet of things: A survey on enabling technologies, protocols, and applications. *IEEE Communications Surveys and Tutorials*, *17*(4), 2347–2376. doi:10.1109/COMST.2015.2444095

Alvi, S. A., Afzal, B., Shah, G. A., Atzori, L., & Mahmood, W. (2015). Internet of multimedia things: Vision and challenges. *Ad Hoc Networks*, *33*, 87–111. doi:10.1016/j.adhoc.2015.04.006

Ashraf, Q. M., & Habaebi, M. H. (2015). Introducing autonomy in internet of things. Recent Advances in Computer Science, 215-221.

Bangerter, B., Talwar, S., Arefi, R., & Stewart, K. (2014). Networks and devices for the 5G era. *IEEE Communications Magazine, 52*(2), 90–96. doi:10.1109/MCOM.2014.6736748

Borthakur, D., Gray, J., Sarma, J. S., Muthukkaruppan, K., Spiegelberg, N., Kuang, H., & Schmidt, R. et al. (2011, June). Apache Hadoop goes realtime at Facebook. In *Proceedings of the 2011 ACM SIGMOD International Conference on Management of data* (pp. 1071-1080). ACM. doi:10.1145/1989323.1989438

Chapman, C., Emmerich, W., Marquez, F. G., Clayman, S., & Galis, A. (2010, April). Elastic service management in computational clouds. In *12th IEEE/IFIP NOMS2010/International Workshop on Cloud Management (CloudMan 2010)* (pp. 19-23). IEEE.

Chapman, C., Emmerich, W., Márquez, F. G., Clayman, S., & Galis, A. (2012). Software architecture definition for on-demand cloud provisioning. *Cluster Computing, 15*(2), 79–100. doi:10.1007/s10586-011-0152-0

Clayman, S. (2010). Lecture Notes in Computer Science: Vol. 6481. *Towards A Service-Based Internet.* doi:10.1007/978-3-642-17694-4_30

Clayman, S., Galis, A., & Mamatas, L. (2010, April). Monitoring virtual networks with lattice. In Network operations and management symposium workshops (NOMS Wksps), 2010 IEEE/IFIP (pp. 239-246). IEEE. doi:10.1109/NOMSW.2010.5486569

Computing, A. (2006). *An architectural blueprint for autonomic computing.* IBM White Paper, 31.

Friess, P. (2013). *Internet of things: converging technologies for smart environments and integrated ecosystems.* River Publishers.

Google. (2010). *Google app engine system status.* Retrieved from http://code.google.com/status/appengine

Hassan, M. M., Song, B., & Huh, E. N. (2009, February). A framework of sensor-cloud integration opportunities and challenges. In *Proceedings of the 3rd international conference on Ubiquitous information management and communication* (pp. 618-626). ACM. doi:10.1145/1516241.1516350

Holub, V., Parsons, T., O'Sullivan, P., & Murphy, J. (2009, June). Run-time correlation engine for system monitoring and testing. In *Proceedings of the 6th international conference industry session on Autonomic computing and communications industry session* (pp. 9-18). ACM. doi:10.1145/1555312.1555317

Hyperic. (2010). *Cloudstatus ® powered by hyperic*. Retrieved from http://www.cloudstatus.com

Medagliani, P., Leguay, J., Duda, A., Rousseau, F., Duquennoy, S., Raza, S., ... Monton, M. (2014). *Internet of Things Applications-From Research and Innovation to Market Deployment*. Academic Press.

Mukherjee, A., Paul, H. S., Dey, S., & Banerjee, A. (2014, March). Angels for distributed analytics in iot. In *Internet of Things (WF-IoT), 2014 IEEE World Forum on* (pp. 565-570). IEEE. doi:10.1109/WF-IoT.2014.6803230

Nimbits. (2014, Sep. 25). Retrieved from http://www.nimbits.com/

Rochwerger, B., Breitgand, D., Levy, E., Galis, A., Nagin, K., Llorente, I. M., & Ben-Yehuda, M. et al. (2009). The reservoir model and architecture for open federated cloud computing. *IBM Journal of Research and Development, 53*(4), 4–1. doi:10.1147/JRD.2009.5429058

Serrano, M., Strassner, J., & Foghlu, M. O. (2009, June). A formal approach for the inference plane supporting integrated management tasks in the Future Internet. In *Integrated Network Management-Workshops, 2009. IM'09. IFIP/IEEE International Symposium on* (pp. 120-127). IEEE. doi:10.1109/INMW.2009.5195947

Shao, J., Wei, H., Wang, Q., & Mei, H. (2010, July). A runtime model based monitoring approach for cloud. In *Cloud Computing (CLOUD), 2010 IEEE 3rd international conference on* (pp. 313-320). IEEE. doi:10.1109/CLOUD.2010.31

Strassner, J., O'Foghlu, M., Donnelly, W., & Agoulmine, N. (2007, July). Beyond the knowledge plane: an inference plane to support the next generation Internet. In *Global Information Infrastructure Symposium, 2007. GIIS 2007. First International* (pp. 112-119). IEEE.

Tsai, C. W., Lai, C. F., Chiang, M. C., & Yang, L. T. (2014). Data mining for Internet of Things: A survey. *IEEE Communications Surveys and Tutorials, 16*(1), 77–97. doi:10.1109/SURV.2013.103013.00206

Wolski, R., Spring, N. T., & Hayes, J. (1999). The network weather service: A distributed resource performance forecasting service for metacomputing. *Future Generation Computer Systems, 15*(5), 757–768. doi:10.1016/S0167-739X(99)00025-4

Xu, X., Huang, S., Chen, Y., Browny, K., Halilovicy, I., & Lu, W. (2014, June). TSAaaS: Time series analytics as a service on IoT. In *Web Services (ICWS), 2014 IEEE International Conference On* (pp. 249-256). IEEE.

KEY TERMS AND DEFINITIONS

Autonomic Computing: The self-managing characteristics of distributed computing resources, adapting to unpredictable changes while hiding intrinsic complexity to operators and users.

Big Data: A term for data sets that are so large or complex that traditional data processing applications are inadequate. Challenges include analysis, capture, data curation, search, sharing, storage, transfer, visualization, querying, updating and information privacy.

Cloud Computing: A kind of Internet-based computing that provides shared processing resources and data to computers and other devices on demand. It is a model for enabling ubiquitous, on-demand access to a shared pool of configurable computing resources (e.g., networks, servers, storage, applications and services), which can be rapidly provisioned and released with minimal management effort.

C-RAN: A centralized, cloud computing-based architecture for radio access networks that supports 2G, 3G, 4G and future wireless communication standards.

Multimedia: Content that uses a combination of different content forms such as text, audio, images, animation, video and interactive content.

Radio Access Network (RAN): Part of a mobile telecommunication system. It implements a radio access technology. Conceptually, it resides between a device such as a mobile phone, a computer, or any remotely controlled machine and provides connection with its core network (CN).

Radio Access Technology (RAT): The underlying physical connection method for a radio based communication network. Many modern phones support several RATs in one device such as Bluetooth, Wi-Fi, and 3G, 4G or LTE.

Chapter 6
5G IoT Industry Verticals and Network Requirements

Massimo Condoluci
King's College London, UK

Maria A. Lema
King's College London, UK

Toktam Mahmoodi
King's College London, UK

Mischa Dohler
King's College London, UK

ABSTRACT

The effective provisioning of industry verticals over the next-to-come 5G systems opens novel business opportunities for telco operators especially when considering the integration of Internet of Things (IoT) devices as enablers of business cases based on remote sensing and control. This chapter highlights the main features of IoT verticals with particular attention on healthcare, smart cities, industry automation and entertainment business cases. The aim of this Chapter is to derive the requirements such IoT verticals pose in terms of design features to be considered in the standardization of 5G systems. This chapter presents the state of the art on the contribution from the research community and standardization bodies to address the 5G design characteristics with particular attention to the features enabling a proper management of IoT-oriented business cases.

DOI: 10.4018/978-1-5225-2799-2.ch006

Copyright © 2018, IGI Global. Copying or distributing in print or electronic forms without written permission of IGI Global is prohibited.

INTRODUCTION

Over the last decade, the Internet of Things (IoT) has gained an always growing importance in the mobile market scenario. Indeed, the availability of data collected from sensors as well as the possibility of extracting knowledge from such data opens new business opportunities and this can be applied to several environments of industry, home, office, city, etc. (Palattella et al, 2016). The IoT ecosystem, as analyzed for instance by Atzori et al. (2010), is based on providing connectivity to machines. This poses additional challenges to mobile networks which have been traditionally designed to provide high data rates for human-type communications (HTC). HTC traffic is usually characterized by the transmission of bursty-based traffic with large packets and non-strict constraints in terms of access delay (i.e., the time between the generation of a packet and its effective transmission) and energy consumption. IoT pushes unprecedented traffic features to be supported over mobile systems due to the set of unique characteristics of the so-called machine-type communications (MTC). MTC traffic is characterized by minimal human intervention, periodic or event-triggered small packets and strict connection time constraints (e.g., short access and data transmission delays) in order to keep low the energy consumption of battery-equipped devices. The main features of MTC traffic are analyzed by Laya et al. (2014), who also provides a comparison of MTC and HTC traffic types.

As briefly mentioned above, current mobile technologies such as Long Term Evolution (LTE) and LTE-Advanced (LTE-A), a.k.a. fourth generation (4G) systems, are designed to deal mainly with HTC traffic. As a consequence, when considering the next-to-come fifth generation (5G) networks, IoT dictates to re-design the transmission procedures to natively handle the simultaneous presence and interaction of HTC and MTC traffic while guaranteeing to meet the requirements of these two very heterogeneous traffic types. Furthermore, disruptive technologies considered to introduce flexibility, customization and re-configurability in 5G networks on both radio and core segments will enable the introduction of enhanced IoT-based services interconnecting people and everything. Indeed, a natural evolution of connecting devices to the Internet, is the remote control of these devices. Machines will be no longer able to only talk to each other. 5G will enable novel industry-related IoT applications in both consumer and business environments, for instance to increase industry automation, remote control and tactile Internet applications (Simsek et al., 2016).

This chapter covers the main trends in the industry to use the IoT to tackle several problems or to improve outcomes: business-to-business (B2B) market, increase in automation and remote control/operation, cost reduction, efficiency improvement.

This chapter also presents 5G use cases highlighting the novel business opportunities for IoT in the next-to-come mobile systems. The aim of this analysis is to recognize the role of MTC in generating an added value to 5G business activity or consumer end. The main industry use cases we will discuss are healthcare, smart cities, industry automation and entertainment.

According to the features of the use cases listed above, in this chapter *we will derive and classify the requirements that above listed use cases push on 5G networks.* Discussed requirements range from QoS (e.g., data rates, latency, jitter, and energy consumption) to more generic constraints from a network point of view. Indeed, 5G networks need to exploit disruptive technologies that can simultaneously provide critical and non-critical MTC, and this dictates requirements in terms of network flexibility and customization.

In addition to the analysis of requirements of 5G use cases, *this chapter provides a survey of the contributions from the research community and standardization bodies to satisfy the requirements of 5G IoT use cases.* We will summarize the available literature by focusing on the recent advances in terms of network slicing, virtualization and softwarisation, solutions for supporting MTC traffic, device multi-connectivity and centralized/cloud radio access network (RAN).

IoT IN THE INDUSTRY: EXPLOITING THE INTERNET CAPABILITIES

Connecting devices to the Internet has enabled a wide range of industrial opportunities due to the availability of data collected from sensors (e.g., sensing devices that measure specific parameters to be sent to remote servers or other machines) as well as the opportunity to remotely send tasks or commands to actuators. As analyzed by Andrews et al. (2014), from an application point of view, 5G networks are expected to *natively* support the traffic generated by devices without the human intervention. Indeed, with the boost of IoT, machines can be connected to provide advantages such as economic savings or safety improvements.

One of the most notorious changes in the design of the new generation of mobile communications, studied for instance by Osseiran et al. (2014), is the inclusion of a variety of use cases and applications that provides more to the society than only enhancing the user broadband experience. Thus, 5G is intended to support a high number of *vertical industries* providing fast and reliable communications. In this section, we will survey different use cases in order to highlight their unique features as well as the requirements they pose in the design of 5G networks. A summary of the features of the 5G IoT verticals discussed in this section is given in Table 1.

Table 1. Features of 5G IoT verticals

	QoS Guarantee	Security and Confidentiality	Network Support	Scalability	Easy Integration and Management	Overhead Reduction for MTC	Time Critical Communications	Non-Time Critical Communications	Remote Control	Seamless Communications	Use of Edge Intelligence
Healthcare	✓	✓	✓								
Smart City				✓	✓	✓					
Industry automation						✓	✓	✓	✓	✓	✓
Entertainment	✓	✓	✓								✓

Healthcare Industry

The healthcare industry has received a lot of attention during the past years, as for instance highlighted by Istepanaian & Zhang (2012). Two major applications are being considered in the 5G context:

- Remote healthcare, i.e., the ability to remotely monitor patients, and precision medicine with the use of bio-connectivity.
- Remote intervention with the use of remote robotic surgery.

The 5G-PPP (2015) has analyzed the bio-connectivity context by highlighting the trend for: *decentralization of hospitals* where medical care can be provided at home or while moving; e.g., *predictive analysis*, electronic medical records, and *the use of embedded systems to perform individual pharmaceutical analysis*. Moreover, in the remote surgery context, the physical aspects need to be virtualised to allow for reliable diagnostics and treatments. In the existing robotic surgery devices, there is currently no feedback for the stiffness or any haptic information and adding these capabilities would reduce the doctor's reliance on video and sound transmission. Above mentioned aspects are discussed by Simsek et al. (2016).

Next generation of mobile communications is the key enabler of the main targets and trends of the healthcare industry providing: cloud-based solutions that improve the accessibility of high-resolution medical data, increased capacity for real-time high-definition video transmission, and robust mobility and low latency communications. Zain et al. (2012) and 5G-PPP (2015) describe some of the major challenges and requirements in the healthcare industry. From a QoS guarantee point of view, aspects such as *reliability, mobility*, and *latency* need to be considered. In addition, delay stability (i.e., *jitter*) is the major requirement for remote interventions. When a robot is operated remotely, and there is a force feedback information being transmitted, the stability of the feedback process can be seriously impaired in presence of substantial time delay. These aspects have been widely discussed as for instance by Anderson & Spong (1989). A further requirement is network support in the form of location tracking (i.e., position accuracy), seamless handovers between different radio access technologies (RATs), routing protocols, as well as MTC capacity. Finally, other requirements are security and confidentiality. These aspects comprise both identity management and privacy protection.

Smart Cities

According to the definitions provided by the International Telecommunication Union-Telecommunication (ITU-T) standardization sector, a smart sustainable city is an innovative city that uses information and communication technologies to improve quality of life, efficiency of urban operation and services, and competitiveness (ITU, 2014). The smart city concept extends the intelligent mobility (IM, a.k.a. intelligent transport systems, ITS) paradigm where cars are connected to each other to increase the level of security and to optimize traffic management by considering the availability of, e.g., enhanced public transportation and emergency services.

A smart city is thus a highly heterogeneous scenario, where MTC and HTC coexist in heterogeneous network deployments. From this point of view, MTC traffic can range from data gathered from road-side sensors (measuring traffic congestion, pollution, traffic light timing, parking availability, etc.) to car-embedded sensors (measuring the status of the car in terms of engine and brakes, for instance, as well as reporting information such as position, mobility, speed, and acceleration) to public transport sensors (deployed to check the position of public buses as well as their status) to public authority sensors. MTC traffic can also be considered in terms of actuators, when commands are sent to, for instance, traffic lights to change light timing to react to a congestion or to provide a quicker path for first aid services in case of an emergency. On the contrary, HTC traffic can be considered in terms of request/ data sent from/to users for, e.g., parking payment. Other examples of HTC is data/ voice traffic among public authority users. As each of the above mentioned types of traffic could be potentially handled with different RATs, a primary characteristic of a smart city is the integration of different communication infrastructures.

Zanella et al. (2014) discuss urban IoT technologies that are close to standardization, and agree that most of smart city services are based on a centralized architecture where data is delivered to a control centre in charge of subsequently processing and storing the received traffic. From a deployment point of view, such a centralized architecture can be either centralized, distributed or cloud-based according to the needs of the specific scenario as well as the availability of network resources in a specific area. A logical centralized architecture is thus considered as an effective solution in order to gather data from different services (traffic management, parking, public transportation, public authorities, etc.) and to globally optimize the smart city. Despite these general requirements, each smart city application may have different challenging key performance indicators (KPIs) to be simultaneously satisfied: city energy consumption, smart lighting, smart parking or smart transportation.

By focusing on the challenges in smart city environments, one of the most demanding services in a smart city is the IM, which dictates for an effective *mobility management* as analyzed for instance by Araniti et al. (2013). Mobility management needs to take into account not only handovers, but also *device discovery* and/or *fast recovery* processes after coverage loss. When extending the IM concept towards autonomous or assisted driving cars, there is a need to continuously monitor the situation outside and inside the car with, thus, a constant information exchange mainly between the different participants of the transport network, i.e., *vehicle to vehicle (V2V)* and *vehicle to infrastructure (V2I)* communications. This asks for *real-time ultra-high reliable communications*, which also are required for other services to increase safety, reduce congestion and pollution.

5G networks need to deal with above listed challenges, as discussed by Andrew et al. (2014), Osseiran et al. (2014) and Condoluci et al. (2015). The intrinsic heterogeneity in smart city environments poses a requirement in terms of quick network reconfiguration according to the current state of traffic, congestion or depending on the service being delivered. Another requirement is scalability, as a large number of devices are expected to be simultaneously connected is a smart city. This aspect, when considering MTC traffic, brings another requirement in terms of overhead reduction in order to increase the utilization of the network. Furthermore, highly loaded networks may impair some stringent QoS requirements, as for example low latency in mission critical MTC. Another key requirements is the easy integration and management, which is necessary to provide seamless experience and efficient use of resources across all available RATs. Finally, security represents a major requirement and this comes from the fact that multiple tenants could share the same network and this could involve security threats.

Industry Automation

Industry automation mainly deals with remote control that, as discussed by Simsek et al. (2016), is an application that can be particularized to many cases: remote control of heavy machineries, factory automation or real-time monitoring of industrial plants.

The IoT has provided powerful solutions to improve industrial systems and applications. In the past, industrial monitoring could be carried out with the use of wireless sensor networks (WSNs), which interconnected a number of intelligent sensors to perform sensing and monitoring. A comprehensive survey on WSNs is given by Al-Fuqaha et al. (2015). The evolution of WSNs has largely contributed to the development of IoT in mobile communications, and industrial applications nowadays include much more than monitoring and tracking. The main competitive trend in the manufacturing business is to evolve into intelligently connected production information systems that can operate beyond the factory premises, and in this context 5G communications represent the natural evolution to WSNs to support several applications enabling huge opportunities. This has been analyzed by Palattella et al. (2016) and 5G-PPP (2015a). The provisioning of these applications pushes the following requirements:

- **Time Critical Process Optimization and Control:** This requirement is necessary to support real-time optimization based on instantly received information from monitoring or interaction between different operators, and remote control of robotic operations.
- **Non-Time Critical Communications:** This assures to provide applications such as non-critical localization of assets and goods, quality control and sensor data collection.
- **Remote Control:** This is mainly required to support augmented reality applications to provide support in production and maintenance.
- **Seamless Communications:** This is required to provide connectivity between different production sites and other parties inside the value chain.
- **Use of Edge Intelligence:** Integrate high processing in mobile edge computing clouds in order to cut delays and overhead.
- Overhead Reduction in MTC.

Real-time cooperation and intervention requires a flexible and converged connectivity that provides seamless experience across multiple mediums, such as wired and fixed networks, multiple vendors, and multiple technologies. In this sense, 5G needs to provide a highly heterogeneous multi-connectivity scenario, where everything is capable of communicating, even in harsh industrial environments. Also it is necessary to have fast, reliable and flexible reconfiguration of QoS and traffic demands to enable fast adaptation to current needs. Examples can be the simultaneous management of applications involving high data transmission due to the use of wearable devices (for instance 3D video or augmented reality content) and applications involving low data transmitted by sensors. Many of these applications will involve massive MTC and mission critical MTC, being the latter more stringent in terms of network requirements: ultra-low latency and ultra-high reliability and availability are essential to provide these types of applications.

Entertainment: Content Delivery and Gaming

The media and entertainment business is experiencing the big changes, mainly because of the behavioral change of individuals, consumers now interact directly with the media and entertainment devices as presented by 5G-PPP (2016). On the other hand, the gaming industry with online games, with increased graphic resolution and simultaneous events happening among different active users involve high level of user real-time interaction, especially when considering the exploitation of enhanced gaming devices humans interact with (glasses, remote controllers, etc.). Gamers want as much realism as possible and also wish to have the most immersive experience while playing.

The gaming industry's efforts are placed in enhancing gamer experience by adding virtual reality and the use of bio-sensing in order to allow the player to detect people in the game, in real or imaginary worlds. Also, motion capture is introduced to interact with objects surrounding, and realistic force feedback. Also, augmented reality, which is expected to revolutionize the gaming industry in general, because of the inherent realism, as it lets the gamer experience real world in tandem with the game played.

Some of the main technical challenges to deliver these new kinds of entertaining services are centered in: *data-rate*, *mobility*, *end-to-end latency*, *coverage* and *reliability*. This brings a requirement in terms of QoS guarantee. Especially when referring to augmented and virtual reality applications, end-to-end latency becomes the most challenging aspect as 15ms to 7ms round trip time (RTT) is the threshold to be considered. Delivering very low end-to-end latency introduces another requirement, i.e., the use of edge intelligence that is bringing closer to the user services and/or process capabilities instead of having them located remotely. Another requirement is in terms of security and confidentiality, in particular to deal with identity management and identification of sources of content to assure that only subscribers access the content. A last requirement is in terms of network support in the form of location tracking (i.e., position accuracy), full integration with non-3GPP systems (radio and fixed), and support of network assisted device-to-device (D2D) communications allowing devices/users to communicate directly by passing the base station (thus, potentially, achieving faster communications).

BUSINESS MODELS AND APPLICATIONS

The integration of healthcare, transport services or entertainment applications generate new business opportunities for network operators. This section provides an overview of the new market opportunities and business models for service providers.

Healthcare

Many mobile operators are active players in offering mobile health services and offer solutions beyond simple connectivity services: content-based wellness information services to consumers or sophisticated end-to-end solutions aimed at improving the efficiency of healthcare systems and workforce. Other players facilitate mobile telemedicine and health call-centers by enabling partnerships with healthcare providers, and they also provide real-time connectivity for devices as well as managed services for monitoring vital body parameters of patients. According to the study done by GSMA (2012), mobile operators are expected to be the key beneficiaries of the expected growth in the mobile health market and command nearly 50% share of the overall market.

Other opportunities and business models in the healthcare industry are providing solutions in hospitals and at home, to deliver enhanced tele-healthcare services. According to the Office for Life Sciences (2015), the remote healthcare market has already started to merge with the mobile health apps market. Disruptive changes could impact the current model of delivery for tele-care and tele-health, and tele-healthcare is likely to converge with mobile Health and connected home solutions. These models could go from mere connectivity provider to adding value by selling complete IoT solutions.

Automotive

The emerging technologies such as 5G and the evolution of complementary industries (such as digital players) have increased the number of potential services that can be offered as analyzed by GSMA (2012a). There has been a change of paradigm in the definition of the business roles between the different players of the automotive industry, but nearly all market analysts agree that there is a strong need for strategic partnerships, in particular cooperation between the telecom players and the car manufacturers. This cooperation enables to complement each other's needs: mobile technology is in great extent one of the main drivers of the change on the way people use cars nowadays and in the future.

Network operators in general play an instrumental role in the development of the connected car services in general. In particular, GSMA (2012a) presents a study on the opportunities of network operators in the connected car market, and highlights the core competencies the operators bring to the value chain:

- **Critical Enablers:** Billing is probably one of the big assets operators bring, and it is as well one critical enabler of the connected car services. Device management, controlling the upgrades or roaming information. Subscription management, added value such as information related to the location to enhance services.

- **Telematics Service Provider (TSP) Platforms:** Activate, maintain and upgrade services. TSPs are expected to gain 11.3% of the connected car market share, and many telecom companies are expanding their presence.
- **Data Collection and Analysis:** Operators can handle big amounts of data that can be analyzed to provide added value in services, such as traffic patterns based on mobile user position.
- Cloud services for connected devices.
- Integration platforms for different service providers, content provision and access to infotainment services.

In general, it is not only about the service but the added value it provides:

- **Infotainment Services:** A number of operators around the globe are already offering content and storage services for in-car entertainment.
- **In-Car Wireless Services:** Provide wireless connectivity inside the car, and facilitate the M2M communication inside the car to collect data from sensors or allow to perform vehicle health records.
- **Connected Car Analytics:** Meaning the collection of vehicle parameters, or driving coaching services for inexperienced drivers. This market opportunity requires collaboration agreements with the automotive industry.
- **Wearables:** Such as safety switch for passenger.

Entertainment

Network operators have a key role as enablers of the fully immersive experience as explained by Pelletier (2016): to be able to support these innovations in the entertainment industry, connectivity providers need to ensure they can cope with the capacity and latency demands. Intelligent traffic management solutions, compression algorithms and investments in ultra-low latency, high-throughput networks will help networks to cope with the demands of VR content. Only such investments will enable most of the immersive applications to flourish, taking entertainment to a new level and opening up new revenue streams for content providers through cloud-based distribution on-demand.

Based on the findings by PwC (2014), entertainment companies have the largest opportunity for growth in the wearable technology market, there is a high number of applications available and very little companies have started to explore these applications. Overall, new business models for network operators need to be centred into adding value to the services provided, which means to collaborate closely with suppliers to ensure good end-to-end service quality that preserves a certain level of customer experience. In this line, the 5G-PPP underlines that collaborative services imply the association of fixed and wireless as well as terrestrial and satellite network service providers to deliver services with common multiservice control layer and assured quality in contrast to competitive services that imply a form of competition between the involved network service providers as analyzed by 5G-PPP (2016).

Industry Automation

Changes in the new industry and business models will change the traditional manufacturing value chain. While traditional players: logistical partners, suppliers of parts, suppliers of sensors and actuators, and manufacturers themselves, are going to still be playing a major role in the industry business, new players that were not part of the traditional value chain will enter the scene: supplier of cyber-security, supplier of data storage and management, supplier of connectivity, supplier of specialized technology, and supplier of automation systems. Nowadays, as analyzed by McKinsey Digital (2015), the majority of players expect new competitors to enter the market: 84% of technology suppliers expect new competitors and 58% of manufacturers expect new competitors.

Telecommunications companies are going to have an instrumental role in this new industrial revolution. The study by McKinsey Digital (2015) recognizes that many of the disruptive technologies are driven by small, innovative companies that have specialized skills in a given field. Another important finding is that it is likely to have an increasing emergence of highly specialized players especially in the telecoms area, providing solutions for data, connectivity and security. Furthermore, the study by McKinsey Digital (2015) shows that new business models are adding value around the whole connected items as to collect, use and share data. Specifically, offering solutions around integration and new services enables manufacturing companies to capture this emerging value in the manufacturing industry. Business models particularly interesting for network operators are around providing technology platforms and data-driven business models.

From the discussions in this section, it becomes clear the huge impact from a business point of view generated by the provisioning of IoT traffic in 5G systems. In the remainder of this chapter, the focus will be on the network architecture of mobile systems in order to investigate how it will possible to handle IoT-related traffic. We will highlight the limitations of current systems in order to highlight why current mobile networks cannot handle the use cases reported above. Afterwards, we will introduce the key aspects to be considered in the design of 5G systems to handle IoT-oriented use cases and finally we will summarize the solutions currently under investigation to properly manage 5G IoT verticals.

OPPORTUNITIES FOR DELIVERY OF IoT THROUGH 5G

Currently deployed mobile networks simply cannot handle the variety of requirements posed by 5G use cases. The 4G systems currently exploited, i.e., LTE and LTE-A, present several limitations to successfully implement the wide number of services being considered for the near future in the different industry verticals. In this section, we briefly highlight the limitations of 4G mobile systems in order to better discuss later the requirements to be taken into account in the design of 5G systems when considering IoT-oriented verticals.

Deployment With 4G Systems

Current mobile communications technologies do not offer the capabilities to easily incorporate a new variety use cases coming from the different industrial needs. From an architectural point of view, the design drivers of 4G systems (e.g., use of static deployment of vendor equipment and use of monolithic functionality at specific network locations) introduce different limitations to successfully support all the new verticals being considered for 5G.

The presence of proprietary black boxes limits the programmability of the network and thus its flexibility. An analysis of this limitation is given by Pentikousis et al. (2013). For instance, Bradai et al. (2015) highlight that elements in the 4G core network are controlled through standardized interfaces and cannot be controlled by APIs. The lack of programmability has a drawback in terms of the introduction of new services which are characterized by high deployment and operational costs (cellular operators have to replace existing equipment even if it is still sufficient for most purposes).

Another aspect underlined by Lee et al. (2013) is related to the configuration and the functionalities of user- and control-plane (U- and C-plane, respectively). In this case, the limitation is that some nodes are designed to implement both U/C-plane functionalities. One example is the packet gateway (PGW) in 4G systems, which is in charge of establishing and managing the bearers that allow a device to be connected with the network in addition to managing data traffic. This aspect introduces complexity and scalability issues. The scalability issue is exacerbated when considering that all the traffic should pass through the PGW, even if the communication is between devices or users attached to the same cell. This exposes the PGW to a huge amount of traffic to be managed and this could potentially cause overload and/or congestion.

Another issue is in terms of signaling traffic. According to Nokia Siemens Networks (2011), signaling is growing 50% faster than data traffic in LTE networks. The 4G core network, namely the evolved packet core (EPC), has a centralized control traffic management, i.e., the Mobility Management Entity (MME), which can reach a traffic volume in the C-plane of about 290,000 messages per second in networks with millions of users. As a consequence, scalability becomes an issue also when considering C-plane traffic. The aspect related to signaling needs to be further investigated when considering IoT-related traffic. Indeed, the maintenance of the U-plane in 4G networks may involve high signaling overhead and this limits the efficiency of the network. This also limits the support of IoT-related services which ask for low energy consumption (in order to save devices' batteries) and signaling overhead (in order to cut the transmission/reception delays as well as to avoid unnecessary energy consumption).

Capabilities for 5G Networks Design

The capabilities to be considered in the design of next-to-come 5G networks are derived according to the requirements of the verticals expected to be supported and by considering the limitation of 4G systems. This dictates for some disruptive architectural changes, which are summarized in the remained of this section.

Nowadays the integration of new services or the change of network topology and architecture (i.e., distributed or centralized) requires the replacement or redistribution of hardware equipment as well as network functionalities. This aspect is particularly challenging for industrial-IoT environments, dictating the support of heterogeneous services to be provided on-demand and to be updated according to the needs of the deployment scenario. As a consequence, one key aspect for 5G networks in supporting IoT industry verticals is the introduction of *flexibility*, which can be achieved by means of the introduction of *programmability*, i.e., by allowing the network functionalities to be flexible. Programmability would directly facilitate the possibility to reconfigure and manage the network by means of having U/C-plane functions that are modular and not strictly associated to one specific location. This will make easier the introduction of new services as well as handling changes in those already supported. In addition, it would enable service-aware QoS (i.e., to dynamically provide QoS on demand according to the need of the supported verticals) by allowing the network to dynamically change the topology or its configuration according to the network status (congestion and traffic demand) as well as the needs of the vertical to be provided. To this end, the new generation system architecture for mobile core needs to shift from the traditional hardware-based to software-based functions that can run in virtual environments. The introduction of softwarization (where network functions run on software instead of a dedicated hardware) and virtualization (where network functions run in virtual environments instead of a dedicated hardware) in the core network allow to create and allocate dedicated functionalities depending on the application needs. This aspect will be treated in more detail in the remainder of this chapter.

As discussed above, complexity is one of the most limiting aspects of 4G systems. This becomes more evident when considering that, for instance, the role of the packet gateway (PGW) in 4G systems: this node represents the edge-node of 4G networks connecting 4G mobile users to external networks. The presence of the PGW as a data anchor point has the already discussed drawback of introducing *scalability* issues but it also reduces the possibility to deliver low-latency services. This underlines the fact that the complexity of 4G systems has a negative impact in the traffic across the network with consequent issues on the verticals that could be provided. When considering IoT-related verticals, many of these dictate the needs to support low latency services. This goal could be achieved by placing network entities or functions closer to the RAN. This has the following advantages: reduction of delays, reduction of the control overhead and higher scalability due to the presence of a higher number of anchor points closer to the devices instead of having one single (or few) anchor points for the whole network. An additional limitation for 4G systems is the centralized management of U/C-planes. This drastically affects the scalability of the network. As a consequence, a key capability to be added to 5G systems is related to the introduction of *distributed U/C-planes*, i.e., functions will be no longer located only in one physical entity but a network function will be distributed across different nodes (and this means less load for the nodes) to allow network entities to scale in a more effective way).

Another aspect to be considered is that the majority of the procedures in 4G systems are triggered by network entities rather than the user equipment (UE). This aspect is controversial when incorporating low-latency services (which are key services in the industrial IoT scenarios) as it adds a lot of complexity when performing active QoS management, based on instantaneous decision making (i.e., congestion, change of traffic prioritization, etc.). As the impossibility to provide instant QoS may seriously impair the ultra-high reliability requirement for 5G IoT verticals, *UE-triggered signaling* procedures should be designed in 5G systems. As seen when discussing IoT in the industry, not all the applications involve the same requirements. This feature could be used to the advantage of reducing the C-plane traffic in the design of 5G networks. For instance, mobility signaling can be dramatically reduced for devices considered to be stationary (this aspect is common to many IoT verticals, especially in industry automation and in remote surgery applications). By considering this aspect, the generation of signaling in the network could be optimized by considering the type of devices as well as the particular service needs. Hence, 5G needs to provide dedicated control signal procedures on a service basis.

In the remainder of this chapter we will provide an insight on how the above mentioned capabilities are expected to be fulfilled in 5G systems.

SOLUTIONS ON THE ROAD TO 5G

The network solutions actually considered in the implementation of 5G systems are summarized in the remainder of this section. Such solutions range from solutions to be applied to both core network and RAN segments to solutions to be considered only in one of these segments.

The core network represents the segment of the network which runs most of the functionalities of a cellular systems. The core network allows the devices to have a bi-directional connectivity towards other devices in the same or in external networks. From a core network point of view, 5G systems are expected to introduce disruptive changes aiming at overcoming the limitations in terms of scalability of 4G systems. In addition, such changes are expected to increase the level of flexibility of the network, which thus means having a flexible network able to support different verticals with heterogeneous features.

The RAN provides access points to the UEs by means of access procedures to allow devices to be synchronized with the network and to perform a connection request. In addition, the RAN handles the procedures relevant to the radio channel exploitation (resource assignment, power management, etc.). From a RAN point of view, 5G systems are expected to introduce flexibility by means of having ad-hoc RAN functionalities designed to handle the specific requirements of the verticals to be supported.

In the remained of this chapter, we will discuss from a technical point of view the novelties that are currently discussed to be introduced in 5G systems, with particular attention to those relevant to 5G IoT verticals.

Network Slicing

In order to handle the requirements of different and heterogeneous verticals in a robust way, there is a need to isolate the different use cases from each other. This means that 5G systems need to handle in a different way different verticals, and this leads to the concept of network slicing. According to the Next Generation Mobile Networks (NGMN) alliance, network slicing primarily targets a partition of the core network, and it is the collection of 5G network functions that are efficiently combined to satisfy one specific business use case, and avoid all unnecessary functionalities. This brings a novel concept in the mobile core, i.e., having a different core network for each network slice to be supported as depicted in Figure 1. Different examples of network slices tailored for different business cases can be in found in NGMN (2015).

All network slices would be different and independently configured. This basically means that a 5G IoT industry automation slices will have its own set of functionalities which could be potentially different from those required to handle

Figure 1. Example of 5G network slicing where two slices have a different configuration in terms of control and data paths and functionalities

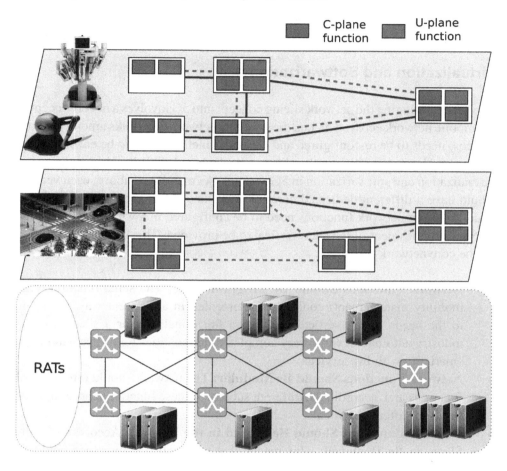

a healthcare slice. One of the key elements of slicing is thus the isolation among the different services, which requires reservation of resources (in terms of link bandwidth as well as storage, memory and computation resources of data centers) in order to fulfill the QoS needs of the vertical to be supported. This involves the concept that 5G systems will dedicate separate resources to serve industry automation and healthcare slices. The isolation concept implements the philosophy of network slicing, i.e., having multiple independent core networks according to the number of different verticals to be provided.

Network slicing also means that that RAN functionalities could be different for each network slice. As a consequence, a network slice tailored for ultra-low latency IoT verticals will implement RAN functionalities allowing to cut delay on the radio interface (for instance, a shorter random access procedure) while a network slice tailored for ultra-reliable IoT verticals will implement RAN functionalities to increase the reliability of data/control packets transmissions (for instance, by pushing the base stations and the devices to exploit more robust modulation and coding schemes).

Virtualization and Softwarization

The need of bringing the network slicing concept into 5G involves a novel concept in the mobile network ecosystem, i.e., the underlay network (i.e., links among network entities) needs to be re-configured and network functions need to be enabled on an on-demand basis according to the slices to be deployed. This has driven the use of virtualization and softwarization in 5G systems. As mentioned above, each vertical would have a different dedicated core network slice created for its own use; this underlines that network functions need to be configured in a way that ensures the QoS accomplishment of the slice/vertical to be provided. This has a set of impacts on the core network functions:

- **Network Functions Should Be Programmable:** The same function (e.g., mobility management) could be implemented in a different way according to the needs of the vertical (i.e., basic functionalities for a slice handling industry automation while very complex functionalities for a slice handling a smart city with IM services).
- **Network Functions Should Be Modular:** The network should offer a set of functions and, accordingly, different subsets of these functions can satisfy the needs of different verticals.
- **Network Functions Should Be Moved in the Network According to the Slices to Be Deployed:** This means that new network functions could be installed to deploy a novel slice to support a novel vertical. The slice needs should be further taken into account when moving network functions (e.g., one network function could be moved from one data center to another of the core network if this would increase the QoS experienced by the users of the slice).

In order to handle the above mentioned features, slicing brings the concept of virtualization into the mobile core. This means that some of the 5G network functions could run in a virtual environment (i.e., virtual machines, VMs) instead of dedicated hardware, and this introduces the possibility to move functionalities across the mobile core. Network function virtualization (NFV) is thus a paradigm at the basis in the design of 5G core, as it will allow the dynamic deployment of virtual network functions (VNFs) or service function chains (SFCs, i.e., a set of VNFs to be executed in a specific order). As a network slice can be seen as one or multiple SFCs, NFV will introduce the possibility to handle the creation of network slices as well as to manage their deployment in the physical infrastructure. A survey on the features and capabilities of NFV is given by Li, Y., & Chen, M. (2015), while the role of NFV in 5G systems is analyzed by Abdelwahab et al. (2015).

Altogether with virtualization, softwarization is another key concept to introduce network slicing in 5G systems. An example of softwarization is Software Defined Networking (SDN), a paradigm where network functions (such as path computation) run in software and managed in a logical central authority referred to as SDN controller. With SDN, the controller is in charge of managing the network entities (i.e., switches) and the related links by defining paths and rules in order to adapt the network topology and the link capabilities according to the need of the provider. SDN thus introduces flexibility in the network management and allows a monitoring and reconfiguration of the network itself. As a consequence, SDN increases the level of flexibility of 5G networks by providing an effective way of installing the paths requested by NFV for the SFCs of a specific slice. In addition, SDN can provide isolation for network slices by means of path separation or traffic isolation (with meters and/or queues) to avoid that the traffic of one slice would affect the performance of another slice. A survey on SDN is given by Kreutz et al. (2015), while the role of SDN in mobile systems is analyzed by Chen et al. (2015). An example which highlights the flexibility of 5G network architecture based on virtualization and softwarisation is depicted in Figure 2.

Figure 2. 5G network architecture enhanced by virtualization and softwarization

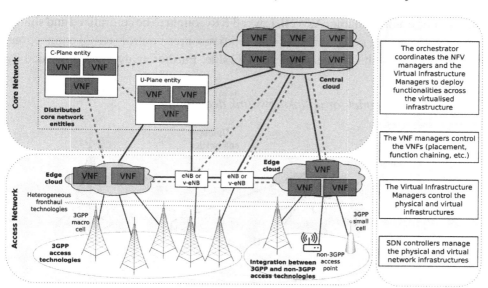

Device Multi-Connectivity

The wide range of services being provided is changing the paradigm of cellular networks, and concepts as common as cells are no longer relevant. In fact, 5G is evolving to a multi-connectivity approach. In a 3GPP perspective, multi-connectivity can be seen as a device sharing resources or more than one BS. 3GPP has already introduced the concept of dual connectivity in Rel. 12 (please, refer to 3GPP, 2012) where one UE will receive information from two separate BSs. In the 4G architecture, the management of this dual connectivity is carried through non ideal backhaul links; in this sense, virtual RANs that coordinate a cluster of antennas can reduce the reliance on this backhaul interface.

Inside the umbrella of multi-connectivity, it is also possible to add full flexibility in the cell association process. Having separate cell associations for UL and DL, a.k.a. downlink and uplink decoupling (DUDe) is a topic that has been covered by the literature lately by Boccardi et al. (2016). This concept, depicted in Figure 3, brings also to the possibility of having a multi-connectivity feature for the device in terms of U/C-plane, as analyzed by Mohamed et al. (2016).

Supporting this solution while maximizing the capacity in 5G systems would require at least a shared medium access control (MAC) layer among both serving cells, since Layer 2 control information needs to be forwarded from one serving cell to another (i.e., hybrid automatic repeat request, HARQ, protocol acknowledgements). 4G systems actually rely on a logical interface, namely the X2 interface, which directly inter-connects the base stations. The current X2 interface among serving cells is not able to provide the required round trip time figures due to the fact that this is a logical interface and most of the times a direct physical interconnection among cells is not available. As well, Layer 3 RRC ought to be centralized and shared among both serving cells, since parallel radio resource control (RRC) connections would add too much complexity in the UE side. Further analysis are provided by

Figure 3. System model for uplink/downlink decoupling

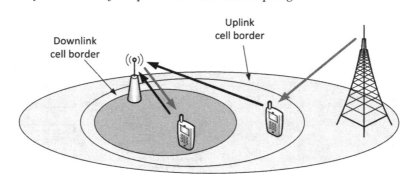

ZTE Corporation (2013). Virtualization and softwarization could help to migrate MAC/RRC entities among the cells involved in the DUDe communications.

Solutions for Supporting MTC Traffic

MTC traffic is characterized by the infrequent/frequent transmission of small data packets sent/received by devices which should save as much as possible energy. The effective support of MTC traffic is thus demanding new solutions in RAN to increase the efficiency of data transmissions from this particular type of terminals in order to reduce power consumption and latency. The following solutions are considered to achieve this goal:

- **Ad-Hoc Network Access Procedure for Transmission of Small Amount of Data:** An example is to dedicate a portion of radio resources in the uplink to a group of MTC devices to transmit their data in a contention manner without establishing a link in advance. The small data bursts can be carried either by implementing predetermined preambles dedicated to this purpose, or by sending the data load in the initial uplink resource allocated for RRC connection requests. However, sending the data along with RRC connection requests has security implications.
- **Data Aggregation to Improve the Efficiency of Data Transmissions:** Data or signaling message aggregation may occur at different locations in the network (e.g. MTC device, MTC gateway, base station, or serving gateway, SGW). Intuitively, this incurs some additional delays and is only applicable to non delay-sensitive MTC applications.

In addition to the above mentioned solutions, there is a consensus in the need for a new radio access interface designed ad-hoc by considering the features of MTC traffic. In this direction, Narrow-Band IOT (NB-IoT) is a technology being standardized by the 3GPP standards body. This technology is a narrowband radio technology specially designed for IoT devices, with particular attention in handling massive MTC access of devices with delay tolerant requirements (e.g., metering, non-critical sensing). The KPIs of NB-IoT are discussed by Gozalvez (2016), and are here summarized:

- **Indoor Coverage:** Enhanced coverage is important in many IoT applications. Simple examples are smart meters, which are often in basements of buildings behind concrete walls. Industrial applications such as elevators or conveyor belts can also be located deep indoors.

- **Low Cost:** The current industry target is for a module cost of less than 5 USD. To enable a positive business case for cellular IoT the total cost of ownership (TCO) including the device must be extremely low.
- **Long Battery Life:** The industry target is a minimum of 10 years of battery operation for simple daily connectivity of small packages.
- **Large Number of Devices:** IoT connectivity is growing significantly faster than normal mobile broadband connections and by 2025 there will be seven billion connected devices over cellular IoT networks. This is equivalent to the current number of global cellular subscriptions.

By going into the details of above listed points, NB-IoT provides 20dB additional link budget enabling about ten times better area coverage. The coverage enhancement can be achieved using a combination of techniques including power boosting of data and reference signals, repetition/retransmission and relaxing performance requirements (e.g. by allowing longer acquisition time or higher error rate). To reduce the cost, NB-IoT is designed to operate with a reduced bandwidth of 200 kHz in downlink and uplink. This, together with low-level modulation and coding schemes, means a reduced throughput based on single resource block operation with consequent lower processing and less memory on the modules compared to other cellular technologies. In addition, by considering that NB-IoT can be deployed in both GSM and LTE frequencies, this lowers the cost of deploying the NB-IoT technology by cutting the spectrum cost from an operator point of view. From a battery consumption point of view, NB-IoT implements an enhanced device power saving mode (PSM). A device that supports PSM will request to be connected for a certain active timer value during attach or tracking area update (TAU) procedures. The active timer determines how long the device remains reachable (by checking for paging according to the regular discontinuous reception, DRX, cycle) for mobile terminated transaction upon transition from connected to idle mode. The device starts the active timer when it moves from connected to idle mode. When the active timer expires, the device moves to power saving mode. In power saving mode, the device is not reachable as it does not check for paging, but it is still registered with the network. The device remains in PSM until a mobile originated transaction (e.g. periodic TAU, uplink data transmission) requires it to initiate any procedure towards the network. By exploiting the above mentioned features, NB-IoT aims to achieve up to 36 years of battery with a daily update of 200 bytes. In reality, taking into account leakage current and battery self-discharge, a battery option of 10 years is more realistic. Finally, in terms of capacity, the target for NB-IoT is to handle up to 55,000 devices per cell.

Centralized/Cloud RAN

The centralized/cloud RAN (C-RAN) is a new architecture for mobile access networks where all the processing of the base station is transferred to a central location. The C-RAN has been conceived to split the base station in two different components: the radio function unit, namely the remote radio head (RRH) which performs the physical transmission/reception of the signals over the radio interface and the digital function unit, a.k.a. base band unit (BBU). The link between the RRHs and the relevant BBU is the generic named as fronthaul, which can be either an optical fibre or a wireless link carrying digitized representations of the baseband data ready for transmission in the RAN. As multiple RRHs can be controlled by one single BBU, this entity has a global overview of the status of all the controlled RRHs and can therefore optimize the radio spectrum exploitation by means of reducing the radio interference and maximizing the spectral efficiency. The C-RAN features are analyzed for instance by Checko et al. (2015).

When considering C-RAN deployments in 5G systems enhanced by virtualization and softwarization, this will therefore involve that the BS's functionalities are softwarized in VMs. Thus, the virtualization enables elastic resource utilization in the cloud that allows a more efficient balancing of processing resources under the fluctuation of capacity demands. The role of virtualization and softwarization is discussed in more details by Dawson et al. (2014) and Pompili et al. (2016). An example of a C-RAN with enhanced functionalities can be found in Figure 4. Advantages of the C-RAN with virtualization of BS functions can be summarized in terms of:

- Added potential for neutral host solutions (i.e., RAN sharing).
- Co-location of CN and RAN functionalities, which could enable low latency interconnection between RAN and core.
- Integration of a RAN service manager that can dynamically switch between RRHs and BBUs based on QoS and instantaneous network states.

The design and the deployment of a software-based virtualized C-RAN architecture are still under investigation. The related challenges have been investigated by Arslan et al. (2015), and can be divided in terms of latency, communication protocol, heterogeneity, reliability and stability. From a latency point of view, the main issue is on the fronthaul network as it deals with very strict delay-sensitive signals from/ to the RRHs. If we consider the LTE frame, novel signals need to be delivered to the RRHs every 1ms (i.e., the LTE's subframe duration). This becomes more challenging in 5G deployments expected to operate also with shorter subframes and this introduces latency-related challenges on the fronthaul. Regarding the communication

Figure 4. Example of a C-RAN enhanced by softwarisation and virtualization
As proposed by Dawson et al. (2014).

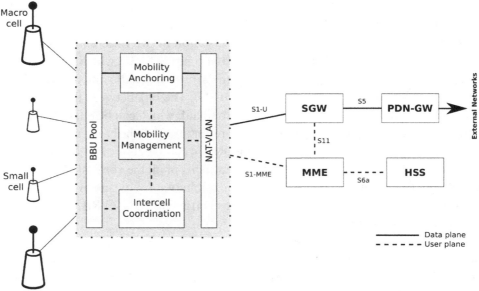

protocols, the issues is that C-RANs are still evolving and there is no consensus on open APIs to send\receive data to\from the RRHs. An admissible trend should be the exploitation of protocols such as the Common Public Radio Interface (CPRI), commonly used to carry signals between the indoor and outdoor units of traditional base stations and tailored to be extended for the fronthaul network. However, integrating such protocols with switch operations and catering to low latencies is still a big challenge to be adequately investigated. The fronthaul network also needs to take into consideration another requirement in terms of heterogeneity due to the fact that the fronthaul interfaces may be composed of a mix of fiber, wireless, and copper links. This thus introduces the need of efficient integration strategies using the bandwidth from the available forms of physical fronthaul to support the logical configurations made by the controller. Reliability is another important requirement for network operators as they need to guarantee the service reliability and service level agreements; this should not be affected when considering SND/NFV deployments. This challenge deals with the fact that the flexibility of service provisioning may require the consolidation and migration of VNFs according to the traffic load as well as the user demand and this may involve reliability degradations.

CONCLUSION

This chapter focused on the support of industry verticals over the next-to-come 5G systems by analyzing the business opportunities that the provisioning of IoT applications opens for telco operators. This chapter highlighted the main features of IoT verticals with particular attention on healthcare, smart cities, industry automation and entertainment business cases. As the proper management of these IoT verticals pushes additional requirements to be considered in the design of 5G systems, this chapter analyzed the capabilities to be introduced in 5G networks from an architectural and a procedural point of view. Finally, this chapter presented the recent advances to handle the requirements that IoT vertical push on 5G systems by considering the enhancements currently under investigation from both a core network and a RAN point of view.

REFERENCES

3. GPP. (2015). *Study on Small Cell enhancements for E-UTRA and E-UTRAN; Higher layer aspects.* Technical Report 36.842.

5G. PPP. (2015a). *5G and e-Health.* White paper.

5G. PPP. (2015b). *5G and the Factories of the Future.* White Paper.

5. GPPP. (2016). *5G and media & entertainment.* White Paper.

Abdelwahab, S., Hamdaoui, B., Guizani, M., & Znati, T. (2016). Network function virtualization in 5G. *IEEE Communications Magazine, 54*(4), 84–91.

Al-Fuqaha, A., Guizani, M., Mohammadi, M., Aledhari, M., & Ayyash, M. (2015). Internet of Things: A Survey on Enabling Technologies, Protocols, and Applications. *IEEE Communications Surveys and Tutorials, 17*(4), 2347–2376. doi:10.1109/COMST.2015.2444095

Anderson, R., & Spong, M. W. (1989). Bilateral control of teleoperators with time delay. *IEEE Transactions on Automatic Control, 34*(5), 494–501. doi:10.1109/9.24201

Andrews, J. G., Buzzi, S., Choi, W., Hanly, S. V., Lozano, A., Soong, A. C. K., & Zhang, J. C. (2014). What Will 5G Be? *IEEE Journal on Selected Areas in Communications, 32*(6), 1065–1082. doi:10.1109/JSAC.2014.2328098

Araniti, G., Campolo, C., Condoluci, M., Iera, A., & Molinaro, A. (2013). LTE for vehicular networking: A survey. *IEEE Communications Magazine, 51*(5), 148–157. doi:10.1109/MCOM.2013.6515060

Arslan, M., Sundaresan, K., & Rangarajan, S. (2015). Software-defined networking in cellular radio access networks: Potential and challenges. *IEEE Communications Magazine*, *53*(1), 150–156. doi:10.1109/MCOM.2015.7010528

Atzori, L., Iera, A., & Morabito, G. (2010). The internet of things: A survey. *Computer Networks*, *54*(15), 2787–2805. doi:10.1016/j.comnet.2010.05.010

Boccardi, F., Andrews, J., Elshaer, H., Dohler, M., Parkvall, S., Popovski, P., & Singh, S. (2016). Why to decouple the uplink and downlink in cellular networks and how to do it. *IEEE Communications Magazine*, *54*(3), 110–117. doi:10.1109/MCOM.2016.7432156

Bradai, A., Singh, K., Ahmed, T., & Rasheed, T. (2015). Cellular software defined networking: A framework. *IEEE Communications Magazine*, *53*(6), 36–43. doi:10.1109/MCOM.2015.7120043

Checko, A., Christiansen, H. L., Yan, Y., Scolari, L., Kardaras, G., Berger, M. S., & Dittmann, L. (2015). Cloud RAN for Mobile Networks. A Technology Overview. *IEEE Communications Surveys and Tutorials*, *17*(1), 405–426. doi:10.1109/COMST.2014.2355255

Chen, T., Matinmikko, M., Chen, X., Zhou, X., & Ahokangas, P. (2015). Software defined mobile networks: Concept, survey, and research directions. *IEEE Communications Magazine*, *53*(11), 126–133. doi:10.1109/MCOM.2015.7321981

Condoluci, M., Sardis, F., & Mahmoodi, T. (2015). Softwarization and Virtualization in 5G Networks for Smart Cities. *EAI International Conference on Cyber Physical Systems, IoT and Sensors Networks*.

Dawson, A. W., Marina, M. K., & Garcia, F. J. (2014). On the Benefits of RAN Virtualisation in C-RAN Based Mobile Networks. *Third European Workshop on Software Defined Networks*. doi:10.1109/EWSDN.2014.37

Gozalvez, J. (2016). New 3GPP Standard for IoT. *IEEE Vehicular Technology Magazine*, *11*(1), 14–20. doi:10.1109/MVT.2015.2512358

GSMA. (2012). *Touching lives through mobile health Assessment of the global market opportunity*. White Paper.

GSMA. (2012a). *Connected Cars: Business Model Innovation*. White Paper.

Istepanaian, R. S. H., & Zhang, Y. T. (2012). Guest Editorial Introduction to the Special Section: 4G Health - The Long-Term Evolution of m-Health. *IEEE Transactions on Information Technology in Biomedicine*, *16*(1), 1–5. doi:10.1109/TITB.2012.2183269 PMID:22271836

ITU. (2014). *Smart Sustainable Cities: An Analysis of Definitions*. ITU.

Kreutz, D., Ramos, F. M. V., Veríssimo, P. E., Rothenberg, C. E., Azodolmolky, S., & Uhlig, S. (2015). Software-Defined Networking: A Comprehensive Survey. *Proceedings of the IEEE, 103*(1), 14–76. doi:10.1109/JPROC.2014.2371999

Laya, A., Alonso, L., & Alonso-Zarate, J. (2014). Is the Random Access Channel of LTE and LTE-A Suitable for M2M Communications? A Survey of Alternatives. *IEEE Communications Surveys and Tutorials, 16*(1), 4–16. doi:10.1109/SURV.2013.111313.00244

Lee, J. H., Bonnin, J. M., Seite, P., & Chan, H. A. (2013). Distributed IP mobility management from the perspective of the IETF: Motivations, requirements, approaches, comparison, and challenges. *IEEE Wireless Communications, 20*(5), 159–168. doi:10.1109/MWC.2013.6664487

Li, Y., & Chen, M. (2015). Software-Defined Network Function Virtualization: A Survey. *IEEE Access, 3*, 2542–2553. doi:10.1109/ACCESS.2015.2499271

McKinsey Digital. (2015). *Industry 4.0 How to navigate digitization of the manufacturing sector*. White Paper.

Mohamed, A., Onireti, O., Imran, M. A., Imran, A., & Tafazolli, R. (2016). Control-Data Separation Architecture for Cellular Radio Access Networks: A Survey and Outlook. *IEEE Communications Surveys and Tutorials, 18*(1), 446–465. doi:10.1109/COMST.2015.2451514

NGMN. (2015). *5G White Paper*. White Paper.

Nokia Siemens Networks. (2011). *Signalling is growing 50% faster than data traffic*. White Paper.

Osseiran, A., Boccardi, F., Braun, V., Kusume, K., Marsch, P., Maternia, M., & Fallgren, M. et al. (2014). Scenarios for 5G mobile and wireless communications: The vision of the METIS project. *IEEE Communications Magazine, 52*(5), 26–35. doi:10.1109/MCOM.2014.6815890

Office for Life Sciences. (2015). *Digital Health in the UK An industry study for the Office of Life Sciences*. White Paper.

Palattella, M. R., Dohler, M., Grieco, A., Rizzo, G., Torsner, J., Engel, T., & Ladid, L. (2016). Internet of Things in the 5G Era: Enablers, Architecture, and Business Models. *IEEE Journal on Selected Areas in Communications, 34*(3), 510–527. doi:10.1109/JSAC.2016.2525418

Pelletier, A. (2016). *Virtual reality: The reality for connectivity providers.* Retrieved July 16, 2016, from http://telecoms.com/opinion/virtual-reality-the-reality-for-connectivity-providers

Pentikousis, K., Wang, Y., & Hu, W. (2013). Mobileflow: Toward software-defined mobile networks. *IEEE Communications Magazine, 51*(7), 44–53. doi:10.1109/MCOM.2013.6553677

Pompili, D., Hajisami, A., & Tran, T. X. (2016). Elastic resource utilization framework for high capacity and energy efficiency in cloud RAN. *IEEE Communications Magazine, 54*(1), 26–32. doi:10.1109/MCOM.2016.7378422

PwC. (2014). *The Wearable Future.* White Paper.

Simsek, M., Aijaz, A., Dohler, M., Sachs, J., & Fettweis, G. (2016). 5G-Enabled Tactile Internet. *IEEE Journal on Selected Areas in Communications, 34*(3), 460–473. doi:10.1109/JSAC.2016.2525398

Zain, A. S. M., Yahya, A., Malek, M. F. A., & Omar, N. (2012). 3GPP Long Term Evolution and its application for healthcare services. *International Conference on Computer and Communication Engineering*, 239-243.

Zanella, A., Bui, N., Castellani, A., Vangelista, L., & Zorzi, M. (2014). Internet of Things for Smart Cities. *IEEE Internet of Things Journal, 1*(1), 22–32. doi:10.1109/JIOT.2014.2306328

ZTE Corporation. (2013). *Comparison between CP solution C1 and C2.* Technical Report.

KEY TERMS AND DEFINITIONS

HTC: The human-type communications (HTC) traffic is the traffic that humans exchange over mobile networks characterized by asynchronous large packets with non-critical delay constraints.

IoT: The Internet of Things (IoT) is the network composed of devices with sensing or actuators capabilities which are connected to each other to enable these objects to collect and exchange data.

MTC: The machine-type communications (MTC) traffic is the traffic that machines send/receive to/from mobile networks characterized by periodic/a-periodic small packets with both critical or non-critical time constraints.

Network Slicing: A design paradigm of 5G systems based on the concept of having multiple logically independent network designed and deployed in order to satisfy the requirements of the service to be provided.

NFV: Network Function Virtualization (NFV) is a paradigm where network functions run in software in a virtual environment instead of running on a physical machine.

QoS: The Quality of Service (QoS) describes the set of features that a specific traffic flow should receive in terms of data rates, delay, packet losses, priority, etc.

SDN: Software Defined Networking (SDN) is a paradigm where network entities (such as switches) are instructed by a central controller which runs in software network functionalities such as path computation and link configuration.

Chapter 7
Wireless Sensor Network With Always Best Connection for Internet of Farming

Ahmed Alahmadi
Al Baha University, Saudi Arabia

Vasuky Mohanan
INTI International College Penang, Malaysia

Tami Alwajeeh
Al Baha University, Saudi Arabia

Rahmat Budiarto
Al Baha University, Saudi Arabia

ABSTRACT

The Internet of Things (IoT) is transforming the agriculture industry and enables farmers to deal with the vast challenges in the industry. Internet of Farming (IoF) applications increases the quantity, quality, sustainability as well as cost effectiveness of agricultural production. Farmers leverage IoF to monitor remotely, sensors that can detect soil moisture, crop growth and livestock feed levels, manage and control remotely the smart connected harvesters and irrigation equipment, and utilize artificial intelligence based tools to analyze operational data combined with 3rd party information, such as weather services, to provide new insights and improve decision making. The Internet of Farming relies on data gathered from sensor of Wireless Sensor Network (WSN). The WSN requires a reliable connectivity to provide accurate prediction of the farming system. This chapter proposes a strategy that provides always best connectivity (ABC). The strategy considers a routing protocol to support Low-power and lossy networks (LLN), with a minimum energy usage. Two scenarios are presented.

DOI: 10.4018/978-1-5225-2799-2.ch007

Copyright © 2018, IGI Global. Copying or distributing in print or electronic forms without written permission of IGI Global is prohibited.

INTRODUCTION

The emerging Internet of Things (IoT) technique provides a new method for access to farmland information technique (Jiao et al., 2013). IoT is the expansion of communication network and internet application, which is a technique to sense the physical world by sensing technology and the intelligent devices through the interconnection, calculation, processing and knowledge mining to achieve the information exchange and seamless links among the persons and devices or among the things and to achieve real-time control of the physical world, accurate management and scientific decision-making (Morais et al., 2008; Wei et al., 2010; Zang et al., 2007)

Internet of Farming (IoF) is the other extreme that lies in the scheme of the Internet of Things (ioT), where intelligent device networks truly belong to the Internet just like any other network. There are applications that will be accessible by the Internet community. Any Internet user/farmer will have access to the information provided by intelligent devices such as telemetry either by directly accessing the device or by means of intermediate servers. There are already very simple forms of Internet access to intelligent devices and the number of these applications will continue to grow. The connectivity model will likely have intermediate servers. The servers will collect data from smart devices and the Internet will connect to these servers, as opposed to the intelligent device, to preserve scarce resources in intelligent device networks and increase scalability.

Smart agriculture and precision farming are taking off, however, could just be the precursors to even greater use of technology in the farming world. BI Intelligence, Business Insider's premium research service, predicts that IoT device installations in the agriculture world will increase from 30 million in 2015 to 75 million in 2020, for a compound annual growth rate of 20%. Given all of the potential benefits of these IoT applications in agriculture, it is understandable that farmers are increasingly turning to agricultural drones and sensors for the future of farming.

The future of farming is in collecting and analyzing big data in agriculture in order to maximize efficiency. But there are far more trends to understand with the IoT, and the Internet of Things will touch many more industries than just farming.

A wireless sensor network (WSN) is a wireless network consisting of spatially distributed autonomous devices that use sensors to monitor physical or environmental conditions. These autonomous devices, known as routers and end nodes, combine with a gateway to create a typical WSN system. The distributed measurement nodes communicate wirelessly to a central gateway, which acts as the network coordinator in charge of node authentication, message buffering, and bridging from the IEEE

802.15.4 wireless network to the wired Ethernet network. Thus, the measurement data can be collected, processed, analyzed, and presented.

Therefore, this chapter initially aims at providing a brief survey on the state of the art in always best connected network concepts and network selection techniques as proposed for Internet of Farming infrastructures. The target behind this survey is to provide a reader with the basic mind-set regarding the design and deployment of always best connected (ABC) methodologies in IoF-specific scenarios. Hence, via this comprehensive survey the chapter targets at enlightening the reader on the applicability of ABC techniques for the IoF scenery as well as to pinpoint on how each proposed methodology from the literature was formulated in order to meet IoF-specific requirements. Nonetheless, in order to facilitate an even more robust understanding to the general audience with respect to the usage of network selection problems, this chapter is also dedicated at presenting a case study regarding an exemplar ABC and network selection technique employed within a controlled experimental IoF test-bed. In particular, the demonstrated ABC approach is mainly concerned with the ABC domain, particularly for the IoF-WSN. The backbone of this technique is derived by the properties of the quality of services (QoS) as well as quality of experience QoE) of nodes and users algorithm within an IoF infrastructure.

BACKGROUND ON ABC NETWORK AND NETWORK SELECTION

Network selection problems have been a major research area for some time (Lahby et al., 2012, Lahby & Adib, 2013). This goes to show that ubiquitous, seamless and Always Best Connected (ABC) network connections are highly sought. Moreover, providing all this for user that can easily go from moving at pedestrian speed to high speed (while in a vehicle) is expected. Mobile Nodes (MNs) with multiple interfaces are currently the norm. This means a MN can connect to different types of access networks. Typically, network selection occurs when handover is imminent. Traditionally, target network to handover to, is chosen based on single criteria such as Required Signal Strength (RSS). Bari & Leung (2009) have shown that network selection based on single criteria is insufficient in serving the user's diverse and changing needs. Also, a context based network selection will better fulfil the ABC criteria as different users may have a different idea of what is ABC (Mohanan et al., 2013). A comprehensive and holistic policy framework for network selection is essential in addressing these issues. Network selection involves fulfilling the requirements of four major stakeholders namely: user, MN, candidate networks (CN) and the active application. A fluid and dynamic network selection policy is important in alleviating the problems that occurs when satisfying different and sometimes conflicting needs of the major stakeholders.

Current network selection solutions (Mohanan et al., 2013) suffer from giving importance to the needs of one or two stakeholders at the expense of others. Moreover, the limited number of attributes collected may not reflect the true situation of a particular stakeholder. Resolving conflicting objectives is not addressed in related work (Mohanan et al., 2013). So far, current researches do not take into account Quality of Experience (QoE) values when selecting target networks. Research in (Ghahfarokhi and Movahhedinia, 2013) uses QoE values to improve network selection but it uses a learning tool to do this hence it is slow in adapting and may give erroneous results while in the process of learning. Most network selection solutions (Labby et al., 2012, Labby & Adib, 2013) use Quality of Service (QoS) values to make this decision. QoS values represent the theoretical values of the said attributes and may not truly mirror what the user experiences in reality. A network selection solution consists of two main tasks that are of assigning weights and performing ranking. Attributes values are collected from various stakeholders in order to determine the status of the said stakeholder. These attributes are assigned weights, reflective of the importance of a particular attribute. In other words, a higher weight is assigned to attributes that have a bigger impact in finding the best target network and vice versa. Ranking of the prospective CNs are done whereby the best network will be top of the list of CNs.

In addition, a context based network selection will better fulfil the ABC criteria as different users may have a different idea of what is ABC (Mohanan et al., 2012; Mohanan et al., 2013). A comprehensive and holistic policy framework for network selection is essential in addressing these issues. Network selection involves fulfilling the requirements of four major stakeholders namely: user, MN, candidate networks (CN) and the active application. A fluid and dynamic network selection policy is important in alleviating the problems that occurs when satisfying different and sometimes conflicting needs of the major stakeholders.

Current network selection solutions (Mohanan et al., 2012; Mohanan et al., 2013) suffer from giving importance to the needs of one or two stakeholders at the expense of others. Moreover, the limited number of attributes collected may not reflect the true situation of a particular stakeholder (Bari and Leung (2009). Resolving conflicting objectives is not addressed in related works (Mohanan et al., 2012; Mohanan et al., 2013). So far, current researches do not take into account Quality of Experience (QoE) values when selecting target networks (Mohanan et al., 2015). A research carried out by Ghahfarokhi and Movahhedinia. (2013) uses QoE values to improve network selection but it uses a learning tool to do this hence it is slow in adapting and may give erroneous results while in the process of learning. Most network selection solutions (Zhang et al., 2010; Savita and Chandraseka

(2011); Labby, Leghris and Adib (2011); Labby, Leghris and Adib (2012); Labby and Adib (2013)) use Quality of Service (QoS) values to make this decision. QoS values represent the theoretical values of the said attributes and may not truly mirror what the user experiences in reality. A network selection solution consists of two main tasks that are of assigning weights and performing ranking. Attributes values are collected from various stakeholders in order to determine the status of the said stakeholder. These attributes are assigned weights, reflective of the importance of a particular attribute. In other words, a higher weight is assigned to attributes that have a bigger impact in finding the best target network and vice versa. Ranking of the prospective CNs are done whereby the best network will be top of the list of CNs.

There are two main ideas in solving network selection problems: Multi Attribute Decision Making (MADM) and Artificial Intelligence (AI) based approaches.

MADM BASED APPROACHES

Various researches have touted MADM based approaches as the answer in solving network selection problems (Charilas and Panagopoulous, (2009); Verma and Singh (2013)). MADM methods seem like a logical choice as MADM algorithms are used to solve decision making problems that involves multiple criteria. MADM based approaches can be further divided into those that are used primarily as a weighting mechanism (i.e. AHP, SAW, MEW, ANP) and those used to perform ranking (i.e. GRA, TOPSIS, ELECTRE and VIKOR). Research by Charilas and Panagopoulous (2010) has shown that MADM based approaches are simple, scalable and efficient in solving NSPs. The only drawback of MADM based approaches is that attribute values must be in crisp and precise numbers. Researchers who argue against the use of MADM based approaches say that it is limiting to assume that all attributes values must be in this format. Hence, the advent of AI based approaches.

AI-BASED APPROACHES

There are a variety of AI-Based methods that have been used to solve network selection problems (Kaleem et al. (2013); Wang et al. (2012); Sasirekha and Ilanzkumaran (2013)). These methods became popular due to the realization that not all attribute values can be expressed in crisp and precise values. More so for user preference values whereby user expresses preferences with regards to certain attributes. It is

Table 1. Fuzzy language variables

FLV	Crisp Values
Very Low	0.0333
Low	0.2000
Medium	0.4000
High	0.6000
Very High	0.8000
Excellent	0.9667

said that users cannot be expected to express the needs using weights. The advocates of these methods say that it is more relatable for users to indicate the preferences using simple language. Therefore, Fuzzy Language Variables (FLVs) were added as part of the network selection strategy. Attribute values can be expressed by using FLV scales such as the one shown in Table 1 adapted from (Kalem et al., 2013).

As detailed in Table 1, the FLV still needs to be converted to an equivalent crisp value as weighting mechanism can only work with crisp numbers. This extra step adds to the complexity of the method. Unfortunately, these methods have been criticized as not being scalable and too complex (Charilas and Panagopoulous (2012). Network selection occurs in a very dynamic environment and an inefficient network selection solution will impede the goal of achieving seamless and ABC network connections. One of the issues in handover is reducing handover delay so much so that the user remains unaware that the connection has been handed over (i.e. seamless). A user's experience while being connected is of paramount importance (ABC) and can only be achieved with an efficient network selection solution. Therefore, other researchers have tried to address this issue by reducing the number of fuzzy rules to increase efficiency (Kaleem, 2012). Figure 1 and 2 summarizes the different types of methods that have been used in network selection.

Figure 1. MADM based approaches

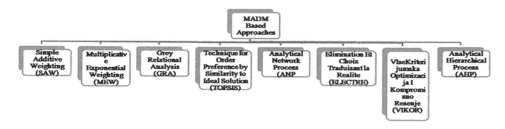

Figure 2. AI based approaches

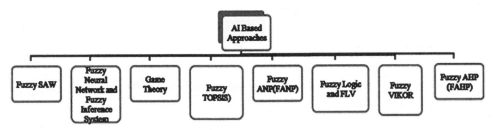

As detailed in (Mohanan et all., 2012; Mohanan et all., 2013), the issue is not so much in the method used to solve network selection problems but the lack of a holistic and comprehensive framework. Problems associated with current approaches towards network selection is a piecemeal approach that only addresses a subset of the problems associated with network selection (Mohanan et all., 2012; Mohanan et all., 2013). Next section details the framework that can solve all aspects of network selection problems and cater for current and future needs in solving network selection problems.

FRAMEWORK FOR CONTEXT BASED NETWORK SELECTION

In order to correctly identify the context on which the network selection occurs, attributes must be collected from all the stakeholders. This would mean that all the four main stakeholders are given equal importance so that the context can be ascertained. The most neglected stakeholder context is users. Related works (Zhang et al., 2010; Savita and Chandraseka (2011); Labby, Leghris and Adib (2011); Labby, Leghris and Adib (2012); Labby and Adib (2013)) assume that as long as QoS requirements are met, that would indirectly translate to a best user experience (ABC). Ironically, for these methods (Zhang et al., 2010; Savita and Chandraseka (2011); Labby, Leghris and Adib (2011); Labby, Leghris and Adib (2012); Labby and Adib (2013)), a user's experience is determined by not taking into account user's preference at all or minimally. This framework suggests that attributes are collected from all stakeholders. Table 2 lists the attributes that are necessary to ensure a holistic and contextual network selection is implemented.

CN's attributes are used to determine the QoS provided by the respective CNs. Generally, all network selection solutions in the literature gives the utmost importance to this stakeholder as CN's attributes is used as a predictor of that network's performance. There are two main ideas on how to determine user's preference: self-learning algorithms through feedback and by explicit indication by

Table 2. List of attributes

MN Attributes	CN Attributes	User Attributes
Velocity	Coverage Area	User Preference
Travelling Trajectory	Delay	User Perceived Quality (UPQ)
Active Application	Packet Loss Ratio	
Dwell Time	Jitter	
	Throughput	
	Security	
	Cost	

the user. Proponents of the former method say that users should not be burdened by forcing them to fill up a questionnaire. Supporters of the latter method states there's no one better qualified to indicate user preference than the users themselves. Common sense dictates explicit input from the user is the best way to determine user's preference. Not only that, each user has his or her own idea of what constitutes ABC for themselves. The challenge here is in the method of acquiring the user's preference. The method must be as simple as possible so that users can understand easily. Users can also change the preference anytime. And these changes can be adapted immediately into the network selection strategy. To the best of the authors' knowledge, no related work used QoE values to support network selection (Mohanan et al., 2015). QoE values were mostly used to improve handover operations (Mohanan et al., 2015). QoE values are essential in determining user's experience in reality. QoE values are usually derived using subjective experiments (Kaleem et al., 2013). These experiments need to be conducted in a controlled laboratory environment with real users. These experiments are accurate but unfortunately require stringent testing conditions and are very expensive. Therefore, objective experiments were designed to overcome these disadvantages. According to (da Silva et all. (2008); Mohamed and Robina (2002)), Pseudo Subjective Quality Assessment (PSQA) used in tandem with Random Neural Networks (RNN) is an accurate reflection of the quality experienced at the user side in real time.

The framework introduced in this chapter combines both QoS and QoE values in order to make the network selection policy more reflective of the context. QoS values are a good predictor of the CN's performance and if the QoE values collected do not correlate with that prediction then QoE values can be used to fine tune the selection policy. Related work shows that the most commonly collected attribute from MN is the active application ((Zhang et al., 2010; Savita and Chandraseka (2011); Labby, Leghris and Adib (2011); Labby, Leghris and Adib (2012); Labby and Adib (2013)). This is because in order to provide the best network connection it is imperative to know what the active running application is. Applications can be grouped under four categories: streaming, interactive, conversational, background. Each of these applications has unique needs (Rinne, 2012) in terms of the QoS requirements. Research in handover techniques (Ceken and Arlan, 2009)] have been suggesting using velocity as means to predict when handover will occur. Researches have also shown that when the MN moves at a high speed, throughput reduces and the number of packets dropped increases (Mohanan et al., 2012; Mohanan et al., 2013).Therefore, velocity of the MN is a very important contributor in determining the MN's context as increasing velocity indicate requirements for throughput and Packet Loss Ratio (PLR) changes as well. Velocity can also be used as a filtering mechanism to exclude unsuitable networks from even being considered as a CN. For example, increasing velocity would render Wireless LANs (WLANs) as not suitable as target network as a fast moving MN will cross the small coverage area of a WLAN very fast, therefore increasing handover frequency. Travelling trajectory combined with velocity and coverage areas of CNs will be useful in calculating dwell time. This is essential in further adducing the best target network for that particular MN (Mohanan, 2013).

Figure 3 illustrates the components of the holistic policy framework for network selection. The algorithm to execute the component A from Figure 3 is shown in Figure 4. Figure 3 shows that the selection policy does not differentiate between homogeneous and heterogeneous handover. A comprehensive network selection policy should be able to handle both types of handover. As shown in Figure 2, the selection policy is dynamic and adaptable to the changing context of the stakeholders. Instead of static weights (Zhang et al., 2010; Savita and Chandraseka (2011); Labby, Leghris and Adib (2011); Labby, Leghris and Adib (2012); Labby and Adib (2013)), dynamic weights are assigned to represent the importance of a particular attribute in finding the best target network. Static weights are predefined weights assigned to QoS attributes based on the type of application running. These techniques may work well previously, but it is not adaptable to the ever changing and volatile environment on which network selection occurs (Mohanan et al., 2012; Mohanan et al., 2013). When MN's velocity surpasses a preset threshold value, weights for attributes such as throughput and packet loss ratio is increased. Also, CNs whose coverage area is small (i.e. WLANS) is removed from the list of CNs considered as a fast moving MN will cross over the coverage area fast therefore it seems prudent to only consider CNs with larger coverage area (i.e. Wireless MANs and WANs). Additionally, whenever UPQ value is lower than a predefined threshold value, weightage for attributes such as jitter and throughput (when the active application is streaming) or jitter and delay (when the active application is conversational) is increased. Travelling trajectory of the MN, its velocity and the coverage area of the CN is used in calculating the duration the MN will spend in a particular CN.

Figure 3. Major components of the framework

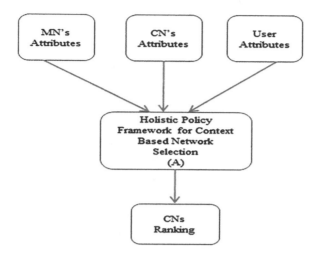

Figure 4. Algorithm for implementing component A of Figure 3 for context based network selection

1. Initial weights is decided with based on active applications
2. Identify prospective CNs
3. Calculate the mobile node's velocity V_{MN}
4. Do checking
    IF V_{MN} > VThreshold
        a) Remove the WLANs from CNs list
        b) Adjust weights fro Throughput and PLR
5. For each CN:
    i) Identify Dwell time DT_{CN}
    ii) IF DT_{CN} < $DT_{Threshold}$
        Remove the CN from the list
        ELSE
        Adjust QoS values collected from the CN
6. IF UPQ_{User} < $UPQ_{Threshold}$ for the active application
        Adjust the weights predefined for the said type of application
7. Choose appropriate GRA formula based on user preference
8. Rank the CNs

The dwell time can be used to fine tune the QoS attribute values. This is essential in situations such as when there is more than one CNs in contention and the dwell time spent in each CN makes a significant difference in the quality of the network connection. Dwell time can also be used as filtering mechanism to weed out those CNs in which the dwell time is below a certain threshold.

WIRELESS SENSOR NETWORK WITH ALWAYS BEST CONNECTION

The wireless sensor network (WSN) consists of spatially distributed autonomous devices that use sensors to monitor a farm as well as to gather environmental data. These autonomous devices, known as routers and end nodes, combine with a gateway to create a typical WSN system. The distributed measurement nodes communicate wirelessly to a central gateway, which acts as the network coordinator in charge of node authentication, message buffering, and bridging from the IEEE 802.15.4 wireless network to the wired or mobile Ethernet network. The design uses three layers: network layer is responsible for communication with the data sink/server; Reliable distributed storage layer is responsible to collect the data using coordinator node (cn); Sensor node layer is responsible to sense the data. The sensor nodes (sn) can be deployed in two different ways using grid topology or random topology as shown in Figure 5.

The block diagram of the wireless sensor design is shown in Figure 6. The sensor able to provide ABC feature through a multiple communication protocols running in the sensor unit. Besides, in order to come up with a low cost sensor design multiple sensors are put in one microcontroller (air temperature, humidity, soil water level, soil humidity). The challenge here is to deal with an efficient battery power usage.

SCENARIO 1: THERE ARE TWO CANDIDATE NETWORK (CNS) TO CHOOSE FROM

In this scenario two candidate networks Network1 and Network2 are available and the attribute values are shown in Table 3.

Grey Relational Analysis (GRA) is the only ranking technique that has three formulas to identify the utility of an attribute. Other ranking techniques describe the utility of an attribute as increasing (i.e throughput) or decreasing monotonically (i.e delay) whereas GRA has an additional third formula that is known as closer-to-desired-value-the-better or nominal-the-best. This third formula is very handy for situations where the selection policy dictates a not so straightforward solution. Also, the attribute values needs to be normalized as the values are of different units. For a network selection problem that has m candidate networks with n attributes, the i_{th} alternative can be translated into its equivalent comparability sequence $X_i = (X_{i1}, X_{i2}, ..., X_{ij}, ... X_{in})$ using one of the following equations where $i = 1,2,..., m$ and $j = 1,2,...n$.(Lampropoulos et al., 2008).

Figure 5. The sensoring components

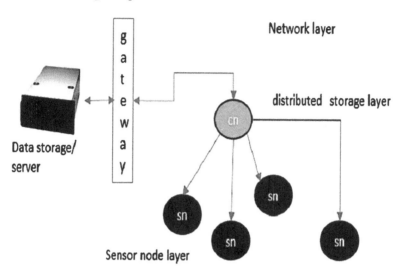

Figure 6. The sensor block diagram

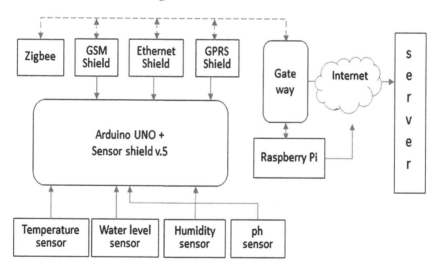

Table 3. Candidate networks attribute values

Candidate Network	Priority	Available Data Rate	Average Delay	Average Packet Error Rate
Network1	20	1 Mbps	50ms	0.01
Network2	10	2Mbps	80ms	0.008

$$X_{ij} = \frac{y_{ij} - Min\{y_{ij}\}}{Max\{y_{ij}\} - Min\{y_{ij}\}} \tag{1}$$

$$X_{ij} = \frac{Max\{y_{ij}\} - y_{ij}\}}{Max\{y_{ij}\} - Min\{y_{ij}\}} \tag{2}$$

$$X_{ij} = 1 - \frac{\left|y_{ij} - y^*_{\ j}\right|}{Max\{Max\{y_{ij}\} - y^*_{\ ij}, \ y^*_{\ ij} - Min\{y_{ij}\}\}} \tag{3}$$

where y_{ij} is the value of alternative *i's* attribute *j* value, $y^*_{\ j}$ refers to the closer to the desired value. Equation 1 is used on the larger the better attributes, equation 2 is for the smaller the better attributes and equation 3 is nominal the best. Equation 1 is used on Available data rate and Priority whereas Equation 2 is used on all the other values. This is to normalize the attribute values so that attributes can be compared objectively to each other. For example, for available data rate, the maximum value is 2 from Network 2 and the minimum value is 1 from Network 1. Using Equation 1, the normalized value for network 1 is (1-1)/(2-1) = 0. The entire normalize values are shown Table 4.

For a CN, if the normalized value for an attribute is nearest to 1, then that CN is the best CN for that particular attribute. Next a reference sequence (network 0) that represents the best alternative where the normalized values are all 1 is defined and is also added to Table 5. The next step is to find the network that has the closest comparability sequence to the reference sequence. This is identified by a grey relational coefficient (GRC). The network with the largest GRC is the best CN. The Equation 4 calculates the GRC (Kuo, Yang and Huang, 2008).

Table 4. Normalized attributes' values

Candidate Network	Priority	Available Data Rate	Average Delay	Average Jitter	Average Packet Error Rate
Network 0	1	1	1	1	1
Network1	1	0	1	0	0
Network2	0	1	0	0	1

$$\gamma\left(x_{0j}, x_{ij}\right) = \frac{\Delta_{\min} + \zeta\Delta_{\max}}{\Delta_{ij} + \zeta\Delta_{\max}} \tag{4}$$

where

$$\Delta_{ij} = |x_{0j} - x_{ij}|$$

$$\Delta_{\min} = \text{Min}\{\Delta_{ij}, i=1,2,..., m; j=1,2,,..., n\},$$

$$\Delta_{\max} = \text{Max}\{\Delta_{ij}, i=1,2,..., m; j=1,2,,..., n\},$$

ζ is the distinguishing coefficient, $\zeta \in [0,1]$

As for example, for $\Delta_{min} = 0$, $\Delta_{max} = 1$ and $\zeta = 0.5$ then the GRC for the available data rate for Network1 is:

$$\gamma_{(\text{Network0, Network1})} = (0+0.5*1)/(1+0.5*1) = 0.5/1.5 = 0.3333.$$

The GRCs for all attributes for both CNs are shown in Table 5.
Next, the grey relational grade between each CN and Network 0 is calculated.
Grey relational grade

$$(\text{Network 0, Network-i}) = \sum_{j=1}^{n} w_j \gamma\left(Network\ 0, Network\ i\right)$$

where w_j refers to the weight of the said attribute, determined by the AHP matrix and geometric mean method as shown in Figure 7.
Thus,

Network 1 grade = 0.304358*1 + 0.043475*0.3333

Table 5. The GRC values

Candidate Network	Priority	Available Data Rate	Average Delay	Average Jitter	Average Packet Error Rate
Network1	1	0.3333	1	0.3333	0.3333
Network2	0.3333	1	0.3333	0.3333	1

Figure 7. The attribute weight values

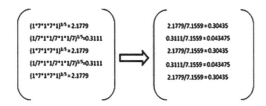

$+ 0.30435*1 + 0.30435*0.3333 + 0.043475*0.3333 = 0.43477$

Network 2 grade $= 0.30435*0.3333 + 0.043475*1$

$+ 0.30435*0.3333 + 0.30435*0.3333 + 0.043475*1 = 0.39127$

Based on the calculated grade, Network1 will be selected as the best network.

SCENARIO 2

Now let's say the node preference has indicated that cost is extremely important means that cost is added to the AHP matrix and Table 7 shows the new matrix.

The geometric mean method is used again to formulate the weights for the attributes as shown in Figure 8.

Equation 1 is used on Priority whereas Equation 2 is used on delay, PER, and cost. Equation 3 will be applied on bit rate. This is because cost is considered very important and usually cost is charged according to the bit rate delivered. Therefore, instead of using larger-the-better equation on bit rate, nominal-the-best is applied to bit rate so as to reduce cost. The attribute values are same as in Table 3 with cost for Network 1 is 0.9 and cost for network 2 is 0.1 added. The normalized values are shown in Table 7.

Table 6. New AHP matrix for the traffic

C1	Priority	Bit Rate	Delay	PER	Cost
Priority	1	7	1	7	1
Bit Rate	1/7	1	1/7	1	1/7
Delay	1	7	1	7	1
PER	1/7	1	1/7	1	1/7
Cost	1	7	1	7	1

Figure 8. The attribute weight values for scenario 2

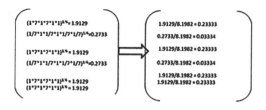

Table 7. Normalized values for scenario 2

Candidate Network	Priority	Available Data Rate	Average Delay	Average Packet Error Rate	Cost
Network 0	1	1	1	1	1
Network1	1	0	1	0	0
Network2	0	0	0	1	1

The normalized value for bit rate is defined using Equation 3 whereby for network 1 it is calculated as shown below. The nominal-the-best value is chosen to be 1.5.

$$1- (| 1 - 1.5| / Max(2 - 1.5, 1.5 - 1)) = 1 - (0.5 / 0.5) = 0$$

Similarly is done for Network 2. GRC is evaluated for Network 1 and 2 and is listed in Table 8.

The final step is to rank the networks based on grey relational grade. Network 1 grade =0.6444 and Network 2 grade = 0.51109.

Based on the grade, this time around Network 1 is again selected as the best network. Even though the same network is selected, it is based on maintaining low cost as well as reasonable bit rate as opposed to the previous scenario whereby only the best (in every way) CN is selected. In the same way as scenario 2 is depicted, the selection policy will be used to dictate the AHP weights as well as the GRA formula to use. There have been many other researchers (Song and Jamlipour (2005); Verma and Singh (2013)) that have defined various enhancements to the use of AHP

Table 8. GRC values for scenario 2

Candidate Network	Priority	Available Data Rate	Average Delay	Average Packet Error Rate	Cost
Network1	1	0.3333	1	0.3333	0.3333
Network2	0.3333	0.3333	0.3333	1	1

and GRA but the enhancements are used to improve the mathematical aspect of the respective solution or to be used in tandem with imprecise attribute values (Labby et al. 2012). However, what the authors do not do is to make the network selection mechanism dynamic and change according to user's, terminal's and CN's context. As shown in Scenario 2, just by including user's preference towards cost, a different grey relational grade is acquired. Similarly, as shown in Figure 2, the selection policy must be dynamic to identify the context on which the network selection occurs.

The initial question was whether QoE or QoS is better for solving NSPs. Even though, research is moving towards QoE, it involves a lot of subjective research in the area of cognitive and behavioral psychology. QoE in the real sense of the definition is very complex and difficult to measure. Therefore, the authors have used UPQ to measure QoE. UPQ does not take into account the subjective aspects of QoE. User's mood is also included as a factor for QoE. How the mood is being measured? If so, the QoE can change even though in every other aspect, the context is the same, just because the user is in a bad mood. UPQ is a concise mechanism for measuring QoE. The authors believe, in reality, the true meaning of QoE cannot be measured objectively and UPQ is a good substitute for this. ABC refers to the best connection experienced by the user. UPQ would be the best measure of this. If the current UPQ is below satisfactory level then this can also trigger a change in the AHP weights and/or GRA formula so that ABC is achieved. In fact, UPQ can also be used as a factor to decide when to handover. When UPQ degrades below an acceptable level, handover can be initiated.

FUTURE RESEARCH DIRECTIONS

Future work would include conducting a survey in determining the best way for users to indicate the users' preference. This survey can also be used to identify whether when given the choice of explicitly indicating preference and the benefits it entails, would users find it burdensome. Also, an extensive analysis needs to be done to identify the least number of attributes that can correctly identify the context of the network selection environment without jeopardizing the quality of the network selection methodology. This extensive analysis is important in reducing the number of attributes in consideration thereby increasing the efficiency of the selection policy. Further works need to be done to find the correlation between velocity and throughput and PLR so that the dynamic weight assignment is accurate. The relationship between dwell time and QoS attributes needs to be established as well. Extensive research needs to be conducted to identify the connection between UPQ value and the QoS attributes as well.

A challenge for 5G networks will be a dramatic increase in the number of devices to be supported. Mobile networks will no longer be concerned primarily with person-to-person communications, as billions of new devices for remote sensing, telemetry and control applications lead to vast numbers of machine-to-machine and person-to-machine interactions, as part of the Internet of Things (IoT). Many of these devices will be simple, low-energy apparatus and in some cases may be located in remote locations or deep inside buildings. While the volume of data involved in each transaction may not be large, the sheer number of devices and transactions will require new approaches, to achieve reliable, efficient and secure communication without compromising the efficiency of other aspects of 5G networks.

A further challenge will be the breadth of requirements across different applications and devices and the need to satisfy all of these efficiently (in terms of both spectrum and energy consumption) and securely. Fast real-time data transmission may be required by some devices in some locations at certain times of day, but the same devices may have much more modest needs for data throughput or latency in other places and at other times. Some devices, such as those involved in remote monitoring or telemetry, may require quite low levels of data transmission and may be tolerant to large delays, but there will be millions of these devices to be served in any given network and in some cases the locations may create coverage challenges. Between the extremes there will be a myriad of variations.

Not only will there be diverse service requirements, however 5G network deployments are unlikely to be uniform across the coverage area. Different technologies, spectrum and architectures will be deployed in different locations, according to the local technical and commercial requirements and the evolution path from legacy equipment. The 5G system must be able to respond dynamically to the requirements of specific devices and applications, applying whichever technologies and spectrum are most suitable and sharing resources with other networks where appropriate. This has implications for the overall architectural design of 5G, as well as the individual technologies and techniques used to deliver services. Context-aware mapping of services to technologies

Advances in individual technologies and techniques will help to address isolated technical targets for 5G. However, 5G is not just about capacity, data rate and latency. It is also about extreme flexibility, to deliver a wide variety of services across a range of environments using disparate technologies in a highly efficient, robust and cost effective way. Achieving the levels of flexibility, agility and efficiency needed by future mobile networks will depend on new architectural approaches, including context-awareness and virtualization.

5G networks will require context-aware mapping of services to technologies, to take a holistic view of the services required in a particular area and the technologies available to deliver them. The network will make dynamic decisions on which resources to use to deliver each service, so as to achieve the necessary quality of service in the most efficient way possible.

CONCLUSION

This chapter has presented a holistic policy framework for context based network selection suitable for various scenarios taking into account the environment of all the important stakeholders involved thereby allowing for the context to be derived. Context based network selection is very vital in order to provide ABC, seamless and ubiquitous network connection. This chapter has shown how the proposed framework can achieve the ABC. Moreover, an implementation methodology is detailed in order to highlight the efficacy of this framework.

Moving from "Always Connected" to "Always Best Connected" is considered critical for next generation networks. This chapter briefly presented a considerable set of enabling technologies that are expected to contribute in converting this vision to reality. It is clear that a number of extensions to today's networks are required, affecting most of the layers of a traditional protocol stack, in order to introduce the required functionality. This functionality, focuses mostly on adding a considerable degree of flexibility to the network for adjusting to different "conditions", in terms of traffic, transmission quality, user preferences, available tariffs, etc. The next big challenge will be to integrate these technologies in a single network architecture, which has the intelligence to perform the required adjustments.

REFERENCES

Sleem, A. E., & Kumar, A. (2005). Handoff management in wireless data networks using topography-aware mobility prediction. *Journal of Parallel and Distributed Computing*, *65*(8), 963–982. doi:10.1016/j.jpdc.2004.12.006

Alkhawlani, M. M., & Alsalem, K. A. (2010), Radio network selection for tight-coupled wireless networks. *Proceedings of the 7th IEEE International Conference on Informatics and Systems (INFOS)*.

Athula, B. (2013). Developing a predictive model of quality of experience for internet video. *Proceedings of the ACM SIGCOMM 2013 Conference*.

Bari, F., & Leung, V. C. M. (2009). Use of non-monotonic utility in multi-attribute network selection, Wireless Technology. *Springer US*, *2009*, 21–39.

Çalhan, A., & Çeken, C. (2010), An adaptive neuro-fuzzy based vertical handoff decision algorithm for wireless heterogeneous networks. *Proceedings of IEEE 21st International Symposium on Personal Indoor and Mobile Radio Communications (PIMRC)*. doi:10.1109/PIMRC.2010.5671693

Ceken, C., & Arslan, H. (2009). An adaptive fuzzy logic based vertical handoff decision algorithm for wireless heterogeneous networks. *Proceedings of the 10th IEEE Annual Wireless and Microwave Technology Conference, WAMICON'09*, 1-9. doi:10.1109/WAMICON.2009.5207312

Charilas, D. E. (2009). Application of Fuzzy AHP and ELECTRE to network selection. Mobile Lightweight Wireless Systems. *Springer Berlin Heidelberg, 2009*, 63–73.

Charilas, D. E., & Athansios, D. P. (2010). Multiaccess radio network enviroments. *Vehicular Technology Magazine, IEEE*, 5(4), 40–49. doi:10.1109/MVT.2010.939107

Charilas, D. E., Athanasios, D. P., & Ourania, I. M. (2012). A Unified Network Selection Framework Using Principal Component Analysis and Multi Attribute Decision Making. *Wireless Personal Communications*, 1–19.

Cherif, W. (2007). A_PSQA: Efficient real-time video streaming QoE tool in a future media internet context. *Multimedia and Expo (ICME), 2011 IEEE International Conference on*. IEEE.

Dutta, A., Das, S., Famolari, D., Ohba, Y., Taniuchi, K., Fajardo, V., & Schulzrinne, H. et al. (2007). Seamless proactive handover across heterogeneous access networks. *Wireless Personal Communications*, 43(3), 837–855. doi:10.1007/s11277-007-9266-3

Ei, T., & Wang, T. (2010). A trajectory-aware handoff algorithm based on GPS information. *Annals of Telecommunications*, 65(7-8), 411-417.

Elnaka, A. M., & Qusay, H. M. (2013), QoS traffic mapping for a multi-participant session in unified communications networks. *Proceedings of 26thAnnual IEEE Canadian Conference on Electrical and Computer Engineering (CCECE)*. doi:10.1109/CCECE.2013.6567743

ETSI Technical Report 102 643 V1.0.2. (n.d.). *Human Factors (HF); Quality of Experience (QoE) requirements for real-time communication services*. ETSI.

ETSI. (2002). *TS. 123 107 V4. 3.0 (2002-01) Universal Mobile Telecommunications System (UMTS); Quality of Service (QoS) concept and architecture (3GPP TS 23.107 version 4.3. 0 Release 4)*. ETSI Technical Specification.

Gakhar, K., Gravey, A., & Leroy, A. (2005) IROISE: a new QoS architecture for IEEE 802.16 and IEEE 802.11 e interworking. *Proceedings of the 2nd International Conference on Broadband Networks (BROADNETS'05)*. doi:10.1109/ICBN.2005.1589787

Ghahfarokhi, S. B., & Movahhedinia, N. (2010). A personalized QoE-aware handover decision based on distributed reinforcement learning. *Wireless Networks*, 1–22.

Gupta, V., & Rohil, M.K. (2012). Enhancing Wi-Fi with IEEE 802.11 u for Mobile Data Offloading. *International Journal of Mobile Network Communications and Telematics, 2*(4).

Herman, H. (2011). Nonlinearity modelling of QoE for video streaming over wireless and mobile network. *Proceedings of the Second IEEE International Conference on Intelligent Systems, Modelling and Simulation (ISMS)*. doi:10.1109/ISMS.2011.55

Huang, Z.-Q., Bai, S-N., & Jaeil, J. (2009). A MIH Services Based Application-Driven Vertical Handoff Scheme for Wireless Networks. *Proceedings of the 5th IEEE International Joint Conference on INC, IMS and IDC,(NCM'09)*. doi:10.1109/NCM.2009.254

IEEE 802.21. (2008). *IEEE standard for local and metropolitan area networks: Media independent handover services*. IEEE.

ITU-T Rec. G.1070. (2007). *Opinion model for videophone applications*. ITU-T.

ITU-T Rec. J.246. (2008). *Perceptual audiovisual quality measurement techniques for multimedia services over digital cable television networks in presence of reduced bandwidth reference*. ITU-T.

ITU-T Rec. J.247. (2008). *Objective perceptual multimedia video quality measurement in the presence of a full reference*. ITU-T.

ITU-T Rec. P.800. (1996). *Methods for subjective determination of transmission quality*. ITU-T.

ITU-T Rec, . (1999). *Subjective video quality assessment method for multimedia applications*. ITU-T.

IEEE Standard 802.21. (2007). *Media Independent Handover Specifications*. IEEE.

Huang, Z.-Q., Bai, S.-N., & Jaeil, J. l. (2009). A MIH services based application-driven vertical handoff scheme for wireless networks. *Proceedings of the 5th IEEE Int'l. Joint Conf. on INC, IMs and IDC*, 1428 – 1430. doi:10.1109/NCM.2009.254

Jiao, J., Ma, H., Qiao, Y., Du, Y., Kong, W., & Wu, Z.-C. (2014). Design of farm environmental monitoring system based on the Internet of Things. *Advance Journal of Food Science and Technology, 6*(3), 368–373.

Kaleem, F., Mehbodniya, A., Islam, A., Yen, K. K., & Adachi, F. (2013). Dynamic target wireless network selection technique using fuzzy linguistic variables. *China Communications, 10*(1), 1–16. doi:10.1109/CC.2013.6457526

Kaloxylos, A., Eigenmann, R., Teye, F., Politopoulou, Z., Wolfert, S., Shrank, C., & Kormentzas, G. et al. (2012). Farm management systems and the future internet era. *Computers and Electronics in Agriculture, 89*, 130–144. doi:10.1016/j.compag.2012.09.002

Kassar, M., Kervella, B., & Pujolle, G. (2008). An overview of vertical handover decision strategies in heterogeneous wireless networks. *Computer Communications, 31*(10), 2607–2620. doi:10.1016/j.comcom.2008.01.044

Klaue, J., Berthold, R., & Adam, W. (2003). Evalvid–A framework for video transmission and quality evaluation. Computer Performance Evaluation. Modelling Techniques and Tools. *Springer Berlin Heidelberg, 2003*, 255–272.

Kuo, Y., Yang, T., & Huang, G.-W. (2008). The use of grey relational analysis in solving multiple attribute decision-making problems. *Computers & Industrial Engineering, 55*(1), 80–93. doi:10.1016/j.cie.2007.12.002

Lahby, M., Leghris, C., & Adib, A. (2012). New multi access selection method using differentiated weight of access interface. *Proceedings of IEEE International Conference on. Communications and Information Technology (ICCIT)*, 237 – 242. doi:10.1109/ICCITechnol.2012.6285799

Lahby, M., & Adib, A. (2013). Network selection mechanism by using M-AHP/GRA for heterogeneous networks. *Proceedings of the 6th Joint IFIP IEEE Wireless and Mobile Networking Conference (WMNC)*, 1-6. doi:10.1109/WMNC.2013.6549009

Lahby, M., Leghris, C., & Abdellah, A. (2013). A Novel Ranking Algorithm Based Network Selection For Heterogeneous Wireless Access. *Journal of Networks, 8*(2), 263–272. doi:10.4304/jnw.8.2.263-272

Lampropoulos, G., & Apostolis, K. (2008). Media-independent handover for seamless service provision in heterogeneous networks. *Communications Magazine, IEEE, 46*(1), 64–71. doi:10.1109/MCOM.2008.4427232

Long, Y., & Guo, D-X. (2012). *A Satellite Heterogeneous Network Selection Algorithm Combining AHP and TOPSIS*. Academic Press.

Makela, J., Ylianttila, M., & Pahlavan, K. (2000). Handoff decision in multi-service networks. *The 11ᵗʰ IEEE International Symposium on Personal, Indoor and Mobile Radio Communications.* doi:10.1109/PIMRC.2000.881503

Márquez-Barja, J., Calafate, C. T., Cano, J.-C., & Manzoni, P. (2011). An overview of vertical handover techniques: Algorithms, protocols and tools. *Computer Communications, 34*(8), 985–997. doi:10.1016/j.comcom.2010.11.010

Menkovski, V., Exarchakos, G., & Liotta, A. (2010). Online QoE prediction. *Proceedings of the Second IEEE International Workshop on Quality of Multimedia Experience (QoMEX).* doi:10.1109/QOMEX.2010.5517692

Mohamed, S., & Rubino, G. (2002). A study of real-time packet video quality using random neural networks. *IEEE Transactions on Circuits and Systems for Video Technology, 12*(12), 1071–1083.

Nguyen, V., & Quoc, T. (2013). *Multi-Criteria Optimization of Access Selection to Improve the Quality of Experience in Heterogeneous Wireless Access Networks.* Academic Press.

Mohanan, V., Budiarto, R., & Zainon, W. N. M. W. (2012). Holistic network selection for wireless mobile nodes in a 4G environment. *Proceedings of the 18th IEEE Asia-Pacific Conference on Communications (APCC).* doi:10.1109/APCC.2012.6388100

Mohanan, V., Budiarto, R., & Osman, M. A. (2013). Holistic network selection using dynamic weights to achieve personalized ABC. *Proceedings of the 19th IEEE Asia-Pacific Conference on Communications (APCC),* 196 – 201. doi:10.1109/APCC.2013.6765941

Mohanan, V., Budiarto, R., & Aldmour, I. (2015). Network Selection Problems-QoE vs QoS Who is the Winner? *Computer Engineering and Applications Journal, 1*(1).

Morais, R., Matos, S. G., Fernandes, M. A., Valente, A. L. G., Soares, S. F. S. P., Ferreira, P. J. S. G., & Reis, M. J. C. S. (2008). Sun, wind and water flow as energy supply for small stationary data acquisition platforms. *Journal of Computer Electronic Agriculture, 64*(2), 120–132. doi:10.1016/j.compag.2008.04.005

Nithyanandan, L., Bharathi, V., & Prabhavathi, P. (2013). User centric network selection in wireless hetnets. *International Journal of Wireless & Mobile Networks, 5*(3).

Piamrat, K. (2011). QoE-aware vertical handover in wireless heterogeneous networks. *Proceedings of the 7th IEEE International Conference on Wireless Communications and Mobile Computing Conference (IWCMC).* doi:10.1109/IWCMC.2011.5982513

ITU-T Rec, . (2008). *Vocabulary for performance and quality of service, Amendment 2: New definitions for inclusion in Recommendation ITU-T P. 10/G. 100* (p. 10). Geneva: Int. Telecomm. Union.

Rein, S., Frank, H. P. F., & Reisslein, M. (2005). Voice quality evaluation in wireless packet communication systems: A tutorial and performance results for RHC. *Wireless Communications, IEEE, 12*(1), 60–67. doi:10.1109/MWC.2005.1404574

Rivera, S. (2013). QoS-QoE correlation neural network modeling for mobile internet services. *Proceedings of IEEE International Conference on. Computing, Management and Telecommunications (ComManTel).* doi:10.1109/ComManTel.2013.6482369

Saaty, T. L. (1990). *Decision making for leaders: the analytic hierarchy process for decisions in a complex world* (Vol. 2). RWS publications.

Saliba, A. J., Beresford, M. A., Ivanovich, M., & Fitzpatrick, P. (2005). User-perceived quality of service in wireless data networks. *Personal and Ubiquitous Computing, 9*(6), 413–422. doi:10.1007/s00779-005-0034-7

Sánchez-Macián, A. (2006). A framework for the automatic calculation of quality of experience in telematic services. *Proceedings of the 13th HP-OVUA Workshop.*

Savitha, K., & Chandrasekar, C. (2011). *Vertical Handover decision schemes using SAW and WPM for Network selection in Heterogeneous Wireless Networks.* arXiv preprint arXiv:1109.4490

Shen, D.-M. (2010), The QoE-oriented Heterogeneous Network Selection Based on Fuzzy AHP Methodology. *Proceeding of the Fourth International Conference on Mobile Ubiquitous Computing, Systems, Services and Technologies (UBICOMM 2010).*

Skorin-Kapov, L. (2013). Survey and Challenges of QoE Management Issues in Wireless Networks. *Journal of Computer Networks and Communications.*

Song, Q.-Y., & Jamalipour, A. (2005). A network selection mechanism for next generation networks. *Proceedings of IEEE International Conference on Communications (ICC 2005), 2.* doi:10.1109/ICC.2005.1494578

Sasirekha, V., & Ilanzkumaran, M. (2013). Heterogeneous wireless network selection using FAHP integrated with TOPSIS and VIKOR. *Proceedings of IEEE Int'l. Conf. on. Pattern Recognition, Informatics and Mobile Engineering (PRIME)*, 399-407. doi:10.1109/ICPRIME.2013.6496510

Stevens-Navarro, E., Martinez-Morales, J. D., & Pineda-Rico, U. (2012). Evaluation of vertical handoff decision algorithms based on MADM methods for heterogeneous wireless networks. *Journal of Applied Research And Technology*, *10*(4), 534–548.

Tara, A.-Y., Sethom, K., & Pujolle, G. (2007). Seamless continuity of service across WLAN and WMAN networks: Challenges and performance evaluation. *Proceedings of the 2nd IEEE/IFIP International Workshop on Broadband Convergence Networks*.

Tran, P. N., & Boukhatem, N. (2008). Comparison of MADM decision algorithms for interface selection in heterogeneous wireless networks. *Proceedings of the 16th IEEE Int'l. Conf. on Software, Telecommunications and Computer Networks, 2008 (SoftCOM 2008)*, 119-124. doi:10.1109/SOFTCOM.2008.4669464

Verma, R., & Singh, N. P. (2013). GRA based network selection in heterogeneous wireless networks. *Wireless Personal Communications*, *72*(2), 1437–1452. doi:10.1007/s11277-013-1087-y

Wang, H.-Q. (2012). Intelligent Access Selection in Cognitive Networks: A Fuzzy Neural Network Approach. *Journal of Computer Information Systems*, *8*(21), 8877–8884.

Wei, Y., Ke, L., & Dong, Z. (2010), Development of wireless intelligent control terminal of greenhouse based on ZigBee. *T. CSAE,* *26*(3), 198-202.

Wu, J.-S., Yang, S.-F., & Hwang, B.-J. (2009). A terminal-controlled vertical handover decision scheme in IEEE 802.21-enabled heterogeneous wireless networks. *International Journal of Communication Systems*, *22*(7), 819–834. doi:10.1002/dac.996

Zang, Q., Yang, X.L., & Zhou, Y.M. (2007). A wireless solution for greenhouse monitoring and control system based on ZigBee technology. *Journal of Zhejiang University Sci. A,* *8*(10), 1584-1587.

KEY TERMS AND DEFINITIONS

AHP: Analytic Hieararchy Process, a multi-crieterion decision making method that allows decision makers to model a complex problem in a hierarchical structure, representing the relationships of the goal, criteria, and alternatives.

Always Best Connected Network: A network that allows a person to have access to applications using the devices and network technologies that best suit the needs or profile at any time.

Context-Aware Network: A form of computer network synthesized of the properties of dumb network and intelligent network architecture.

GRA: Grey Relational Analysis, an analysis method that uses a specific concept of information and defines situations with no perfect information.

IoF: Internet of Farming, the implementation of Internet of Thing in agriculture with the aims to support precision agriculture to increase productivity.

NSP: Network Selection Problem, selecting an optimum network connection by a mobile node from available network connections with multiple criteria.

Chapter 8
Smart Real-Time Internet-of-Things Network Monitoring System

Adil Fahad Alharthi
Albaha University, Saudi Arabia

Mohammed Yahya Alzahrani
Albaha University, Saudi Arabia

Ismat Aldmour
Albaha University, Saudi Arabia

Deris Stiawan
Universitas Sriwijaya, Indonesia

Muhammad Fermi Pasha
Monash University Malaysia, Malaysia

Rahmat Budiarto
Albaha University, Saudi Arabia

ABSTRACT

The network traffic of the Internet became huge and more complex due to the expansion of the Internet technology in supporting the convergence of IP networks, Internet of Things, and social networks. As a consequence, a more sophisticated network monitoring tool is desired in order to prevent an enterprise network from malware attacks, to maintain its availability as high as possible at any time, and to maintain the network's healthiness. This chapter offers a development of real-time network monitoring tool platform. The research component of this chapter attempts to answer the challenges of making the monitoring tool become smarter and more accurate by applying artificial intelligence techniques. In addition, a research on buffering techniques to speed up the traffic data acquisition process and micro-controller unit design for sensor-based applications are also carried out. In the development component, some ground works has already been done such as network traffic packets capturing modules, and packets decoding modules. The system development uses Java Eclipse platform.

DOI: 10.4018/978-1-5225-2799-2.ch008

Copyright © 2018, IGI Global. Copying or distributing in print or electronic forms without written permission of IGI Global is prohibited.

INTRODUCTION

In today's world, not only computers are connected to the Internet, other devices such as smartphones, smart cars, sensors, home appliances, and so on, are also connected to the Internet. This, so called Internet of Things, makes the network traffics become more complex and vulnerable. Computer networks provide the shared resources, accounting, e-mail, Internet and Intranet that is used within organizations. It helps business to reduce cost, streamlines processes, and facilitates the sharing of information and the same time opens new vulnerabilities.

Most computer networks provide a lot of features that can be used to help the running of a business however, if a problem occurs within the network itself, the productivity of the company is severely affected. Therefore, it is important to find the cause of the problem as soon as possible. Such a task can normally be very tedious in a complex network.

Many commercial network monitoring tools and software are available today, vary from as simple as only monitoring segments of network up to systems with sophisticated capabilities such as visualization of nodes activities, IDS and intelligent engine to analyze the traffic as well as to predict requirements for future system development.

The traffic on the network may be generated by thousands of devices and thousands of software drivers and applications. Without the proper tools that can interpret, analyze and display network traffic and any related problems, a network administrator is limited to the time-consuming trial and error method to try to identify a problem. With a network analyzer application, such problems can be immediately detected and resolved. Nonetheless, a simple network analyzer application is no longer enough. To keep a network performs at top-notch condition, a network administrator needs a tool that has ability to

- Have intelligence built in.
- Even of tracking and resolving some of the problems on its own.
- Detect network viruses and provide the early warning needed.
- Point out the sources of the virus, and close it if possible.
- Provide intrusion detection and warning.
- Work in all IP platforms, including IPv4 and IPv6.
- Cross platform that support any Operating systems.
- Capture and monitor traffic from devices attached to Internet.

Autonomous intrusion agents, commonly referred to as 'worms', are fast becoming a popular method of network and system compromise. The most famous start to the history of network worms is the Morris worm, which quickly crippled a substantial portion of the 1988 Internet. Worms have been a persistent security threat on the Internet, though for most of this history they focused on Windows hosts.

A real-time smart network monitoring and security platform will be implemented as a product named InstaMon.

InstaMon performs real time data collection of network traffic that flows on a local area network (LAN) segment and analyzes the data that is decoded, performs statistical calculation and displays the analyzed data. The objective is to create an intelligent tool to assist network and system administrators by anticipating and giving intelligent information for preventive measures to be taken so that damages as a result of system or network down time that can be very costly is minimized. Real-time network analysis helps to detect and resolve network faults and performance problems quickly. It even has the power to analyze multi-topology, multi-protocol networks—automatically.

BACKGROUND

With the additional traffic generated by the Internet of Things, computer networks traffic are growing at a drastic rate and thus network administrators can no longer monitor network problems by only relying on the traditional method such as Simple Network Management Protocol (SNMP) and Remote Monitoring (RMON). What network administrators need is the latest passive monitoring approach. Because as the number of hosts increase number of SNMP agents increase as well, which will result in a massive amount of traffic pumped to the network due to the fact that SNMP based tools are active in nature.

There are few of ways to monitor/protect network segments. InstaMon will initially tap into a network segment using passive capturing method (Matthews, Cottrell, & Salomoni, 1999). This will give the administrator access to traffic statistics of a network segment. Secondly for network devices with an internal RMON (Remote MONitoring) probe, the RMON Extension™ gives an access to the information gathered internally by the network devices. Finally for network devices with internal SNMP agents, the SNMP Extension™ gives an access to SNMP alerts (traps) and current status of the network devices. InstaMon uses the first method to monitor a network segment. The reason is that it is the most compatible method supported by all the switches.

Not all features used by the network analyzer to monitor a network are built into network devices.

The reasons are:

1. As for SNMP 1, it reports only whether devices are functioning properly. This can prove to be too vague and does not pinpoint the problem-causing device. Industry has attempted to define a new set of protocols called SNMP 2 that can provide additional information upon recognition of a problem. However, standardization efforts have not been successful.

2. Although, RMON can prove to be a very useful network-monitoring tool, it is still plagued with various problems besides high costs. Even with the introduction of RMON 2, a problem with incompatibility between vendor implementations has still not been alleviated. Because of this, RMON tool vendors have been adding propriety extensions to their products to make them more attractive to network managers who are demanding more functionality. There is still much risk of becoming dependent on a single vendor.

3. The passive approach, which is what InstaMon uses, does not increase the traffic on the network for the measurements, unlike SNMP and RMON where the polling required to collect the data and the traps and alarms (SNMP and RMON) all generate network traffic, which can be substantial. The general passive approach is extremely valuable in network trouble-shooting, however it is limited in certain ability to emulate error scenarios or isolating problems arising from other networks. Thus, in order to overcome these limitations, InstaMon uses an advanced passive approach. That is why an advance network traffic monitoring application such as InstaMon is needed to overcome the problem faced today.

4. With the Internet of Things coming into the picture, the current Internet traffic become more complex. More intelligent technique to detect anomaly in the network is needed. This chapter considers intelligent agent, evolving connectionist system, and computer forensics techniques to be incorporated into the Instamon in order to provide more accuracy in anomaly detection strategy.

INTERNET OF THINGS MONITORING SYSTEM

As technologies are changing and advancing rapidly, new technologies have emerged which were not anticipated previously. These new technologies are gaining popularity, and are predicted to create the de facto standards in their respective areas. These include Wi-Fi or WLAN (IEEE 802.11b) and Internet Protocol version 6- IPv6 (Lohith et al. 2011). As a potential commercial product, InstaMon must encompass all these technologies in order to be a successful product. InstaMon will be using a modular architecture as a measure to allow it to modularly incorporate rapidly changing network technologies as shown in the diagram in Figure 1. This modularity would allow changes to be confined to an affected module instead of the whole product, minimizing the development cost and reducing the time to release the product.

Instamon consists of 4 main modules: Real-time network monitoring, Intelligent engine to detect anomaly, Network Security (Intrusion detection and network forensics), and Internet of Things Applications and monitoring. The overall structure of the project is shown in Figure 2.

Real-Time Network Monitoring

Packet Driver, a low-level capturing component for network monitoring application, which interacts directly with the Network Interface Card (NIC) running in the operating system kernel level, provides interface for user level application as shown in the diagram in Figure 3.

The packet driver is the major component of network monitoring application such as InstaMon, basically it provides high level Application Program Interface (API) for capturing wireless packet (A set of routines provides to network monitoring application such as InstaMon to direct the performance of packet capturing procedures by a computer's operating system). One disturbingly powerful aspect of packet drivers is their ability to place the hosting machine's network adapter into "promiscuous

Figure 1. Overall architecture of the proposed Instamon

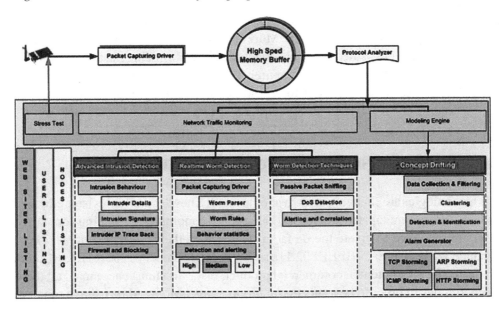

Figure 2. Development of InstaMon: a real-time smart network monitoring and security platform

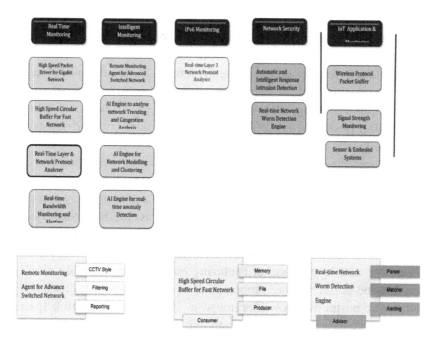

Figure 3. Packet drivers in Instamon

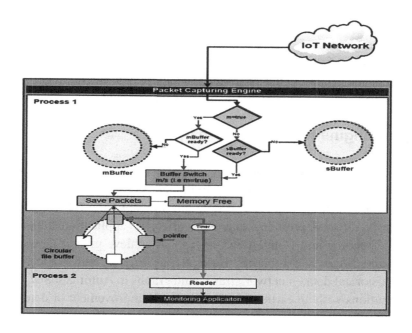

mode". Network adapters running in promiscuous mode receive not only the data directed to the machine hosting the sniffing software, but also all the traffic on the physically connected local network. It must provide high-speed packet capturing mechanism, which allows network-monitoring application to capture gigabits of information flowing in the computer network (3Com, 1990).

This module also focuses on the implementation of a circular buffer technology to enhance the capability of the capturing engine. A circular buffer is an efficient method of temporary storage allocation which entails the rotation of data through an array of buffer positions. In a circular buffer, the data writer advances one step every time new data is entered into the buffer. Once the end of the buffer is reached, this process is restarted once again from the beginning of the buffer. Data reading is done in the exact same manner. A circular buffer holds several advantages when compared to a conventional buffer. Firstly, it ensures approximately constant-time insertion and removal of data values. In addition, it also avoids the producer-consumer conundrum by enabling the packet analyzer to read up the packets from the circular file buffer in a smooth and efficient manner. This process is done concurrently with the insertion of data by the packet capturing engine. Careful calibration is done to ensure that the buffer writing process is done marginally faster than the packet analysis to avoid buffer overflow (Parameswar, 1996). All these will help to ensure a highly efficient capturing engine. Instamon is also designed to have capability to monitor IPv6 traffic.

Some concerns on the modules include: Network Driver Interface Specification (NDIS) version 5 whereby it is the de facto standard of interacting with NIC (Note: NDIS is a standard defined by Microsoft and 3Com), high-speed memory buffer to handle the large amount of data stream coming from the NIC, high speed packet filter to reduce the information passing from the NIC to computer's main memory, and the bottleneck of the I/O bus or Peripheral Component Interconnect (PCI) bus in the handling Gigabits of data (McCanne & Jacobson, 1992).

Intelligent Engine to Detect Anomaly

In years people have dream of one day, when computer handle all daily activities using intelligence as similar to human intelligent. The dream is realized by the arrival of Artificial Intelligent (AI). People are now applying AI technologies to the solution of difficult problems across a variety of application domains such as Network Trending and Congestion Analysis to achieve greater automation in network maintenances and supports. Basically, an Engine with AI technologies will tracks historical data on network traffic and graphs it. Automatically, compare current operations with an earlier benchmark, track improvement or deterioration of performance over a period of months or years, and predict when additional bandwidth or server resources will be needed.

It will also detect problem conditions to a network automatically. Using trending data, it can give early warning of a possible problem. Automatically define triggers with each with many adjustments and sub-trigger settings, as well as an offset-based, user-defined trigger. Each trigger can have an associated action, which includes pop-up message windows, activating captures, starting/appending logs, executing external programs (for example, page or send email), etc. In short, AI engines apply the technology of AI to generate a network trend using recorded network traffic information such as network utilization, broadcast traffic percentage and protocol distribution. Using artificial intelligent again, current network trend is compare against history trend, and with the help of predefined probabilistic model it can alert the network administrator in the situation of network anomalies such as network congestion, broadcast abnormality.

Concerns to be considered include: neural network paradigms, knowledge-based systems, evolutionary algorithms, and optimization techniques in providing above mentioned feature; graphing and data recording technique to provide network trend presentation; software alarm for network error using AI techniques

The Evolving Clustering Method (ECM) is an online clustering method that performs well on one-pass partitioning of an input space. ECMc is a method to partition scarce input. ECMm is a clustering method for the purpose of clustering network traffic data streams. ECMm algorithm is a combination of ECM algorithm and its extension ECMc so that it can use the number of cluster created in previous process and optimize its cluster center in online mode. By having the advantages of ECM with a fast one-past online clustering and ECMc which optimize the cluster center, ECMm can perform online network traffic clustering with optimum results. There are 2 scenarios to show how ECMm work in clustering network traffic data input stream. The first scenario is the condition where ECMm is first-time run in the particular network and no profile has been created before. In this condition, ECMm works in one-pass clustering by creating and updating clusters in online mode. The ECMm is used to detect outliers if the current traffics collection is noisy and not attack-free. The second scenario is the condition where all the profiles have been created, where ECMm normally does after its first running.

ECMm is focused on component-level design and input-output data format. The ECMm algorithm is constructed into several components such as Objective function, Optimization function, Update cluster function, Main function, Create Cluster function. These components are representing some repeating process in the algorithm itself and each component is implemented as a separate function. The designs of these functions are following the theme of low coupling and high cohesion. Figure 4 shows the work flow of the ECM.

Figure 4. ECMm work flow

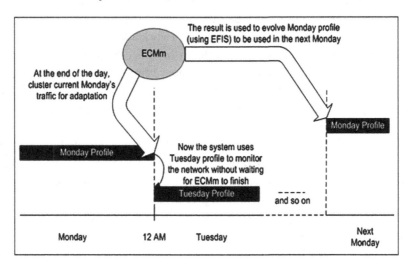

As for the input-output format, for the input, ECMm is fed with cumulative information every 5 minutes which contains the time when the traffic is captured. Total network traffic data (packets) at that time interval, and its total byte. This information is extracted from the collected network traffic data streams. As for the output, information about the cluster center and its radius, a matrix that maps the inputs index into the cluster where it belongs, the objective value and the input itself after being normalized is included. Figure 5 illustrates the clustering process and Figure 6 shows the snapshots of clustering results

Figure 5. Clustering process

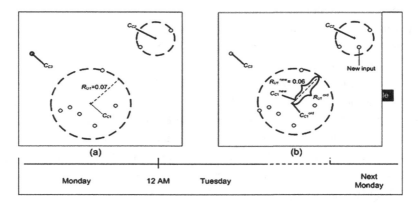

Figure 6. Snapshot of clustering results

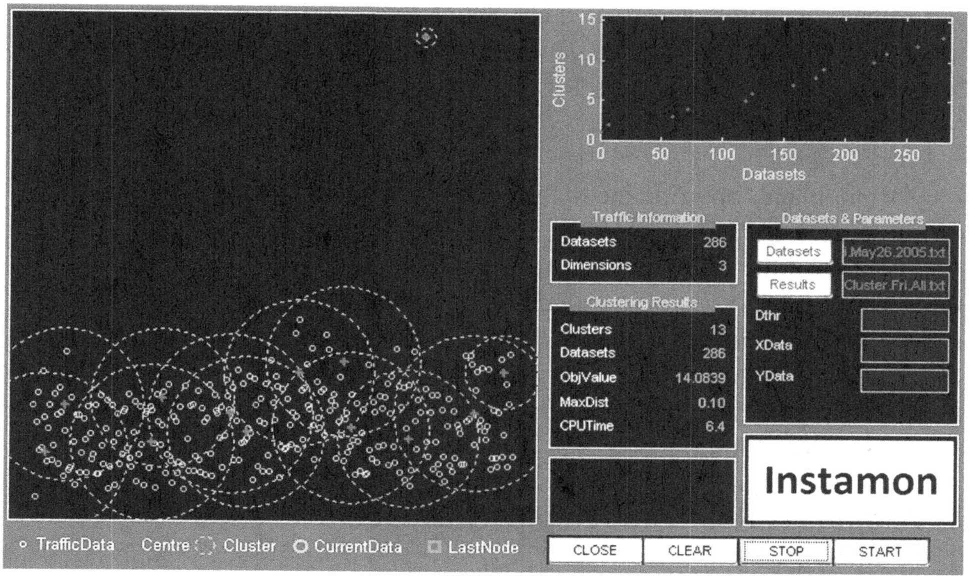

IoT Network Security

Malina et all. (2016) states that an IoT security is the area of endeavor concerned with safeguarding connected devices and networks in the Internet of things (IoT). Much of the increase in IoT communication comes from computing devices and embedded sensor systems used in industrial machine-to-machine (M2M) communication, home and building automation, vehicle to vehicle communication and wearable computing devices.

The idea of networking appliances and other objects is relatively new, security has not always been considered in product design. IoT products are often sold with old and unpatched embedded operating systems and software. Furthermore, purchasers often fail to change the default passwords on smart devices -- or if they do change them, fail to select sufficiently strong passwords. To improve security, an IoT device that needs to be directly accessible over the Internet, should be segmented into its own network and have network access restricted. The network segment should then be monitored to identify potential anomalous traffic, and action should be taken if there is a problem (Tankard, 2015; Razzaque et al., 2016).

The main motivation behind this security module is the existence of a big number of attacks and viruses that severely affect the performance of computer networks. Such attacks include overloading the network with dummy packets which will then destroy the efficiency of the network. In general, network security systems have some common objectives to fulfill. This chapter focuses on certain areas which are part of these common objectives. This section looks at the area of security policy which has to be adopted by any organization that are implementing and maintaining computer networks. Based on the security policy, an intrusion detection system that will perform the following tasks:

- Monitor and capturing the traffic on the network to be used later.
- Filter the traffic based on the source and destination IP addresses and the content of the packet (data).
- Detect attacks to the system using the Misuse and Anomaly Detection method.
- Employing neural network techniques to minimize false positive and maximizing the ability to learn from detected scenarios.
- Adopting fuzzy logic algorithm for abnormal activities to minimize the possibilities of intruders.

AI Engine for Real-Time Anomaly Detection

The explosion number of IoT applications also raises new issues, where various devices with multi-platform converge into one centralized, interconnected, shared, multi user, multi devices and flexible network. Research works by Microsoft (1991) and Stalling (1999) declare main issues on IoT. Growing number of internetwork network establish a heterogeneous network which is more complex than before. With various devices attached in the network, it will rise up technical problems in monitoring, managing, surveying and early detection of the network itself.

This sub-module utilizes EFIS: An Evolvable-Neural Based Fuzzy Inference System for Network Traffic Anomaly Detection. EFIS is an evolvable-neural based fuzzy inference system for profile creation and network traffic anomaly detection in online mode. It utilizes the evolving connectionist system framework which makes it able to evolve in open space to deal with concept drift problem and continuously monitor the network traffic to detect anomaly in online and lifelong mode. The idea of EFIS comes from a combination of features and structure of HyFIS and DENFIS model so that it is more suitable for network traffic data. The main feature of EFIS is that it is adaptable and the membership functions of the fuzzy predicates and the fuzzy rules can be adapted if necessary. EFIS structure has 2 main parts. The first one is the Profile Creation and Management (PCM) module which created and extracts rules from ECMm results, and the second one is the Neuro-Fuzzy Model (NFM) module which is a 5 layer neural network-based fuzzy system. Figure 7

Figure 7. Intrusion detection system model

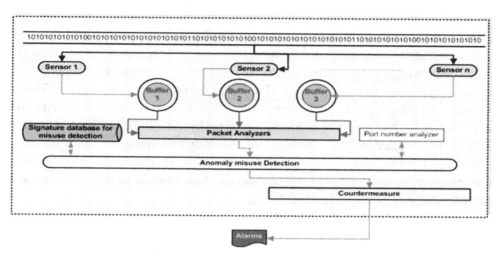

depicts the intrusion detection system model. The Monitor process consists of Capturing, Buffering and Analyzing Network packets. The sensors monitor and capture every packet in the network. For the buffering, the packets will be saved in a circular buffer for fast processing and overcoming any packet lose and to enhance the system performance. Figure 8 illustrates the rule extraction process in the EFIS

Figure 8. Rule extraction process in EFIS

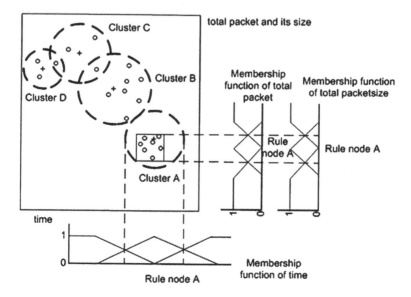

SNMP-Based Anomaly Detection

There are some solutions from a various IoT Infrastructure vendors with various standards that should be integrated. Unfortunately, due to the reason of incompatibility, not all of the things be able to adapt because they use their own proprietary technologies even though these technologies are claimed to be multiplatform support. These various technology also has encouraged the appearance of heterogeneous network information. Research works conducted conducted by (Zhenhui et al. (2014); Hyunho et al. (2014); Sakakibara et al. (2009)) mentioned that the heterogeneous IoT network must have services, with the following characteristics: (i) network transparency, (ii) transparency on the location of the service, (iii) transparency of data formats, and (iv) transparency of control protocols.

A problem related to the fact where each IoT device has a different Simple Network Management Protocol (SNMP) versions have been discussed in Yongqi et al. (2013) and Sanchez et al. (2013). The SNMP Protocol is used for capturing inbound-outbound packet load to a monitoring application. However, the existing monitoring applications only support monitoring in a single version of the SNMP protocol. An IoT network with monitoring and early anomaly detection system can prevent system failure which in turn will increase the reliability of the IoT network itself. Authors in Sanchez et al. (2013) and Tavares et al. (2014), proposed a network monitoring application with SNMP trap. The application is already informative but yet be able to perform the monitoring task if the SNMP protocol used is different versions and it merely focuses on network traffic. Besides, works by Aydin et al. (2009) and Wang et al. (2009) confirmed that the profiles of the system network activity (user, host, server and last mile connections) can be also as an indicator to any conditions occured in the network, such as: (i) utilization reaches 95% of the total traffic in a long period of time, which is typically only 40% in the peak time, (ii) increased use of memory continuously on the main Server, (iii) data access on a server outside normal hours, (iv) some devices attempt to connect and synchronize.

In the development of IoT monitoring system for detecting failures, the SNMP protocol is the main issues, where several heterogeneous network devices use different versions of SNMP which have different characteristics and features (SNMPv1, SNMPv2 and SNMPv3). That is the reason why messages format from the SNMP become the main attention. Extracting raw data from SNMP must be done to get the "Object Identifier" of the device.

The design consists of two phases:

1. Deploying a network monitoring system for observing IoT network with heterogeneous devices,
2. Deploying early system for detecting errors based on device profiles and activities. In fact, there are several stages to design monitoring and detection system, including: data agent input, trapping the agent, storing that data into database, repeating on trapping the agent steps in case of data error and finally displaying data.

The first step is by paying attention to the monitoring of the process of "Get-Request" between managers and agents which getting some messages that occur in the process. The format of the messages from the "request and response" are: (1) Version, (2) Community name, (3) a Command (4) Request ID, (5) Error Status, (6) Error Index, and (7) value of the variable from the object.

This work refers to research works done previously by Yongqi et al. (2013) and Tavares t al. (2014) that focused on trapping traffic in SNMP and used the approaching method of SNMP messages format. SNMP has a Protocol Data Unit (PDU) as part of that message, and has five types of PDU: GetRequest PDU, GetNextRequest PDU, SetRequest PDU, GetResponse PDU and Trap PDU. Figure 9 shows example of the raw data packets that are successfully extracted from the traffic on the experimental network. SNMP is able to be installed in Raspberry "sysORDescr = STRING: The MIB module for SNMPv2 entities".

Figure 9. SNMP raw data

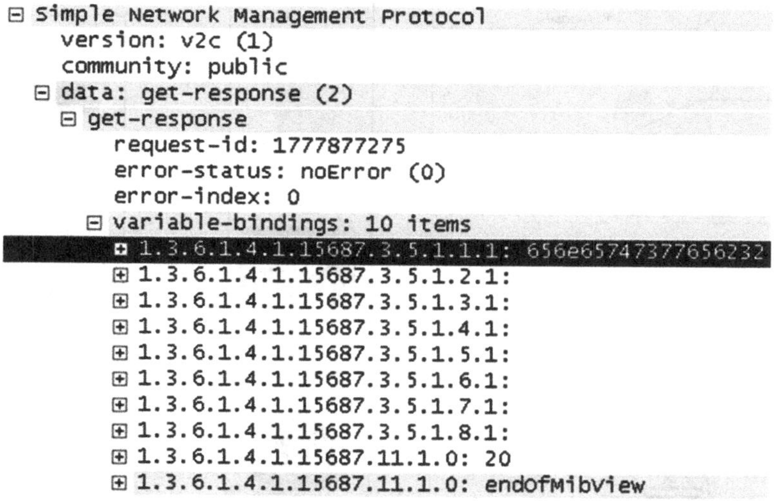

```
⊟ Simple Network Management Protocol
    version: v2c (1)
    community: public
⊟ data: get-response (2)
  ⊟ get-response
      request-id: 1777877275
      error-status: noError (0)
      error-index: 0
    ⊟ variable-bindings: 10 items
      ⊞ 1.3.6.1.4.1.15687.3.5.1.1.1: 656e65747377656232
      ⊞ 1.3.6.1.4.1.15687.3.5.1.2.1:
      ⊞ 1.3.6.1.4.1.15687.3.5.1.3.1:
      ⊞ 1.3.6.1.4.1.15687.3.5.1.4.1:
      ⊞ 1.3.6.1.4.1.15687.3.5.1.5.1:
      ⊞ 1.3.6.1.4.1.15687.3.5.1.6.1:
      ⊞ 1.3.6.1.4.1.15687.3.5.1.7.1:
      ⊞ 1.3.6.1.4.1.15687.3.5.1.8.1:
      ⊞ 1.3.6.1.4.1.15687.11.1.0: 20
      ⊞ 1.3.6.1.4.1.15687.11.1.0: endofMibView
```

Experiment

A network environment is setup at our computer network Laboratory as illustrated in Figure. 10. The network consists of two components: network peripherals and devices, in order to represent an IoT network. The topology of the experimental network is set up in such a way, so an application system to monitor and to detect anomaly on multi-platform devices attached to an IoT network can be deployed.

Device Specification and Configuration

The network pheriperals are: (1) two Cisco routers as a data packets forwarder at layer 3 (Network Layer), (2) two switches, and (3) one wireless access point router (WiFi 2.4 Ghz with AP-OpenWRT 802.11g) to provide WiFi service access from mobile devices.

The devices attached to the experimental network include:

1. Two servers to run multiple applications including Web server, database server, and other application servers with the following specifications: Intel Core

Figure 10. Experimental setup

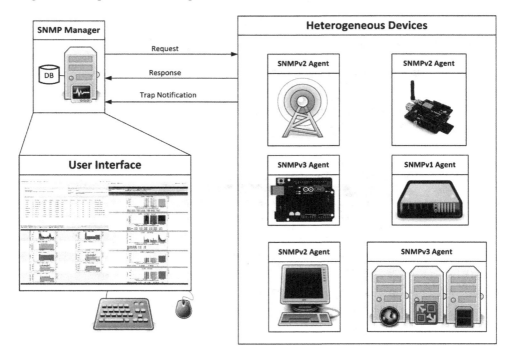

2 duo, 4048MB RAM, 320 GB Storage, Operating system: Ubuntu Server 14.04.3 LTS 64bit.

2.   Three PCs Workstation users which do the user profile with Windows 7 Operating System (OS): Intel Core 2 Quad Processor Q9500, 2048MB RAM DDR3, 500GB HD.

3.   One server as network monitoring MIB host,

4.   One cloud computing server for running virtual hosts running on Debian OS (Proxmox): Intel Xeon, 12048 MB, 1TB HD

5.   Sensors to sensing room condition:

a.   Two Raspberry Pi: ARM Processor, Storage MMCard 8GB, 1 port Ethernet, Raspbian OS.

b.   Three Xbee S1 module: 3.3V @ 50mA, 250kbps Max data rate, 1mW output (+0dBm)

c.   Three M2303 Sensor and smoke sensor

Experiment Scenario

- Perform ping, tracer command and access to multiple servers
- Perform servers testing in running its daemon and enable by restarting it every time testing
- Measure traffic load to determine performance threshold values either in time or number of data packets
- Three PC users access to Web and application servers as well as cloud server. Set two times of treatment activities and performing (i) access separately to that three servers, (ii) access simultaneously, and (iii) random access with a specified time interval
- Memory and CPU usage will be used as measurement to enable a trap in the traffic by the agent,
- Running application of the monitoring system to receive data packages from any agent,
- Perform filtering to distinguish normal traffic from a failure, by separating and dividing the data traffic in several stages; based on time, target machine and used tools
- Pumping in data packet into the experimental network using Packet Generator (packgen) and real active users achieve a normal real world traffic
- Capturing raw traffic data using TCPdump to produce pcap files
- Enabling all services/daemons in target machines and restarting them before each test to ensure the same starting conditions

- Configuring sensors' option configuration LINUX-RASPI: Downed Device Detection SNMP Uptime, Timeout Value 400, Retry 1, SNMP Ver 3, Community public, Port 161, Timeout 10,
- Monitoring the network traffic using IPtraf and Collasoft Capsa.

Experimental Results

A network mapping matrix of interconnection traffic and summary data information are shown in Figure 11 and Figure 12. This traffic obtained during the experimental observation.

Figure 13 shows Raspberry device status from SNMP agent and displayed with graph. The system will inform real-time with elapse time of 5 seconds (adjustable) after the agent cannot response request from SNMP agent. Meanwhile, if the status is down, automatically will be updated in the system. Similarly, the graph will show up and down graphic to depict traffic activity from those devices.

The summary status visualization depicts for all device sensors that are most indicative of a pending failure, and the predictive strength of each devices.

Figure 14 shows a graph which describes about the traffic profiles of a user and CPU processing usage percentage in the experimental IoT network. The same graphic flow between the incoming and outgoing traffic of CPU/memory usage on

Figure 11. Overall traffic

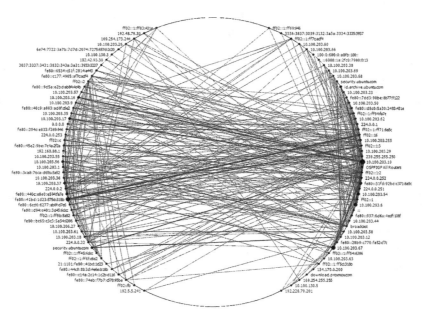

Figure 12. Overall protocol used

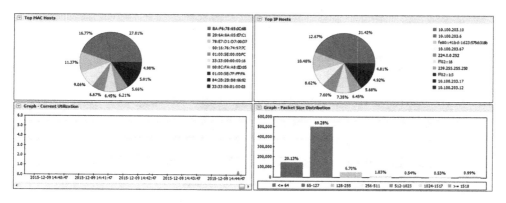

Figure 13. Device status vizualization

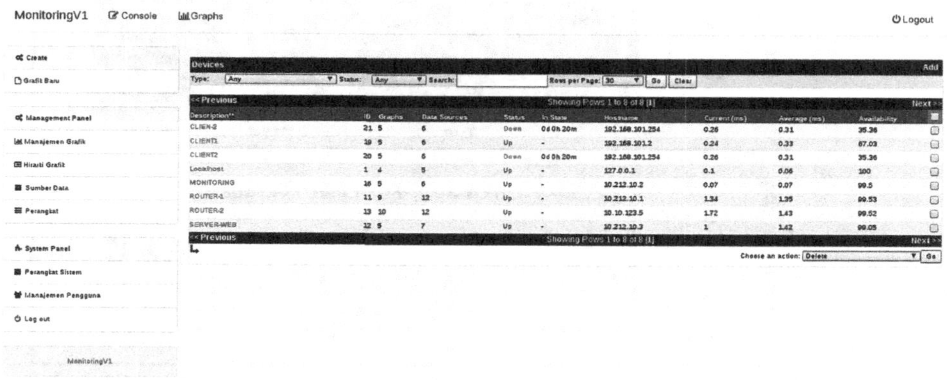

the monitored server are analyzed. Thus, it is possible to set a basic threshold value to trigger an allert in the notification system. For example, the network administrator may set the value of the threshold value network traffic as if "the traffic load < 500 Kbps or > 150 Mbps = usage processor > 45 percent" then the system will trigger an alert as an anomaly notification.

Network Forensics

What is unique about InstaMon as compared to other tools is that it does not only provide a centralised troubleshooting system: Centralised Monitoring Console, it also provides remote agent to monitor each remote segment and thin clients to protect each individual computer. This interesting and unique distributed architecture

Figure 14. Snapshot of traffic profile in a period of an observation time

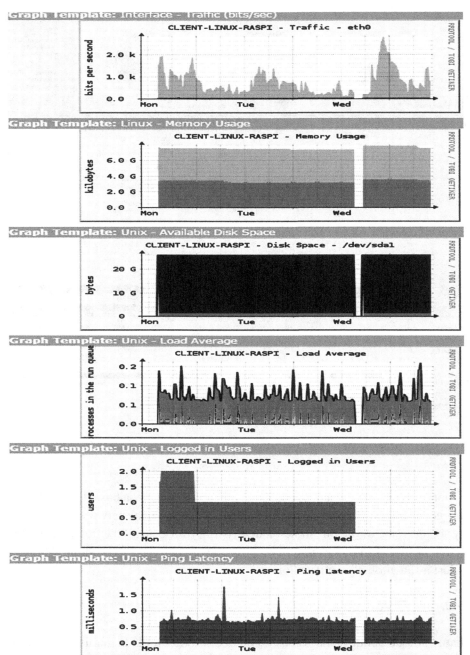

creates a complete protected environment for the organisations servers, devices and the network itself. InstaMon is also a cross platform analysis and troubleshooting tool that means even if an organisation uses a mix of Windows and Linux based computers, devices and servers, Instamon would still be able to fully monitor and protect the network. The remote agent will constantly monitor the remote segment providing the CCTV Style to network administrators and enabling them to review the history at any time and at anywhere. For instance if administrator detected something went wrong at any specific time let say at 3 am, the network administrator will still be able to login and review what happened at that specific time and date.

FUTURE RESEARCH DIRECTIONS

The future of IoT and its impact on networking and network performance monitoring focus on concerns around IP addressing space and the need for Internet Service Providers (ISPs) to switch to Interent Protocol version 6 (IPv6) on a large scale. This is a perfectly valid concern – by some estimates, 30 billion devices will be online by 2020. This is the only main factor to consider when it comes to how IoT will impact the performance of networks around the world. The customer's expectations of network service is constantly changing as new technologies emerge that facilitate faster, more reliable connectivity. The following are some area of researches and development to enhance the capability of the future IoT network monitoring system to keep high availabitily of the network.

1. **Buffering System:** With the tremendous increase of traffic produced by billions of device connect to the network, it is a challange to avoid packet dropped by the packet capturing module. A fast and efficient buffering mechanism is one of the research opportunity to be carried out.
2. **Distributed Monitoring:** With the aims to not increasing the traffic with additional traffic to monitor, a distributed monitoring mechanism is recommended. The mechanism will keep local traffic in local probe and regulary will update the main/center monitoring system. The challenge are include: autonomousity, bottle-neck traffic in some segments, and synchronization.
3. **Layer-2 IDS:** Security is the main concern in WSNs especially in WSNs application designed for military and healthcare. Securing WSNs is a great challenge since broadcast nature of wireless commination, limited resources, unattended environment where sensor nodes vulnerable to physical attack (Abduvaliyev et al. (2013); Wang & Lu (2014)). Prevention countermeasures

like authentication, cryptography and other key management that known as first line of defiance can enhance the security of WSNs. Nevertheless, prevention solution cannot be stand alone to prevent all possible attacks Wang & Lu (2014). Thus Intrusion Detection System in Layer-2 (Data Link Layaer). that known as second line of defiance is extremely needed in order to detect attacks that pass prevention solutions (Abduvaliyev et al. (2013); Miranda et al. (2014)). Examples of attacks are given as follows.

a.   **Collision:** When to node try to send out at identical frequency at the same time, the data portion will be changed due to packet collision. As consequence, packet will be rejected because of mismatch checksum (Buch (2011)).

b.   **Exhaustion:** In this attack, adversary consumes all energy resources of the targeted node and disturbs the media access control protocol (MAC), by engaging the channel to send and receive unnecessary data. (Miranda et al. (2014); Khan (2014))

c.   **Sybil Attack:** A malicious node in this attack spoofs the identity of other legitimate nodes (either MAC or IP). WSNs nodes work cooperatively and malicious node in this attack disturbs this cooperation. (Patel et al. (2013); Salehi et al. (2013))

4.   **Adaptive System:** Due to the facts that new services and applications in IoT keep coming, the profile or the network traffic may change more frequently. The monitoring mechanism in the future also needs to be able to adapt to a new trend of the traffic quickly.

CONCLUSION

This chapter presents the development of smart real-time IoT network monitoring tool platform. The chapter is divided into 2 components: Research and Development. The research component attempts to answer the challenges of making the monitoring tool becomes smarter and more accurate by applying artificial intelligent techniques. The IoT carries a tsunami of data. IoT rollouts bring a proliferation of cheap, distributed sensors – resulting in a huge volume of data in a short amount of time. Thus, a research on buffering techniques to speed up the traffic data acquisition process and micro-controller unit design for sensor-based applications are introduced. The proposed system utilizes available existing elementary components such as network traffic packets capturing, packet filtering and packets decoding modules.

Malwares are becoming smart and sophisticated. Now, the same malwares may attack smart TV connected to Internet. This matter triggers the need of a system that is capable to monitor in real time fashion to detect any anomalies in the network and to pinpoint the sources of the malwares. The proposed monitoring system uses intelligent techniques for clustering the network traffic to distinguish anomalies from normal traffics and machine learning for adaptively learning the network traffic changes and adapt accordingly. An insider attack is one of the biggest threats faced by modern enterprise networks. Thus, the proposed monitoring system is also acts as CCTV. The monitoring system uses Java Eclipse platform.

Experiments using an IoT testbed are conducted to reveal attacks/anomalies patterns.

REFERENCES

Abduvaliyev, A., Pathan, A.-S. K., Zhou, J., Roman, V., & Wong, W.-C. (2013, January). On the vital areas of intrusion detection systems in wireless sensor networks. *IEEE Communications Surveys and Tutorials*, *15*(3), 1223–1237. doi:10.1109/SURV.2012.121912.00006

Aydın, M. A., Zaim, A. H., & Ceylan, K. G. (2009). A hybrid intrusion detection system design for computer network security. *Computers & Electrical Engineering*, *35*(3), 517–526. doi:10.1016/j.compeleceng.2008.12.005

Buch, D., & Jinwala, D. (2011). Detection of wormhole attacks in wireless sensor network. *Proceedings of the 3rd International Conference on Advances in Recent Technologies in Communication and Computing (ARTCom 2011)*. doi:10.1049/ic.2011.0042

3.   Corn/Microsoft LAN Manager, Network Driver Interface Specification (NDIS) Version 2.01 (FINAL). (1990).

Hyunho, P., Ho, L.-H., & Seung-Hwan, L. (2014). IEEE 802 standardization on heterogeneous network interworking. *Proceedings of the 16th International Conference on Advanced Communication Technology (ICACT)*, 1140-1145.

Khan, F. (2014). Secure communication and routing architecture in wireless sensor networks. *Proceedings of IEEE 3rd Global Conference on Consumer Electronics (GCCE)*. doi:10.1109/GCCE.2014.7031298

Lohith, Y. S., Brinda, M. C., Anand, S. V. R., & Hegde, M. (2011). 6PANVIEW: A Network Monitoring System for the Internet of Things. *Proceedings of the Asia-Pacific Advanced Newtork*, *32*(0), 106–109. doi:10.7125/APAN.32.13

Malina, L., Hajny, J., Fujdiak, R., & Hosek, J. (2016, June). On perspective of security and privacy-preserving solutions in the internet of things. *Computer Networks, 102*, 83–95. doi:10.1016/j.comnet.2016.03.011

Matthews, W., Cottrell, L., & Salomoni, D. (2001, April). *Passive and Active Monitoring on a High Performance Research Network*. Academic Press.

McCanne, S., & Jacobson, V. (1992, December). *The BSD Packet Filter: A New Architecture for User-level Packet Capture*. Lawrence Berkeley Laboratory.

Miranda, J., Gomes, T., Abrishambaf, R., Loureiro, F., Mendes, J., Cabral, J., & Monteiro, J. (2014). A Wireless Sensor Network for collision detection on guardrails. *Proceedings of IEEE 23rd International Symposium on Industrial Electronics (ISIE)*. doi:10.1109/ISIE.2014.6864824

Parameswar, S. K., & Pooch, U. W. (1996). *Universal Packet Analyser - A Network Packet Filtering tool.* Department of Computer Science, Texas A&M University, Technical Report 96-008 (TR 96-008).

Patel, V., Taghavi, M., Bakhtiyari, K., & Júnior, J. C. (2013). An intrusion detection and prevention system in cloud computing: A systematic review. *Journal of Network and Computer Applications, 36*(1), 25–41. doi:10.1016/j.jnca.2012.08.007

Razzaque, M. A., Milojevic-Jevric, M., Palade, A., & Clarke, S. (2016). Middleware for Internet of Things: A Survey. *IEEE Internet of Things Journal, 3*(1), 70–95. doi:10.1109/JIOT.2015.2498900

Sakakibara, H., Nakazawa, J., & Tokuda, H. (2009). PBN: A seamless network infrastructure of heterogeneous network nodes. *Proceedings of the Sixth International Conference on Networked Sensing Systems (INSS)*. doi:10.1109/INSS.2009.5409912

Salehi, S. A., Razzaque, M., Naraei, P., & Farrokhtala, A. (2013). Detection of sinkhole attack in wireless sensor networks. *Proceedings of IEEE International Conference on Space Science and Communication (IconSpace)*. doi:10.1109/IconSpace.2013.6599496

Sánchez, R., Herrero, Á., & Corchado, E. (2013, October). Visualization and clustering for SNMP intrusion detection. *Cybernetics and Systems, 44*(6-7), 505–532. doi:10.1080/01969722.2013.803903

Stalling, W. (1999). SNMP, SNMPv2, SNMPv3 and RMON 1 and 2 (3rd ed.). Addison Wesley Longman.

Tankard, C. (2015, September). The security issues of the Internet of Things. *Computer Fraud & Security, 2015*(9), 11–14. doi:10.1016/S1361-3723(15)30084-1

Tavares Guimaraes, V., Lessa dos Santos, G., da Cunha Rodrigues, G., Zambenedetti Granville, L., & Rockenbach Tarouco, L. M. (2014). A collaborative solution for SNMP traces visualization. *Proceedings of International Conference on, 2014, International Conference on Information Networking (ICOIN)*, 458-463. doi:10.1109/ICOIN.2014.6799724

Wang, C. Y., Chou, S.-T., & Chang, H.-C. (2009. Emotion and motivation: understanding user behavior of Web 2.0 Application. *Proceedings of IEEE Computer Society Seventh Annual Communication Networks and Services Research Conference*, 1341-1346. doi:10.1109/ITNG.2009.205

Wang, L., & Lu, F. (2014). Intrusion detection system based on integration of neural network for wireless sensor network. *Journal of Software Engineering*, 8(4), 225–238. doi:10.3923/jse.2014.225.238

Wong, E. (1997, August). *Network Monitoring Fundamentals and Standards*. Academic Press.

Yongqi, H., Yun, Z., Taihao, L., & Liying, C. (2013). Research of network monitoring based on SNMP. *Proceedings of Third International Conference on Instrumentation, Measurement, Computer, Communication and Control (IMCCC)*, 411-414.

Zhenhui, Y., Keeney, J., Van Der Meer, S., Hogan, G., & Muntean, G. M. (2014). Context-aware heterogeneous network performance analysis: Test-bed development. *Proceedings of IEEE International Conference on Pervasive Computing and Communications Workshops (PERCOM Workshops)*, 472-477.

KEY TERMS AND DEFINITIONS

Anomaly Traffic: A deviation from the normal traffic pattern for example a flood of UDP packets or a new service appearing on the network.

Intrusion Detection System: A system (usually in the form of device or software application) that monitors a network for malicious activity or policy violations. The system reports the detected anomaly or violation to system administrator or centrally collected using a security information and event management (SIEM) system.

Network Traffic: The amount of data moving across a network at a given point of time. Network data is mostly encapsulated in network packets, which provide the load in the network. Network traffic is the main component for network traffic measurement.

Traffic Visualization System: A system to display the captured network traffic, so system administrator can view current situation in the network.

Chapter 9
Sensor Cloud:
A Cloud–Based Sensor Network Data Gathering and Processing Platform

Seyed Amin Hosseini Seno
Ferdowsi University of Mashhad, Iran

Fatemeh Banaie
Ferdowsi University of Mashhad, Iran

ABSTRACT

With the advancement of wireless sensor networks (WSN) and the increasing use of sensors in various industrial, environmental and commercial fields, it is difficult to store and process the volume of generated data on local platforms. Cloud computing provides scalable resources to perform analysis of online as well as offline data streams generated by sensor networks. This can help to overcome the weakness of WSN in combining and analyzing heterogeneous and large numbers of sensory data. This chapter presents a comprehensive survey on state-of-the-art results in the context of cloud –enabled large-scale sensor networks. The chapter also discusses the objectives, architecture and design issues of the generic sensor-cloud platform.

INTRODUCTION

The global sensor market represents an increasing use of wireless sensors in a wide variety of applications, including process automation, monitoring service, health and vehicular networking. The growth of this market is expected to reach more than $190 billion at the compounded annual growth rate of 11% by 2021[1]. These global sensor networks provide remote sensing application, which is known as Internet of Thing (IoT). However, traditional WSNs are domain specific and task-oriented,

DOI: 10.4018/978-1-5225-2799-2.ch009

Copyright © 2018, IGI Global. Copying or distributing in print or electronic forms without written permission of IGI Global is prohibited.

which lead to inefficient and redundant deployments of sensor nodes (Khan et al., 2016). Moreover, the limitations of WSNs (Mao et al, 2012; Tu & Blum, 2009) in the terms of battery life, processing and storage capacity would probably impact the service performance, and converges towards designing better data and communication management system for WSN (Madria et al., 2014).

Connecting the large scale WSN to the cloud platform can provide meaningful information to the users by processing and analyzing the vast amount of collected data from multiple locations. This idea helps to alleviate the limitations of sensor nodes using the extensive cloud resources. The resulting sensor-cloud platform enables a new kind of services and applications that are the hart of next-generation smart environment.

Sensor-cloud Infrastructure (SCI) refers to the advent of cloud computing (Buyya et al., 2009) for a new generation of ubiquitous monitoring and effective control of the on-field distributed WSNs. It is a new dimension of cloud computing for the efficient management of sensor network resources (Alamri et al. 2013). SCI provides services in the form of virtual network slices of the shared infrastructure, which lead to the convenient and on-demand access to a shared pool of resources by virtualizing the physical sensors on a cloud platform. Likewise, virtualization allows users to use sensors without worrying about their locations and specifications (Yuriyama & Kushida, 2010). As shown in Figure 1, sensor-cloud architecture is composed of three layers:

- *Physical sensors layer* that performs sensing and forwards the sensed data to the sensor-cloud.
- *Sensor-cloud Infrastructure* that provides SaaS by virtualizing physical sensors as virtual sensors.
- *Applications layer* that uses the sensed information provisioned by sensor-cloud service provider (SCSP) to serve on-demand requests of End-users.

Such an integration brings mutual benefits to both WSN and cloud computing. For WSNs, it can provide sensing data to multiple applications at the same type, instead of the application specific model. In addition, it takes the advantages of the powerful processing and the storage abilities of cloud computing for sensing data. For cloud computing, it will enrich the existing cloud platform with a new service paradigm, named as Sensing-as-a-Service (SaaS). This service enables the cloud platform to provide physical sensors as a service to the End-users, rather than a typical hardware (Zeng et al. 2013). This chapter presents a comprehensive survey on state-of-the-art results in the context of cloud –enabled large-scale sensor networks. The survey helps new researchers entering the domain of sensor-cloud by providing a comprehensive survey on recent developments.

Figure 1. The layered architecture of the sensor-cloud

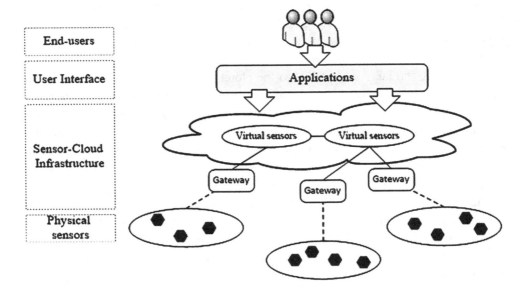

BACKGROUND

The concept of sensor-cloud has as introduced by several researches (Yuriyama & Kushida, 2010; Madria et al., 2014) whereas decoupling of WSN owners and the users lead to access sensors and deploy remote sensing application through cloud platform. According to Lan (2010), sensor- cloud can be defined as follows:

An infrastructure that allows truly pervasive computation using sensors as an interface between physical and cyber worlds, the data-compute clusters as the cyber backbone and the internet as the communication medium.

The goal of sensor-cloud is to develop a cloud based platform that provides truly pervasive computation using sensors as an interface between the physical and cyber world, computation resources as the cyber backbone and the Internet as the communication medium (Hussain Shah, 2013). SCI provides an easy and scalable access to every kind of distributed sensor and actuator device. These devices may be located at different places such as homes, offices, cars, and outdoor areas. As a result, it significantly minimizes the cost of IT resources and WSN infrastructure by allowing the trading of resources among multiple service providers and application level users (Eggert et al., 2014).

A theoretical model has been presented by Misra et al. (2014), which studies the performance improvement of sensor-cloud over traditional WSNs. According to their results, in most cases SCI outperforms the traditional WSNs in the terms of energy consumption, lifetime, cost and fault tolerance. A sensor-cloud allows on-demand sensing services by effectively collecting and processing information from various sensor networks. Users can easily gather, access, process, analyze, store, and search huge amounts of sensor data from different applications using accumulated computational and storage resources on sensor-cloud infrastructure.

In this infrastructure, physical sensors are virtualized as virtual sensors on the cloud environment. Services are provisioned automatically to the end users whenever they require using virtual sensors, which are part of IT resources (Yuriyama & Kushida, 2010). This interactive model processes and minimizes the number of requests sent to physical sensors using request aggregation methods. To fully take advantage of the sensor-cloud services, IT resources and physical sensors should be prepared prior to the operation of sensor-cloud infrastructure (Yuriyama et al., 2011).

An Overview of Cyber Physical Cloud, Internet of Things, and Sensor Cloud

Developing sensor network applications demands a new set of tools to overcome the inherent limitations of sensors in the terms of computational and memory resource shortage. These applications often generate a huge amount of data from multiple sources that has to be stored and processed. As widely recognized, the traditional approaches usually suffer from flexibility, scalability, data diversity, cost controlling and on demand provisioning of the applications. Hence, researchers have investigated the integration of WSNs with large scale distributed computing infrastructures, as, for instance, sensor-cloud (Yuriyama & Kushida, 2010) and sensor grid (Cuzzocrea & Saccà, 2013). Sensor grid provides processing procedures over sensor data, while cloud is used to analyze processed data (Cuzzocrea et al., 2013). Due to recent trends, integrating sensor network with cloud is becoming a very hot topic in distributed systems research (Sakr et al. 2011). In this context, there are three topical research areas which are highly inter-related (Sehgal et al., 2014):

- Cyber Physical Cloud (CPC),
- Internet of Thing (IoT),
- Sensor-Cloud (SC).

Sensors and cloud are the integral part of these three areas. Cyber physical systems (CPSs) build a relation between virtual world and physical world by embedding sensors to the physical world (Wu et al., 2011). CPS consists of one or more sensors that collect data by monitoring the environment. Based on input data, outcome is determined and actuators react to this information by performing appropriate actions (Wu et al., 2011). CPC is simply a CPS that integrated with cloud for computation and communication (Phuong et al., 2011).

IoT is a novel technical hierarchy system, which aims at connecting a variety of things or objects for providing the pervasive presence around us of things. The term "thing" encompasses anything from Radio Frequency Identification (RFID) tags, sensors, and actuators to mobile phones, laptops and super computers [40]. IoT is aimed at connecting the devices to the Internet infrastructure, whereas CPS focuses on achieving certain goals on particular application using sensing and actuation capabilities of devices. In other words, CPS systems do not need to be connected to the Internet for in order to work working (Salim & Haque, 2015).

Sensor-Cloud (SC) applies virtualization and abstraction techniques in the form of virtual sensors. A virtual sensor is an abstract sensor that enables the decoupling of the physical sensors from the applications running on top of them. These sensors are provided as a service to end users (Yuriyama & Kushida, 2010). Unlike the IoT that provides services through the Internet, SC builds a cloud of virtual Sensors on top of physical sensors (Madria et al. 2014). Table 1 depicts the key similarities and differences between CPC, IoT and SC respectively (Wu et al., 2011).

In this way, the authors' perspective moves toward sensor-cloud (SC) as compared to CPC and IoT. Sensor-cloud means more than simply interconnecting and hyperlinking sensors. It provides scalable services by virtualizing and managing sensors according to the user needs. The purpose is to implement services to provide indexing and querying methods applied to every kind of distributed sensor.

Table 1. A brief comparison of the SC, CPS, and IoT

Instance	Brief Description of the Case
Using of the Cloud computing	• CPC uses cloud for computation and storage. • IoT connects the devices to the Internet Infrastructure, and uses cloud for processing huge amount of data. • SC uses cloud for provisioning of sensors, computing and storing of data.
Aim & Scope	• CPC enriches the relation between virtual world and physical world • IoT connects things and provides services through the Internet. • SC builds a cloud of virtual sensors on top of the physical sensors.
Real Time Systems	• In CPC, data must be sensed and decision must be taken in real time. • The IoT devices communicate their status with other devices in real time. • Data must be provided to the users within well-defined timing limits else users will be required to pay more.
On-demand services	• Resources cannot instantly provisioned and removed in CPC. • IoT cannot increase/decrease the number of devices on demand. • In SC, virtual sensors are provisioned automatically on demand whenever user requests.
Domain	Applications in CPC are domain specific, but IoT and SC provide inter-domain services.

SENSOR CLOUD

Sensor-Cloud Infrastructure results from the convergence of distributed wireless sensor networks and cloud computing. These combination takes advantage of the ubiquitous sensing abilities of sensors and the unlimited computing resources of the cloud. In SC, sensors are not only simple endpoints, but are smart sensing and computing resources that can be reached with the cloud platform. In this new paradigm, service functionality can be dynamically allocated across distributed platform in order to maximize service performance, and minimize operational costs.

The main advantages of SC with respect to the traditional domain-specific sensor networks are:

- **Location Awareness:** Virtualization technologies allow sharing heterogenous physical sensors among different applications without worrying about their location and specification.
- **Scalability:** Integrating sensor nodes with the cloud allows the number of connected devices and services to be scaled without having to invest heavily in these additional hardware resources.
- **High Flexibility:** The property of sharing the heterogenous infrastructure among multiple users provides much flexibility for users. The users can easily access data from anywhere and use random applications as many times as the users want, under a flexible usage environment.
- **Reduced Operational Cost:** Collaboration within SCI enables consumers to communicate and share a huge amount of sensor data more easily compared to the traditional methods. The collaboration helps to reduce costs, as the services are charged per usage metrics.

SCI hence emerges as an ideal platform for the implementation of smart services in the context of smart applications. The following section therefore provides a brief overview of some essential aspects of the enabling technologies for this infrastructure.

Sensor Network: Overview

A wireless sensor network (WSN) consists of a large number of autonomous sensor nodes with sensing, computational, and wireless communications capabilities. These nodes are usually scattered in a sensor field, and cooperatively monitor physical or environmental conditions. The development of WSN was mainly derived by military applications. However, it is now applied in various areas for commercial and industrial use, including environment and habitat monitoring, industrial process monitoring and control, as well as the healthcare industry (Tiwari et al., 2007).

With the proliferation of various kinds of sensor networks, a large amount of heterogeneous data with different characteristics will be collected. Different types of sensor nodes have various energy and computational capabilities, and are used for a variety types of smart environment. In particular, typical sensor networks are designed to serve a specific application and snub the possibilities of sharing resources with other applications. This can lead to unnecessary replication of sensing infrastructure (Rutakemwa, 2013).

To allow users to utilize many sources of data simultaneously, a framework is needed to define the geometric, dynamic, and observational characteristics of sensors such as location, accuracy and type of sensor nodes. Virtualization in sensor networks can provide flexibility and cost effective solutions for the availability and performance of physical sensors. They do this by allowing heterogeneous sensor nodes to coexist over the common physical sensor substrate (Khan et al. 2016).

Virtualization in Sensor Network

In the field of wireless sensor network (WSN), Virtualization of Sensor Network (VSN) is quite a new research approach. A virtual sensor network is formed by providing logical connectivity among a subset of sensor nodes that are dedicated to a certain task or application at any given time (Motaharul et al., 2012). A VSN is a logical subset of a WSN, which is required for serving the particular application with two or more nonadjacent sensor nodes. In fact, it abstracts the complexities of setting communication link between nodes. Sensor-cloud, on the contrary, delivers Se-aaS by virtualizing the physical resources (Madria et al.,2014).

WSN virtualization can be categorized into two classes: Node-level virtualization and Network-level virtualization. In the former, multiple application may run tasks concurrently on a single node. In Network-level virtualization, a subset of a WSN's nodes is dedicated to one application at a given time (Khan et al., 2016).

Virtual sensors are software sensors that are built on top of actual physical sensors. The sensors have some data processing functions for complex queries. These functions combine and process sensed data from a group of heterogeneous sensors (Misra et al., 2014). Each virtual sensor is created from one or more physical sensors based on the performed task. Users can freely create and use virtual sensors as if the users owned the sensors. These sensors are accessed on-demand and deployed when the sensors are active request for using data (Misra et al, 2014). The relationship between virtual sensors and physical sensors is illustrated in Figure 2.

Figure 2. The relation between virtual and physical sensors

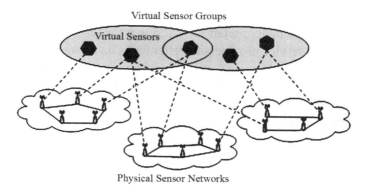

Virtual Sensor Network Design Space

The design goals of virtualization technology in wireless sensor network have been addressed by different research groups. The design criteria should be considered in materializing the issues behind sensor network virtualization.

1. **Secure Sharing of Sensor Network:** Secure and safe sharing of sensor resources is the most important opportunity behind sensor network virtualization. It is very cost effective to have one single sensor network, which serve multiple purposes. Different application level users can utilize a single physical infrastructure through virtualization (Motaharul et al., 2012). Security constraints and privacy policies must be used to guarantee correct behavior in the shared network (Efstratiou, 2010).

2. **Flexibility:** Traditional sensor networks lack enough flexibility for processing sensor information. Virtualization in sensor networks must provide flexibility to support several heterogeneous and independent applications with different requirements in the same infrastructure (Akyildiz et al., 2006).

3. **Heterogeneity:** As sensor data must be accessed from various types of users, such as PC, smartphone, and tablets, heterogeneity is a significant issue in designing virtual sensor networks. In this context, heterogeneity comes from two perspectives: heterogeneity of the underlying sensor network technologies and heterogeneity of end user devices. It demands to make effective and seamless usage of sensor resources and services in an integrated VSN service platform (Motaharul et al. 2012).

4. **Scalability:** Virtualization is a promising technique for achieving the coexistence of multiple sensor networks. Scalability is an essential part of this equation.

Infrastructure Providers must be able to accommodate a very large and increasing number of nodes without affecting their performance.

5. **Manageability:** A major part of VSN design is the separating of infrastructure providers from service providers to better focus on their core service oriented business. VSN modularizes network management tasks and introduces accountability into the network (Motaharul et al. 2012).

Sensor Description

There have been relatively few studies concentrate on the management of physical sensors. To use physical sensors, end users need to know the specifications of sensors such as geometric, dynamic, and observational characteristics. Besides, a mapping process between physical and virtual sensors is needed to describe how to translate user's commands to the corresponding physical sensors (Yuriyama & Kushida, 2010).

The Sensor Web Enablement (SWE) initiative of the Open Geospatial Consortium (OGC) defines the sensor model language (SensorML) (Botts et al., 2007) to provide standard models for physical sensor's description and measurement processes in an XML-based structure. SensorML was developed for representing metadata for any physical sensors like location, accuracy, and type of sensor. Sensors are modeled as processes that convert real phenomena to data. In particular, SensorML provides a functional model for sensors, rather a detailed description of hardware. Observations and Measurement (O&M) is also defined to encode sensor data measured. Sensor nodes should be standardized using SensorML due to the heterogeneous specifications of the sensor nodes (Misra et al. 2014).

Cloud Computing: Overview

Cloud computing relies on sharing of resources to achieve better use of various distributed resources, higher throughput and large scale computation (Asnani et al. 2013)). The U.S. NIST defines the concept of cloud computing as follow:

Cloud computing is a model for enabling convenient, on demand network access to a share pool of configurable computing resources (e.g., networks, servers, storage, applications, and services) that can be rapidly provisioned and released with minimal management effort or service provider interaction (Mell et al., 2011).

Cloud computing provides on demand network access to storage, processing power, development platforms and software. In cloud computing paradigm, these resources can be stored centrally, and accessed as a service rather than deployed locally (Dihal et al., 2013). End users of cloud computing use the servers with no concern about the location of the servers. Virtualization is the base technology for cloud computing, which abstracts away the details of hardware and supplies virtualized resources for high-level applications. It raises the utilization of resources by allocating the resources in a scalable manner. Hence, it is suitable for processing of the large volume of data (Quinton et al., 2012; Caytiles et al., 2012). Cloud computing allows the systems and users to use following three services (Zhang et al. 2010):

1. **Software as a Service (SaaS):** In this model, the cloud vendor delivers their applications as a service over the internet, e. g. Rackspace[2], and SAP business ByDesign[3].
2. **Platform as a Service (PaaS):** PaaS refers to providing software or development environment, on which the clients can create their cloud services and applications such as operating systems (e. g. Google App Engine[4], and Microsoft Windows Azure[5]).
3. **Infrastructure as a Service (IaaS):** IaaS provides basic storage and computing capabilities, usually in terms of VMs. In this sense, consumers can easily run and deploy applications without a need to manage and control underlying infrastructure. Amazon EC2[6], and GoGrid[7] are the examples of IaaS.

Cloud computing provides several salient features that make it different from traditional service computing, as follows (Dihal et al., 2013).

1. **Shared Resource Pooling:** The resources are dynamically assigned to multiple resource consumers from a pool of computing resources that provides much flexibility to infrastructure providers for managing the resources.
2. **Ubiquitous Network Access:** Services hosted in the cloud are generally exposed as web services. Hence, the services can easily be accessible with the help of mobile phone, laptop and PDA using secure internet connection.
3. **Measured Service:** Cloud computing services leverage a metering capability which automatically enables to control and optimize resource usage (e.g. storage, processing, computing). Monitoring and controlling the utilized services in cloud computing provides transparency for providers and consumers of the services.
4. **Dynamic Resource Provisioning:** One of the important features of cloud computing is the ability to access necessary computational resources and releasing them when not needed on the fly. Dynamic resource provisioning allows providers to provision on demand services, which considerably lower the operating costs.
5. **Multi-Tenancy:** Multi-tenancy provides the ability of sharing resources and costs across a large pool of users. In cloud environment, multiple services

owned by different providers coexist in a single data center, and share resources among cloud service consumers.

One of important issue in sensor cloud is integration between cloud computing and physical sensor networks. In the next part a layered view description of this integration is explained.

SOLUTIONS AND RECOMMENDATIONS

The increasing amount in the number of sensors and smart applications will inevitably lead to excessive network load, end-to-end delay and power consumption. A promising solution is to use distributed cloud environment in managing and optimizing the smart services. Recent advances in virtualization and programmability enable the sensor cloud to efficiently host and manage huge sensory data in highly distributed cloud networking architecture. These highly virtualized heterogenous platform provide increased flexibility in service provisioning, and a clear advantage in meeting the latency, cost and location awareness constraints.

The Layered Architecture and Life Cycle of Sensor Cloud

The layered architecture and life cycle of sensor-cloud infrastructure is illustrated in Figure 3. As shown, several users can access and utilize the sensor data through this infrastructure. A user can request the required service instances by selecting the appropriate service template. The service instances are automatically provisioned to the End-user by virtualizing the physical sensors as virtual sensors. Service templates are prepared by SCSPs as service catalog. Users can add or delete service templates when required. The sensed information is retrieved from physical sensor nodes and used to serve the application based on user demand (Yuriyama & Kushida, 2010).

Sensor Cloud Applications

Sensors are fundamental elements for gathering and processing data in monitoring systems. Monitoring is a process to observe a state or changes in states over time. The application of monitoring plays an important role in collecting sufficient information to achieve the desired outcome. The integration of wireless sensor networks with cloud computing makes it easy to share and analyze the data needed to real-time decisions. This combination provides sensor data as a service (SaaS) and sensor event as a service (SEaaS) over the Internet. Furhtermore, it makes sense for large number of applications such as environmental monitoring including,

Figure 3. The life cycle of SCI and its layered structure

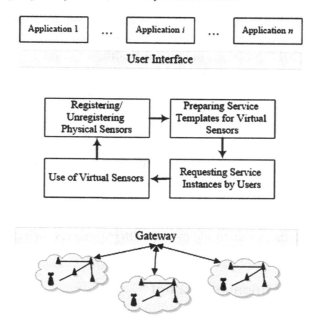

weather forecasting, earth observation, health monitoring, military services, smart home monitoring, industry monitoring and etc. Users require continuous monitoring of the environment to get information about a situation such as disaster, pollution, earthquake and etc. The following is a brief overview of some of the applications.

1. Ubiquitous Healthcare Monitoring

There is an increasing demand for daily monitoring of health condition at home. Sensor networks are widely used in health monitoring applications. This system uses a number of wearable sensor nodes that are capable of sensing, processing and communicating several physiological signs. Recently, commercially available devices for health care are networked using monitoring platforms. The wearable miniaturized nodes simplify the supervision of patients' health by collecting patient's health-related data for tracking blood sugar, body temperature, and other repository conditions. Consequently, it reduces health cost and improves quality of life by providing continuous remote patient supervision both in and out of hospital conditions (Lounis et al., 2012). Lounis et al. (2012) proposes an architecture for collecting and accessing large amount of data generated by medical sensor network. The proposed architecture provides an access control mechanism, which allows implementing complex and dynamic security policies for medical applications.

Misra et al., (2013) study the optimal gateway selection problem in SCI for real-time patient monitoring system. The authors show how the user requests can be mapped and serviced by gateway to access data from cloud platform optimally.

Hii & Chung (2011) propose a ubiquitous healthcare solution on android mobile devices, which monitor ECG vital sings in real time. EGC data is transmitted from patient's body to a smart phone through WSN technology. As shown in Figure 4, the proposed system is divided into two modes, real-time mode and the store and forward mode. In real-time, ECG signals are immediately available on smart phone device. Heart conditions can be captured and analyzed immediately by patient. In second case, medical data are transferred to the web server by mobile phone for further analysis. The data can be stored and accessed at a later time as well.

Hii & Chung (2011) believe that this technology has greatly increased the diagnostic power, and can be easily applied with wearable devices and smart phones. In the future, the authors plan to add more health parameters such as blood pressure, body temperature to provide more precise monitoring.

2. Agriculture and Irrigation Control

Sensor-cloud infrastructure is an open, flexible and reconfigurable platform, which is suitable for precision agriculture services such as air/soil monitoring, precise

Figure 4. System design of real-time monitoring system
Hii & Chung, 2011.

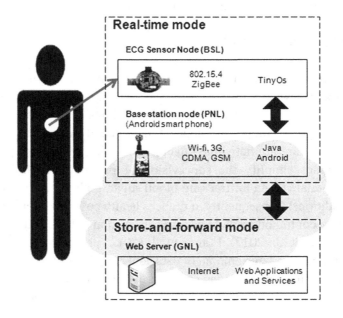

monitoring of the growth status and so forth. The field owner tracks the health of their crops using the several sensor nodes including air sensor, temperature sensor, soil moisture and temperature sensors, which are deployed in the field. Several Sensor-Cloud infrastructures have been envisioned for agricultural applications (Mahesh et al., 2014).

For instance, the authors in (Kim et al., 2014) proposed agriculture SCI for providing various agricultural services using WSNs. The authors also proposed a hierarchical source routing (HSR), aggregation gradient routing (AGR), and a priority-based data transmission technique in order to provide reliable transmission of packets with high priority in large-scale WSNs. The work presented in (Wang et al., 2014) proposed a heterogeneous sensor data management scheme in Internet of Thing for agriculture based on cloud computing. It is based on two-tier storage structure of a distributed database, and accesses it using MapReduce model. Authors in (Li et al., 2013) came up with a novel data aggregation approach to estimate ground water balance average water availability. The authors develop an intelligent android based mobile application, which helps Australian farmers to decide how much water to buy and use for their potential future irrigation and crop growth. Efficient management of water usage is essential due to the high electricity costs in Australia.

3. Weather Forecasting

Weather forecasting applies scientific knowledge to predict future atmospheric conditions for a given location. Each weather station is equipped with sensor nodes, which sense the weather conditions (e.g. rain, wind speed/direction, humidity, and temperature) and provide their sensed data to cloud for processing. As the gathered data by these sensors is huge, it is difficult to maintain and analyze it using the traditional reporting and data mining approaches. Sensor-cloud enables users to manage and analyze weather and location data more efficiently (Dash et al., 2010).

4. Military Use

In military purposes, sensor networks are used in battlefields for surveillance of enemies, targeting, monitoring of weapons and equipment, battle damage assessment and nuclear etc. The data being collected from these applications have sensitive information and need top level of security. Sensor-cloud provides a solution for this problem by providing a secure infrastructure exclusively for military applications (Dash et al., 2010). For example, Mils-cloud (Misra et al., 2014) is a sensor-cloud architecture, which is proposed to integrate the tri-services on a common platform for better command and control. This architecture improves the real time situational awareness of the battlefield and provides scalable and flexible access to resources.

5. Transport Monitoring

With the constant increasing of the vehicular traffic around the world, wireless sensor networks based intelligent transportation systems have emerged as the cost-effective technology for transport monitoring. This technology enables a new range of smart city applications including basic management such as car navigation, traffic signal control system, parking guidance and information system, dynamic traffic light and etc. (Dash et al., 2010). Sensory data is gathered and transmitted to the cloud for central fusion and processing. The gathered data provides more accurate information than achieved by a single sensor node. An instance of these systems is a travel recommendation system (Yerva et al., 2012) that provides the information on how enjoyable the place would be on the day for travel. This system employs a combination of cloud technologies, including Hadoop[8], HBase[9], and GSN (Aberer et al., 2006) that allows blending heterogeneous social and sensor data for analysis and extraction of information.

FUTURE RESEARCH DIRECTIONS

Sensor-cloud creates an environment, by which dynamic resource allocation for efficient sharing of services among multiple users is achieved. It unites multiple heterogeneous sensor networks on a platform to provide users with seamless access to the sensor data and efficient utilization of the resources. Although, cloud facilitates better collaboration and information sharing, it adds additional complexity to the design and implementation of services. On the other hand, there are several issues such as event processing and management, pricing, energy efficiency, and security and privacy issues that need to be considered while designing this platform. Therefore, a more comprehensive research effort is still required to meet the requirements of integrating sensor network and cloud computing.

Motivated by above mentioned reasons, interesting direction for future work include designing and implementing event matching algorithms of improved computational complexity, and studying the benefit of distributed optimization techniques to enable flexibility and agility in service provisioning while reduces the overall system costs.

CONCLUSION

The integration of the distributed WSNs and cloud computing enables a new class of services and applications in the field of smart environment. These applications utilize cloud-enabled sensing data resources to provide remote sensing abilities. With the predicted explosion in the number of connected devices, cloud architecture is tending to be a promising solution for managing and optimizing the huge amount of gathered data. Sensor-cloud infrastructure provides a federated platform, which enables open, scalable, cost-effective and easy to use network of sensors for numerous applications. This chapter provided a brief overview of the state of the art and current proposal in SCI, as well as enabling technology to this end. It has shown the potential of sensor-cloud to scale by employing computing platforms and sensing resources to provide sensing as a service. Besides, a layered architecture of sensor-cloud is presented, and technical design objectives of sensor networks for developing this infrastructure is described in detail.

REFERENCES

Aberer, K., Hauswirth, M., & Salehi, A. (2006). A middleware for fast and flexible sensor network deployment. VLDB, 1199–1202.

Akyildiz, I. F., Melodia, T., & Chowdhury, K. R. (2006). A Survey on Wireless Multimedia Sensor Networks. *Computer Networks*. doi: .2006.10.00210.1016/j.commnet

Alamri, A., Ansari, W. S., Hassan, M. M., Hossain, M. S., Alelaiwi, A., & Hossain, M. A. (2013). A Survey on Sensor-Cloud: Architecture, Applications, and Approaches. *International Journal of Distributed Sensor Networks, 2013*, 1–18.

Asnani, M., Verma, A., Bijve, S., & Bakariya, B. (2013). A Sketch on Security Issues and Concerns of Cloud Enviroment: Review. *International Conference on Cloud, Big Data and Trusted.*

Botts, M., & Robin, A. (2007). OpenGIS sensor model language (SensorML) implementation specification, OpenGIS Implementation Specification OGC 07-000. The Open Geospatical Consortium.

Buyya, R., Yeoa, C. S., Venugopala, S., Broberga, J., & Brandic, I. (2009). Cloud Computing and Emerging IT Platforms: Vision, Hype, and Reality for Delivering Computing as the 5th Utility. *Future Generation Computer Systems, 25*(6), 599–616. doi:10.1016/j.future.2008.12.001

Caytiles, R. D., Lee, S., & Park, B. (2012). Cloud computing: The next computing paradigm. *International Journal of Multimedia and Ubiquitous Engineering, 7*, 297–302.

Cuzzocrea, A., Fortino, G., & Rana, O. (2013). Managing Data and Processes in Cloud-Enabled Larg-Scale Sensor Networks: State-of-The-Art and Future Research Directions. *13th IEEE/ACM International Symposium on Cluster, Cloud, and Grid computing*. doi:10.1109/CCGrid.2013.116

Cuzzocrea, A., & Saccà, D. (2013). Exploiting Compression and Approximation Paradigms for Effective and Efficient OLAP over Sensor Network Readings in Data Grid Environments. *Concurrency and Computation*. doi:10.1002/cpe.2982

Dash, S. K., Mohapatra, S., & Pattnaik, P. K. (2010). A survey on Applications of Wireless Sensor Network Using Cloud Computing. *International Journal of Computer Science & Emerging Technologies*, *1*(4).

Dihal, S., Bouwman, H., Reuver, M., de Warnier, M., & Carlsson, C. H. (2013). Mobile cloud computing: State of the art and outlook. *Info*, *15*(1), 4-16.

Efstratiou, C. (2010). Challenges in Supporting Federation of Sensor Networks. *NSF/FIRE Workshop on Federating Computing Resources*.

Eggert, M. (2014). *Sensor Cloud: Towards the Interdisciplinary Development of a Trustworthy Platform for Globally Interconnected Sensors and Actuators*. Trusted Cloud Computing.

Hill, P. Ch., & Chung, W. Y. (2011). A Comprehensive Ubiquitous Healthcare Solution on an Android Mobile Device. *Sensors (Basel, Switzerland)*, *11*(12), 6799–6815. doi:10.3390/s110706799 PMID:22163986

Hussain Shah, S., Kabeer Khan, F., Ali, W., & Khan, J. (2013). A New Framework to Integrate Wireless Sensor Networks with Cloud Computing. *Aerospace Conference*. IEEE.

ID MTL. (2016, 8 July). Retrieved from https://ville.montreal.qc.ca/idmtl/en/the-development-of-new-generation-sensors-driven-by-research-and-leading-edge-smes-in-montreal

Islam, M., & Huh, E. (2012). Virtualization in Wireless Sensor Network; Challenges and Opportunities. *Journal of Networks*, *7*(3).

Islam, M., Hassan, M. M., Lee, G.-W., & Huh, E.-N. (2012). A Survey on Virtualization of Wireless Sensor Networks. *Sensors (Basel, Switzerland)*, *12*(2), 2175–2207. doi:10.3390/s120202175 PMID:22438759

Khan, I., Belqasmi, F., Glitho, R., Crespi, N., Morrow, M., & Polakos, P. (2016). Wireless Sensor Network Virtualization: A Survey. *IEEE Communication Survey & Tutorials*, *18*(1).

Kim, K., Lee, S., Yoo, H., & Kim, D. (2014). Agriculture Sensor-Cloud Infrastructure and Routing Protocol in the Physical Sensor Network Layer. *International Journal of Distributed Sensor Networks.*

Lan, K. T. (2010) What's Next? Sensor+Cloud? In *Proceeding of the 7th International Workshop on Data Management for Sensor Networks* (pp. 978–971). ACM Digital Library.

Li, C. (2013). Mobile Application Based Sustainable Irrigation Water Usage Decision Support System: An Intelligent Sensor CLOUD Approach. *Sensors (Basel, Switzerland).*

Lounis, A., Hadjidj, A., Bouabdallah, A., & Challa, Y. (2012). *Secure and Scalable Cloud-based Architecture for e-Health Wireless Sensor Networks. Computer Communications and Networks.* ICCCN.

Lounis, A., Hadjidj, A., Bouabdallah, A., & Challal, Y. (2012). Secure and Scalable Cloud-based Architecture for e-Health Wireless Sensor Networks. *International Conference on Computer Communications and Networks (ICCCN)*. doi:10.1109/ICCCN.2012.6289252

Madria, S., Kumar, V., & Dalvi, R. (2014). Sensor Cloud: A Cloud of Virtual Sensors. *IEEE Software, 31*(2), 70–77. doi:10.1109/MS.2013.141

Mahesh, D. S., Savitha, S., & Dinesh, K. (2014). A Cloud Computing Architecture with Wireless Sensor Networks for Agricultural Applications. *International Journal of Computer Networks and Communications Security, 2*(1).

Mao, Koksal, & Shroff. (2012). Near Optimal Power and Rate Control of Multi-Hop Sensor Networks With Energy Replenishment: Basic Limitations With Finite Energy and Data Storage. *IEEE Trans. Autom. Control, 7*, 815–829.

Mell, P., & Grance, T. (2009). *Draft nist working definition of cloud computing* (vol. 15). Academic Press.

Misra, S., Bera, S., Mondal, A., Tirkey, R., Chao, H., & Chattopadhyay, S. (2013). Optimal gateway selection in sensor-cloud framework for health monitoring. *IET Wireless Sensor Systems, 4*(2), 61–68. doi:10.1049/iet-wss.2013.0073

Misra, S. Chatterjee, S. Obaidat, M. S. (2014). On Theoretical Modeling of Sensor Cloud: A Paradigm Shift From Wireless Sensor Network. *IEEE System Journal.*

Misra, S., Singh, A., Chatterjee, S., & Obaidat, M. S. (2014). *Mils-Cloud: A Sensor-Cloud-Based Architecture for the Integration of Military Tri-Services Operations and Decision Making*. IEEE System Journal.

Pande, P., & Padwalkar, A. R. (2014). Internet of Things-A Future of Internet: A Survey, *International Journal of Advanced Research in Computer Science and Management Studies, 2*(2).

Phuong, L. T. (2011). Energy Efficiency based on Quality of Data for Cyber Physical System. *IEEE International Conferences on Internet of Things, and Cyber, Physical and Social Computing.*

Quinton, C., Rouvoy, R., & Duchien, L. (2012). Leveraging feature models to configure virtual appliances. *Proceedings of the 2nd International Workshop on Cloud Computing Platforms (CloudCP '12).* doi:10.1145/2168697.2168699

Rutakemwa, M. (2013). From Physical to Virtual Wireless Sensor Networks Using Cloud Computing. *International Journal of Research in Computer Science, 3*(1), 19–25.

Sakr, S., Liu, A., Batista, D. M., & Alomari, M. (2011). A Survey of Large Scale Data Management Approaches in Cloud Environments. *IEEE Communications Surveys and Tutorials, 13*(3), 311–336. doi:10.1109/SURV.2011.032211.00087

Salim, F., & Haque, U. (2015). Urban computing in the wild: A survey on large scale participation and citizen engagement with ubiquitous computing, cyber physical systems, and Internet of Things. *International Journal of Human-Computer Studies, 81*, 31–48. doi:10.1016/j.ijhcs.2015.03.003

Sehgal, V. K., Patrik, A., & Rajpoot, L. (2014). A Comparative Study of Cyber Physical Cloud, Cloud of Sensors and Internet of Things: Their Ideology, Similarities and Differences. *IEEE International Advanced Computing Conference (IACC).* doi:10.1109/IAdCC.2014.6779411

Tiwari, A., Ballal, P., & Lewis, F. (2007). Energy-efficient wireless sensor network design and implementation for condition-based maintenance. *ACM Transactions on Sensor Networks, 3*(1), 1. doi:10.1145/1210669.1210670

Tu, Z., & Blum, R. S. (2009). On the Limitations of Random Sensor Placement for Distributed Signal Detection. *IEEE Trans. Aerospace Electron, 45*(2), 555–563. doi:10.1109/TAES.2009.5089541

Wang, H., Lin, G., Wang, J., Gao, W., Chen, Y., & Duan, Q. (2014). Management of Big Data in the Internet of Things in Agriculture Based on Cloud Computing, *Applied. Mechanics of Materials, 548-549*, 1438–1444. doi:10.4028/www.scientific.net/AMM.548-549.1438

Wu, F.-J., Kao, Y.-F., & Tseng, Y.-C. (2011). From wireless sensor networks towards cyber physical systems. *Pervasive and Mobile Computing, 7*(4), 397–413. doi:10.1016/j.pmcj.2011.03.003

Yerva, S. R., Saltarin, J., Hoyoung, J., & Abere, K. (2012). Social and Sensor Data Fusion in the Cloud. *13th International Conference on Mobile Data Management (MDM)*. doi:10.1109/MDM.2012.52

Yuriyama, M., & Kushida, T. (2010). Sensor-Cloud Infrastructure: Physical Sensor Management with Virtualized Sensors on Cloud Computing. *13th International Conference on Network-based Information Systems*. doi:10.1109/NBiS.2010.32

Yuriyama, M., Kushida, T., & Itakura, M. (2011). A new model of accelerating service innovation with sensor-cloud infrastructure. *Proceedings of the annual SRII Global Conference (SRII'11)*, 308–314. doi:10.1109/SRII.2011.42

Zeng, D., Miyazaki, T., Guo, S., Tsukahara, T., Kitamichi, J., & Hayashi, T. (2013). *Evolution of Software-Defined Sensor Networks*. Mobile Ad-hoc and Sensor Networks. doi:10.1109/MSN.2013.60

Zhang, Q., Cheng, L., & Boutaba, R. (2010). Cloud Computing: State-of-the-art and research challenges. *Journal of Internet Services and Applications, 1*(1), 7–18. doi:10.1007/s13174-010-0007-6

KEY TERMS AND DEFINITIONS

Cloud Computing: A share pool of configurable computing resources (e.g., networks, servers, storage, applications, and services) that can be rapidly provisioned and released with minimal management effort.

Cost Effective: Providing required QoS without costing a lot of money.

Energy Efficiency: Using less energy to provide the same service.

Sensor-Cloud Infrastructure: An infrastructure that sharing the sensor resources among different users.

Smart Applications: A smart application is a function of sensing, actuation, and control in order to describe and analyze a situation, and make decisions based on the available data in a predictive or adaptive manner.

ENDNOTES

[1]   https://ville.montreal.qc.ca/idmtl/en/the-development-of-new-generation-sensors-driven-by-research-and-leading-edge-smes-in-montreal.

[2]   Dedicated Server, Managed Hosting, Web Hosting by Rackspace Hosting, http://www.rackspace.com.

[3]   SAP Business ByDesign,www.sap.com/sme/solutions/businessmanagement/ businessbydesign/ index.epx.

[4]   Google App Engine, http://code.google.com/ appengine.

[5]   Windows Azure, www.microsoft.com/azure.

[6]   Amazon Elastic Computing Cloudaws.amazon.com / ec2.

[7]   Cloud Hosting, Cloud Computing and Hybrid Infrastructure from GoGrid, http://www.gogrid.com.

[8]   Apache Hadoop, http://wiki.apache.org/hadoop.

[9]   "Hbase," http://hbase.apache.org.

Chapter 10
Internet of Things (IoT) Security and Privacy

Muawya N. Al Dalaien
Higher Colleges of Technology, UAE

Salam A. Hoshang
Higher Colleges of Technology, UAE

Ameur Bensefia
Higher Colleges of Technology, UAE

Abdul Rahman A. Bathaqili
Higher Colleges of Technology, UAE

ABSTRACT

In recent years the Internet of Things (IoT) has rapidly become a revolutionary technological invention causing significant changes to the way both corporate computing systems, and even household gadgets and appliances, are designed and manufactured. The aim of this chapter is to highlight the security and privacy issues that may affect the evolution of IoT technology. The privacy issues are discussed from customer perspectives: first, the IoT privacy concern where the privacy debates on IoT and the IoT privacy that reflected from users' perspective based on the examination of previous researches results. In addition, the different architectures for IoT are discussed. Finally, the chapter discusses the IoT security concern by collecting, analyzing and presenting the major IoT security concerns in the literature as well as providing some potential solutions to these concerns.

DOI: 10.4018/978-1-5225-2799-2.ch010

Copyright © 2018, IGI Global. Copying or distributing in print or electronic forms without written permission of IGI Global is prohibited.

INTRODUCTION

IoT refers to networked interconnection of everyday objects, which are equipped with some ubiquitous intelligence. The word "Thing" in IoT has always been subject to different interpretations; Haller et al. (2009) defines IoT as an active physical object participating in any business process.

The number of connected devices is continuously growing where, on average, everyone around the world has roughly two connected devices at a given time. This indicates that the number of connected devices actually outnumber the number of people around the world (Evans, 2011). It is expected that in 2020 the number of "connected" devices reach 26 billion devices (Gartner, 2013). This abundance of units in addition to their predominance in our daily lives raises a number of security and privacy concerns. In this chapter, the authors attempt to give an overview of these security and privacy anxieties.

This chapter is organized into different sections. The chapter begins by addressing the IoT background and its domains of application and assessing its maturity and the various research directions. The second part of the chapter is dedicated to describing the current privacy and security concerns in IoT; number of various IoT architectures is described along with their potential security breaches using several case studies.

BACKGROUND

The convenience, ease of access and interactive communication with a wide variety of devices including home appliances, surveillance cameras, monitoring sensors & displays, and vehicles and, enabled by the IoT technology is expected to boost the development of even more cutting-age smart application of this technology to provide new services to citizens' corporates and public authorities. Such new services would both utilize and generate enormous variety and large amount of data.

This paradigm spans across many different application domains, such as home automation, industrial automation, healthcare, automotive, intelligent energy management and smart grids, traffic management, and many others (Sundmaeker et al. 2010). In theory, every single domain in peoples' life could find some opportunities to exploit IoT in some ways to its advantage or solve some of its problems.

In a recent study, (Mitchell et.al, 2013) Cisco calculated potential value of the IoT if applied in 21 core use cases spanning five areas of business (employee productivity, customer experience, asset utilization, supply chain and logistics and innovation). It was found that the IoT has the potential to deliver $14.4 trillion of value (net profits) for private sector companies globally, between 2013 and 2022. This value is based on the ability to secure lower costs while gaining higher revenues from IoT strategies and applications. The study used cases that cover areas such as smart grid, smart buildings, connected healthcare and patient monitoring, smart factories, connected private education, connected ground vehicles, connected marketing and advertising, and connected gaming and entertainment (Mitchell et al. 2013).

However, not all applications seem to be equally achievable in the near future. While, the traceability of agricultural animals for instance and their movements during outbreaks of contagious diseases, utilizing IoT real-time detection technologies is one of those relatively simple applications. Considering the required technologies are already available and the existence of financial interest for the stakeholders, such applications are already in use today (Sundmaeker et al. 2010).

However, building 'Smart Cities' is more complex. Some of the goals of Smart Cities are to make more efficient use of the public resources and to increase the quality of the offered services to the citizens while reducing the operational costs of public administration and elevate citizens' happiness as the case in Dubai. These objectives can be achieved by the deployment of a communication infrastructure that provides simple, unified and cost-effective access to some public services, therefore creating potential synergies and increasing transparency to the citizens. In such a way, Smart Cities may bring many benefits to the management and optimization of the traditional public services. The improvements include traffic management, smart roads, smart parking, smart lighting, surveillance and maintenance of public areas, preservation of cultural heritage, waste management, pollution control, and others (Zanella et al. 2014).

Despite its complexity, the direction toward Smart Cities is of particular interest, as it responds to the strong push of several governments worldwide, to adopt IoT solutions for the management of public affairs. In 2013, the Smart City project was launched in Dubai, as part of UAE's strategic vision to place itself as a tourism and business hub in the region, which in turn necessitates continuous pioneering of technology (Nagraj, 2013). Since then, constant efforts to achieve the vision are taking place, one of which was an annual IoT event, bringing together government, industry and technology leaders from around the world, to discuss how to create smart ecosystems utilizing mature IoT technologies

INTERNET OF THINGS MATURITY

The ultimate vision for IoT will not just connect our homes, hospitals, schools and streets, but will enable completely new ranges of interactions, services, and efficiencies. However, such a diverse field of applications makes the identification of solutions that are capable of satisfying the requirements of every possible application scenario quite challenging. This difficulty has led to the appearance of different and often incompatible proposals for the practical realization of IoT systems. From a technical perspective, the realization of an IoT network, together with the necessary backend network services and devices, still lacks a proven best practic due to its novelty and complexity. In addition to the technical difficulties, the adoption of the IoT paradigm by industry and organizations is also hindered by the lack of a clear and internationally accepted business model that can attract investments to promote the deployment of these technologies (Zanella et al. 2014).

It is important to note that the comprehensive vision of the Internet of Things is still in the imagination phase (Newman, 2015). The actual realistic visualization is still evolving, with considerable interest and enthusiasm from different parties, including researchers, technology firms, corporate and government sectors. Moreover, just like any evolutionary process, today's Internet of Things faces many challenges and setbacks reminiscent of the Internet development in the early 90's, where many vendors included Internet connectivity features into their products or services, without fully understanding how the technology was supposed to work.

According to Gartner, the IoT concept has reached the peak of its hype in mid-2014, however most of its sub-technologies will need at least few more years before gaining mainstream adoption. Gartner places IoT in the hype phase referred to as 'Peak of Inflated Expectations'. It further describes this stage: "During this phase of overenthusiasm and unrealistic projections, a flurry of well-publicized activity by technology leaders' results in some successes, but more failures, as the technology is pushed to its limits (LeHong & Velosa, 2014).

Amid the momentum and enthusiasm, there are still several challenges that can be categorized into three major potential obstacles to IoT transformation: standardization and compatibility issues, the ambiguity of vision and data security threats. If technology firms could overcome these hurdles, the outcomes will be revolutionary (Texas Instruments, 2014) (Sharma, 2013).

Standardization challenges mainly arise from the difficulties of developing and integrating Internet of Things applications. Functionality in highly distributed architectures, such as 'pervasive computing' environments, involves many disparate parts, supposedly communicating together in a coordinated, seamless pattern. When comparing this with the Internet predecessor, there is an enormous leap in complexity when moving to Internet of Things applications. This complexity is partially due to the infinite diversity of people's preferences, interactions, and consumption patterns. This complication is even multiplied by the variety of deployment environments (Williams, 2015).

INTERNET OF THINGS RESEARCH DIRECTIONS

Since the rise of the IoT concept, a significant quantity of research work and literature has been written about it, especially in the last few years. The spectrum of research required to achieve the scale of IoT envisioned above requires a substantial amount of research in various directions.

According to (Stankovic, 2014), the research efforts related to the IoT up to date are diverse and fragmented. In some cases, they are discussed under the 'Internet of Things' title. In other cases, they might be studied within other research fields, such as 'Wireless Sensor Networks', 'Mobile Computing', 'Pervasive Computing' or most recently, the 'Cyber-Physical Systems'. As technology and solutions progress in any of these fields, there is an increasing overlap and merger of concepts and research domains. Narrow definitions for each of those fields will no longer be appropriate.

Regardless of the research field, the range of research topics required to achieve the envisioned IoT was broadly categorized by the author into one of eight topic areas:

1. **Massive Scaling:** In this research direction, researchers study the introduction and connectivity of the new billions and trillions of 'things' to the Internet; How to name, authenticate, maintain, protect, use and support such a large scale of objects is a question that is yet to be answered.
2. **Architecture and Dependencies:** In this domain, researchers attempt to find a standard architecture that enables easy connectivity, control, communications and useful applications. What will be the platform, or probably platforms, that support the IoT vision is another question that requires further investigation before reaching a fruitful conclusion.
3. **Creating Knowledge and Big Data:** Since collecting raw data alone does not magically create the envisioned value of IoT, it is necessary to develop techniques that convert this raw data into usable knowledge. However, there are several challenges to doing that including difficulties in gathering, storing, correlating, data mining and business intelligence, which all need to be studied further.
4. **Robustness:** In this domain, researchers are expected to find technical solutions for the IoT-enabled devices and infrastructure issues, to ensure it is ready to be utilized consistently and reliably.
5. **Openness:** With every 'thing' connected in one massive network, products from different manufacturers and using different technologies should be able to communicate together as seamlessly as possible. Nowadays, this is considered still a major challenge with different proprietary technologies being frequently used.

6.   **Human-in-the-Loop:** Fully automated solutions might be easier to secure and control than those that involve human beings since behavioral and psychological actions cannot be as simply anticipated. Solutions should still be developed for systems that would incorporate human interaction.

7.   **Security:** The scope of security risks in the IoT world, will not be limited to computers, which will necessitate the introduction of innovative techniques to mitigate the security risks, a mission that would not be simple with infinite types of 'things' being continuously introduced into the Internet.

8.   **Privacy:** Maintaining individual's privacy in an IoT world is extremely complicated, considering a huge amount of information is actually on the Internet today, and a lot more is added daily (Stankovic, 2014).

In the remaining sections of this chapter, the authors will be focusing on the category of privacy and security concerns related to the IoT consumers.

INTERNET OF THINGS SECURITY ARCHITECTURE

Many researchers addressed the IoT security threats from the point of view of a traditional network systems, others focus on the IoT systems features such as: their massive interconnectivity size of different types of IoT devices, the heterogeneity of their nodes, the complexity and the magnitudes of their networks; the security challenges are much bigger (Airehrour et al., 2016).

Whatever is the point of view in considering the IoT security concerns, to fully grasp these concerns we need to better understand the IoT architecture as most of the security breaches are deep rooted in the IoT architecture. A typical IoT architecture is proposed by (Leo et al., 2014) t is built around three main layers: Perception layer, Network layer and the Application layer as shown in Figure 1.

- **Perception Layer:** Represent the sensors used to acquire the data from the external environment such as RFID tags.

- **Network Layer:** Represent all the units embedded in the routing and the transmission data to other devices or applications. Different technologies may be used such as WiFi, LTE, Bluetooth, 3G and Zigbee (Mahmoud et al., 2015).

- **Application Layer:** In this layer the data are stored and processed to produce benefits to users. Thus, this layer is in charge to verify and guaranty the authenticity, confidentiality and integrity of these data.

Figure 1. IoT security architecture
Li, 2012.

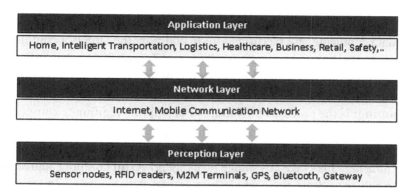

The following section describes each of the above layers in more details.

Perception Layer Security Issues

This layer represents the hardware used to acquire the data from the external environment. In most of the IoT systems, the perception layer is provided by Radio Frequency Identification (RFID), Wireless Sensor Network (WSN), Near Field Communication (NFC) and Bluetooth low energy (Billure, 2015).

RFID uses electromagnetic fields to authenticate automatically tags attached to objects. According to Bolic, (2010), this technology is widely used due to its wide range of advantages.

On the contrary, the NFC is exclusively a RFID short-range wireless communication, thus the device and the tags need to touch each other or to be very close to enabling the communication. Despite the fact that this technology is new it is widely used in mobile phones and payments technologies (Roland, 2015).

This layer is very sensitive since it is exposed to the external environment which makes it vulnerable. Many authors (Zhao et al., 2013; Alajmi, 2014; Rangstone, 2016) addressed the WSN security issues categorization where the most common one is the Denial of Service (DoS). The DOS attack disrupts the wireless transmission by introducing noise or collisions at the receiver side. The attack drains the resources available to the victim node by transferring extra needless data (Alajmi, 2014), which prevents users to accessing services. Riecker in 2014 gave a well-documented survey about this attack and it effects.

Network Layer Security Issues

This layer is subject to different types of attacks such as flooding, spoofing, network sniffing, data capturing and modification. In addition, the DoS is a common attack in this layer due to the numerous protocols in use (Billure, 2015). According to (Lee et al., 2014), attacks in Network Layer can be summarized as Follows:

- **Jamming:** is the process of avoiding or corrupting legitimate communication between sensor nodes by sending radio frequency signal in a wireless channel so that the channel will be completely blocked (Ganeshkumar et al., 2016). The attackers may take advantage by using powerful jamming source pushing the receiver to drain their whole battery and thus leading to a serious DoS. The Jammers can be categorized into four categories (Thakur et al., 2013): constant jammer (continuously emits RF signals of random bits in the channel), random jammer (alters between sending RF signals and periods of inactivity), reactive jammer (inactive if the channel is Idle) and deceptive Jammer (continuously injects series packets to the channel).
- **Tampering:** In a study conducted by (Wurm et al., 2016), the authors studied a commonly used sensor in IoT: Haier SmartCase that has been designed to read all the user's surrounding information such as: smoke detector, door lock state, remote power switch, etc. A simple UART connection coupled to an emulator and the device serial number were enough to allow the authors (attackers) to get access and to modify all the major parameters of that device. This tampering attack example shows how vulnerable the IoT systems can be if the hacker gets physical access to the device. Different tampering attacks exist (Lee et al. 2014):
  - **Injection Attacks:** In this case, the attacker injects malicious code in the device software, and since this device is already deployed in the network, this may lead to the disruption of the whole smart network.
  - **Extraction of Security Information:** The attacker may also extract sensitive information from the device such as encryption keys
  - **Duplication of a Device:** In such case, the attacker could duplicate all the features of a genuine device by creating a malicious one. Thus, this malicious device may run malicious software to other genuine devices in the network to degrade or stop their functionalities.

Application Layer Security Issues

In this layer, the IoT event-driven communications rely on the open eXtensible Messaging and Presence Protocol (XMPP) (Sicari et al., 2015). However, some commands such as XMPPloit, which is command-line exploit tool, attack the XMPP connections by exploiting the vulnerabilities at the client and the server side (Billure, 2015). Such attacks decrypt the client communications making all the messages exchanged readable by the attackers.

INTERNET OF THINGS DATA PRIVACY CONCERNS

Among all of the challenges ahead of IoT adoption, data privacy threats are probably the most significant concerns for the consumer community (Miller, 2015). With all the bulk of information that is collected about every individual as a specific outcome of IoT, it is hard to know, and even harder to control, who knows what information about other consumers. Data is being collected from surveillance cameras, the location determining GPS devices, personal data from smart appliances, personal networks and social media communications, online browsing and shopping preferences, and much more. This collected data can be a serious source of concern for many people as there is always a possibility that it can end up in the wrong hands (Miller, 2015).

Although the 'Internet of Things' term was first introduced in 1999 (New Cause for Concern, 2013), most of the available research work and write-ups about IoT privacy were written after the year 2012. One of the earliest studies in this domain was conducted by Weber (2010), In this study, the author presented a partial vision for the applications of IoT, limiting it to supply chain networks – probably due to the insufficient realization of the IoT at the time. Interestingly, Weber reached several conclusions and suggestions that are similar to recent research works.

In addition, the article outlines four elements for privacy that any enterprise practicing IoT should consider. Those elements are Resilience to attacks, Data Authentication, Access control and Client privacy. The article concludes emphasizing the importance of developing an adequate legal framework that can cater for the new challenges of IoT from different perspectives (Weber, 2010).

Privacy in Distributed/Centralized Services

There is no single strategy for realizing the vision of the IoT, as services can be provisioned in various ways. However, eventually the Internet of Things will take one of two shapes: Services can either be provisioned using centralized architectures, where data is retrieved by a single central entity, which will process it into information, combine it, and provide it to the customers. Alternatively, services could be supplied through distributed architectures, which delegates the decision-making authority to entities located in the lower levels, and entities at the edge of the network exchange information and collaborate with each other in a dynamic way (Proffitt, 2013).

The authors in (Romana et al., 2013) propose some solutions to the privacy issues, based on the two different architectures for IoT. The authors recommend the distributed architecture over the centralized type, highlighting its security and privacy advantages, such as Openness and Scalability. If present trends continue, as they are today, data to and from devices will primarily be trapped within centralized silos. Eventually, companies and vendors will be able to interconnect those silos, rendering all the protocol differences and incompatibilities.

The researchers also suggest some mitigation methods for the security and privacy risks associated with the distributed approach. One example is the negative impact on trust resulting from the enormous size and heterogeneity of the IoT. To enable trust between any two communicating entities, the authors propose to mandate the implementation of efficient cryptographic and identity management algorithms (Romana et al., 2013).

Another solution is proposed by (Banerjee et al. 2014). In the study, the authors developed a privacy-aware slotted channel access mechanism, through which the IoT nodes from different operators or trust domains can share wireless channel without actually exposing their identities, therefore minimizing consumer's concerns about their privacy being compromised in a multi-trust-domain IoT environment.

However, data would remain difficult to share than it should ideally be, given the need to keep building new links between the different silos. It would have to travel farther and might be subject to congestion at hubs, resulting in slowing down services. Nevertheless, this setup would be much closer to a real Internet of Things than the centralization of data, which could raise more security and privacy concerns.

Data Privacy From Customers Perspective

The importance of developing a security legal frameworks that takes users' privacy into consideration, comes from the fact that many people still consider the Internet today a complex and dark place. It is believed that some people might be aware, to some extent at least, that their personal data on the Internet is being exploited, and their search histories are tracked. However, the current behavior of online services today does not provide enough mechanisms for individuals to have oversight and control of their personal information (Turow et al. 2015).

An important question is whether privacy will change as we enter the era of IoT. It can be fairly assumed that the new hyper-connected IoT world will potentially result in data privacy getting much worse (Baldini et al. 2015). That is because more services and more 'things' mean more data gets generated and exchanged. This increase in data volume and complexity might plausibly result in less control. It is a reasonable assumption, and it leaves data privacy at risk (Singh and Powles, 2014).

On the other hand, some people might consider that as a tradeoff, as long as it will result in a simpler, safer and more convenient lifestyle. In fact, some analysts argue that such vast data collecting comes with performance-enhancing wizardry, which might be welcomed by the next generation of workers. The majority of those who will be joining the workforce in 2025 are teenagers today and have grown up sharing everything, starting with pictures of their pets to their relationship status on social media (Kobie, 2015).

So, will the provision of IoT-related services be beneficial enough for future users in making them comfortable in giving up more of their privacy? Do they trust the manufacturers of activity trackers, connected cars, smart homes, and the like to keep the security of their data and to be transparent in their utilization of that data and even any possible sale down the line to a third party? Without appropriate mechanisms to ensure consumers privacy in place, adoption rates of IoT can slowdown. This fact was clearly identified in TRUSTe's research (TRUSTe, 2013), which concluded that consumer privacy concerns could hinder the growth of the IoT market. That result was revealed from a study held in the U.S. and Great Britain, which tried to explore the consumer views about privacy in the context of IoT. The survey showed that around half the surveyed users already knew that smart devices are being used for collecting data about their personal activities. However, just around a fifth of the population believed that IoT benefits outweighed the privacy concerns.

Several similar studies were conducted in different regions and by different researchers, some of which will be discussed in the following sections.

Ponemon Institute Study

This study was carried out by Ponemon Institute, an independent, data privacy specialized, research center, and sponsored by Trend Micro to determine if consumers are worried about how Internet of Things (IoT) is affecting their privacy and security (Ponemon Institute, 2015).

In this study, 1,903 consumers in the US, Europe, and Japan were surveyed. The study also attempted to understand the respondents' perceptions of the worth of their personal information such as health information, purchasing habits, credit history, and browsing reports.

Based on the survey results, the respondents were categorized into three different profiles:

1. **Privacy-Centric:** This group of respondents (around 20% of the sample) tends to change their behaviors when they experience situations that make them worry about the security and privacy of their personal information.

2. **Privacy Sensitive:** Those respondents (61% of the sample) believe data privacy is important but will rarely change any of their behaviors or information sharing practices, even if they experience a situation that affects the security or privacy of their personal information.
3. **Privacy Complacent:** This group (the remaining 19%) is the least concerned about privacy and data security. These respondents do not care even if their sensitive information is shared or even sold.

Some key findings of Ponemon's research are listed below:

- Mobility, data breaches, and social media increase users concerns about privacy.
- In IoT and Social Media, most respondents are more concerned about security than privacy.
- Until today, respondents do not believe that benefits of IoT outweigh their privacy concerns.
- Most respondents (75%) believe that they have limited control over their personal information.
- Little information is provided on how smart devices protect and use personal Information.
- Respondents would like to receive some compensation and information about the smart devices they are using.
- Personal information does have value to those surveyed.
- Respondents would provide their personal information willingly in exchange for money if they trust the company.

Ponemon study included several instrumental questions, from which the following were used in this research.

- What smart devices consumers use or plan to use?
    ◦ Smartphones, Tablets, Smart TV, kitchen appliance, fitness tracker, etc.
- What personal information consumers believe is collected about them:
    ◦ Email address, Home address, Name, Physical location, Browser history, Gender, Photos & Videos, Friends and Family members, Health Condition, Date of Birth, etc.
- What protections are in place to protect your personal information?
    ◦ My data is shared only with trusted parties
    ◦ I can turn off tracking activities
    ◦ My personal information is encrypted
    ◦ I can remotely disable the device that is lost or stolen

- Does your employer have the right to access personal data on your smart device if you use it at work or connect to your employer's Internet?
- Do you have control over how your personal data is used?
- What do you believe companies do with your personal data?
  - ○ The data is used to understand my preferences.
  - ○ The data is used to understand other consumers' preferences.
  - ○ The data is sold to those collecting it for unknown purposes.
  - ○ The data is used to provide me with better security.
  - ○ I do not know how companies use my personal data.

Pew Research Center

This research is one of a series of studies that examined the Americans' digital-privacy-related perceptions and behaviors (Madden & Rainie, 2015). The research was carried out by Pew Research Center, a public opinion polling, and demographic research center, through an online survey of 498 adults and revealed the following key findings:

- Most Americans hold strong views about the importance of privacy in their everyday lives.
- Permission and publicness are important features that influence views on surveillance. Permission refers to the prior authorization from the individual to be watched or heard while Publicness refers to the belief in the individual's right to move around freely in public without being identified.
- Americans have little confidence that their collected data will remain private and secure. Only small minorities say they are "very confident" their personal records maintained by these organizations will continue to be private and secure.
- A slight percentage has changed their behavior to avoid being regularly tracked, but many were already engaged in common or less technical privacy-enhancing measures. Advanced measures on the other hand, such as the use of proxy servers and encryption are less popular.
- Most want limits on the duration that records of their activity can be retained. However, there is a wide variation in the length of time that respondents feel is reasonable for organizations to store their data.
- Respondents who have greater awareness of the U.S. federal monitoring programs are more likely to believe that certain information should not be saved for any length of time
- Although respondents agree on the importance of government collecting some data as part of anti-terrorism efforts, 65% of the American adults

believe there are not adequate limits on the telephone and Internet data that the government collects.

- 55% of Americans support the idea of anonymity for certain online activities.
- Even as respondents expect online anonymity, most assume that determined individuals and organizations could uncover private details.
- Pew Research study included several instrument questions, from which the following were used in this research:
  - Rate how important is the following?
    - Being in control of who can get information about the respondent
    - Being in control of what information is collected about the respondent
    - Not being disturbed at home
    - Not being monitored at work
  - What behavior have been engaged with to ensure the privacy?
    - Clearing cookies or browser history
    - Refusing to provide information that was not relevant
    - Using a temporary username or email address
    - Giving inaccurate or misleading information about the respondent
    - Deciding not to use a website because being asked for some personal information
    - Used encryption or other advanced method of security
  - Which entities to trust for maintaining the privacy?
    - Promotion Agencies, Search engines, cellular telephone companies, government agencies, credit card companies, etc.

Annenberg School Study

This study aimed to understand American's opinions about a variety of online and offline privacy issues. The Annenberg survey was conducted in the period between February and March 2015 and carried out by Princeton Survey Research Associates International. The Research Center conducted telephone interviews with a nationally representative sample which was either English or Spanish speaking and constituted of about 1,506 adult Internet users living in the United States (Turow et al, 2015).

The research results indicated that marketers are misrepresenting the majority of Americans by claiming that Americans willingly give out the personal information as a trade-off for benefits received. To the contrary, the survey revealed that most Americans do not believe that 'data for discounts' is a fair deal.

Some key results of the study are the following:

- 91% of the respondents disagree that "If companies provide me a discount, it is an acceptable deal for them to collect information about me without informing me."
- 71% disagree that "It is fair for an online or physical store to monitor what I am doing online when I am there, in exchange for letting me use the store's wireless Internet, or WiFi, without charge."
- 55% disagree that "It is okay if a store where I shop uses my information to create an image of me that can improve the services provided to me."

Further analysis of these responses indicates that only a very small percentage of Americans agree with the overall concept of tradeoffs. In fact, only about 4% agree with all three propositions. In contrast to the marketers' claims, the study findings also suggest that Americans' willingness to provide personal information cannot be explained by the public's poor knowledge of the ins and outs of digital commerce. In fact, people who knew more about ways their personal information could be used were more likely to accept some discounts in exchange for their data when presented with a real-life scenario.

Altimeter Group Survey

Altimeter Group, a research and consulting firm specialized on technology disruption, conducted an online survey of 2,062 American consumers to determine the consumers' perceptions around the Internet of Things privacy. Companies may point to a complex user experience, legal complexity, or other reason for 'streamlining' registration processes, communications about privacy, or minimizing notifications of data use. However, this study concluded that there is a massive gap between consumer awareness and industry practices with regards to privacy (Groopman & Etlinger, 2015).

Some of the key findings of Altimeter research include the following:

1. The top concern for consumers was found to be: Who is seeing customer data? Consumers are worried about the companies that share their data: 78% of consumers are highly concerned about firms that sell the consumers' data to third parties.
2. Half of the consumers expressed their extreme discomfort with the use and sale of consumers' data in connected 'real world' environments. Older generations demonstrated higher concern although strong discomfort is common across all age groups.
3. Consumers want more information and engagement around privacy. Since trust and understanding of the methods of data collection and privacy protections

are low, consumers are highly interested in more detailed information and more frequent notifications about consumer private data.

4.   Although most consumers accepted monetary compensation in exchange for consumer data, other also demanded that in the form of time, energy, and convenience.

5.   Technological awareness is a core indicator of expectations around notifications, service, communications and trust.

Altimeter study included several instrument questions, from which the following were used in the research:

- "Which of the following devices does the consumer own today that connect to the Internet?"
  - **Choices Included:** Smartphones, Tablets, Smart TV, Wearables, Cars, Connected Appliance, etc.
- "How much of an Understanding does the consumer feel consumer have today about how companies are using the consumer data?"
- "How much does the consumer Trust companies are using the data securely and protecting consumer privacy?"
- "How much Interest does consumer have in understanding how companies are using your data?"
- Rate your level of comfort of sharing information related to the following fields:
  - Your body, your home, public spaces, etc.
- "How important is it to the consumer for companies to notify consumer when the portals are collecting consumer data?"
- Which of the following reasons does consumer find most compelling to share the data?
  - Getting Promotions, getting information, etc.

CONCLUSION

IoT is enabling easy access and interactive communication with a wide variety of services and devices including home appliances, surveillance cameras, monitoring sensors and displays, vehicles and so on. IoT is expected to boost the development of some potential applications. The potential value of the IoT can span from employee productivity, customer experience, asset utilization, supply chain and logistics to innovation. Data security and privacy could be breached through a vast number of causes.

This chapter highlighted the security and privacy concern that may affect the evolution of IoT technology. Further, the chapter discussed IoT privacy issues from customer perspectives.

Furthermore, this chapter discoursed the diverse and fragmented research directions of IoT where several studies conceding data privacy from customers' perspective and solutions were outlined.

REFERENCES

Airehrour, D., Gutierrez, J., & Ray, S. K. (2016). Secure routing for internet of things: A survey. *Journal of Network and Computer Applications*, *66*(1), 198–213. doi:10.1016/j.jnca.2016.03.006

Alajmi, N. (2014). Wireless Sensor Networks Attacks and Solutions. *International Journal of Computer Science and Information Security*, *12*(7), 37–40.

Baldini, G., Peirce, T., Botterman, M., Talacchini, M. C., Pereira, A., & Handte, M. (2015). *IoT Governance, Privacy and Security Issues*. European Commission. Retrieved from http://www.internet-of-things-research.eu/pdf/IERC_Position_Paper_IoT_Governance_Privacy_Security_Final.pdf

Banerjee, D., Dong, B., Taghizadeh, M., & Biswas, S. (2014). Privacy-Preserving Channel Access for Internet of Things. *IEEE Internet of Things Journal, 1*(5).

Billure, R., Tayur, T. M., & Mahesh, V. (2015). Internet of Things - a study on the security challenges. *Advance Computing Conference (IACC), 2015 IEEE International*, 247-252. doi:10.1109/IADCC.2015.7154707

Bolic, M., Simplot-Ryl, D., & Stojmenovic, I. (2010). *RFID Systems: Research Trends and Challenges*. Wiley Editions. doi:10.1002/9780470665251

Evans, A. (2011). *The Internet of Things - How the next evolution of the internet is changing everything. Cisco Internet Business Solutions Group*. IBSG.

Ganeshkumar, P., Vijayakumar, K. P., & Anandaraj, M. (2016). A novel jammer detection framework for cluster-based wireless sensor networks. *EURASIP Journal of Wireless Communication and Networking, 35*(1).

Gartner Inc. (2013). *Forecast: The Internet of Things, Worldwide*. Author.

Groopman, J., & Etlinger, S. (2015). *Consumer Perceptions of Privacy in the Internet of Things*. Altimeter Group.

Haller, S., Karnouskos, S., & Schroth, C. (2009). The Internet of Things in an Enterprise Context. *Lecture Notes in Computer Science*, *5468*, 14–28. doi:10.1007/978-3-642-00985-3_2

IBM Center for Applied Insights. (2014). *The next phase of the Internet: The Internet of Things*. Retrieved from http://ibmcai.com/2014/06/25/the-next-phase-of-the-internet-the-internet-of-things/

Kobie, N. (2015). What will the privacy and security landscape look like in 2025? *The Guardian*. Retrieved from http://www.theguardian.com/media-network/2015/sep/07/privacy-security-landscape-2025

Lee, C., Zappaterra, L., Choi, K., & Hyeong-Ah, C. (2014). Securing smart home: Technologies, security challenges, and security requirements. *Communications and Network Security (CNS), 2014 IEEE Conference on*, 67-72.

LeHong, H., & Velosa, A. (2014). *Hype Cycle for the Internet of Things, 2014*. Gartner. Retrieved from http://www.gartner.com/technology/reprints.do?id=1-27LJLAK&ct=150119&st=sb

Leo, M., Battisti, F., Carli, M., & Neri, A. (2014). A federated architecture approach for Internet of Things security. *Euro Med Telco Conference (EMTC)*, 1-5. doi:10.1109/EMTC.2014.6996632

Madden, M., & Rainie, L. (2015). *Americans' Attitudes About Privacy, Security, and Surveillance*. Pew Research Center.

Mahmoud, R., Yousuf, T., Aloul, F., & Zualkernan, I. (2015). Internet of things (IoT) security: Current status, challenges and prospective measures. *10th International Conference for Internet Technology and Secured Transactions (ICITST)*, 336-341. doi:10.1109/ICITST.2015.7412116

Miller, M. (2015). *The Internet of Things: How Smart TVs, Smart Cars, Smart Homes, and Smart Cities Are Changing the World*. Que. Retrieved from http://proquest.safaribooksonline.com.ezproxy.hct.ac.ae/book/hardware-and-gadgets/9780134021300/15dot-smart-problems-big-brother-is-watching-you/ch15_html

Mitchell, S., Villa, N., Weeks, M. S., & Lange, A. (2013). *The Internet of Everything for Cities*. Cisco Systems Incorporation.

Nagraj, A. (2013). *Dubai's Ruler Announces New 'Smart City' Plan*. Retrieved from http://gulfbusiness.com/2013/10/dubais-ruler-announces-new-smart-city-plan/#.VXplK8-qpBe

New Cause for Concern: 'Internet of Things'. (2013). *Privacy Journal, 39*(11).

Newman, J. (2015). *The IoT is like the internet of the 1990's*. Retrieved from Fast Company (Sector ForeCasting): http://www.fastcompany.com/3044375/sector-forecasting/the-future-of-the-internet-of-things-is-like-the-internet-of-the-1990s

Ponemon Institute. (2015). *Privacy and Security in a Connected Life*. Ponemon Institute© Research.

Proffitt, B. (2013). *What's Holding Up The Internet Of Things?* Retrieved from http://readwrite.com/2013/06/14/whats-holding-up-the-internet-of-things?goback=. gde_73311_member_250004900

Rangstone, P. K., & Sharma, B. (2016). Survey on Issues In Wireless Sensor Networks: Attacks and Countermeasures. *International Journal of Computer Science and Information Security, 14*(4), 262–269.

Riecker, M., Thies, D., & Hollick, M. (2014). Measuring the impact of denial-of-service attacks on wireless sensor networks. *39th Annual IEEE Conference on Local Computer Networks*, 296-304. doi:10.1109/LCN.2014.6925784

Roland, M. (2015). *Security issues in mobile NFC devices*. Cham: Springer. doi:10.1007/978-3-319-15488-6

Romana, R., Zhoua, J., & Lopezb, J. (2013). *On the features and challenges of security and privacy in distributed Internet of things*. Academic Press.

Sharma, R. (2013). Five Challenges For The Internet of Things Ecosystem. *Forbes*. Retrieved from http://www.forbes.com/sites/rakeshsharma/2013/11/12/five-challenges-for-the-the-internet-of-things-ecosystem/

Sicari, S., Rizzardi, A., Grieco, L. A., & Coen-Porisini, A. (2015). Security, privacy and trust in Internet of Things: The road ahead. *Computer Networks, 76*(1), 146–164. doi:10.1016/j.comnet.2014.11.008

Singh, J., & Powles, J. (2014, July 28). The internet of things - the next big challenge to our privacy. *The Guardian*. Retrieved from http://www.theguardian.com/technology/2014/jul/28/internet-of-things-privacy

Stankovic, J. A. (2014). Research Directions for the Internet of Things. *IEEE Internet of Things Journal, 1*(1).

Sundmaeker, H., Guillemin, P., Friess, P., & Woelfflé, S. (2010). *Internet of Things Application Domains. In Vision and Challenges for Realising the Internet of Things* (pp. 49–56). European Commission.

Texas Instruments. (2014). *The Internet of Things: Opportunities & Challenges*. Retrieved from http://www.ti.com/ww/en/internet_of_things/pdf/14-09-17-IoTforCap.pdf

Thakur, N., & Sankaralingam, A. (2013). Introduction to Jamming Attacks and Prevention Techniques using Honeypots in Wireless Networks. *International Journal of Computer Science and Information Technology & Security, 3*(2).

TRUSTe. (2013). *Announcing the 2013 TRUSTe Transparency Report*. TRUSTe. Retrieved from http://www.truste.com/blog/2014/05/29/internet-of-things-industry-brings-data-explosion-but-growth-could-be-impacted-by-consumer-privacy-concerns/

Turow, J., Hennessy, M., & Draper, N. (2015). *The Tradeoff Fallacy*. The University of Pennsylvania, Annenberg School for Communication.

Weber, R. H. (2010). Internet of Things – New security and privacy challenges. *Computer Law & Security Report, 26*(1), 23–30. doi:10.1016/j.clsr.2009.11.008

Williams, O. (2015). *Creating standards for the internet of things – live webchat*. Retrieved from http://www.theguardian.com/media-network/2015/jul/21/standards-internet-of-things-iot-webchat#comment-56518730

Wurm, J., Hoang, K., Arias, O., Sadeghi, A. R., & Jin, Y. (2016). Security analysis on consumer and industrial IoT devices. *21st Asia and South Pacific Design Automation Conference (ASP-DAC)*, 519-524. doi:10.1109/ASPDAC.2016.7428064

Zanella, A., Vangelista, L., Bui, N., Castellani, A., & Zorzi, M. (2014). Internet of Things for Smart Cities. *IEEE Internet of Things Journal, 1*(1).

Zhao, K., & Ge, L. (2013). A Survey on the Internet of Things Security. *Computational Intelligence and Security (CIS), 9th International Conference on*, 663-667.

KEY TERMS AND DEFINITIONS

Data Security: The measures taken to keep data protected from unauthorized access and/or manipulation to prevent privacy.

Privacy: The condition when individuals are free from secret surveillance or annoyed by other people or systems.

Radio Frequency Identification (RFID): The technology that utilizes radio waves to identify objects.

Sensor: A device that detects variations in the environment or system's conditions to cause an adequate response.

Smart City: Integrating Internet of Things applications with various type of information technology systems to manage cities assets, engage citizens and provide services.

Wireless Sensor Network: A wireless network which consists of devices connected with sensors to screen objects or environmental states.

Compilation of References

Abdelwahab, S., Hamdaoui, B., Guizani, M., & Znati, T. (2016). Network function virtualization in 5G. *IEEE Communications Magazine*, *54*(4), 84–91.

Abduvaliyev, A., Pathan, A.-S. K., Zhou, J., Roman, V., & Wong, W.-C. (2013, January). On the vital areas of intrusion detection systems in wireless sensor networks. *IEEE Communications Surveys and Tutorials*, *15*(3), 1223–1237. doi:10.1109/SURV.2012.121912.00006

Aberer, K., Hauswirth, M., & Salehi, A. (2006). A middleware for fast and flexible sensor network deployment. VLDB, 1199–1202.

Airehrour, D., Gutierrez, J., & Ray, S. K. (2016). Secure routing for internet of things: A survey. *Journal of Network and Computer Applications*, *66*(1), 198–213. doi:10.1016/j.jnca.2016.03.006

Akyildiz, I. F., Melodia, T., & Chowdhury, K. R. (2006). A Survey on Wireless Multimedia Sensor Networks. *Computer Networks*. doi: .2006.10.00210.1016/j.commnet

Akyildiz, I. F., Melodia, T., & Chowdhury, K. R. (2007). A survey on wireless multimedia sensor networks. *Computer Networks*, *51*(4), 921–960. doi:10.1016/j.comnet.2006.10.002

Alajmi, N. (2014). Wireless Sensor Networks Attacks and Solutions. *International Journal of Computer Science and Information Security*, *12*(7), 37–40.

Alamri, A., Ansari, W. S., Hassan, M. M., Hossain, M. S., Alelaiwi, A., & Hossain, M. A. (2013). A Survey on Sensor-Cloud: Architecture, Applications, and Approaches. *International Journal of Distributed Sensor Networks*, *2013*, 1–18.

Al-Fuqaha, A., Guizani, M., Mohammadi, M., Aledhari, M., & Ayyash, M. (2015). Internet of things: A survey on enabling technologies, protocols, and applications. *IEEE Communications Surveys and Tutorials*, *17*(4), 2347–2376. doi:10.1109/COMST.2015.2444095

Al-Joumayly, M. A., & Behdad, N. (2011, December). Wideband Planar Microwave Lenses Using Sub-Wavelength Spatial Phase Shifters. *IEEE Transactions on Antennas and Propagation*, *59*(12), 4542–4552. doi:10.1109/TAP.2011.2165515

Alkhawlani, M. M., & Alsalem, K. A. (2010), Radio network selection for tight-coupled wireless networks. *Proceedings of the 7th IEEE International Conference on Informatics and Systems (INFOS)*.

Alliance, W. F. (2009). *Wi-fi peer-to-peer (p2p) technical specification v1. 0*. Wi-Fi Alliance.

Alvi, S. A., Afzal, B., Shah, G. A., Atzori, L., & Mahmood, W. (2015). Internet of multimedia things: Vision and challenges. *Ad Hoc Networks, 33*, 87–111. doi:10.1016/j.adhoc.2015.04.006

Anderson, R., & Spong, M. W. (1989). Bilateral control of teleoperators with time delay. *IEEE Transactions on Automatic Control, 34*(5), 494–501. doi:10.1109/9.24201

Andreev, S., Galinina, O., Pyattaev, A., Gerasimenko, M., Tirronen, T., Torsner, J., & Koucheryavy, Y. et al. (2015). Understanding the IoT connectivity landscape: A contemporary M2M radio technology roadmap. *IEEE Communications Magazine, 53*(9), 32–40. doi:10.1109/MCOM.2015.7263370

Andrews, J. G., Buzzi, S., Choi, W., Hanly, S. V., Lozano, A., Soong, A. C. K., & Zhang, J. C. (2014). What Will 5G Be? *IEEE Journal on Selected Areas in Communications, 32*(6), 1065–1082. doi:10.1109/JSAC.2014.2328098

Anritsu. (2015). *Understanding 5G*. Retrieved from https://pages.anritsu-emearesponse.com/Understanding-5G-Guide.html

Araniti, G., Campolo, C., Condoluci, M., Iera, A., & Molinaro, A. (2013). LTE for vehicular networking: A survey. *IEEE Communications Magazine, 51*(5), 148–157. doi:10.1109/MCOM.2013.6515060

Archer, D. H. (1984, September). Lens-fed multiple beam arrays. *Microwave Journal, 27*, 171.

Archoverview. (n.d.). *Named-data.net online*. Retrieved from http://named-data.net/project/archoverview/

Arslan, M., Sundaresan, K., & Rangarajan, S. (2015). Software-defined networking in cellular radio access networks: Potential and challenges. *IEEE Communications Magazine, 53*(1), 150–156. doi:10.1109/MCOM.2015.7010528

Asadi, A., Wang, Q., & Mancuso, V. (2014). A survey on device-to-device communication in cellular networks. *IEEE Communications Surveys and Tutorials, 16*(4), 1801–1819. doi:10.1109/COMST.2014.2319555

Ashraf, Q. M., & Habaebi, M. H. (2015). Introducing autonomy in internet of things. Recent Advances in Computer Science, 215-221.

Asnani, M., Verma, A., Bijve, S., & Bakariya, B. (2013). A Sketch on Security Issues and Concerns of Cloud Enviroment: Review. *International Conference on Cloud, Big Data and Trusted.*

Astely, D., Dahlman, E., Fodor, G., Parkvall, S., & Sachs, J. (2013). LTE release 12 and beyond. *IEEE Communications Magazine, 51*(7), 154–160. doi:10.1109/MCOM.2013.6553692

Athula, B. (2013). Developing a predictive model of quality of experience for internet video. *Proceedings of the ACM SIGCOMM 2013 Conference.*

Atzori, L., Iera, A., & Morabito, G. (2010). The internet of things: A survey. *Computer Networks*, *54*(15), 2787–2805. doi:10.1016/j.comnet.2010.05.010

Aydın, M. A., Zaim, A. H., & Ceylan, K. G. (2009). A hybrid intrusion detection system design for computer network security. *Computers & Electrical Engineering*, *35*(3), 517–526. doi:10.1016/j.compeleceng.2008.12.005

Baid, A., Vu, T., & Raychaudhuri, D. (2012, March). Comparing alternative approaches for networking of named objects in the future Internet. In *Computer Communications Workshops (INFOCOM WKSHPS), 2012 IEEE Conference on* (pp. 298-303). IEEE. doi:10.1109/INFCOMW.2012.6193509

Baldini, G., Peirce, T., Botterman, M., Talacchini, M. C., Pereira, A., & Handte, M. (2015). *IoT Governance, Privacy and Security Issues*. European Commission. Retrieved from http://www.internet-of-things-research.eu/pdf/IERC_Position_Paper_IoT_Governance_Privacy_Security_Final.pdf

Banerjee, D., Dong, B., Taghizadeh, M., & Biswas, S. (2014). Privacy-Preserving Channel Access for Internet of Things. *IEEE Internet of Things Journal*, *1*(5).

Bangerter, B., Talwar, S., Arefi, R., & Stewart, K. (2014). Networks and Devices for the 5G Era. *IEEE Communications Magazine*, *52*(2), 90–96. doi:10.1109/MCOM.2014.6736748

Bari, F., & Leung, V. C. M. (2009). Use of non-monotonic utility in multi-attribute network selection, Wireless Technology. *Springer US*, *2009*, 21–39.

Bauer, M. (2013). *Catalogue of IoT Naming, Addressing and Discovery Schemes*. IERC Projects V1.7. IERC-AC2-D1.

Billure, R., Tayur, T. M., & Mahesh, V. (2015). Internet of Things - a study on the security challenges. *Advance Computing Conference (IACC), 2015 IEEE International*, 247-252. doi:10.1109/IADCC.2015.7154707

Bliss, D. W., Parker, P., & Margetts, A. R. (2007). Simultaneous Transmission and Reception for Improved Wireless Network Performance. *IEEE/SP 14th Workshop on Statistical Signal Processing*, 478–482. doi:10.1109/SSP.2007.4301304

Boccardi, F., Andrews, J., Elshaer, H., Dohler, M., Parkvall, S., Popovski, P., & Singh, S. (2016). Why to decouple the uplink and downlink in cellular networks and how to do it. *IEEE Communications Magazine*, *54*(3), 110–117. doi:10.1109/MCOM.2016.7432156

Boccardi, F., Heath, R. W., Lozano, A., Marzetta, T. L., & Popovski, P. (2014, February). Five disruptive technology directions for 5G. *IEEE Communications Magazine*, *52*(2), 74–80. doi:10.1109/MCOM.2014.6736746

Bolic, M., Simplot-Ryl, D., & Stojmenovic, I. (2010). *RFID Systems: Research Trends and Challenges*. Wiley Editions. doi:10.1002/9780470665251

Boric-Lubecke, O., Lubecke, V. M., Jokanovic, B., Singh, A., Shahhaidar, E., & Padasdao, B. (2015, Oct). Microwave and wearable technologies for 5G. *Telecommunication in Modern Satellite, Cable and Broadcasting Services (TELSIKS), 2015 12th International Conference on,* 183-188. doi:10.1109/TELSKS.2015.7357765

Boroujeny, B. F. (2011, April). OFDM versus filter bank multicarrier. *IEEE Signal Processing Magazine, 28*(3), 92–112. doi:10.1109/MSP.2011.940267

Borthakur, D., Gray, J., Sarma, J. S., Muthukkaruppan, K., Spiegelberg, N., Kuang, H., & Schmidt, R. et al. (2011, June). Apache Hadoop goes realtime at Facebook. In *Proceedings of the 2011 ACM SIGMOD International Conference on Management of data* (pp. 1071-1080). ACM. doi:10.1145/1989323.1989438

Boskovic, N., Jokanovic, B., Oliveri, F., & Tarchi, D. (2015). High gain printed antenna array for FMCW radar at 17 GHz. *Telecommunication in Modern Satellite, Cable and Broadcasting Services (TELSIKS), 2015 12th International Conference on,* 164-167. doi:10.1109/TELSKS.2015.7357760

Boskovic, N., Jokanovic, B., & Nesic, A. (2015). Frequency scanning antenna arrays with pentagonal dipoles of different impedances. *Serbian Journal of Electrical Engineering, 12*(1), 99–108. doi:10.2298/SJEE1501099B

Botts, M., & Robin, A. (2007). OpenGIS sensor model language (SensorML) implementation specification, OpenGIS Implementation Specification OGC 07-000. The Open Geospatial Consortium.

Bradai, A., Singh, K., Ahmed, T., & Rasheed, T. (2015). Cellular software defined networking: A framework. *IEEE Communications Magazine, 53*(6), 36–43. doi:10.1109/MCOM.2015.7120043

Brady, J., Behdad, N., & Sayeed, A. M. (2013, July). Beamspace MIMO for Millimeter-Wave Communications: System Architecture, Modeling, Analysis, and Measurements. *IEEE Transactions on Antennas and Propagation, 61*(7), 3814–3827. doi:10.1109/TAP.2013.2254442

Brizzolara, D. (2013). Future trends for automotive radars: Towards the 79 GHz band. *ITU News Magazine,* (4).

Buch, D., & Jinwala, D. (2011). Detection of wormhole attacks in wireless sensor network. *Proceedings of the 3rd International Conference on Advances in Recent Technologies in Communication and Computing (ARTCom 2011).* doi:10.1049/ic.2011.0042

Buckl, C., Sommer, S., Scholz, A., Knoll, A., Kemper, A., Heuer, J., & Schmitt, A. (2009, May). Services to the field: An approach for resource constrained sensor/actor networks. In *Advanced Information Networking and Applications Workshops, 2009. WAINA'09. International Conference on* (pp. 476-481). IEEE.

Buyya, R., Yeoa, C. S., Venugopala, S., Broberga, J., & Brandic, I. (2009). Cloud Computing and Emerging IT Platforms: Vision, Hype, and Reality for Delivering Computing as the 5th Utility. *Future Generation Computer Systems, 25*(6), 599–616. doi:10.1016/j.future.2008.12.001

Çalhan, A., & Çeken, C. (2010), An adaptive neuro-fuzzy based vertical handoff decision algorithm for wireless heterogeneous networks. *Proceedings of IEEE 21st International Symposium on Personal Indoor and Mobile Radio Communications (PIMRC)*. doi:10.1109/PIMRC.2010.5671693

Caytiles, R. D., Lee, S., & Park, B. (2012). Cloud computing: The next computing paradigm. *International Journal of Multimedia and Ubiquitous Engineering, 7*, 297–302.

Ceken, C., & Arslan, H. (2009). An adaptive fuzzy logic based vertical handoff decision algorithm for wireless heterogeneous networks. *Proceedings of the 10th IEEE Annual Wireless and Microwave Technology Conference, WAMICON'09*, 1-9. doi:10.1109/WAMICON.2009.5207312

Chapman, C., Emmerich, W., Marquez, F. G., Clayman, S., & Galis, A. (2010, April). Elastic service management in computational clouds. In *12th IEEE/IFIP NOMS2010/International Workshop on Cloud Management (CloudMan 2010)* (pp. 19-23). IEEE.

Chapman, C., Emmerich, W., Márquez, F. G., Clayman, S., & Galis, A. (2012). Software architecture definition for on-demand cloud provisioning. *Cluster Computing, 15*(2), 79–100. doi:10.1007/s10586-011-0152-0

Charilas, D. E. (2009). Application of Fuzzy AHP and ELECTRE to network selection. Mobile Lightweight Wireless Systems. *Springer Berlin Heidelberg, 2009*, 63–73.

Charilas, D. E., Athanasios, D. P., & Ourania, I. M. (2012). A Unified Network Selection Framework Using Principal Component Analysis and Multi Attribute Decision Making. *Wireless Personal Communications*, 1–19.

Charilas, D. E., & Athansios, D. P. (2010). Multiaccess radio network enviroments. *Vehicular Technology Magazine, IEEE, 5*(4), 40–49. doi:10.1109/MVT.2010.939107

Checcacci, P., Russo, V., & Scheggi, A. (1970, November). Holographic antennas. *IEEE Transactions on Antennas and Propagation, 18*(6), 811–813. doi:10.1109/TAP.1970.1139788

Checko, A., Christiansen, H. L., Yan, Y., Scolari, L., Kardaras, G., Berger, M. S., & Dittmann, L. (2015). Cloud RAN for Mobile Networks. A Technology Overview. *IEEE Communications Surveys and Tutorials, 17*(1), 405–426. doi:10.1109/COMST.2014.2355255

Chen, S., Beach, M., & McGeehan, J. (1998). Division-free duplex for wireless applications. In IEEE. *Electronics Letters, 34*(2), 147–148. doi:10.1049/el:19980022

Chen, T., Matinmikko, M., Chen, X., Zhou, X., & Ahokangas, P. (2015). Software defined mobile networks: Concept, survey, and research directions. *IEEE Communications Magazine, 53*(11), 126–133. doi:10.1109/MCOM.2015.7321981

Cherif, W. (2007). A_PSQA: Efficient real-time video streaming QoE tool in a future media internet context. *Multimedia and Expo (ICME), 2011 IEEE International Conference on*. IEEE.

Choi. (2012, November). Beyond full duplex wireless. *Proceedings of Forty Sixth Signals, Systems and Computers (ASILOMAR) Conference*, 40 – 44. doi:10.1109/ACSSC.2012.6488954

Choi, J. I., Jain, M., Srinivasan, K., Levis, P., & Katti, S. (2010). Achieving single channel, full duplex wireless communication. *Proceedings of the sixteenth annual international conference on Mobile computing and networking*, 1–12. doi:10.1145/1859995.1859997

Choudhury, D. (2015, May). 5G wireless and millimeter wave technology evolution: An overview. *2015 IEEE MTT-S International Microwave Symposium*, 1-4. doi:10.1109/MWSYM.2015.7167093

Clayman, S., Galis, A., & Mamatas, L. (2010, April). Monitoring virtual networks with lattice. In Network operations and management symposium workshops (NOMS Wksps), 2010 IEEE/IFIP (pp. 239-246). IEEE. doi:10.1109/NOMSW.2010.5486569

Clayman, S. (2010). Lecture Notes in Computer Science: Vol. 6481. *Towards A Service-Based Internet*. doi:10.1007/978-3-642-17694-4_30

Computing, A. (2006). *An architectural blueprint for autonomic computing*. IBM White Paper, 31.

Condoluci, M., Sardis, F., & Mahmoodi, T. (2015). Softwarization and Virtualization in 5G Networks for Smart Cities. *EAI International Conference on Cyber Physical Systems, IoT and Sensors Networks*.

Coskun, V., Ozdenizci, B., & Ok, K. (2013). A survey on near field communication (NFC) technology. *Wireless Personal Communications*, *71*(3), 2259–2294. doi:10.1007/s11277-012-0935-5

Cuzzocrea, A., Fortino, G., & Rana, O. (2013). Managing Data and Processes in Cloud-Enabled Larg-Scale Sensor Networks: State-of-The-Art and Future Research Directions. *13th IEEE/ACM International Symposium on Cluster, Cloud, and Grid computing*. doi:10.1109/CCGrid.2013.116

Cuzzocrea, A., & Saccà, D. (2013). Exploiting Compression and Approximation Paradigms for Effective and Efficient OLAP over Sensor Network Readings in Data Grid Environments. *Concurrency and Computation*. doi:10.1002/cpe.2982

Dash, S. K., Mohapatra, S., & Pattnaik, P. K. (2010). A survey on Applications of Wireless Sensor Network Using Cloud Computing. *International Journal of Computer Science & Emerging Technologies*, *1*(4).

Dawson, A. W., Marina, M. K., & Garcia, F. J. (2014). On the Benefits of RAN Virtualisation in C-RAN Based Mobile Networks. *Third European Workshop on Software Defined Networks*. doi:10.1109/EWSDN.2014.37

Dihal, S., Bouwman, H., Reuver, M., de Warnier, M., & Carlsson, C. H. (2013). Mobile cloud computing: State of the art and outlook. *Info*, *15*(1), 4-16.

Doré, J. B., Berg, V., Cassiau, N., & Kténas, D. (2014). FBMC receiver for multi-user asynchronous transmission on fragmented spectrum. *EURASIP Journal on Advances in Signal Processing, 41*. doi:10.1186/1687-6180-2014-41

Duarte, M. (2012, April). *Full-duplex Wireless: Design, Implementation and Characterization* (Ph.D. Thesis). Rice University.

Dutta, A., Das, S., Famolari, D., Ohba, Y., Taniuchi, K., Fajardo, V., & Schulzrinne, H. et al. (2007). Seamless proactive handover across heterogeneous access networks. *Wireless Personal Communications, 43*(3), 837–855. doi:10.1007/s11277-007-9266-3

Efstratiou, C. (2010). Challenges in Supporting Federation of Sensor Networks. *NSF/FIRE Workshop on Federating Computing Resources.*

Eggert, M. (2014). *Sensor Cloud: Towards the Interdisciplinary Development of a Trustworthy Platform for Globally Interconnected Sensors and Actuators.* Trusted Cloud Computing.

Ei, T., & Wang, T. (2010). A trajectory-aware handoff algorithm based on GPS information. *Annals of Telecommunications, 65*(7-8), 411-417.

Elnaka, A. M., & Qusay, H. M. (2013), QoS traffic mapping for a multi-participant session in unified communications networks. *Proceedings of 26thAnnual IEEE Canadian Conference on Electrical and Computer Engineering (CCECE).* doi:10.1109/CCECE.2013.6567743

Ericsson White Paper. (2016, April). *5G Radio Access.* Available from https://www.ericsson.com/res/docs/whitepapers/wp-5g.pdf

Ericsson. (n.d.). *Whitepaper: Release, L. T. E. 13.* Retrieved June 1, 2016, from http://www.ericsson.com/res/docs/whitepapers/150417-wp-lte-release-13.pdf

ETSI Technical Report 102 643 V1.0.2. (n.d.). *Human Factors (HF); Quality of Experience (QoE) requirements for real-time communication services.* ETSI.

ETSI. (2002). *TS. 123 107 V4. 3.0 (2002-01) Universal Mobile Telecommunications System (UMTS); Quality of Service (QoS) concept and architecture (3GPP TS 23.107 version 4.3. 0 Release 4).* ETSI Technical Specification.

EU FP7 Internet of Things Architecture Project. (2014, Sep. 18). Retrieved from http://www.iot-a.eu/public

Evans, A. (2011). *The Internet of Things - How the next evolution of the internet is changing everything. Cisco Internet Business Solutions Group.* IBSG.

FAQ. (n.d.). *Opendaylight online.* Retrieved from http://www.opendaylight.org/project/faq#1

FCC. (2016). Use of Spectrum Bands Above 24 GHz for Mobile Radio Services, et al. Federal Communications Commission.

Fettweis, G. (2012). A 5G Wireless Communications Vision. *Microwave Journal, 55*(12), 24–39.

Fettweis, G., & Alamouti, G. (2014, February). 5G: Personal Mobile Internet beyond What Cellular Did to Telephony. *IEEE Communications Magazine, 52*(2), 140–145. doi:10.1109/MCOM.2014.6736754

Fettweis, G., Denzin, F., Michailov, N., Schlöder, K., Seul, D., Wolff, I., & Zimmermann, E. (2011). *Wireless M2M – Wireless Machine-to-Machine Communications.* VDE Position Paper.

Finkelzeller, K. (2003). *The RFID handbook*. Academic Press.

Friess, P. (2013). *Internet of things: converging technologies for smart environments and integrated ecosystems*. River Publishers.

Gakhar, K., Gravey, A., & Leroy, A. (2005) IROISE: a new QoS architecture for IEEE 802.16 and IEEE 802.11 e interworking. *Proceedings of the 2nd International Conference on Broadband Networks (BROADNETS'05)*. doi:10.1109/ICBN.2005.1589787

Ganeshkumar, P., Vijayakumar, K. P., & Anandaraj, M. (2016). A novel jammer detection framework for cluster-based wireless sensor networks. *EURASIP Journal of Wireless Communication and Networking, 35*(1).

Gao, X., Edfors, O., Rusek, F., & Tufvesson, F. (2011, Sept). Linear Pre-Coding Performance in Measured Very-Large MIMO Channels. *Vehicular Technology Conference (VTC Fall), 2011 IEEE*, 1-5. doi:10.1109/VETECF.2011.6093291

Gartner Inc. (2013). *Forecast: The Internet of Things, Worldwide*. Author.

Ghahfarokhi, S. B., & Movahhedinia, N. (2010). A personalized QoE-aware handover decision based on distributed reinforcement learning. *Wireless Networks*, 1–22.

Google. (2010). *Google app engine system status*. Retrieved from http://code.google.com/status/appengine

Gozalvez, J. (2016). New 3GPP Standard for IoT. *IEEE Vehicular Technology Magazine, 11*(1), 14–20. doi:10.1109/MVT.2015.2512358

Groopman, J., & Etlinger, S. (2015). *Consumer Perceptions of Privacy in the Internet of Things*. Altimeter Group.

GSMA Intelligence Report. (2014). *ANALYSIS Understanding 5G: Perspectives on future technological advancements in mobile*. Available from http://www.gsma.com/network2020/volte/understanding-5g-perspectives-on-future-technological-advancements-in-mobile-gsmai-report-3/

GSMA. (2012). *Touching lives through mobile health Assessment of the global market opportunity*. White Paper.

GSMA. (2012a). *Connected Cars: Business Model Innovation*. White Paper.

Gupta, A., & Jha, R. K. (2015). A survey of 5G network: Architecture and emerging technologies. *IEEE Access, 3*, 1206-1232.

Gupta, V., & Rohil, M. K. (2012). Enhancing Wi-Fi with IEEE 802.11 u for Mobile Data Offloading. *International Journal of Mobile Network Communications and Telematics, 2*(4).

Haleplidis, E., Pentikousis, K., Denazis, S., Salim, J. H., Meyer, D., & Koufopavlou, O. (2015, January). *Software-Defined Networking (SDN): Layers and Architecture Terminology*. RFC 7426, IETF, ISSN 2070-1721.

Haller, S., Karnouskos, S., & Schroth, C. (2009). The Internet of Things in an Enterprise Context. *Lecture Notes in Computer Science, 5468*, 14–28. doi:10.1007/978-3-642-00985-3_2

Hammad, H. F., Antar, Y. M., & Freundorfer, A. P. (2001). Uni-planar slot antenna for TM slab mode excitation. *Electronics Letters, 37*(25), 1. doi:10.1049/el:20011009

Hansen, R. C. (2009). *Phased Array Antennas*. Hoboken, NJ: Wiley. doi:10.1002/9780470529188

Hassan, M. M., Song, B., & Huh, E. N. (2009, February). A framework of sensor-cloud integration opportunities and challenges. In *Proceedings of the 3rd international conference on Ubiquitous information management and communication* (pp. 618-626). ACM. doi:10.1145/1516241.1516350

Heath, R. W., González-Prelcic, N., Rangan, S., Roh, W., & Sayeed, A. M. (2016, April). An Overview of Signal Processing Techniques for Millimeter Wave MIMO Systems. *IEEE Journal of Selected Topics in Signal Processing, 10*(3), 436–453. doi:10.1109/JSTSP.2016.2523924

Herman, H. (2011). Nonlinearity modelling of QoE for video streaming over wireless and mobile network. *Proceedings of the Second IEEE International Conference on Intelligent Systems, Modelling and Simulation (ISMS)*. doi:10.1109/ISMS.2011.55

Hill, P. Ch., & Chung, W. Y. (2011). A Comprehensive Ubiquitous Healthcare Solution on an Android Mobile Device. *Sensors (Basel, Switzerland), 11*(12), 6799–6815. doi:10.3390/s110706799 PMID:22163986

Holub, V., Parsons, T., O'Sullivan, P., & Murphy, J. (2009, June). Run-time correlation engine for system monitoring and testing. In *Proceedings of the 6th international conference industry session on Autonomic computing and communications industry session* (pp. 9-18). ACM. doi:10.1145/1555312.1555317

Huang, Z.-Q., Bai, S-N., & Jaeil, J. (2009). A MIH Services Based Application-Driven Vertical Handoff Scheme for Wireless Networks. *Proceedings of the 5th IEEE International Joint Conference on INC, IMS and IDC,(NCM'09)*. doi:10.1109/NCM.2009.254

Huawei Technologies. (2010). *Behaviour Analysis of Smartphone, White Paper*. Available from http://www.huawei.com/en/static/hw-001545.pdf

Hussain Shah, S., Kabeer Khan, F., Ali, W., & Khan, J. (2013). A New Framework to Integrate Wireless Sensor Networks with Cloud Computing. *Aerospace Conference*. IEEE.

Hyperic. (2010). *Cloudstatus ® powered by hyperic*. Retrieved from http://www.cloudstatus.com

Hyunho, P., Ho, L.-H., & Seung-Hwan, L. (2014). IEEE 802 standardization on heterogeneous network interworking. *Proceedings of the 16th International Conference on Advanced Communication Technology (ICACT)*, 1140-1145.

IBM Center for Applied Insights. (2014). *The next phase of the Internet: The Internet of Things*. Retrieved from http://ibmcai.com/2014/06/25/the-next-phase-of-the-internet-the-internet-of-things/

ID MTL. (2016, 8 July). Retrieved from https://ville.montreal.qc.ca/idmtl/en/the-development-of-new-generation-sensors-driven-by-research-and-leading-edge-smes-in-montreal

IEEE 802.15 Working Group for WPAN. (n.d.). Retrieved June 1, 2016, from http://ieee802.org/15

IEEE 802.21. (2008). *IEEE standard for local and metropolitan area networks: Media independent handover services.* IEEE.

IEEE Standard 802.21. (2007). *Media Independent Handover Specifications.* IEEE.

Imbert, M., Romeu, J., Jofre, L., Papió, A., & Flaviis, F. D. (2014, July). Switched-beam antenna array for 60 GHz WPAN applications. *2014 IEEE Antennas and Propagation Society International Symposium (APSURSI)*, 1672-1673. doi:10.1109/APS.2014.6905162

IMT2020. (2015, July). Available from https://www.itu.int/en/ITU-T/gsc/19/Documents/201507/GSC-19_307_Research_Activities_of_IMT-2020_%20(5G)_Promotion%20Group.pptx

Islam, M., & Huh, E. (2012). Virtualization in Wireless Sensor Network; Challenges and Opportunities. *Journal of Networks, 7*(3).

Islam, M., Hassan, M. M., Lee, G.-W., & Huh, E.-N. (2012). A Survey on Virtualization of Wireless Sensor Networks. *Sensors (Basel, Switzerland), 12*(2), 2175–2207. doi:10.3390/s120202175 PMID:22438759

Istepanaian, R. S. H., & Zhang, Y. T. (2012). Guest Editorial Introduction to the Special Section: 4G Health - The Long-Term Evolution of m-Health. *IEEE Transactions on Information Technology in Biomedicine, 16*(1), 1–5. doi:10.1109/TITB.2012.2183269 PMID:22271836

ITU. (2014). *Smart Sustainable Cities: An Analysis of Definitions.* ITU.

ITU. (2015 July). *ITU towards IMT for 2020 and beyond.* Available from http://www.itu.int/en/ITU-R/study-groups/rsg5/rwp5d/imt-2020/Pages/default.aspx

ITU-R. (2015, September). *IMT Vision – Framework and overall objectives of the future development of IMT for 2020 and beyond.* Available from https://www.itu.int/dms_pubrec/itu-r/rec/m/R-REC-M.2083-0-201509-I!!PDF-E.pdf

ITU-T Rec, . (1999). *Subjective video quality assessment method for multimedia applications.* ITU-T.

ITU-T Rec, . (2008). *Vocabulary for performance and quality of service, Amendment 2: New definitions for inclusion in Recommendation ITU-T P. 10/G. 100* (p. 10). Geneva: Int. Telecomm. Union.

ITU-T Rec. G.1070. (2007). *Opinion model for videophone applications.* ITU-T.

ITU-T Rec. J.246. (2008). *Perceptual audiovisual quality measurement techniques for multimedia services over digital cable television networks in presence of reduced bandwidth reference.* ITU-T.

ITU-T Rec. J.247. (2008). *Objective perceptual multimedia video quality measurement in the presence of a full reference.* ITU-T.

ITU-T Rec. P.800. (1996). *Methods for subjective determination of transmission quality.* ITU-T.

IWPC. (2014, April 2). *IWPC Ultra High Capacity Networks White Paper Version 1.1.* Available from http://www.iwpc.org/WhitePaper.aspx?WhitePaperID=17

Jain, M., Choi, J., Kim, T. M., Bharadia, D., Seth, S., Srinivasan, K., & Sinha, P. et al. (2011). Practical, real-time full duplex wireless. *Proceedings of the seventeenth annual international conference on Mobile computing and networking*, 301–312. Doi:10.1145/2030613.2030647

Jiao, J., Ma, H., Qiao, Y., Du, Y., Kong, W., & Wu, Z.-C. (2014). Design of farm environmental monitoring system based on the Internet of Things. *Advance Journal of Food Science and Technology*, *6*(3), 368–373.

Johnson, M. C., Brunton, S. L., Kundtz, N. B., & Kutz, J. N. (2015, April). Sidelobe Canceling for Reconfigurable Holographic Metamaterial Antenna. *IEEE Transactions on Antennas and Propagation*, *63*(4), 1881–1886. doi:10.1109/TAP.2015.2399937

Kaleem, F., Mehbodniya, A., Islam, A., Yen, K. K., & Adachi, F. (2013). Dynamic target wireless network selection technique using fuzzy linguistic variables. *China Communications*, *10*(1), 1–16. doi:10.1109/CC.2013.6457526

Kaloxylos, A., Eigenmann, R., Teye, F., Politopoulou, Z., Wolfert, S., Shrank, C., & Kormentzas, G. et al. (2012). Farm management systems and the future internet era. *Computers and Electronics in Agriculture*, *89*, 130–144. doi:10.1016/j.compag.2012.09.002

Kasparick, M., Wunder, G., Jung, P., & Maryopi, D. (2014 May). Bi-orthogonal Waveforms for 5G Random Access with Short Message Support. *European Wireless 2014- Conference Proceedings of 20th European Wireless, 1*(6), 14-16.

Kassar, M., Kervella, B., & Pujolle, G. (2008). An overview of vertical handover decision strategies in heterogeneous wireless networks. *Computer Communications*, *31*(10), 2607–2620. doi:10.1016/j.comcom.2008.01.044

Khan, I., Belqasmi, F., Glitho, R., Crespi, N., Morrow, M., & Polakos, P. (2016). Wireless Sensor Network Virtualization: A Survey. *IEEE Communication Survey & Tutorials*, *18*(1).

Khan, R., Khan, S. U., Zaheer, R., & Khan, S. (2012, December). Future internet: the internet of things architecture, possible applications and key challenges. In *Frontiers of Information Technology (FIT), 2012 10th International Conference on* (pp. 257-260). IEEE. doi:10.1109/FIT.2012.53

Khan, F. (2014). Secure communication and routing architecture in wireless sensor networks. *Proceedings of IEEE 3rd Global Conference on Consumer Electronics (GCCE).* doi:10.1109/GCCE.2014.7031298

Khan, I., Belqasmi, F., Glitho, R., Crespi, N., Morrow, M., & Polakos, P. (2016). Wireless sensor network virtualization: A survey. *IEEE Communications Surveys and Tutorials*, *18*(1), 553–576. doi:10.1109/COMST.2015.2412971

Khojastepour, M. A., Sundaresan, K., Rangarajan, S., Zhang, X., & Barghi, S. (2011). The case for antenna cancellation for scalable full-duplex wireless communications. *Proceedings of the 10th ACM Workshop on Hot Topics in Networks*, *17*, 1–17. doi:10.1145/2070562.2070579

Kim, K., Lee, S., Yoo, H., & Kim, D. (2014). Agriculture Sensor-Cloud Infrastructure and Routing Protocol in the Physical Sensor Network Layer. *International Journal of Distributed Sensor Networks*.

Klaue, J., Berthold, R., & Adam, W. (2003). Evalvid–A framework for video transmission and quality evaluation. Computer Performance Evaluation. Modelling Techniques and Tools. *Springer Berlin Heidelberg*, *2003*, 255–272.

Kobie, N. (2015). What will the privacy and security landscape look like in 2025? *The Guardian*. Retrieved from http://www.theguardian.com/media-network/2015/sep/07/privacy-security-landscape-2025

Kreutz, D., Ramos, F. M. V., Veríssimo, P. E., Rothenberg, C. E., Azodolmolky, S., & Uhlig, S. (2015). Software-Defined Networking: A Comprehensive Survey. *Proceedings of the IEEE*, *103*(1), 14–76. doi:10.1109/JPROC.2014.2371999

Kuo, Y., Yang, T., & Huang, G.-W. (2008). The use of grey relational analysis in solving multiple attribute decision-making problems. *Computers & Industrial Engineering*, *55*(1), 80–93. doi:10.1016/j.cie.2007.12.002

Kushalnagar, N., Montenegro, G., & Schumacher, C. (2007). *IPv6 over low-power wireless personal area networks (6LoWPANs): Overview, assumptions, problem statement, and goals* (No. RFC 4919). RFC.

Lahby, M., & Adib, A. (2013). Network selection mechanism by using M-AHP/GRA for heterogeneous networks. *Proceedings of the 6th Joint IFIP IEEE Wireless and Mobile Networking Conference (WMNC)*, 1-6. doi:10.1109/WMNC.2013.6549009

Lahby, M., Leghris, C., & Abdellah, A. (2013). A Novel Ranking Algorithm Based Network Selection For Heterogeneous Wireless Access. *Journal of Networks*, *8*(2), 263–272. doi:10.4304/jnw.8.2.263-272

Lahby, M., Leghris, C., & Adib, A. (2012). New multi access selection method using differentiated weight of access interface. *Proceedings of IEEE International Conference on. Communications and Information Technology (ICCIT)*, 237 – 242. doi:10.1109/ICCITechnol.2012.6285799

Lampropoulos, G., & Apostolis, K. (2008). Media-independent handover for seamless service provision in heterogeneous networks. *Communications Magazine, IEEE*, *46*(1), 64–71. doi:10.1109/MCOM.2008.4427232

Lan, K. T. (2010) What's Next? Sensor+Cloud? In *Proceeding of the 7th International Workshop on Data Management for Sensor Networks* (pp. 978–971). ACM Digital Library.

Laya, A., Alonso, L., & Alonso-Zarate, J. (2014). Is the Random Access Channel of LTE and LTE-A Suitable for M2M Communications? A Survey of Alternatives. *IEEE Communications Surveys and Tutorials*, *16*(1), 4–16. doi:10.1109/SURV.2013.111313.00244

Lee, C., Zappaterra, L., Choi, K., & Hyeong-Ah, C. (2014). Securing smart home: Technologies, security challenges, and security requirements. *Communications and Network Security (CNS), 2014 IEEE Conference on*, 67-72.

Lee, J. H., Bonnin, J. M., Seite, P., & Chan, H. A. (2013). Distributed IP mobility management from the perspective of the IETF: Motivations, requirements, approaches, comparison, and challenges. *IEEE Wireless Communications*, *20*(5), 159–168. doi:10.1109/MWC.2013.6664487

Lee, W., Kim, J., & Yoon, Y. J. (2011, February). Compact Two-Layer Rotman Lens-Fed Microstrip Antenna Array at 24 GHz. *IEEE Transactions on Antennas and Propagation*, *59*(2), 460–466. doi:10.1109/TAP.2010.2096380

LeHong, H., & Velosa, A. (2014). *Hype Cycle for the Internet of Things, 2014*. Gartner. Retrieved from http://www.gartner.com/technology/reprints.do?id=1-27LJLAK&ct=150119&st=sb

Lehpamer, H. (2008). *Millimeter-Wave Radios in Backhaul Networks. Tech. rep*. Communication Infrastructure Corporation.

Leo, M., Battisti, F., Carli, M., & Neri, A. (2014). A federated architecture approach for Internet of Things security. *Euro Med Telco Conference (EMTC)*, 1-5. doi:10.1109/EMTC.2014.6996632

Li, C. (2013). Mobile Application Based Sustainable Irrigation Water Usage Decision Support System: An Intelligent Sensor CLOUD Approach. *Sensors (Basel, Switzerland)*.

Li, M., Al-Joumayly, M. A., & Behdad, N. (2013, March). Broadband True-Time-Delay Microwave Lenses Based on Miniaturized Element Frequency Selective Surfaces. *IEEE Transactions on Antennas and Propagation*, *61*(3), 1166–1179. doi:10.1109/TAP.2012.2227444

Li, Y., & Chen, M. (2015). Software-Defined Network Function Virtualization: A Survey. *IEEE Access*, *3*, 2542–2553. doi:10.1109/ACCESS.2015.2499271

Lohith, Y. S., Brinda, M. C., Anand, S. V. R., & Hegde, M. (2011). 6PANVIEW: A Network Monitoring System for the Internet of Things. *Proceedings of the Asia-Pacific Advanced Newtork*, *32*(0), 106–109. doi:10.7125/APAN.32.13

Long, Y., & Guo, D-X. (2012). *A Satellite Heterogeneous Network Selection Algorithm Combining AHP and TOPSIS*. Academic Press.

Lounis, A., Hadjidj, A., Bouabdallah, A., & Challal, Y. (2012). Secure and Scalable Cloud-based Architecture for e-Health Wireless Sensor Networks. *International Conference on Computer Communications and Networks (ICCCN)*. doi:10.1109/ICCCN.2012.6289252

Lounis, A., Hadjidj, A., Bouabdallah, A., & Challa, Y. (2012). *Secure and Scalable Cloud-based Architecture for e-Health Wireless Sensor Networks. Computer Communications and Networks.* ICCCN.

Madden, M., & Rainie, L. (2015). *Americans' Attitudes About Privacy, Security, and Surveillance.* Pew Research Center.

Madria, S., Kumar, V., & Dalvi, R. (2014). Sensor Cloud: A Cloud of Virtual Sensors. *IEEE Software, 31*(2), 70–77. doi:10.1109/MS.2013.141

Mahesh, D. S., Savitha, S., & Dinesh, K. (2014). A Cloud Computing Architecture with Wireless Sensor Networks for Agricultural Applications. *International Journal of Computer Networks and Communications Security, 2*(1).

Mahmoud, R., Yousuf, T., Aloul, F., & Zualkernan, I. (2015). Internet of things (IoT) security: Current status, challenges and prospective measures. *10th International Conference for Internet Technology and Secured Transactions (ICITST)*, 336-341. doi:10.1109/ICITST.2015.7412116

Mahmoud, S. F., Antar, Y. M., Hammad, H. F., & Freundorfer, A. P. (2003). Optimum excitation of surface waves on planar structures. *Antennas and Propagation Society International Symposium, 2*, 88-91. doi:10.1109/APS.2003.1219186

Mailloux, R. J. (2007). *Electronically Scanned Arrays.* Williston, VT: Morgan & Claypool.

Makela, J., Ylianttila, M., & Pahlavan, K. (2000). Handoff decision in multi-service networks. *The 11th IEEE International Symposium on Personal, Indoor and Mobile Radio Communications.* doi:10.1109/PIMRC.2000.881503

Malina, L., Hajny, J., Fujdiak, R., & Hosek, J. (2016, June). On perspective of security and privacy-preserving solutions in the internet of things. *Computer Networks, 102*, 83–95. doi:10.1016/j.comnet.2016.03.011

Mao, Koksal, & Shroff. (2012). Near Optimal Power and Rate Control of Multi-Hop Sensor Networks With Energy Replenishment: Basic Limitations With Finite Energy and Data Storage. *IEEE Trans. Autom. Control, 7*, 815–829.

Márquez-Barja, J., Calafate, C. T., Cano, J.-C., & Manzoni, P. (2011). An overview of vertical handover techniques: Algorithms, protocols and tools. *Computer Communications, 34*(8), 985–997. doi:10.1016/j.comcom.2010.11.010

Marzetta, T. (2006, October), How much training is required for multiuser MIMO. *Proceedings of Fortieth Signals, Systems and Computers (ASILOMAR) Conference*, 359 – 363. doi:10.1109/ACSSC.2006.354768

Marzetta, T. (2010, November). Noncooperative cellular wireless with unlimited numbers of base station antennas. *IEEE Transactions on Wireless Communications, 9*(1), 3590–3600. doi:10.1109/TWC.2010.092810.091092

Matthews, W., Cottrell, L., & Salomoni, D. (2001, April). *Passive and Active Monitoring on a High Performance Research Network*. Academic Press.

McCanne, S., & Jacobson, V. (1992, December). *The BSD Packet Filter: A New Architecture for User-level Packet Capture*. Lawrence Berkeley Laboratory.

McKinsey Digital. (2015). *Industry 4.0 How to navigate digitization of the manufacturing sector*. White Paper.

McMillan, R. W. (2006). Terahertz imaging, millimeter-wave radar. In *Advances in sensing with security applications* (pp. 243–268). Heidelberg, Germany: Springer. doi:10.1007/1-4020-4295-7_11

Medagliani, P., Leguay, J., Duda, A., Rousseau, F., Duquennoy, S., Raza, S., ... Monton, M. (2014). *Internet of Things Applications-From Research and Innovation to Market Deployment*. Academic Press.

Meinel, H. H. (2014, April). Evolving automotive radar #x2014; From the very beginnings into the future. *The 8th European Conference on Antennas and Propagation (EuCAP 2014)*, 3107-3114. doi:10.1109/EuCAP.2014.6902486

Mell, P., & Grance, T. (2009). *Draft nist working definition of cloud computing* (vol. 15). Academic Press.

Menkovski, V., Exarchakos, G., & Liotta, A. (2010). Online QoE prediction. *Proceedings of the Second IEEE International Workshop on Quality of Multimedia Experience (QoMEX)*. doi:10.1109/QOMEX.2010.5517692

Menzel, W., & Moebius, A. (2012, July). Antenna Concepts for Millimeter-Wave Automotive Radar Sensors. *Proceedings of the IEEE*, *100*(7), 2372–2379. doi:10.1109/JPROC.2012.2184729

METIS. (2015). *Scenarios, requirements and KPIs for 5G mobile and wireless system*. Document number: ICT-317669-METIS/D1.1. Available from https://www.metis2020.com/wp-content/uploads/deliverables/METIS_D1.1_v1.pdf

Michailow, N., Matthe, M., Gaspar, I. S., Caldevilla, A. N., Mendes, L. L., Festag, A., & Fettweis, G. P. (2014, September). Generalized Frequency Division Multiplexing for 5th Generation Cellular Networks. *IEEE Transactions on Communications*, *62*(9), 3045–3061. doi:10.1109/TCOMM.2014.2345566

Militano, L., Araniti, G., Condoluci, M., Farris, I., & Iera, A. (2015). *Device-to-device communications for 5G internet of things*. EAI.

Miller, M. (2015). *The Internet of Things: How Smart TVs, Smart Cars, Smart Homes, and Smart Cities Are Changing the World*. Que. Retrieved from http://proquest.safaribooksonline.com.ezproxy.hct.ac.ae/book/hardware-and-gadgets/9780134021300/15dot-smart-problems-big-brother-is-watching-you/ch15_html

Milosevic, V., Jokanovic, B., & Bojanic, R. (2013, August). Effective Electromagnetic Parameters of Metamaterial Transmission Line Loaded With Asymmetric Unit Cells. *IEEE Transactions on Microwave Theory and Techniques, 61*(8), 2761–2772. doi:10.1109/TMTT.2013.2268056

Milosevic, V., Radovanovic, M., Jokanovic, B., Boric-Lubecke, O., & Lubecke, V. M. (2016, Oct., accepted paper). Tx Leakage Cancellation Using Antenna Image Impedance for CW Radar Applications. *2016 European Microwave Conference (EuMC).* doi:10.1109/EuMC.2016.7824370

Miranda, J., Gomes, T., Abrishambaf, R., Loureiro, F., Mendes, J., Cabral, J., & Monteiro, J. (2014). A Wireless Sensor Network for collision detection on guardrails. *Proceedings of IEEE 23rd International Symposium on Industrial Electronics (ISIE).* doi:10.1109/ISIE.2014.6864824

Misra, S. Chatterjee, S. Obaidat, M. S. (2014). On Theoretical Modeling of Sensor Cloud: A Paradigm Shift From Wireless Sensor Network. *IEEE System Journal.*

Misra, S., Bera, S., Mondal, A., Tirkey, R., Chao, H., & Chattopadhyay, S. (2013). Optimal gateway selection in sensor-cloud framework for health monitoring. *IET Wireless Sensor Systems, 4*(2), 61–68. doi:10.1049/iet-wss.2013.0073

Misra, S., Singh, A., Chatterjee, S., & Obaidat, M. S. (2014). *Mils-Cloud: A Sensor-Cloud-Based Architecture for the Integration of Military Tri-Services Operations and Decision Making.* IEEE System Journal.

Mitchell, S., Villa, N., Weeks, M. S., & Lange, A. (2013). *The Internet of Everything for Cities.* Cisco Systems Incorporation.

mmMagic. (2016, April). *Architectural aspects of mm-wave radio access integration with 5G ecosystem.* Available from https://bscw.5g-mmmagic.eu/pub/bscw.cgi/d100702/mm-wave_architecture_white_paper.pdf

Mohamed, A., Onireti, O., Imran, M. A., Imran, A., & Tafazolli, R. (2016). Control-Data Separation Architecture for Cellular Radio Access Networks: A Survey and Outlook. *IEEE Communications Surveys and Tutorials, 18*(1), 446–465. doi:10.1109/COMST.2015.2451514

Mohamed, S., & Rubino, G. (2002). A study of real-time packet video quality using random neural networks. *IEEE Transactions on Circuits and Systems for Video Technology, 12*(12), 1071–1083.

Mohanan, V., Budiarto, R., & Aldmour, I. (2015). Network Selection Problems-QoE vs QoS Who is the Winner? *Computer Engineering and Applications Journal, 1*(1).

Mohanan, V., Budiarto, R., & Osman, M. A. (2013). Holistic network selection using dynamic weights to achieve personalized ABC. *Proceedings of the 19th IEEE Asia-Pacific Conference on Communications (APCC),* 196 – 201. doi:10.1109/APCC.2013.6765941

Mohanan, V., Budiarto, R., & Zainon, W. N. M. W. (2012). Holistic network selection for wireless mobile nodes in a 4G environment. *Proceedings of the 18th IEEE Asia-Pacific Conference on Communications (APCC).* doi:10.1109/APCC.2012.6388100

Morais, R., Matos, S. G., Fernandes, M. A., Valente, A. L. G., Soares, S. F. S. P., Ferreira, P. J. S. G., & Reis, M. J. C. S. (2008). Sun, wind and water flow as energy supply for small stationary data acquisition platforms. *Journal of Computer Electronic Agriculture, 64*(2), 120–132. doi:10.1016/j.compag.2008.04.005

Mukherjee, A., Paul, H. S., Dey, S., & Banerjee, A. (2014, March). Angels for distributed analytics in iot. In *Internet of Things (WF-IoT), 2014 IEEE World Forum on* (pp. 565-570). IEEE. doi:10.1109/WF-IoT.2014.6803230

Nagraj, A. (2013). *Dubai's Ruler Announces New 'Smart City' Plan*. Retrieved from http://gulfbusiness.com/2013/10/dubais-ruler-announces-new-smart-city-plan/#.VXplK8-qpBe

New Cause for Concern: 'Internet of Things'. (2013). *Privacy Journal, 39*(11).

Newman, J. (2015). *The IoT is like the internet of the 1990's*. Retrieved from Fast Company (Sector ForeCasting): http://www.fastcompany.com/3044375/sector-forecasting/the-future-of-the-internet-of-things-is-like-the-internet-of-the-1990s

NGMN Alliance. (2016). *NGMN 5G White Paper*. Available from https://www.ngmn.org/uploads/media/NGMN_5G_White_Paper_V1_0.pdf

NGMN Alliance. (2016). *NGMN 5G White Paper*. Retrieved from https://www.ngmn.org/

NGMN. (2015). *5G White Paper*. White Paper.

Nguyen, V., & Quoc, T. (2013). *Multi-Criteria Optimization of Access Selection to Improve the Quality of Experience in Heterogeneous Wireless Access Networks*. Academic Press.

Nimbits. (2014, Sep. 25). Retrieved from http://www.nimbits.com/

Nithyanandan, L., Bharathi, V., & Prabhavathi, P. (2013). User centric network selection in wireless hetnets. *International Journal of Wireless & Mobile Networks, 5*(3).

Nokia Networks. (2015). *Nokia Networks white paper - 5G Radio Access System Design Aspects*. Available from http://resources.alcatel-lucent.com/asset/200009

Nokia Siemens Networks. (2011). *Signalling is growing 50% faster than data traffic*. White Paper.

Nokia Siemens Networks. (2011). *Understanding Smartphone Behavior in the Network, White Paper*. Available: http://www.nokiasiemensnetworks.com/sites/default/files /document/Smart_Lab_WhitePaper_27012011_low-res.pdf

Office for Life Sciences. (2015). *Digital Health in the UK An industry study for the Office of Life Sciences*. White Paper.

Openflow, D. (n.d.). *Opennetworking online*. Retrieved https://www.opennetworking.org/sdn-resources/openflow

Osseiran, A., Boccardi, F., Braun, V., Kusume, K., Marsch, P., Maternia, M., & Fallgren, M. et al. (2014). Scenarios for 5G mobile and wireless communications: The vision of the METIS project. *IEEE Communications Magazine, 52*(5), 26–35. doi:10.1109/MCOM.2014.6815890

Palattella, M. R., Dohler, M., Grieco, A., Rizzo, G., Torsner, J., Engel, T., & Ladid, L. (2016). Internet of Things in the 5G Era: Enablers, Architecture, and Business Models. *IEEE Journal on Selected Areas in Communications, 34*(3), 510–527. doi:10.1109/JSAC.2016.2525418

Pande, P., & Padwalkar, A. R. (2014). Internet of Things-A Future of Internet: A Survey, *International Journal of Advanced Research in Computer Science and Management Studies, 2*(2).

Parameswar, S. K., & Pooch, U. W. (1996). *Universal Packet Analyser - A Network Packet Filtering tool.* Department of Computer Science, Texas A&M University, Technical Report 96-008 (TR 96-008).

Pasley, J. (2005). How BPEL and SOA are changing Web services development. *IEEE Internet Computing, 9*(3), 60–67. doi:10.1109/MIC.2005.56

Patel, V., Taghavi, M., Bakhtiyari, K., & Júnior, J. C. (2013). An intrusion detection and prevention system in cloud computing: A systematic review. *Journal of Network and Computer Applications, 36*(1), 25–41. doi:10.1016/j.jnca.2012.08.007

Pelletier, A. (2016). *Virtual reality: The reality for connectivity providers.* Retrieved July 16, 2016, from http://telecoms.com/opinion/virtual-reality-the-reality-for-connectivity-providers

Pentikousis, K., Wang, Y., & Hu, W. (2013). Mobileflow: Toward software-defined mobile networks. *IEEE Communications Magazine, 51*(7), 44–53. doi:10.1109/MCOM.2013.6553677

Phuong, L. T. (2011). Energy Efficiency based on Quality of Data for Cyber Physical System. *IEEE International Conferences on Internet of Things, and Cyber, Physical and Social Computing.*

Piamrat, K. (2011). QoE-aware vertical handover in wireless heterogeneous networks. *Proceedings of the 7th IEEE International Conference onWireless Communications and Mobile Computing Conference (IWCMC).* doi:10.1109/IWCMC.2011.5982513

Pompili, D., Hajisami, A., & Tran, T. X. (2016). Elastic resource utilization framework for high capacity and energy efficiency in cloud RAN. *IEEE Communications Magazine, 54*(1), 26–32. doi:10.1109/MCOM.2016.7378422

Ponemon Institute. (2015). *Privacy and Security in a Connected Life.* Ponemon Institute© Research.

Proffitt, B. (2013). *What's Holding Up The Internet Of Things?* Retrieved from http://readwrite.com/2013/06/14/whats-holding-up-the-internet-of-things?goback=.gde_73311_member_250004900

PwC. (2014). *The Wearable Future.* White Paper.

Qmee. (n.d.). Blog.Qmee.Com online. Retrieved from http://blog.qmee.com/online-in-60-seconds-infographic-a-year-later/

Quinton, C., Rouvoy, R., & Duchien, L. (2012). Leveraging feature models to configure virtual appliances. *Proceedings of the 2nd International Workshop on Cloud Computing Platforms (CloudCP '12)*. doi:10.1145/2168697.2168699

Radunovic, B., Gunawardena, D., Key, P., Singh, A. P. N., Balan, V., & Dejean, G. (2009). *Rethinking Indoor Wireless: Low power, Low Frequency, Full-duplex*. Technical report, Microsoft Research. Available from https://www.microsoft.com/en-us/research/wp-content/uploads/2016/02/TR-1.pdf

Rangstone, P. K., & Sharma, B. (2016). Survey on Issues In Wireless Sensor Networks: Attacks and Countermeasures. *International Journal of Computer Science and Information Security*, *14*(4), 262–269.

Rappaport, T., Shu Sun, , Mayzus, R., Hang Zhao, , Azar, Y., Wang, K., & Gutierrez, F. et al. (2013). Millimeter Wave Mobile Communications for 5G Cellular: It Will Work. *IEEE Access*, *1*, 335–349. doi:10.1109/ACCESS.2013.2260813

Ravi, S. Y., & Mohan, J. (2015). A Survey Paper On 5G Cellular Technologies - Technical & Social Challenges. *International Journal of Emerging Trends in Electrical and Electronics*, *11*(2), 98–100.

Razzaque, M. A., Milojevic-Jevric, M., Palade, A., & Clarke, S. (2016). Middleware for Internet of Things: A Survey. *IEEE Internet of Things Journal*, *3*(1), 70–95. doi:10.1109/JIOT.2015.2498900

Rein, S., Frank, H. P. F., & Reisslein, M. (2005). Voice quality evaluation in wireless packet communication systems: A tutorial and performance results for RHC. *Wireless Communications, IEEE*, *12*(1), 60–67. doi:10.1109/MWC.2005.1404574

Riecker, M., Thies, D., & Hollick, M. (2014). Measuring the impact of denial-of-service attacks on wireless sensor networks. *39th Annual IEEE Conference on Local Computer Networks*, 296-304. doi:10.1109/LCN.2014.6925784

Rivera, S. (2013). QoS-QoE correlation neural network modeling for mobile internet services. *Proceedings of IEEE International Conference on. Computing, Management and Telecommunications (ComManTel)*. doi:10.1109/ComManTel.2013.6482369

Roberts, D. A., Kundtz, N., & Smith, D. R. (2009, September). Optical lens compression via transformation optics. *Optics Express*, *17*(19), 16535–16542. doi:10.1364/OE.17.016535 PMID:19770868

Rochwerger, B., Breitgand, D., Levy, E., Galis, A., Nagin, K., Llorente, I. M., & Ben-Yehuda, M. et al. (2009). The reservoir model and architecture for open federated cloud computing. *IBM Journal of Research and Development*, *53*(4), 4–1. doi:10.1147/JRD.2009.5429058

Roh, W., Seol, J. Y., Park, J., Lee, B., Lee, J., Kim, Y., & Aryanfar, F. et al. (2014, February). Millimeter-wave beamforming as an enabling technology for 5G cellular communications: Theoretical feasibility and prototype results. *IEEE Communications Magazine*, *52*(2), 106–113. doi:10.1109/MCOM.2014.6736750

Roland, M. (2015). *Security issues in mobile NFC devices*. Cham: Springer. doi:10.1007/978-3-319-15488-6

Romana, R., Zhoua, J., & Lopezb, J. (2013). *On the features and challenges of security and privacy in distributed Internet of things*. Academic Press.

Rusch, C., Schäfer, J., Guian, H., & Zwick, T. (2014, April). 2D-scanning holographic antenna system with Rotman-lens at 60 GHz. *The 8th European Conference on Antennas and Propagation (EuCAP 2014)*, 196-199. doi:10.1109/EuCAP.2014.6901725

Rusch, C., Schäfer, J., Gulan, H., Pahl, P., & Zwick, T. (2015, April). Holographic mmW-Antennas With rm TE_0 and rm TM_0 Surface Wave Launchers for Frequency-Scanning FMCW-Radars. *IEEE Transactions on Antennas and Propagation, 63*(4), 1603–1613. doi:10.1109/TAP.2015.2400458

Rutakemwa, M. (2013). From Physical to Virtual Wireless Sensor Networks Using Cloud Computing. *International Journal of Research in Computer Science, 3*(1), 19–25.

Rysavy Research. (2014, May). How will 5G compare to fiber, cable or DSL. *Fierce Wireless*. Available from http://www.rysavy.com/Articles/2014-05-5G-Comparison-Wireline.pdf

Saaty, T. L. (1990). *Decision making for leaders: the analytic hierarchy process for decisions in a complex world* (Vol. 2). RWS publications.

Sahai, A., Patel, G., & Sabharwal, A. (2011). *Pushing the limits of Full-duplex: Design and Real-time implementation*. Available from arXiv.org:1107.0607

Sahai, A., Patel, G., & Sabharwal, A. (2012). Asynchronous Full-duplex Wireless. *Proceedings of Fourth International Conference on Communication Systems and Networks (COMSNETS 2012)*, 1–9. doi:10.1109/COMSNETS.2012.6151328

Sakakibara, H., Nakazawa, J., & Tokuda, H. (2009). PBN: A seamless network infrastructure of heterogeneous network nodes. *Proceedings of the Sixth International Conference on Networked Sensing Systems (INSS)*. doi:10.1109/INSS.2009.5409912

Sakr, S., Liu, A., Batista, D. M., & Alomari, M. (2011). A Survey of Large Scale Data Management Approaches in Cloud Environments. *IEEE Communications Surveys and Tutorials, 13*(3), 311–336. doi:10.1109/SURV.2011.032211.00087

Salehi, S. A., Razzaque, M., Naraei, P., & Farrokhtala, A. (2013). Detection of sinkhole attack in wireless sensor networks. *Proceedings of IEEE International Conference on Space Science and Communication (IconSpace)*. doi:10.1109/IconSpace.2013.6599496

Saliba, A. J., Beresford, M. A., Ivanovich, M., & Fitzpatrick, P. (2005). User-perceived quality of service in wireless data networks. *Personal and Ubiquitous Computing, 9*(6), 413–422. doi:10.1007/s00779-005-0034-7

Salim, F., & Haque, U. (2015). Urban computing in the wild: A survey on large scale participation and citizen engagement with ubiquitous computing, cyber physical systems, and Internet of Things. *International Journal of Human-Computer Studies*, *81*, 31–48. doi:10.1016/j.ijhcs.2015.03.003

Sánchez-Macián, A. (2006). A framework for the automatic calculation of quality of experience in telematic services. *Proceedings of the 13th HP-OVUA Workshop*.

Sánchez, R., Herrero, Á., & Corchado, E. (2013, October). Visualization and clustering for SNMP intrusion detection. *Cybernetics and Systems*, *44*(6-7), 505–532. doi:10.1080/0196972 2.2013.803903

Sarkar, C., Nambi, S. A. U., Prasad, R. V., & Rahim, A. (2014, March). A scalable distributed architecture towards unifying IoT applications. In *Internet of Things (WF-IoT), 2014 IEEE World Forum on* (pp. 508-513). IEEE. doi:10.1109/WF-IoT.2014.6803220

Sasirekha, V., & Ilanzkumaran, M. (2013). Heterogeneous wireless network selection using FAHP integrated with TOPSIS and VIKOR. *Proceedings of IEEE Int'l. Conf. on. Pattern Recognition, Informatics and Mobile Engineering (PRIME)*, 399-407. doi:10.1109/ICPRIME.2013.6496510

Savitha, K., & Chandrasekar, C. (2011). *Vertical Handover decision schemes using SAW and WPM for Network selection in Heterogeneous Wireless Networks*. arXiv preprint arXiv:1109.4490

Sayeed, A. M. (2002, October). Deconstructing multiantenna fading channels. *IEEE Transactions on Signal Processing*, *50*(10), 2563–2579. doi:10.1109/TSP.2002.803324

Schurig, D., Mock, J. J., & Smith, D. R. (2006). Electric-field-coupled resonators for negative permittivity metamaterials. *Applied Physics Letters*, *88*(4), 041109. doi:10.1063/1.2166681

Sehgal, V. K., Patrik, A., & Rajpoot, L. (2014). A Comparative Study of Cyber Physical Cloud, Cloud of Sensors and Internet of Things: Their Ideology, Similarities and Differences. *IEEE International Advanced Computing Conference (IACC)*. doi:10.1109/IAdCC.2014.6779411

Serrano, M., Strassner, J., & Foghlu, M. O. (2009, June). A formal approach for the inference plane supporting integrated management tasks in the Future Internet. In *Integrated Network Management-Workshops, 2009. IM'09. IFIP/IEEE International Symposium on* (pp. 120-127). IEEE. doi:10.1109/INMW.2009.5195947

Shao, J., Wei, H., Wang, Q., & Mei, H. (2010, July). A runtime model based monitoring approach for cloud. In *Cloud Computing (CLOUD), 2010 IEEE 3rd international conference on* (pp. 313-320). IEEE. doi:10.1109/CLOUD.2010.31

Shariatmadari, H., Ratasuk, R., Iraji, S., Laya, A., Taleb, T., Jäntti, R., & Ghosh, A. (2015). Machine-type communications: Current status and future perspectives toward 5G systems. *IEEE Communications Magazine*, *53*(9), 10–17. doi:10.1109/MCOM.2015.7263367

Sharma, R. (2013). Five Challenges For The Internet of Things Ecosystem. *Forbes*. Retrieved from http://www.forbes.com/sites/rakeshsharma/2013/11/12/five-challenges-for-the-the-internet-of-things-ecosystem/

Shen, D.-M. (2010), The QoE-oriented Heterogeneous Network Selection Based on Fuzzy AHP Methodology. *Proceeding of the Fourth International Conference on Mobile Ubiquitous Computing, Systems, Services and Technologies (UBICOMM 2010).*

Sicari, S., Rizzardi, A., Grieco, L. A., & Coen-Porisini, A. (2015). Security, privacy and trust in Internet of Things: The road ahead. *Computer Networks, 76*(1), 146–164. doi:10.1016/j.comnet.2014.11.008

Simsek, M., Aijaz, A., Dohler, M., Sachs, J., & Fettweis, G. (2016). 5G-Enabled Tactile Internet. *IEEE Journal on Selected Areas in Communications, 34*(3), 460–473. doi:10.1109/JSAC.2016.2525398

Singh, J., & Powles, J. (2014, July 28). The internet of things - the next big challenge to our privacy. *The Guardian.* Retrieved from http://www.theguardian.com/technology/2014/jul/28/internet-of-things-privacy

Skorin-Kapov, L. (2013). Survey and Challenges of QoE Management Issues in Wireless Networks. *Journal of Computer Networks and Communications.*

Sleem, A. E., & Kumar, A. (2005). Handoff management in wireless data networks using topography-aware mobility prediction. *Journal of Parallel and Distributed Computing, 65*(8), 963–982. doi:10.1016/j.jpdc.2004.12.006

Slovic, M., Jokanovic, B., & Kolundzija, B. (2006). High Efficiency Patch Antenna for 24 GHz Anticollision Radar. *Microwave Review, 12*(1), 50-53.

Soldani, D., & Manzalini, A. (2015). Horizon 2020 and beyond: On the 5G operating system for a true digital society. *IEEE Vehicular Technology Magazine, 10*(1), 32–42. doi:10.1109/MVT.2014.2380581

Song, Q.-Y., & Jamalipour, A. (2005). A network selection mechanism for next generation networks. *Proceedings of IEEE International Conference on Communications (ICC 2005), 2.* doi:10.1109/ICC.2005.1494578

Spiess, P., Karnouskos, S., Guinard, D., Savio, D., Baecker, O., De Souza, L. M. S., & Trifa, V. (2009, July). SOA-based integration of the internet of things in enterprise services. In *Web Services, 2009. ICWS 2009. IEEE International Conference on* (pp. 968-975). IEEE.

Stalling, W. (1999). SNMP, SNMPv2, SNMPv3 and RMON 1 and 2 (3rd ed.). Addison Wesley Longman.

Stankovic, J. A. (2014). Research Directions for the Internet of Things. *IEEE Internet of Things Journal, 1*(1).

Stevens-Navarro, E., Martinez-Morales, J. D., & Pineda-Rico, U. (2012). Evaluation of vertical handoff decision algorithms based on MADM methods for heterogeneous wireless networks. *Journal of Applied Research And Technology, 10*(4), 534–548.

Strassner, J., O'Foghlu, M., Donnelly, W., & Agoulmine, N. (2007, July). Beyond the knowledge plane: an inference plane to support the next generation Internet. In *Global Information Infrastructure Symposium, 2007. GIIS 2007. First International* (pp. 112-119). IEEE.

Sundmaeker, H., Guillemin, P., Friess, P., & Woelfflé, S. (2010). *Internet of Things Application Domains. In Vision and Challenges for Realising the Internet of Things* (pp. 49–56). European Commission.

Sun, S., Rappaport, T. S., Heath, R. W., Nix, A., & Rangan, S. (2014). MIMO for millimeter-wave wireless communications: Beamforming, spatial multiplexing, or both? *IEEE Communications Magazine, 52*(12), 110–121. doi:10.1109/MCOM.2014.6979962

Tankard, C. (2015, September). The security issues of the Internet of Things. *Computer Fraud & Security, 2015*(9), 11–14. doi:10.1016/S1361-3723(15)30084-1

Tara, A.-Y., Sethom, K., & Pujolle, G. (2007). Seamless continuity of service across WLAN and WMAN networks: Challenges and performance evaluation. *Proceedings of the 2nd IEEE/IFIP International Workshop on Broadband Convergence Networks.*

Tavares Guimaraes, V., Lessa dos Santos, G., da Cunha Rodrigues, G., Zambenedetti Granville, L., & Rockenbach Tarouco, L. M. (2014). A collaborative solution for SNMP traces visualization. *Proceedings of International Conference on, 2014, International Conference on Information Networking (ICOIN)*, 458-463. doi:10.1109/ICOIN.2014.6799724

Tekkouk, K., Ettorre, M., Sauleau, R., & Casaletti, M. (2012, March). Folded Rotman lens multibeam antenna in SIW technology at 24 GHz. *2012 6th European Conference on Antennas and Propagation (EUCAP)*, 2308-2310. doi:10.1109/EuCAP.2012.6206347

Texas Instruments. (2014). *The Internet of Things: Opportunities & Challenges*. Retrieved from http://www.ti.com/ww/en/internet_of_things/pdf/14-09-17-IoTforCap.pdf

Thakur, N., & Sankaralingam, A. (2013). Introduction to Jamming Attacks and Prevention Techniques using Honeypots in Wireless Networks. *International Journal of Computer Science and Information Technology & Security, 3*(2).

Tiwari, A., Ballal, P., & Lewis, F. (2007). Energy-efficient wireless sensor network design and implementation for condition-based maintenance. *ACM Transactions on Sensor Networks, 3*(1), 1. doi:10.1145/1210669.1210670

Tran, P. N., & Boukhatem, N. (2008). Comparison of MADM decision algorithms for interface selection in heterogeneous wireless networks. *Proceedings of the 16th IEEE Int'l. Conf. on Software, Telecommunications and Computer Networks, 2008 (SoftCOM 2008)*, 119-124. doi:10.1109/SOFTCOM.2008.4669464

TRUSTe. (2013). *Announcing the 2013 TRUSTe Transparency Report*. TRUSTe. Retrieved from http://www.truste.com/blog/2014/05/29/internet-of-things-industry-brings-data-explosion-but-growth-could-be-impacted-by-consumer-privacy-concerns/

Tsai, C. W., Lai, C. F., Chiang, M. C., & Yang, L. T. (2014). Data mining for Internet of Things: A survey. *IEEE Communications Surveys and Tutorials, 16*(1), 77–97. doi:10.1109/SURV.2013.103013.00206

Tseng, C. H., Chen, C. J., & Chu, T. H. (2008). A Low-Cost 60-GHz Switched-Beam Patch Antenna Array With Butler Matrix Network. *IEEE Antennas and Wireless Propagation Letters, 7,* 432–435. doi:10.1109/LAWP.2008.2001849

Turow, J., Hennessy, M., & Draper, N. (2015). *The Tradeoff Fallacy.* The University of Pennsylvania, Annenberg School for Communication.

Tu, Z., & Blum, R. S. (2009). On the Limitations of Random Sensor Placement for Distributed Signal Detection. *IEEE Trans. Aerospace Electron, 45*(2), 555–563. doi:10.1109/TAES.2009.5089541

University of Bristol. (2016, May 17). *Bristol and Lund once again set new world record in 5G wireless spectrum efficiency.* Retrieved from http://www.bristol.ac.uk/engineering/news/2016/bristol-and-lund-set-new-world-record-in-5g-wireless.html

Vakilian, V., Wild, T., Schaich, F., Brink, S. T., & Frigon, J. F. (2013, December). Universal-Filtered Multi-Carrier Technique for Wireless Systems Beyond LTE. *Proceedings of 9th International Workshop on Broadband Wireless Access(Globecom'13).* doi:10.1109/GLOCOMW.2013.6824990

Verma, R., & Singh, N. P. (2013). GRA based network selection in heterogeneous wireless networks. *Wireless Personal Communications, 72*(2), 1437–1452. doi:10.1007/s11277-013-1087-y

Vieira, J., Malkowsky, S., Nieman, K., Miers, Z., Kundargi, N., Liu, L., & Tufvesson, F. (2014). *A flexible 100-antenna testbed for massive MIMO. In 2014 IEEE Globecom Workshops* (pp. 287–293). GC Wkshps.

Wang, C. Y., Chou, S.-T., & Chang, H.-C. (2009. Emotion and motivation: understanding user behavior of Web 2.0 Application. *Proceedings of IEEE Computer Society Seventh Annual Communication Networks and Services Research Conference,* 1341-1346. doi:10.1109/ITNG.2009.205

Wang, H., Lin, G., Wang, J., Gao, W., Chen, Y., & Duan, Q. (2014). Management of Big Data in the Internet of Things in Agriculture Based on Cloud Computing, *Applied. Mechanics of Materials, 548-549,* 1438–1444. doi:10.4028/www.scientific.net/AMM.548-549.1438

Wang, H.-Q. (2012). Intelligent Access Selection in Cognitive Networks: A Fuzzy Neural Network Approach. *Journal of Computer Information Systems, 8*(21), 8877–8884.

Wang, L., & Lu, F. (2014). Intrusion detection system based on integration of neural network for wireless sensor network. *Journal of Software Engineering, 8*(4), 225–238. doi:10.3923/jse.2014.225.238

Weber, R. H. (2010). Internet of Things – New security and privacy challenges. *Computer Law & Security Report, 26*(1), 23–30. doi:10.1016/j.clsr.2009.11.008

Wei, Y., Ke, L., & Dong, Z. (2010), Development of wireless intelligent control terminal of greenhouse based on ZigBee. *T. CSAE, 26*(3), 198-202.

Wei, L., Hu, R. Q., Qian, Y., & Wu, G. (2014, December). Key elements to enable millimeter wave communications for 5G wireless systems. *IEEE Wireless Communications, 21*(6), 136–143. doi:10.1109/MWC.2014.7000981

What-is-ccn. (n.d.). *ccnx.org online.* Retrieved from http://ccnx.org/what-is-ccn/

Wild, T. (2011, Sep). Comparing coordinated multi-point schemes with imperfect channel knowledge. *Proceedings of IEEE VTC Fall 2011.* doi:10.1109/VETECF.2011.6092923

Williams, O. (2015). *Creating standards for the internet of things – live webchat.* Retrieved from http://www.theguardian.com/media-network/2015/jul/21/standards-internet-of-things-iot-webchat#comment-56518730

Wolski, R., Spring, N. T., & Hayes, J. (1999). The network weather service: A distributed resource performance forecasting service for metacomputing. *Future Generation Computer Systems, 15*(5), 757–768. doi:10.1016/S0167-739X(99)00025-4

Wong, E. (1997, August). *Network Monitoring Fundamentals and Standards.* Academic Press.

Wu, M., Lu, T. J., Ling, F. Y., Sun, J., & Du, H. Y. (2010, August). Research on the architecture of Internet of things. In *Advanced Computer Theory and Engineering (ICACTE), 2010 3rd International Conference on* (Vol. 5, pp. V5-484). IEEE.

Wu, X., Tavildar, S., Shakkottai, S., Richardson, T., Li, J., Laroia, R., & Jovicic, A. (2013). FlashLinQ: A synchronous distributed scheduler for peer-to-peer ad hoc networks. *IEEE/ACM Transactions on Networking (TON), 21*(4), 1215-1228.

Wu, F.-J., Kao, Y.-F., & Tseng, Y.-C. (2011). From wireless sensor networks towards cyber physical systems. *Pervasive and Mobile Computing, 7*(4), 397–413. doi:10.1016/j.pmcj.2011.03.003

Wu, J.-S., Yang, S.-F., & Hwang, B.-J. (2009). A terminal-controlled vertical handover decision scheme in IEEE 802.21-enabled heterogeneous wireless networks. *International Journal of Communication Systems, 22*(7), 819–834. doi:10.1002/dac.996

Wunder, G., Jung, P., & Wang, C. (2014, June). Compressive Random Access for Post-LTE Systems. *IEEE ICC Workshop on Massive Uncoordinated Access Protocols,* 539-544. doi:10.1109/ICCW.2014.6881254

Wurm, J., Hoang, K., Arias, O., Sadeghi, A. R., & Jin, Y. (2016). Security analysis on consumer and industrial IoT devices. *21st Asia and South Pacific Design Automation Conference (ASP-DAC),* 519-524. doi:10.1109/ASPDAC.2016.7428064

Xu, X., Huang, S., Chen, Y., Browny, K., Halilovicy, I., & Lu, W. (2014, June). TSAaaS: Time series analytics as a service on IoT. In *Web Services (ICWS), 2014 IEEE International Conference On* (pp. 249-256). IEEE.

Yang, Z., Yue, Y., Yang, Y., Peng, Y., Wang, X., & Liu, W. (2011, July). Study and application on the architecture and key technologies for IOT. In *Multimedia Technology (ICMT), 2011 International Conference on* (pp. 747-751). IEEE.

Yerva, S. R., Saltarin, J., Hoyoung, J., & Abere, K. (2012). Social and Sensor Data Fusion in the Cloud. *13th International Conference on Mobile Data Management (MDM)*. doi:10.1109/MDM.2012.52

Yongqi, H., Yun, Z., Taihao, L., & Liying, C. (2013). Research of network monitoring based on SNMP. *Proceedings of Third International Conference on Instrumentation, Measurement, Computer, Communication and Control (IMCCC)*, 411-414.

Yuriyama, M., & Kushida, T. (2010). Sensor-Cloud Infrastructure: Physical Sensor Management with Virtualized Sensors on Cloud Computing. *13th International Conference on Network-based Information Systems*. doi:10.1109/NBiS.2010.32

Yuriyama, M., Kushida, T., & Itakura, M. (2011). A new model of accelerating service innovation with sensor-cloud infrastructure. *Proceedings of the annual SRII Global Conference (SRII'11)*, 308–314. doi:10.1109/SRII.2011.42

Zain, A. S. M., Yahya, A., Malek, M. F. A., & Omar, N. (2012). 3GPP Long Term Evolution and its application for healthcare services. *International Conference on Computer and Communication Engineering*, 239-243.

Zanella, A., Vangelista, L., Bui, N., Castellani, A., & Zorzi, M. (2014). Internet of Things for Smart Cities. *IEEE Internet of Things Journal, 1*(1).

Zanella, A., Bui, N., Castellani, A., Vangelista, L., & Zorzi, M. (2014). Internet of Things for Smart Cities. *IEEE Internet of Things Journal, 1*(1), 22–32. doi:10.1109/JIOT.2014.2306328

Zang, Q., Yang, X.L., & Zhou, Y.M. (2007). A wireless solution for greenhouse monitoring and control system based on ZigBee technology. *Journal of Zhejiang University Sci. A, 8*(10), 1584-1587.

Zeng, D., Miyazaki, T., Guo, S., Tsukahara, T., Kitamichi, J., & Hayashi, T. (2013). *Evolution of Software-Defined Sensor Networks*. Mobile Ad-hoc and Sensor Networks. doi:10.1109/MSN.2013.60

Zhang, Q., Cheng, L., & Boutaba, R. (2010). Cloud Computing: State-of-the-art and research challenges. *Journal of Internet Services and Applications, 1*(1), 7–18. doi:10.1007/s13174-010-0007-6

Zhao, K., & Ge, L. (2013). A Survey on the Internet of Things Security. *Computational Intelligence and Security (CIS), 9th International Conference on*, 663-667.

Zhenhui, Y., Keeney, J., Van Der Meer, S., Hogan, G., & Muntean, G. M. (2014). Context-aware heterogeneous network performance analysis: Test-bed development. *Proceedings of IEEE International Conference on Pervasive Computing and Communications Workshops (PERCOM Workshops)*, 472-477.

Zhou, B., Hu, H., Huang, S. Q., & Chen, H. H. (2013). Intracluster device-to-device relay algorithm with optimal resource utilization. *IEEE Transactions on Vehicular Technology, 62*(5), 2315–2326. doi:10.1109/TVT.2012.2237557

ZTE Corporation. (2013). *Comparison between CP solution C1 and C2*. Technical Report.

About the Contributors

Vasuky Mohanan is a lecturer at Inti College University, Malaysia. She obtained her M.Sc in computer science from Universiti Sains Malaysia, Malaysia. She is also currently as PhD candidate at the university. Her area of expertises include: programming paradigms, programming languages, algorithm analysis, wireless networking, semantic grammar for machine interpretation, routing algorithms.

Rahmat Budiarto is currently working as a full professor at Department of Computer Science, College of Computer and Information Technology, Albaha University, Saudi Arabia. He received his master and doctor of engineering degrees in the area of intelligent systems from Nagoya Instititute of Technology, Japan, in 1995 and 1998, respectively. He has published more than 250 research papers. His research interests include future internet, information security, wireless sensor networks, intelligent systems and cloud computing.

Ismat Aldmour is currently in Al Baha University in Saudi Arabia in its Computer Engineering and Science Department. He worked in universities in Jordan and UAE as well. He got his PhD from the University of Glamorgan (currently University of South Wales), Wales, UK, in the area of mobile wireless communications systems in 2008. His MSc and BSc were from the university of Jordan, Jordan in the field of Electrical Engineering/ Communications. He assumed a number of a non- academic positions including a research engineer/ Head of Electrical testing at the Royal Scientific Society of Jordan. His current research interests include energy efficiency in mobile wireless networks and 5G networks in general.

* * *

Ahmed Alahmadi is an Assistant Professor in the department of computer science and engineering at Al Baha University, Saudi Arabia and a Member of IEEE. He in 2014 obtained his PhD in Computer science at La Trobe University. Since then, he has published several peer-reviewed research papers. He has made significant contributions in various research areas, including eHealth, IoT, and cloud computing. And now Dr. Alahmadi is the Dean of the college of computer science and IT in Al Baha University.

Adil Alharthi received the B.S. degree in computer science from King Abdulaziz University, Jeddah, Saudi Arabia, in 2003, the M.S. (Hons.) degree from RMIT University, Melbourne, Australia, in 2008, and the Ph.D. degree in computer science from the University of RMIT. He is currently an Assistant Professor with the College of Computer Science and Information Technology, Al Baha University, Al Baha, Saudi Arabia. His research interests are in the areas of wireless sensor networks, mobile networks, and ad-hoc networks with an emphasis on data mining, statistical analysis/modeling, and machine learning.

Tami Alwajeeh is a lecturer in Al Baha University, College of Computer Science and Information Technology, Al Baha University, Saudi Arabia. After finishing his master of computer science in 2012 from United States, he joined King Khalid University and moved to Al Baha University. His current research interests include artificial intelligent, fast learning, deep learning and machine learning.

Mohammed Yahya Alzahrani is currently working as Assistant Professor and the Head of the IT department, School of Computer Science and IT, Al Baha University, Saudi Arabia. He received his Master and PhD in Computer Science from Heriot-Watt University, UK, in 2010 and 2015, respectively. His research interests include: formal methods, model checking, information security, software verification, data mining.

Fatemeh Banaie received her M.Sc. Degree in software computer engineering in 2012, from Engineering department of Ferdowsi University of Mashhad. She is currently a Ph.D. student at Ferdowsi University of Mashhad. Her research interests are in the general area of Computer networking, Sensor virtualization, Cloud computing, Sensor-Cloud, Internet of Things and Machine type communications.

Ameur Bensefia is an Assistant Professor at the Higher Colleges of Technology in UAE. He earned his PhD in Computer Science in 2004 from Rouen University (France) and his master degree in Computer Engineering and Automatic Control from the University of Haute Alsace (France). His reserach interests cover different areas mainly in image processing and documents analysis but he is also involved in other areas of research such as the virtual environment and the IoT concerns.

Olga Borić-Lubecke received the B.Sc. from the University of Belgrade in 1989, the M.S. from Caltech in 1990, and the Ph.D. from UCLA in 1995, all in electrical engineering. Since 2003, she has been with the University of Hawaii at Manoa, where she is currently a Professor of Electrical Engineering. Prior to UH, she was a Member of the Technical Staff with Bell Labs, Lucent. From 1996 to 1998 she was at RIKEN, in Sendai, Japan. From 1995 to 1996 she was at NASA, JPL. She has authored or coauthored about 200 journal and conference publications, two books and several book chapters, and two patents. Dr. Borić -Lubecke was co-recipient of the Emerging Technology Award at TechConnect 2007, and co-founded Kai Medical and Adnoviv. She was the adviser for student paper competition awards at the 2001 IEEE IMS, 2001 IEEE EMBC, and 2003 IEEE IMS (First Place). She served as associate editor for the IEEE Microwave and Wireless Components Letters and for the IEEE EMBC from 2012 to 2015, and currently serves as associate editor for the IEEE Transactions on Microwave Theory and Techniques. Prof. Borić –Lubecke is an IEEE Fellow and Foreign Member of the Academy of Engineering of Serbia.

Massimo Condoluci is currently post-doctoral research associate at the Centre for Telecommunications Research, Department of Informatics, King's College London, UK. He received the M.Sc. degree in Telecommunications Engineering and the Ph.D. in Information Technology in 2011 and 2016, respectively, from the University Mediterranea of Reggio Calabria, Italy. His main current research interests include softwarisation, virtualization, mobility management, group-oriented and machine-type communications over 5G systems.

Mischa Dohler is full Professor in Wireless Communications at King's College London, Head of the Centre for Telecommunications Research, co-founder and member of the Board of Directors of the smart city pioneer Worldsensing, Fellow and Distinguished Lecturer of the IEEE, and Editor-in-Chief of the Transactions on Emerging Telecommunications Technologies. He is a frequent keynote, panel and tutorial speaker. He has pioneered several research fields, contributed to numerous wireless broadband and IoT/M2M standards, holds a dozen patents, organized and chaired numerous conferences, has more than 200 publications, and authored several books. He has a citation h-index of 37. He acts as policy, technology and entrepreneurship adviser, examples being Richard Branson's Carbon War Room, the House of Lords UK, the EPSRC ICT Strategy Advisory Team, the European Commission, the ISO Smart City working group, and various start-ups. He is also an entrepreneur, angel investor, passionate pianist and fluent in 6 languages. He has talked at TEDx. He had coverage by national and international TV & radio; and his contributions have featured on BBC News and the Wall Street Journal.

Salam A. Hoshang has over 25 years of international academic and business IT consulting including more than 20 years of university lecturing experience in Europe, Germany, Thailand and the UAE. He has been working as Graduate Studies & Research Faculty member in the Masters of Information Systems Management Program at the Higher Colleges of Technology (HCT) since January 2012. He had academic positions from Head of Department to Dean. Dr Hoshang is interested in Smart Cities and Systems, RFID Technologies and Applications, IoT, Applied Information Technology, Innovation and Technology Management including data privacy and security.

Seyed Amin Hosseini Seno received his B.Sc and M.Sc. degree in Computer Engineering from Ferdowsi University of Mashhad, Iran in 1990 and 1998 respectively and his Ph.D from Universiti Sains Malaysia, Penang, Malaysia in 2010. He is currently Head of Virtual Learning Center at the Ferdowsi University of Mashhad and academic member of Computer Engineering Department. His research interests include Wireless and Sensor Networks, Network protocols, QoS and Network Security.

Branka Jokanovic (M'89) received the Dipl. Ing., M.Sc. and Ph.D. degrees in electrical engineering at the University of Belgrade, Faculty of Electrical Engineering, Belgrade, Serbia, in 1977, 1988, and 1999, respectively. She is currently a Research Professor at the Institute of Physics, University of Belgrade, Serbia. Before she joined the Photonic Center, Institute of Physics, she was the Head of the Microwave Department, Institute IMTEL, Belgrade. Her current research interests include modelling, simulation and characterization of microwave and photonic metamaterials for wireless communications and sensors. Dr. Jokanovic was one of the founders of the Yugoslav IEEE MTT-S Chapter and its chairperson from 1989 to 2000. She also founded the Yugoslav Association for Microwave Techniques and Technology in 1994 and initiated the Yugoslav MTT journal Microwave Review for which she was the editor for six years (1994-2000). She received the IMTEL Institute Award for Scientific Contribution in 1996, the 2000 IEEE Third Millennium Award, the YUMTT Distinguished Service Award in 2005 and Aleksandar Marincic Award in 2013. Dr Jokanovic is a corresponding member of the Serbian Academy of Engineering Sciences.

Maria A. Lema is currently a post-doctoral researcher working on the 5G Tactile Internet project sponsored by Ericsson. She obtained her PhD in Mobile communications from Universitat Politecnica de Catalunya in 2015. She worked as a research intern on DVB-T in the Wicomtec group until she obtained her M.Sc. in

Telecommunications in 2010, when she joined the group as research staff, where she worked in Spanish and European research projects on radio resource management to maximize performance in 4G radio access networks. Her major topic of research in her PhD was LTE-A system level studies, in concrete uplink studies with carrier aggregation techniques. Nowadays, her research interests are 4G/5G Radio Access Network, Internet of Things and the Tactile Internet.

Victor Lubecke received his Ph.D. degree in electrical engineering from Caltech in 1995. He is currently a Professor of Electrical Engineering at the University of Hawaii, Manoa. From 1998 to 2003, Dr. Lubecke was with Bell Laboratories, Lucent Technologies, where his research focused on remote sensing for biomedical and industrial applications, and on microelectromechanical systems (MEMS) and 3-D wafer-scale integration for wireless and optical communications. From 1987-96, he was with the NASA Jet Propulsion Laboratory (JPL), and from 1996-98, he was with the Institute for Physical and Chemical Research (RIKEN), Japan, where his research involved terahertz and MEMS technologies for space remote sensing and communications. Dr. Lubecke is an IEEE Fellow, and emeritus Distinguished Microwave Lecturer of the Microwave Theory and Techniques Society, and Topic Editor for Transactions on Terahertz Science and Technology. He holds 7 U.S. patents, has published over 200 peer-reviewed research articles, and co-founded two high-tech start-up companies. His current research interests include remote sensing, biomedical sensors, MEMS, heterogeneous integration, and microwave/terahertz radio.

Toktam Mahmoodi is with the academic faculty of the Centre for Telecommunications Research (CTR) in King's College London. She is one of the leading members of the Tactile Internet Lab at King's College London and principal and co-investigator of number of research projects funded by telecom industries, UK Research Councils and European Commission, on subjects such as low-latency communications, SDN and NFV, and eHealth. She was visiting research scientist with F5 Networks, in San Jose, CA, in 2013, post-doctoral Research Associate in the ISN research group at Electrical and Electronic Engineering department of Imperial College during 2010 and 2011, and Mobile VCE researcher from 2006 to 2009. She has also worked in mobile and personal communications industry, from 2002-2006, and in an R&D team on developing DECT standard for WLL applications. Toktam has a BSc. degree in Electrical Engineering from Sharif University of Technology, Iran, and a PhD degree in Telecommunications from King's College London, UK. She is senior member of the IEEE, and member of the ACM.

Vojislav Milosevic was born in Belgrade, Serbia, on April 5, 1986. He received the Dipl. Ing. and M.Sc. degrees in electrical engineering from the University of Belgrade, Belgrade, Serbia, in 2009 and 2012, respectively, where he is currently working toward the Ph.D. degree.

Ahmed M. Mostafa is an Assistant Professor at Electronics, Communications, and Computers Engineering Department, Helwan University, Egypt. He obtained his PhD degree in Computer Engineering from Helwan University, Egypt, 2012. He also obtained his Msc and Bsc degrees from Helwan University, Egypt, in 2007 and 2001 respectively. His research interest includes multi-core systems, real time systems, network-on-chip, distributed systems, Internet of Things, and cloud computing.

Muawya Naser is a faculty member in the Dept. Computer and Information Science, Khalifa City Women's Colleges, Higher Collges of Technology HCT, UAE. He received a M.Sc. degree in computer science and a Ph.D. degree in network security. His research interests are in the field of protocols design, lightweight cryptography, cryptanalysis etc. Nowadays, his research is focused on radio frequency identification systems (RFID).

Muhammad Fermi Pasha is currently working as Senior Lecturer and Coordinator of Computer Science Program at School of Information Technology, Monash University, Malaysia Campus. He received his master and PhD in Computer Science from Universiti Sains Malaysia in 2006 and 2010, respectively. His research interests include: evolving system, neocortex memory modeling, adaptive network security and traffic analysis, neuroimaging, medical image analysis platform, healthcare and radiology IT.

Deris Stiawan is senior lecturer in Faculty of Computer Science Universitas Sriwijaya, Indonesia. He is member of IEEE and senior member of IAES since 2009. In 2011, he holds Certified Ethical Hacker (CEH) & Certified Hacker Forensic Investigator (CHFI) licensed from EC-Council. He received PhD in Computer Science from Universiti Teknologi Malaysia in 2014. His professional profile has derived to computer and network security fields, focused on network attack and intrusion prevention / detection system.

Ravi Sekhar Yarrabothu received his B.Tech in Electronics and Communications Engineering from Acharya Nagarjuna University in 1997. He received his M.Tech in Computer Science and Technology from Indian Institute of Technology, Roorkee in 1999. He is Currently working as Associate Professor at Vignan's University at Department of ECE in Guntur, India, since September 2014. Prior to academics, he is having more than 15 years of rich experience in the Wireless Communication Industry working on Protocols, System Development and Integration for LTE, GSM/GPRS, W-CDMA (UMTS), TD-SCDMA, GMR-3G, WiMAX (IEEE 802.16e), CDMA One, and CDMA 2000. He started his career as ASE at Tata Consultancy Services and worked as Senior Manager at Smartplay Technolgies, before moving in to academics. He has worked with the companies like TCS, Aeroflex, Huawei, Ubinetics, NextWave, Hughes Network Systems, Qualcomm, Broadcom, Intel. He is a member of IEEE member since 1999.

Index

Purchase Print, E-Book, or Print + E-Book

IGI Global books can now be purchased from three unique pricing formats:
Print Only, E-Book Only, or Print + E-Book. Shipping fees apply.

www.igi-global.com

Recommended Reference Books

ISBN: 978-1-4666-6042-7
© 2014; 1,727 pp.
List Price: $1,756

ISBN: 978-1-4666-6571-2
© 2015; 927 pp.
List Price: $404

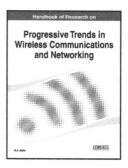

ISBN: 978-1-4666-5170-8
© 2014; 592 pp.
List Price: $304

ISBN: 978-1-4666-7401-1
© 2015; 362 pp.
List Price: $156

ISBN: 978-1-4666-4916-3
© 2014; 398 pp.
List Price: $164

ISBN: 978-1-4666-5003-9
© 2014; 580 pp.
List Price: $152

Looking for free content, product updates, news, and special offers?
Join IGI Global's mailing list today and start enjoying exclusive perks sent only to IGI Global members.
Add your name to the list at **www.igi-global.com/newsletters**.

Publishing Information Science and Technology Research Since 1988

 www.igi-global.com   Sign up at www.igi-global.com/newsletters   f facebook.com/igiglobal   t twitter.com/igiglobal

Stay Current on the Latest Emerging Research Developments

Become an IGI Global Reviewer for Authored Book Projects

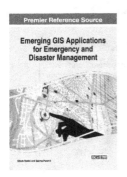   

The overall success of an authored book project is dependent on quality and timely reviews.

In this competitive age of scholarly publishing, constructive and timely feedback significantly decreases the turnaround time of manuscripts from submission to acceptance, allowing the publication and discovery of progressive research at a much more expeditious rate. Several IGI Global authored book projects are currently seeking highly qualified experts in the field to fill vacancies on their respective editorial review boards:

Applications may be sent to:
development@igi-global.com

Applicants must have a doctorate (or an equivalent degree) as well as publishing and reviewing experience. Reviewers are asked to write reviews in a timely, collegial, and constructive manner. All reviewers will begin their role on an ad-hoc basis for a period of one year, and upon successful completion of this term can be considered for full editorial review board status, with the potential for a subsequent promotion to Associate Editor.

If you have a colleague that may be interested in this opportunity,
we encourage you to share this information with them.

www.igi-global.com

InfoSci®-Books

A Database for Progressive Information Science and Technology Research

Maximize Your Library's Book Collection!

Invest in IGI Global's InfoSci®-Books database and gain access to hundreds of reference books at a fraction of their individual list price.

The InfoSci®-Books database offers unlimited simultaneous users the ability to precisely return search results through more than 75,000 full-text chapters from nearly 3,400 reference books in the following academic research areas:

Business & Management Information Science & Technology • Computer Science & Information Technology
Educational Science & Technology • Engineering Science & Technology • Environmental Science & Technology
Government Science & Technology • Library Information Science & Technology • Media & Communication Science & Technology
Medical, Healthcare & Life Science & Technology • Security & Forensic Science & Technology • Social Sciences & Online Behavior

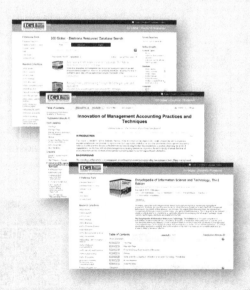

Peer-Reviewed Content:
- Cutting-edge research
- No embargoes
- Scholarly and professional
- Interdisciplinary

Award-Winning Platform:
- Unlimited simultaneous users
- Full-text in XML and PDF
- Advanced search engine
- No DRM

Librarian-Friendly:
- Free MARC records
- Discovery services
- COUNTER4/SUSHI compliant
- Training available

To find out more or request a free trial, visit:
www.igi-global.com/eresources

www.igi-global.com

IGI Global Proudly Partners with

Enhance Your Manuscript with
eContent Pro's Professional and Academic
Copy Editing Service

Additional Services

Expert Translation

eContent Pro Translation provides professional translation services across key languages around the world. Our expert translators will work to provide a clear-cut translation of your document, while maintaining your original meaning and ensuring that your document is accurately and professionally translated.

Professional Proofreading

eContent Pro Proofreading provides fast, high-quality, affordable proofreading that will optimize the accuracy and readability of your document, ensuring that its contents are communicated in the clearest way possible to your readers.

IGI Global Authors Save 20% on eContent Pro's Services!

Scan the QR Code to Receive Your 20% Discount

The 20% discount is applied directly to your eContent Pro shopping cart when placing an order through IGI Global's referral link. Use the QR code to access this referral link. eContent Pro has the right to end or modify any promotion at any time.

Email: customerservice@econtentpro.com

econtentpro.com

Information Resources Management Association

Become an IRMA Member

Members of the **Information Resources Management Association (IRMA)** understand the importance of community within their field of study. The Information Resources Management Association is an ideal venue through which professionals, students, and academicians can convene and share the latest industry innovations and scholarly research that is changing the field of information science and technology. Become a member today and enjoy the benefits of membership as well as the opportunity to collaborate and network with fellow experts in the field.

IRMA Membership Benefits:

- **One FREE Journal Subscription**

- **30% Off Additional Journal Subscriptions**

- **20% Off Book Purchases**

- Updates on the latest events and research on Information Resources Management through the IRMA-L listserv.

- Updates on new open access and downloadable content added to Research IRM.

- A copy of the Information Technology Management Newsletter twice a year.

- A certificate of membership.

IRMA Membership $195

Scan code or visit **irma-international.org** and begin by selecting your free journal subscription.

Membership is good for one full year.

www.irma-international.org

Printed in the United States
By Bookmasters